# RENT-A-GiRLFRiEND

VOLUME **12**

## REIJI MIYAJIMA

# CONTENTS

## RATING 95

## MY GIRLFRIEND AND WHAT I'M CAPABLE OF 4

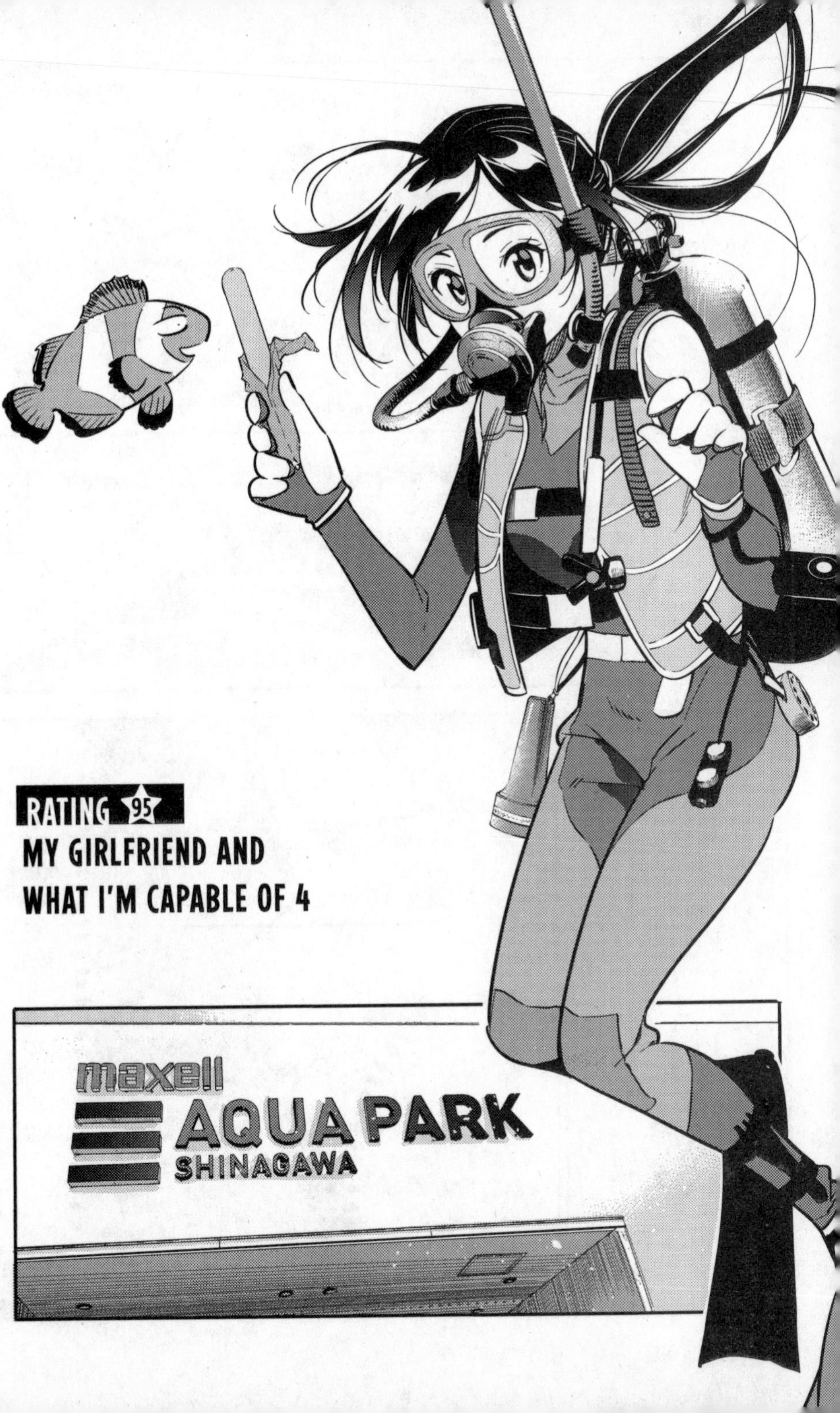
maxell
AQUA PARK
SHINAGAWA

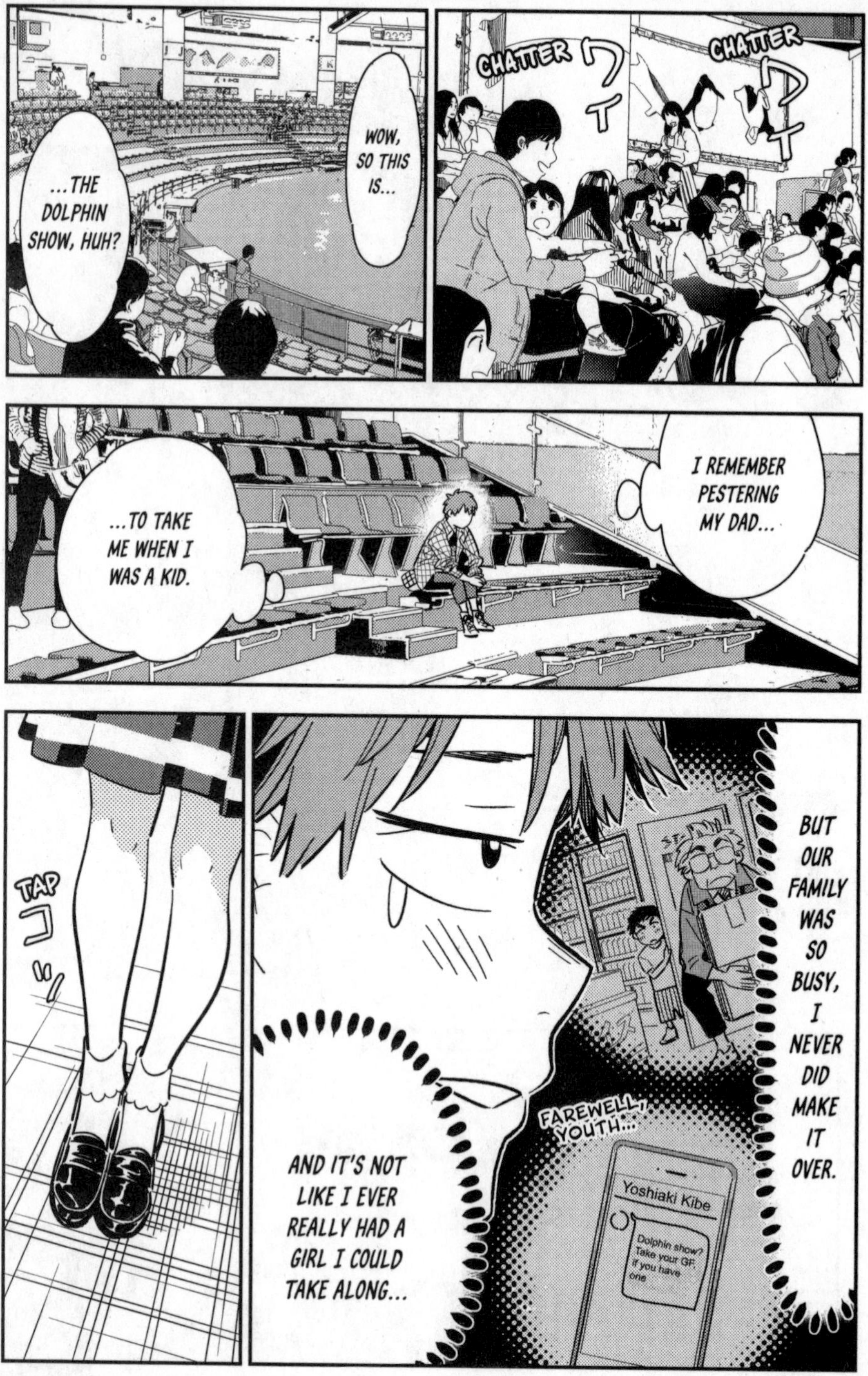
CHATTER
ワイ
CHATTER
ワイ
WOW, SO THIS IS...
...THE DOLPHIN SHOW, HUH?
I REMEMBER PESTERING MY DAD...
...TO TAKE ME WHEN I WAS A KID.
BUT OUR FAMILY WAS SO BUSY, I NEVER DID MAKE IT OVER.
FAREWELL, YOUTH...
Yoshiaki Kibe
Dolphin show? Take your GF, if you have one
AND IT'S NOT LIKE I EVER REALLY HAD A GIRL I COULD TAKE ALONG...
TAP
コッ

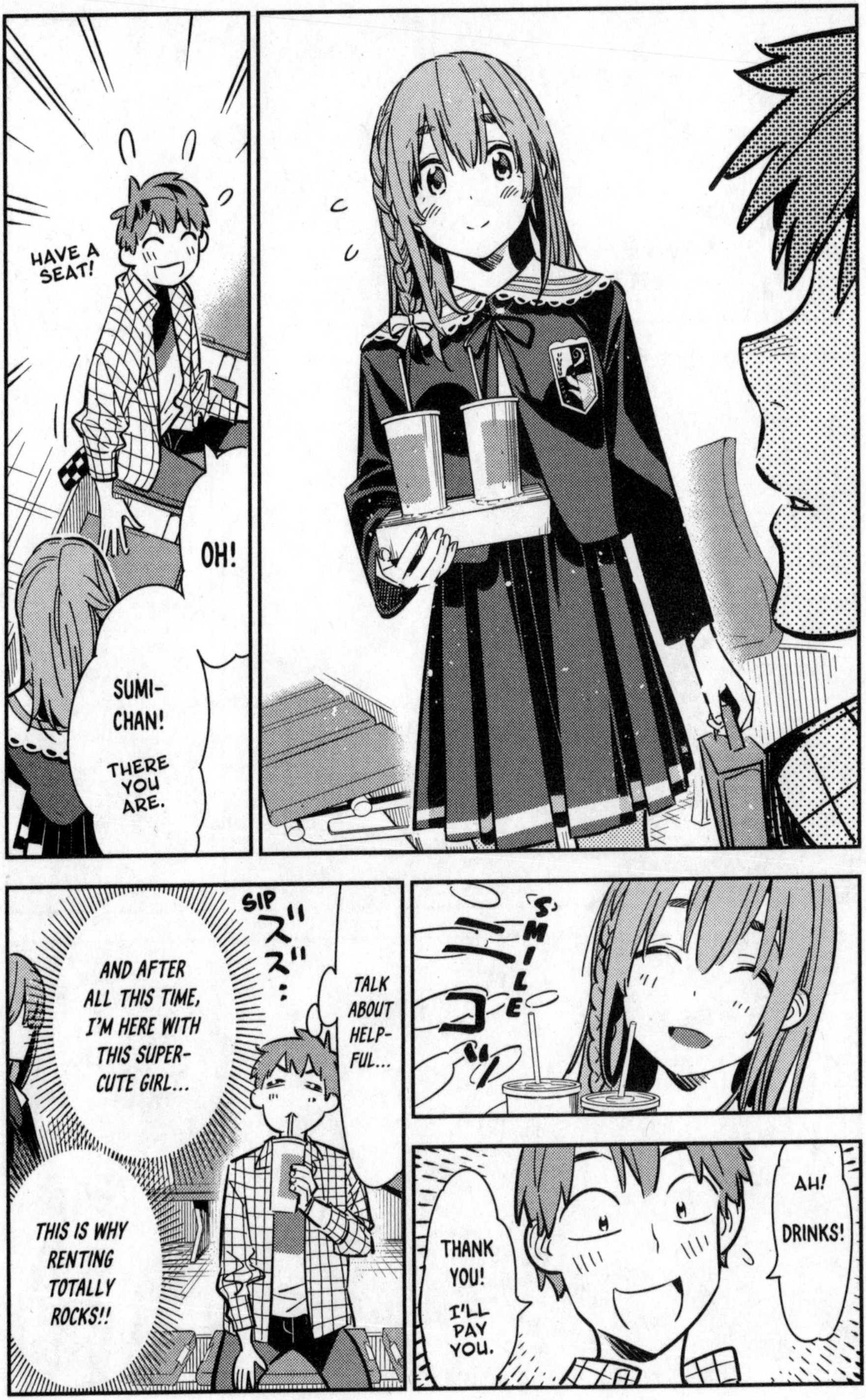

OH!
SUMI-CHAN!
THERE YOU ARE.
HAVE A SEAT!
SMILE
AH!
DRINKS!
THANK YOU!
I'LL PAY YOU.
TALK ABOUT HELPFUL...
SIP
AND AFTER ALL THIS TIME, I'M HERE WITH THIS SUPER-CUTE GIRL...
THIS IS WHY RENTING TOTALLY ROCKS!!

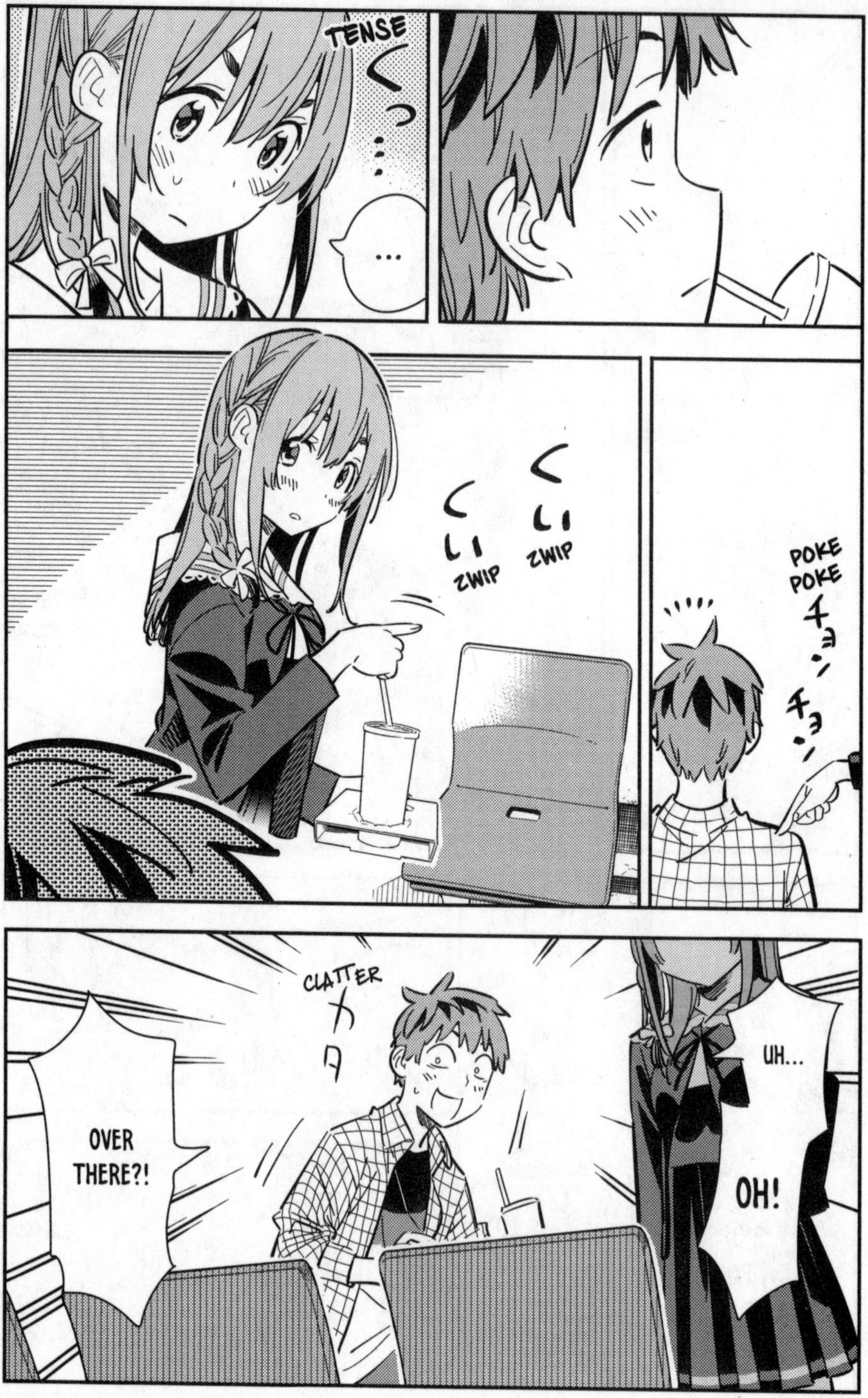
TENSE
くっ…
...
POKE POKE
チョン チョン
くい くい
ZWIP ZWIP
UH...
OH!
CLATTER
カタ
OVER THERE?!

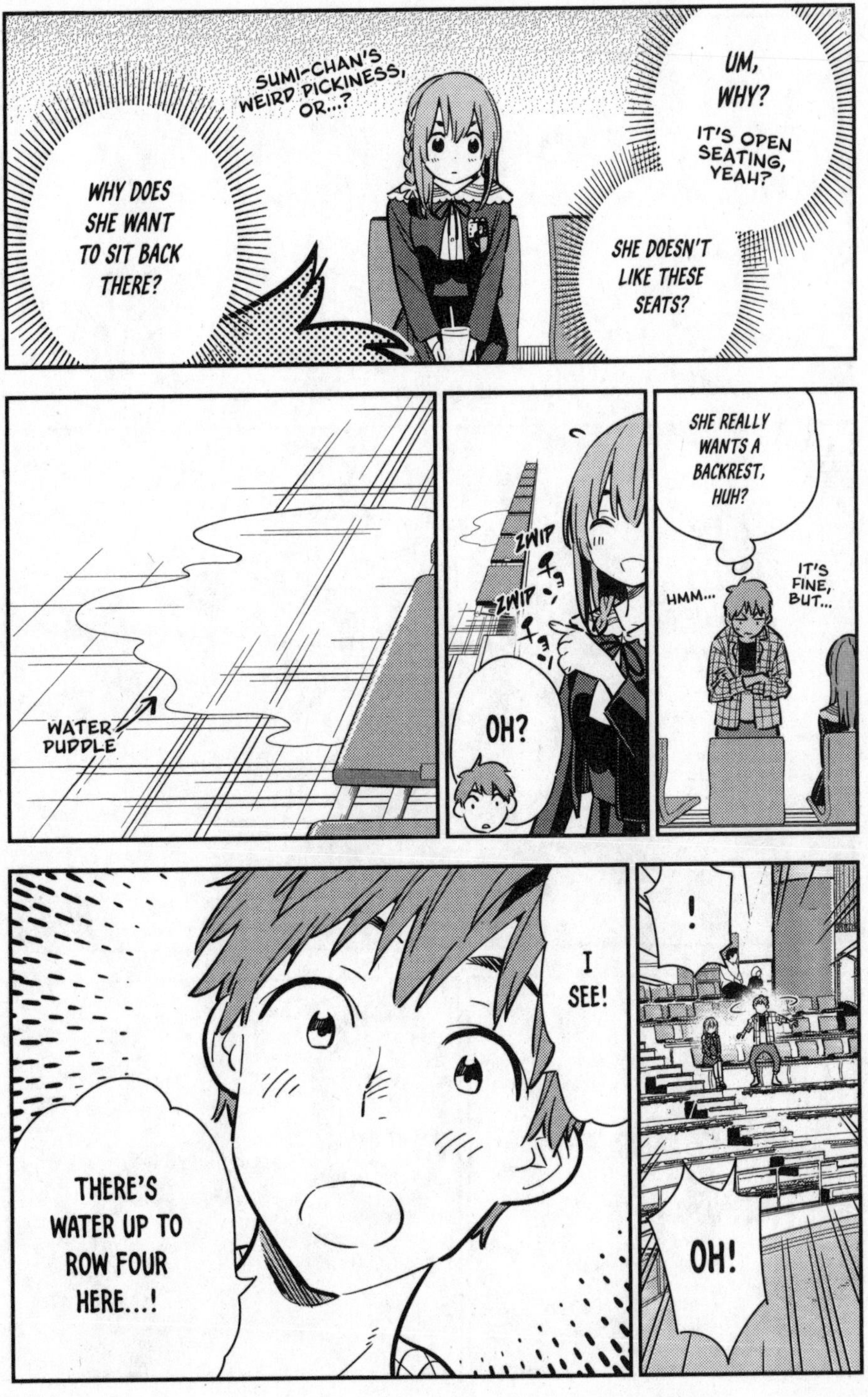
UM, WHY?
IT'S OPEN SEATING, YEAH?
SHE DOESN'T LIKE THESE SEATS?
SUMI-CHAN'S WEIRD PICKINESS, OR...?
WHY DOES SHE WANT TO SIT BACK THERE?
SHE REALLY WANTS A BACKREST, HUH?
IT'S FINE, BUT...
HMM...
ZWIP
ZWIP
OH?
WATER PUDDLE
!
OH!
I SEE!
THERE'S WATER UP TO ROW FOUR HERE...!

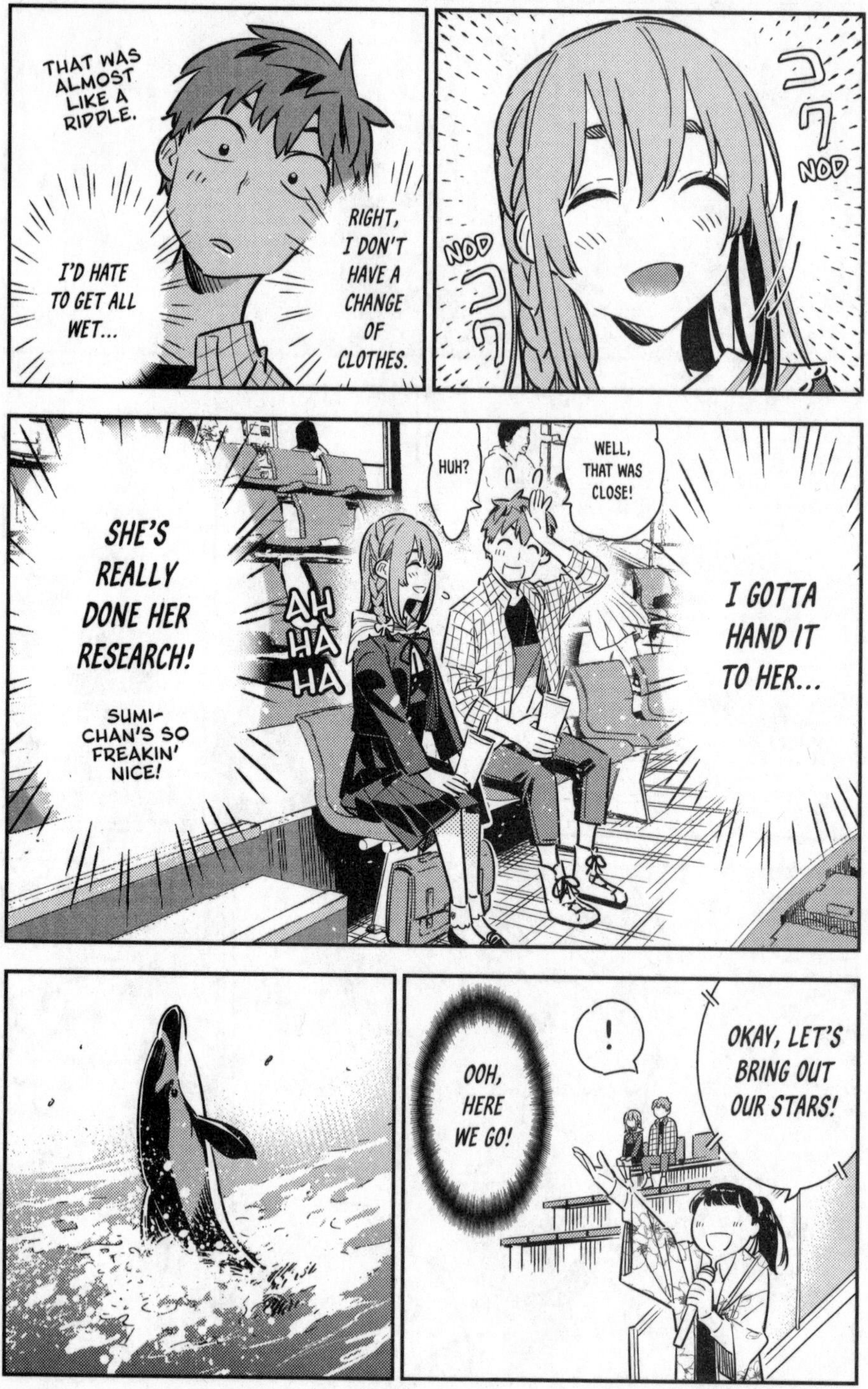
コク
NOD
NOD
コク
THAT WAS ALMOST LIKE A RIDDLE.
RIGHT, I DON'T HAVE A CHANGE OF CLOTHES.
I'D HATE TO GET ALL WET...
I GOTTA HAND IT TO HER...
WELL, THAT WAS CLOSE!
HUH?
AH HA HA
SHE'S REALLY DONE HER RESEARCH!
SUMI-CHAN'S SO FREAKIN' NICE!
OKAY, LET'S BRING OUT OUR STARS!
!
OOH, HERE WE GO!

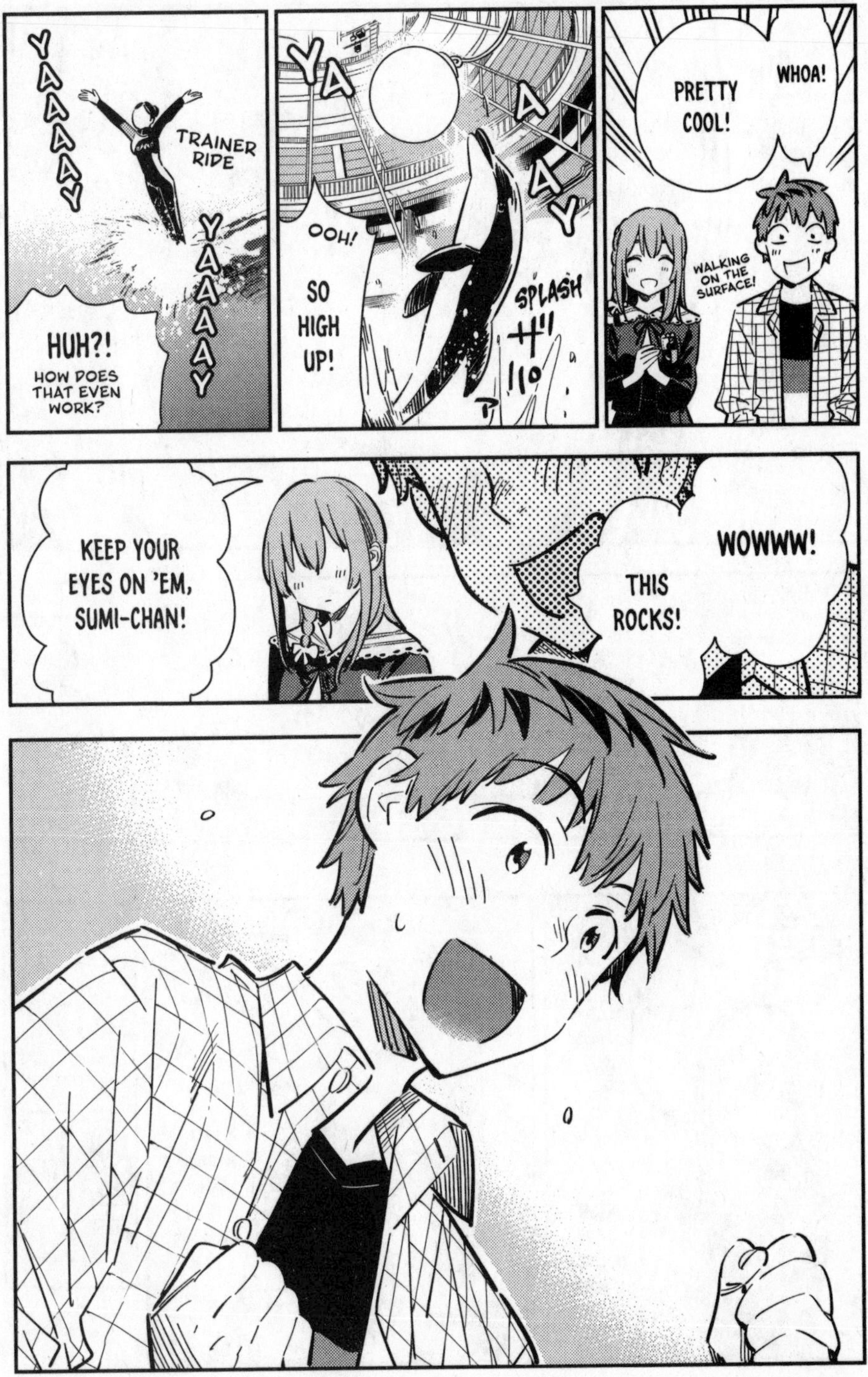
WHOA!
PRETTY COOL!
WALKING ON THE SURFACE!
YA
A
A
Y
OOH!
SO HIGH UP!
SPLASH
YAAAAY
TRAINER RIDE
YAAAAAY
HUH?!
HOW DOES THAT EVEN WORK?
WOWWW!
THIS ROCKS!
KEEP YOUR EYES ON 'EM, SUMI-CHAN!

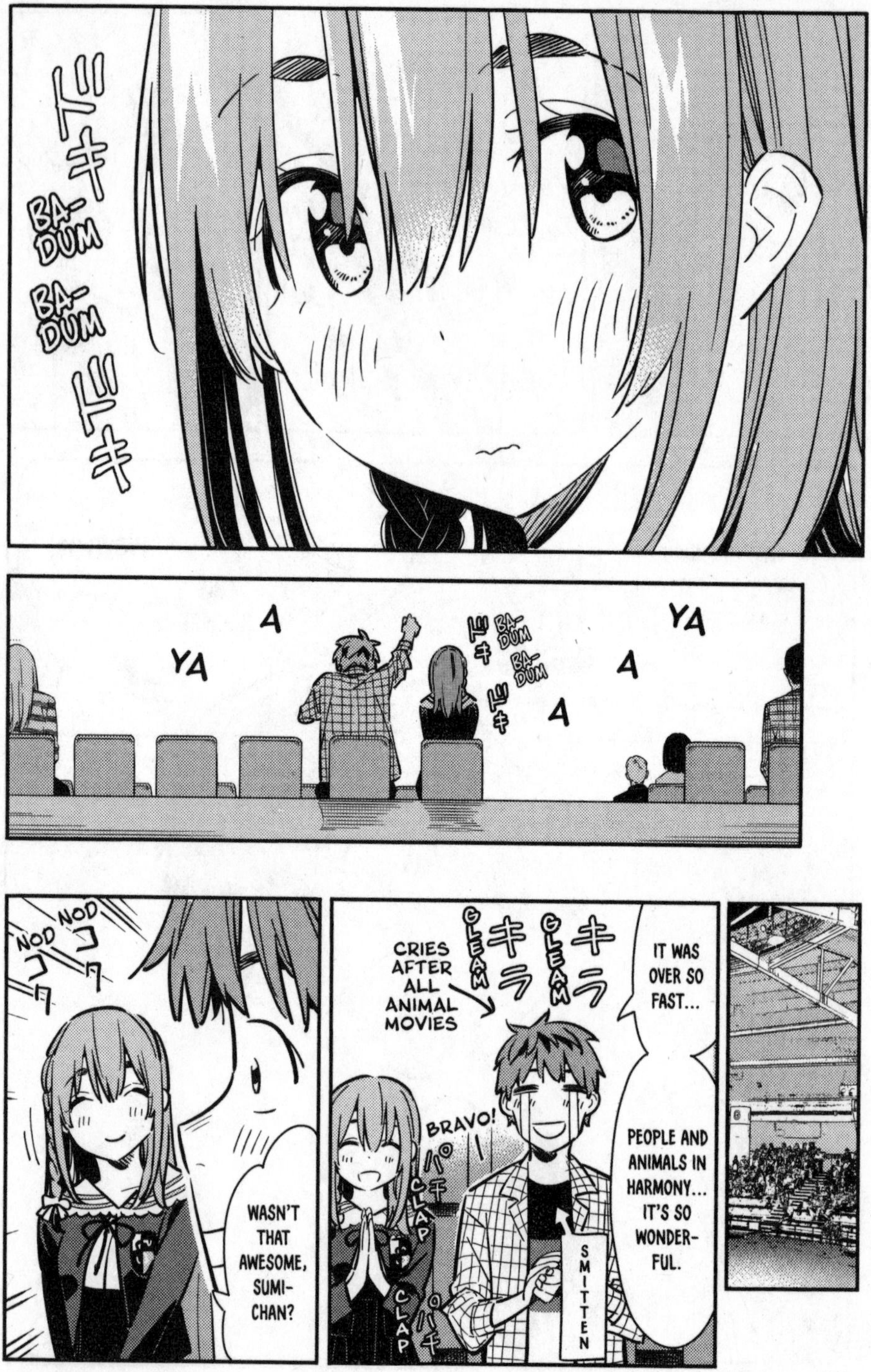
ドキ
BA-DUM
BA-DUM
ドキ
YA
A
A
A
YA
A
ドキ BA-DUM
BA-DUM ドキ
IT WAS OVER SO FAST...
PEOPLE AND ANIMALS IN HARMONY... IT'S SO WONDER-FUL.
キラ GLEAM
キラ GLEAM
CRIES AFTER ALL ANIMAL MOVIES
BRAVO!
パチ CLAP
パチ CLAP
SMITTEN
NOD コク
NOD コク
WASN'T THAT AWESOME, SUMI-CHAN?

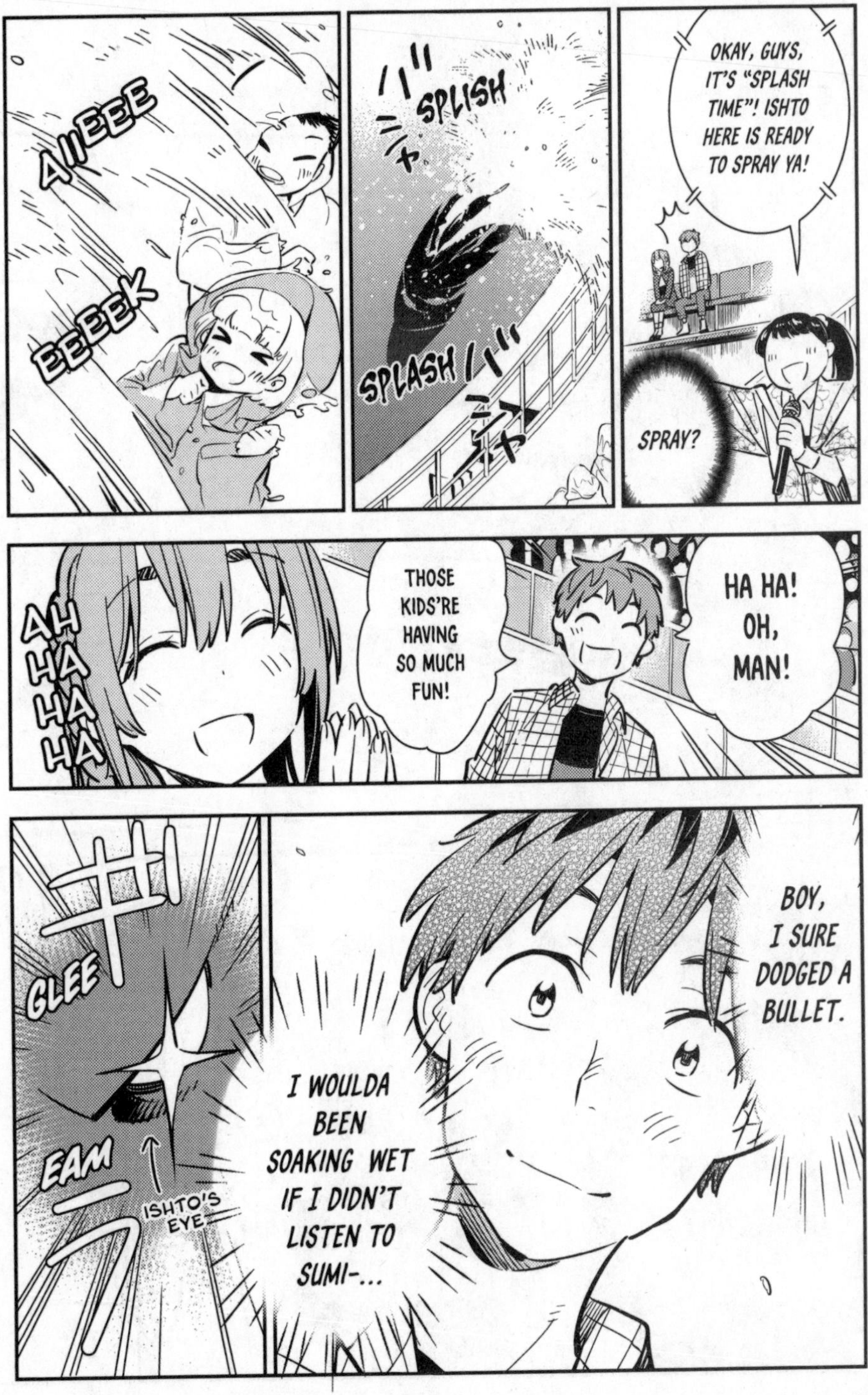
OKAY, GUYS, IT'S "SPLASH TIME"! ISHTO HERE IS READY TO SPRAY YA!
SPRAY?
SPLISH
SPLASH
AIIEEE
EEEEK
HA HA! OH, MAN!
THOSE KIDS'RE HAVING SO MUCH FUN!
AH HA HA HA HA
BOY, I SURE DODGED A BULLET.
I WOULDA BEEN SOAKING WET IF I DIDN'T LISTEN TO SUMI-...
GLEE
EAM
ISHTO'S EYE

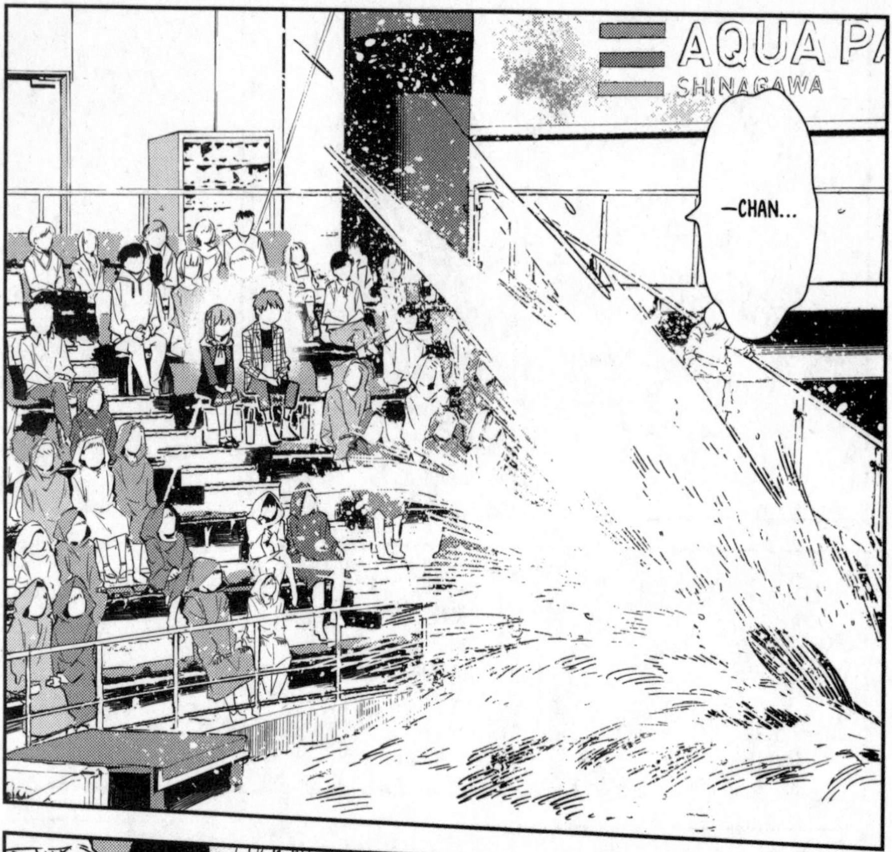
AQUA PA
SHINAGAWA
—CHAN...
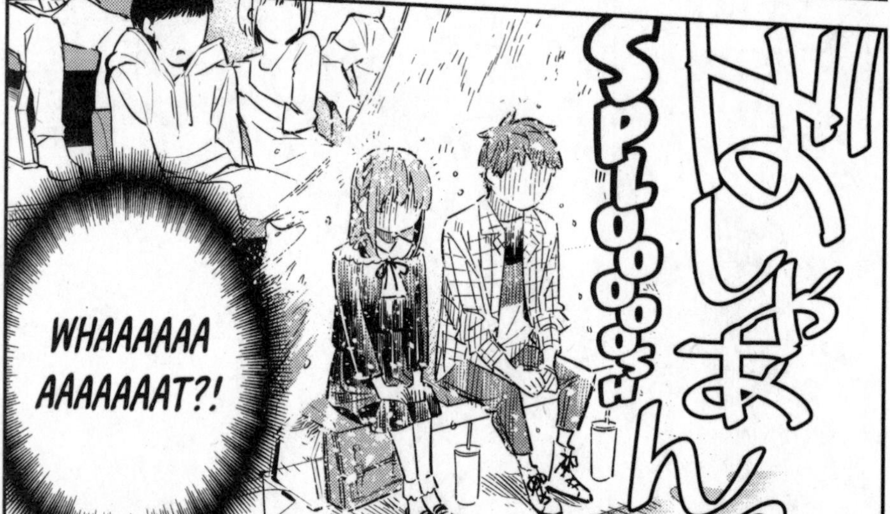
ばしゃんっ
SPLOOOOSH
WHAAAAAAA AAAAAAAT?!

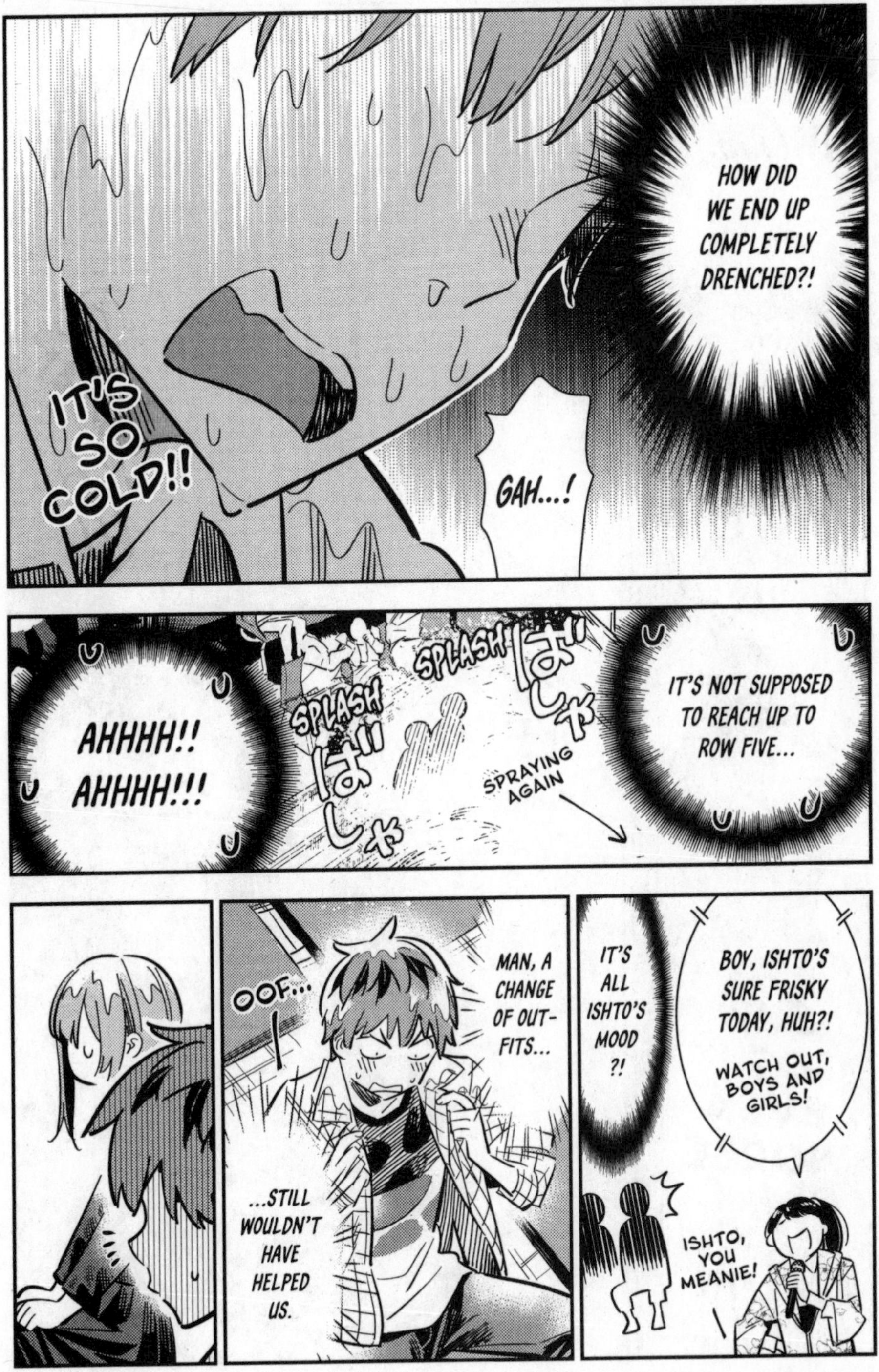
HOW DID WE END UP COMPLETELY DRENCHED?!
GAH...!
IT'S SO COLD!!
IT'S NOT SUPPOSED TO REACH UP TO ROW FIVE...
SPRAYING AGAIN
SPLASH ばしゃ
SPLASH ばしゃ
AHHHH!! AHHHH!!!
BOY, ISHTO'S SURE FRISKY TODAY, HUH?!
WATCH OUT, BOYS AND GIRLS!
IT'S ALL ISHTO'S MOOD?!
ISHTO, YOU MEANIE!
MAN, A CHANGE OF OUT-FITS...
OOF...
...STILL WOULDN'T HAVE HELPED US.

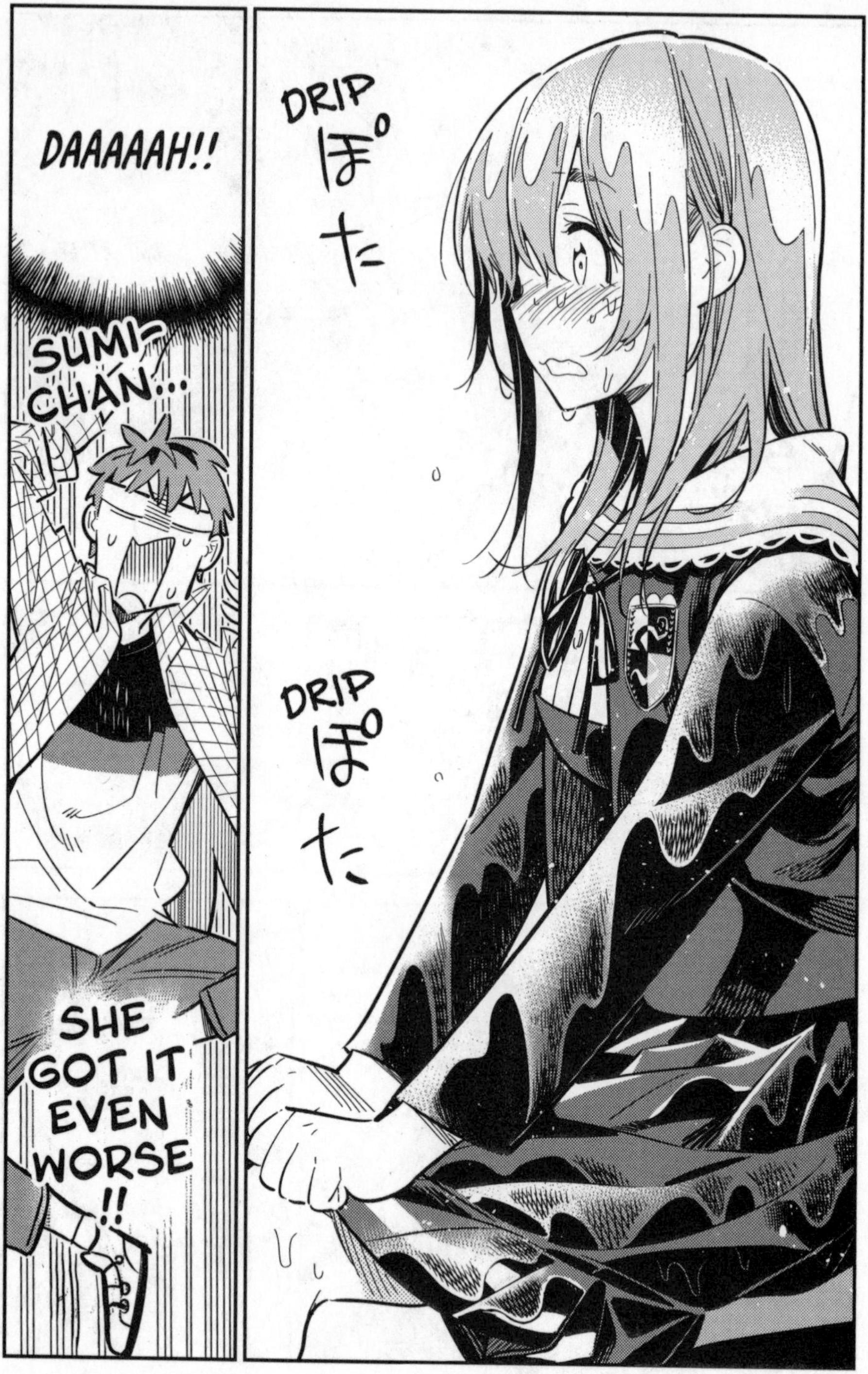
DRIP
ぽた
DRIP
ぽた
DAAAAAH!!
SUMI-CHAN...
SHE GOT IT EVEN WORSE!!

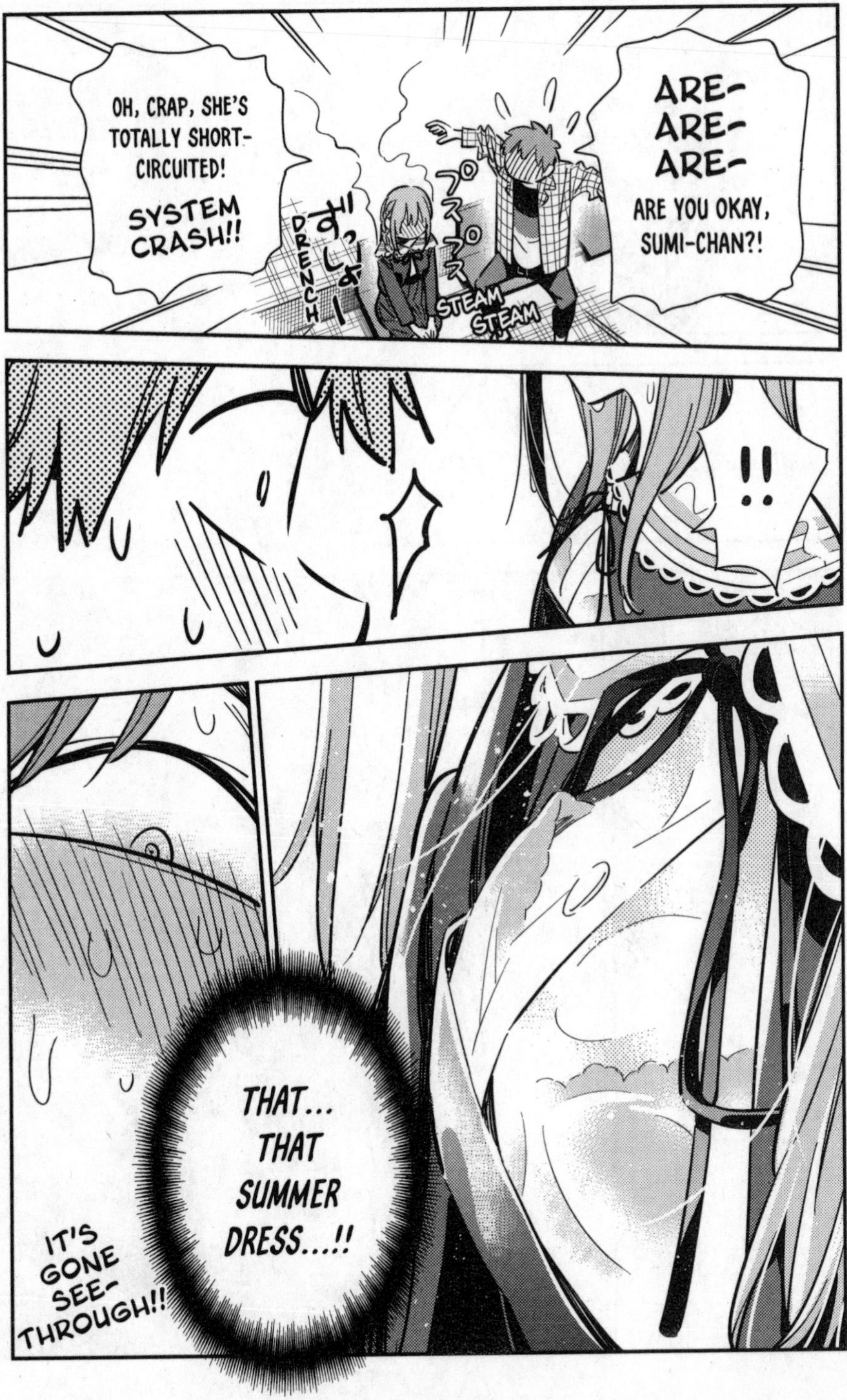
ARE- ARE- ARE-
ARE YOU OKAY, SUMI-CHAN?!
プスプス
STEAM STEAM
ずっしょー
DRENCH
OH, CRAP, SHE'S TOTALLY SHORT-CIRCUITED!
SYSTEM CRASH!!
!!
THAT... THAT SUMMER DRESS...!!
IT'S GONE SEE-THROUGH!!

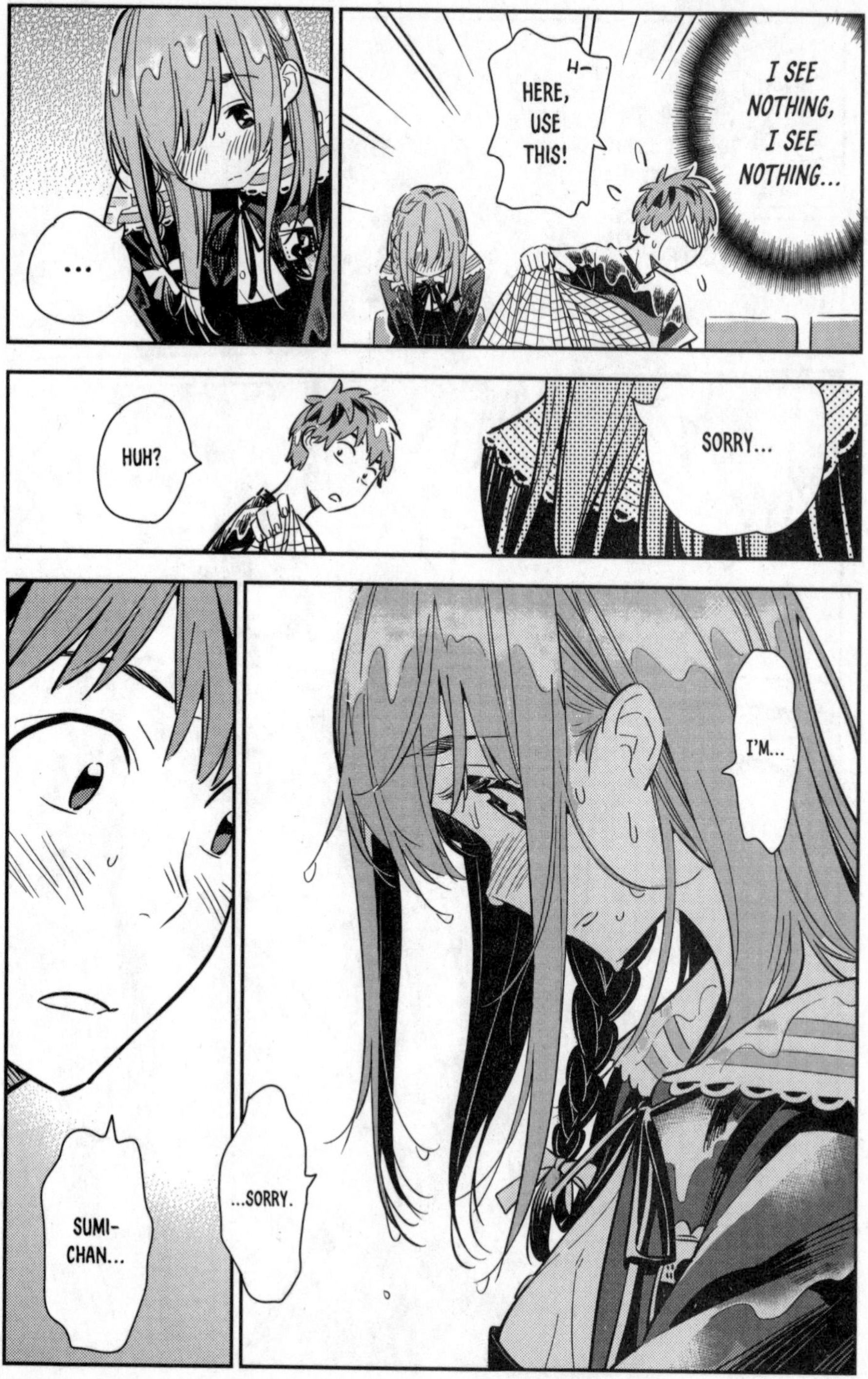
I SEE NOTHING, I SEE NOTHING...
H- HERE, USE THIS!
...
SORRY...
HUH?
I'M...
...SORRY.
SUMI-CHAN...

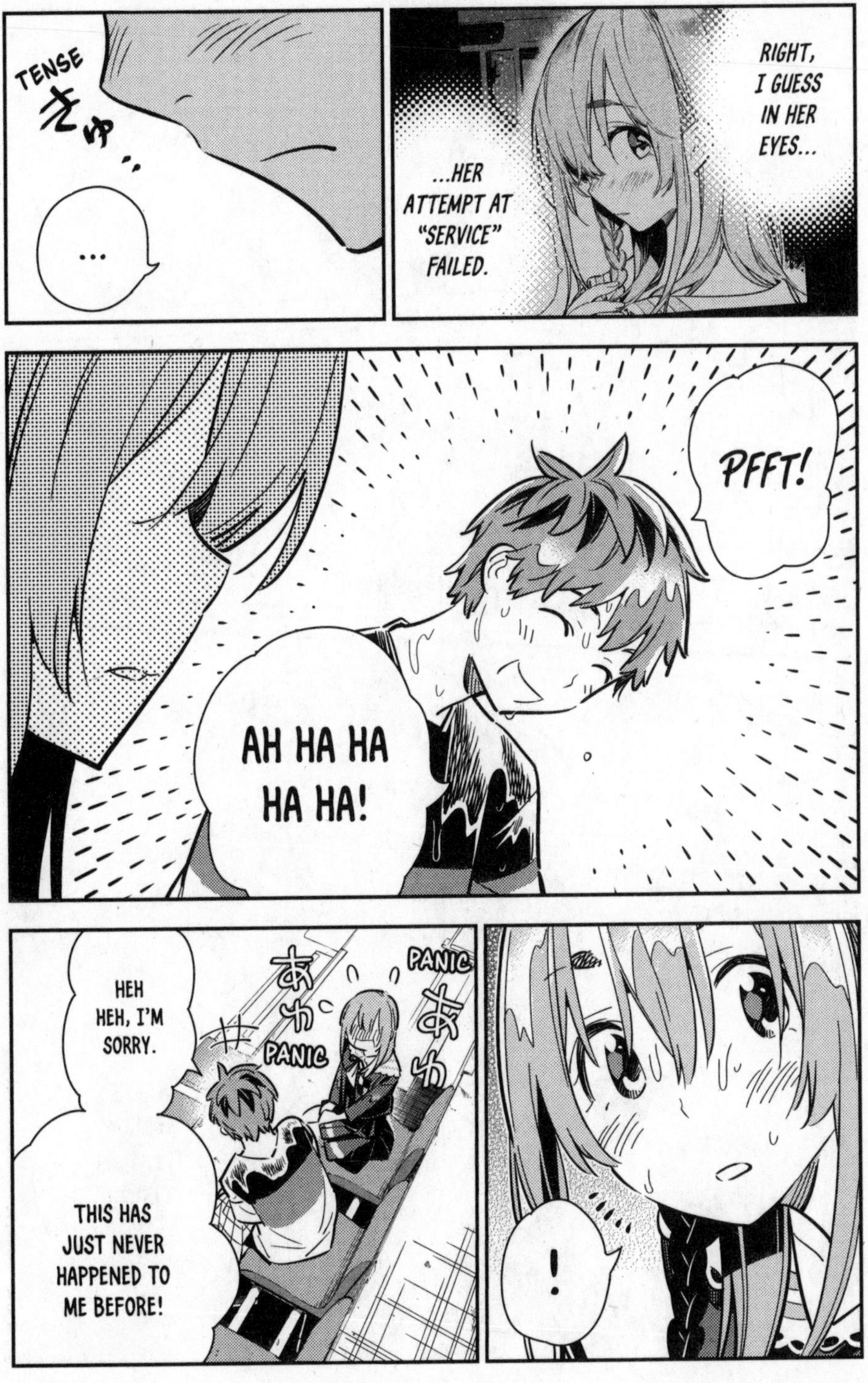
RIGHT, I GUESS IN HER EYES...
...HER ATTEMPT AT "SERVICE" FAILED.
TENSE
きゅ
...
PFFT!
AH HA HA HA HA!
!
PANIC
あわ
PANIC
あわ
HEH HEH, I'M SORRY.
THIS HAS JUST NEVER HAPPENED TO ME BEFORE!

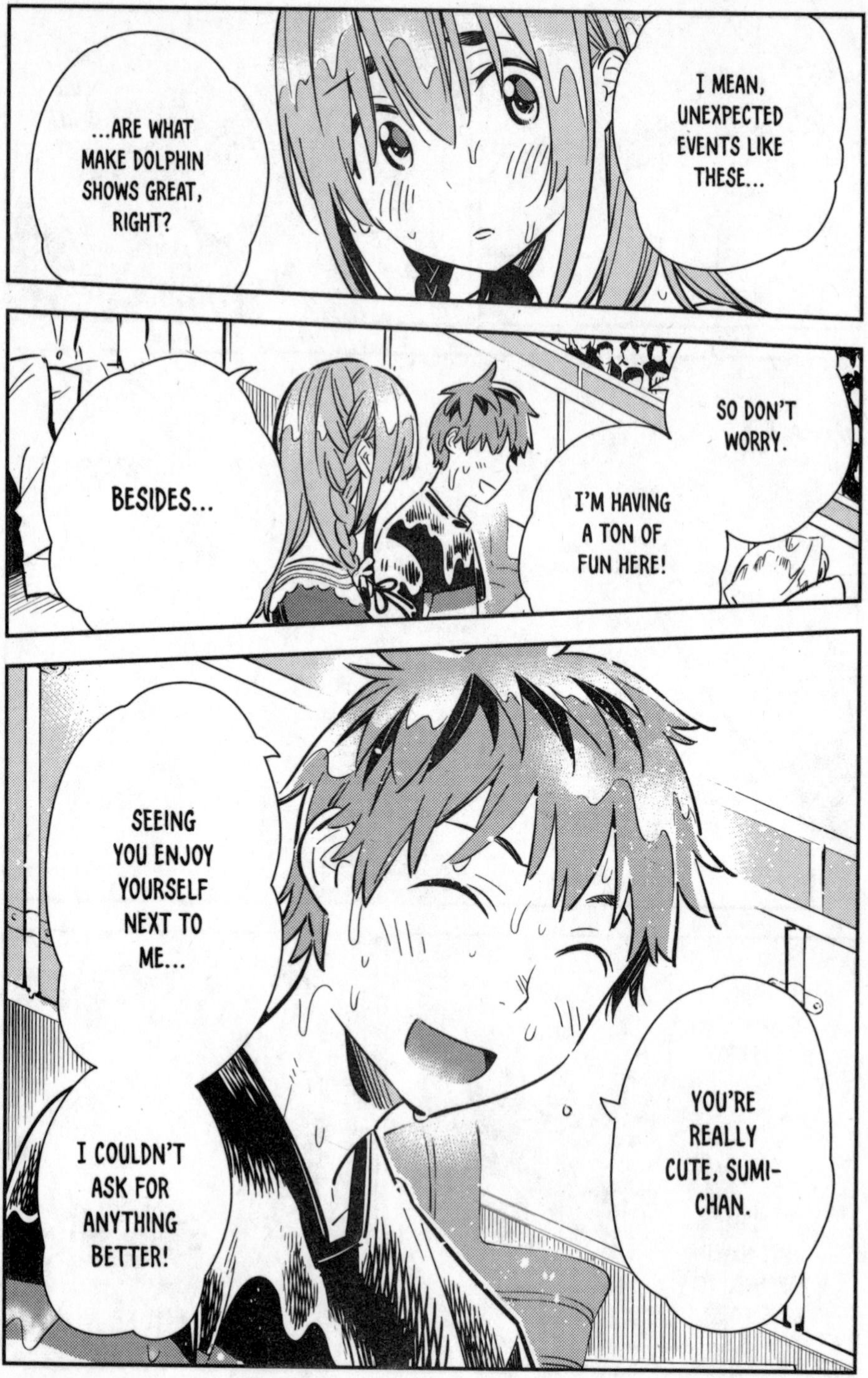
I MEAN, UNEXPECTED EVENTS LIKE THESE...
...ARE WHAT MAKE DOLPHIN SHOWS GREAT, RIGHT?
SO DON'T WORRY.
I'M HAVING A TON OF FUN HERE!
BESIDES...
SEEING YOU ENJOY YOURSELF NEXT TO ME...
I COULDN'T ASK FOR ANYTHING BETTER!
YOU'RE REALLY CUTE, SUMI-CHAN.

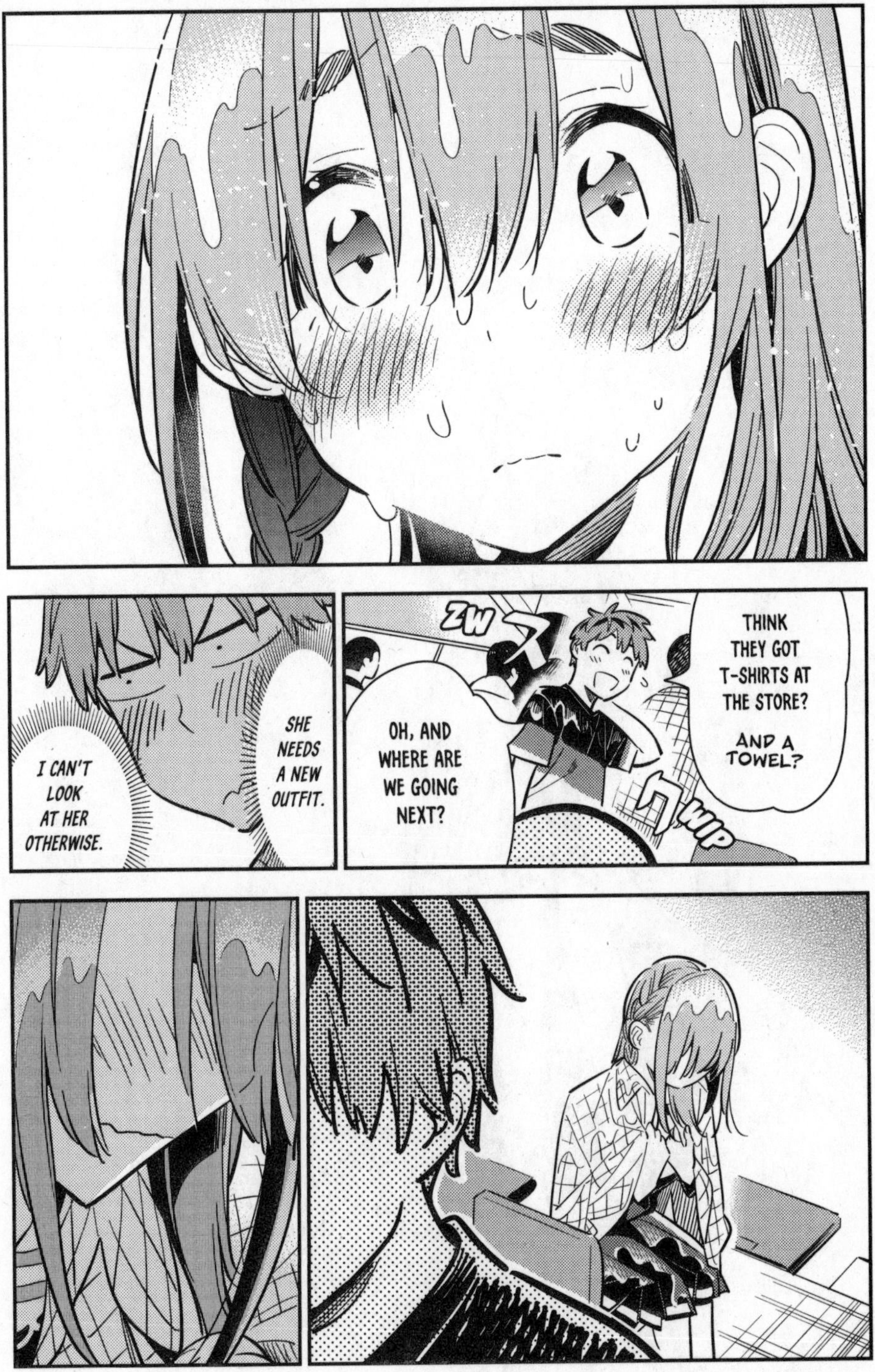
THINK THEY GOT T-SHIRTS AT THE STORE?
AND A TOWEL?
ZW
OH, AND WHERE ARE WE GOING NEXT?
WIP
SHE NEEDS A NEW OUTFIT.
I CAN'T LOOK AT HER OTHERWISE.

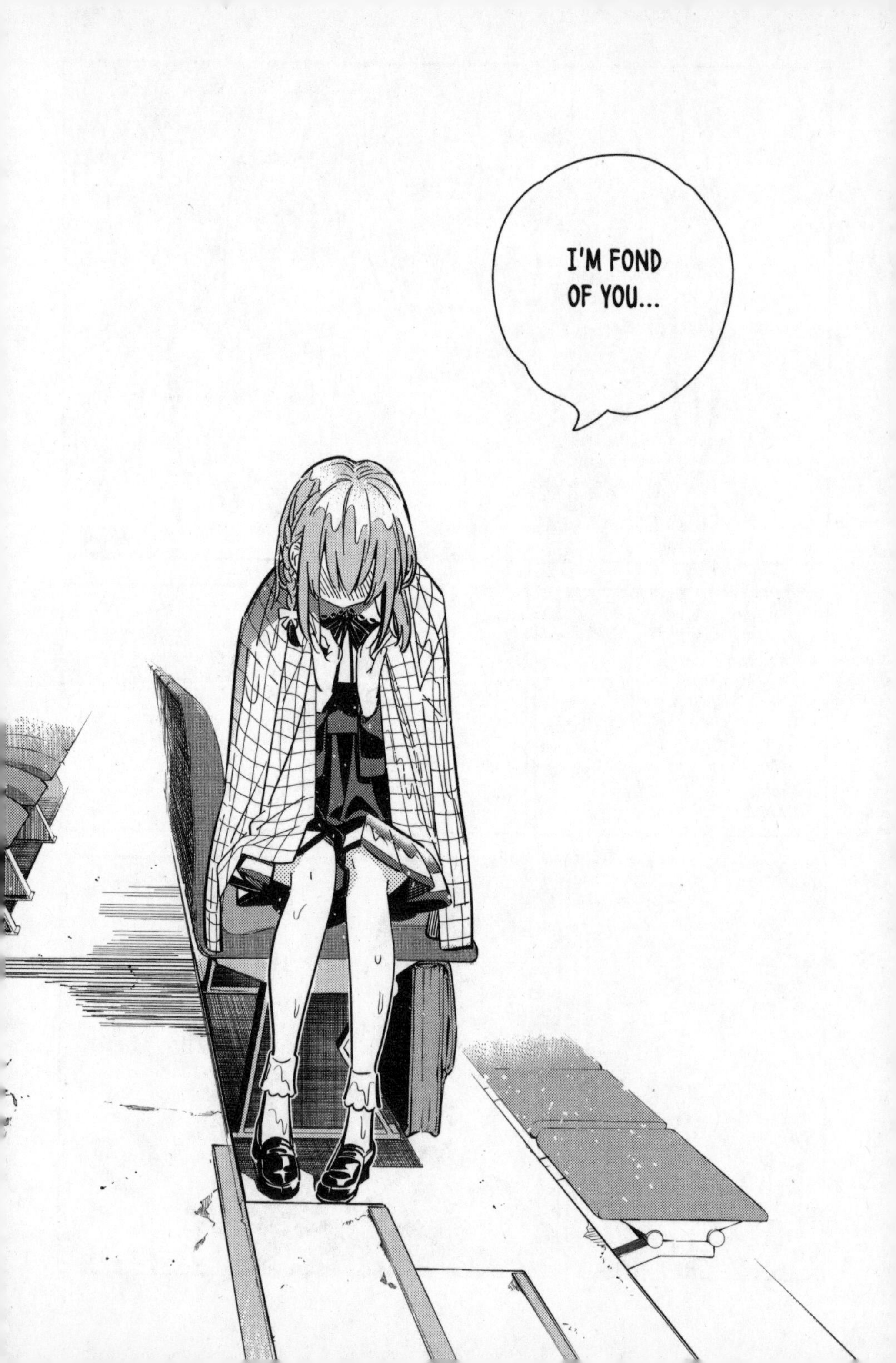
I'M FOND OF YOU...

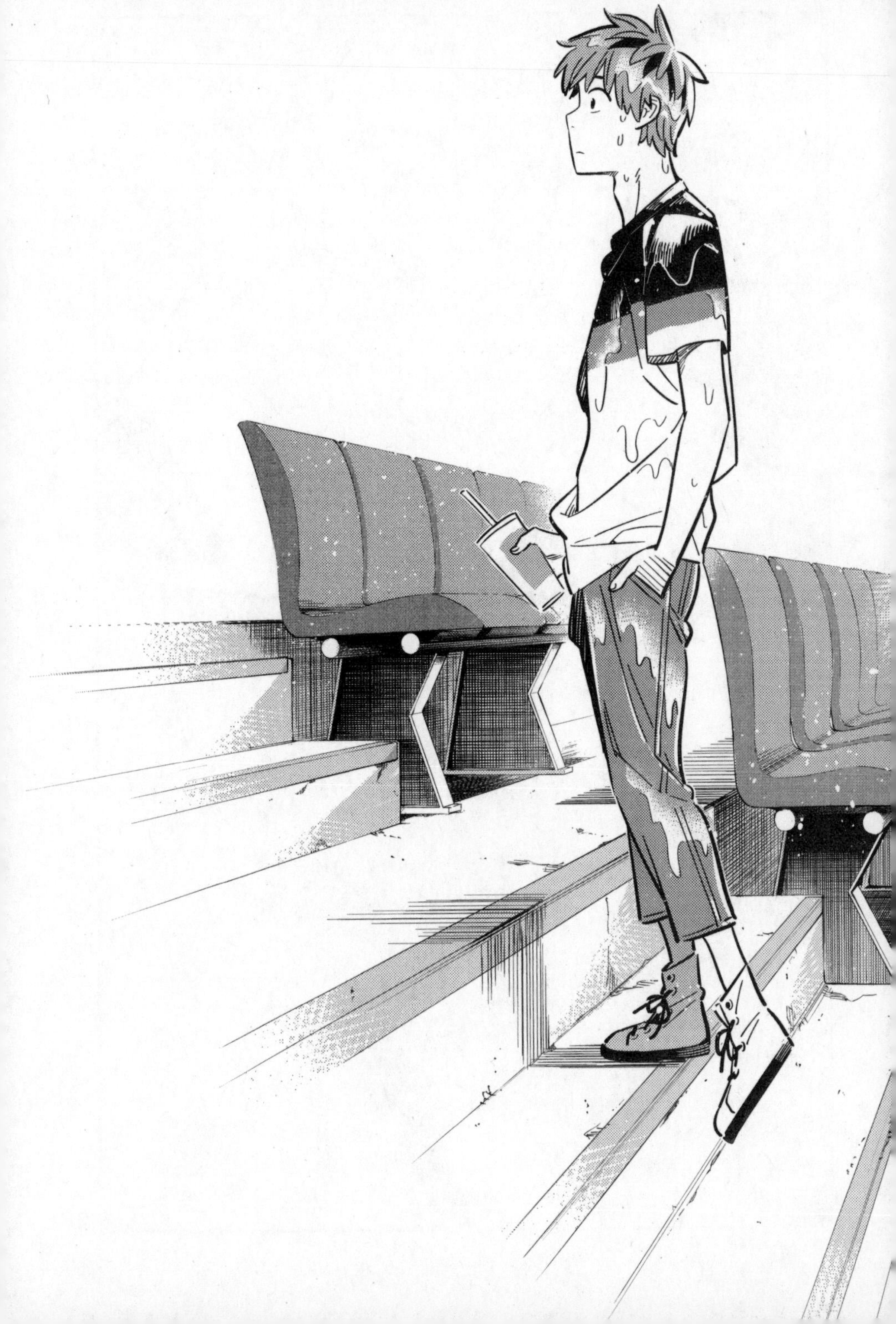

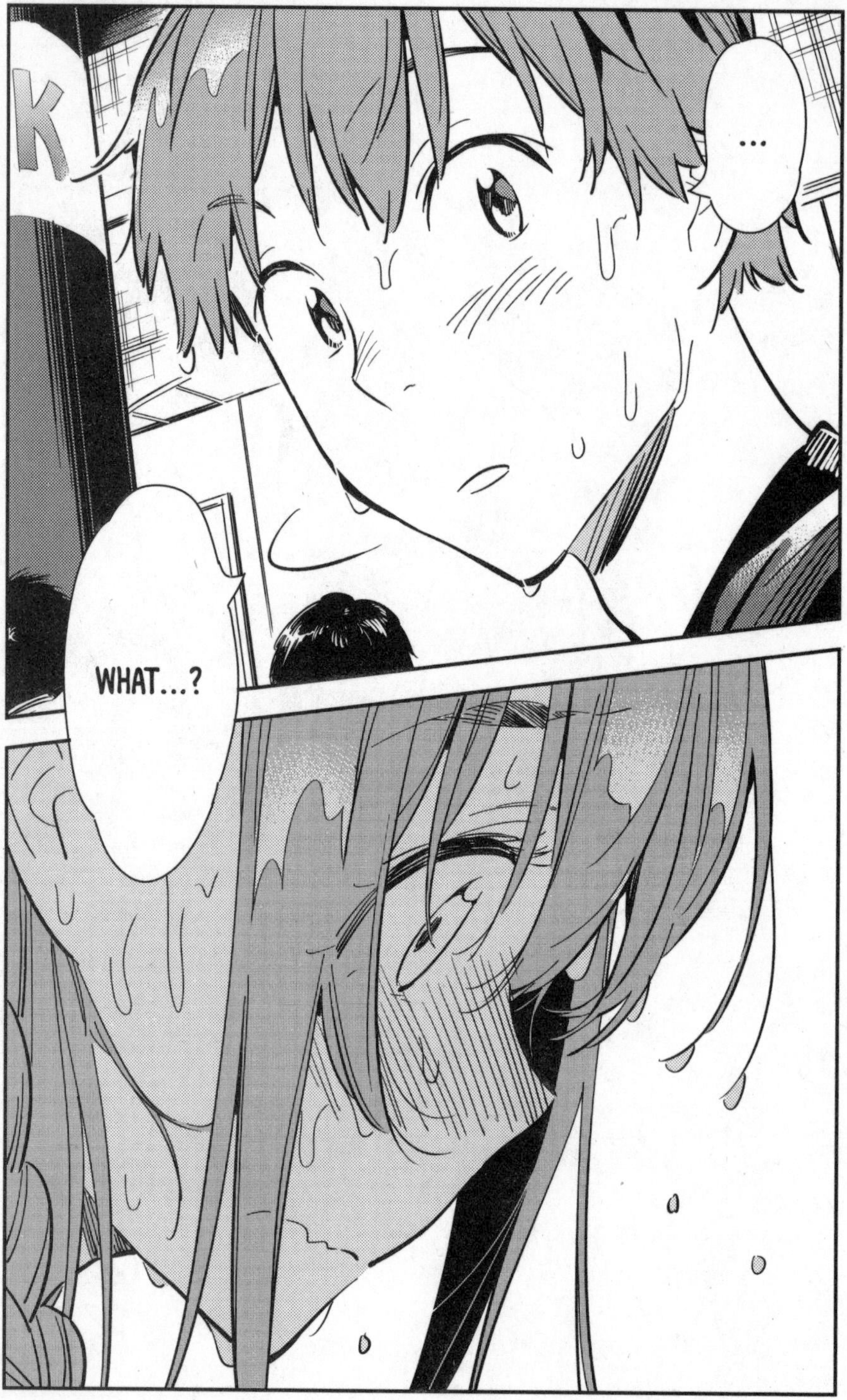
...
WHAT...?

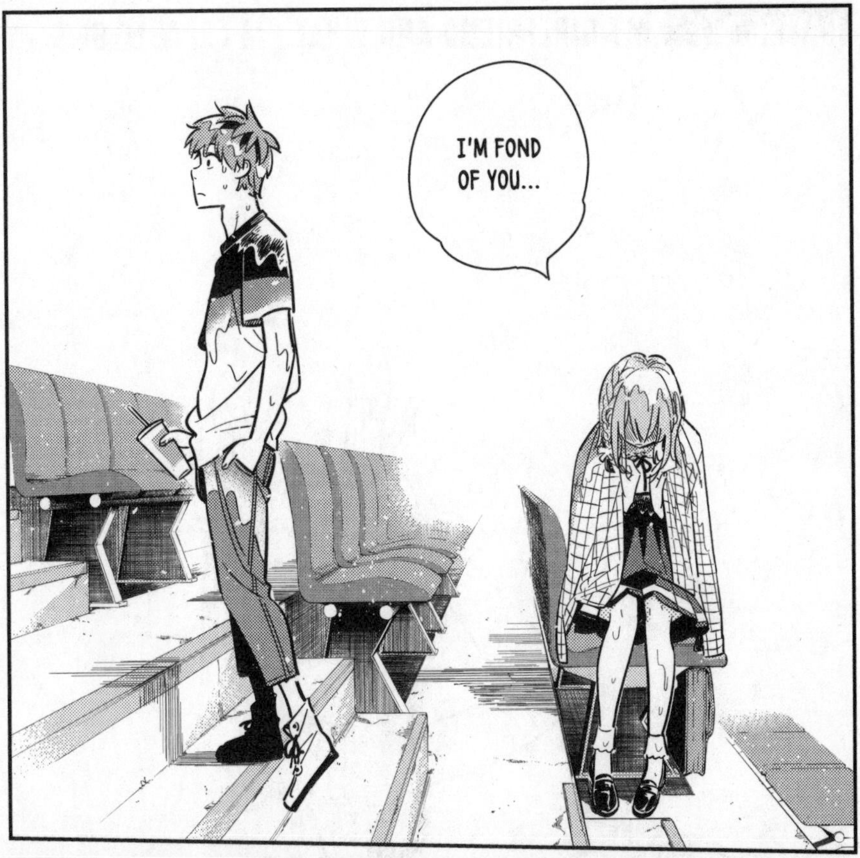
I'M FOND OF YOU...

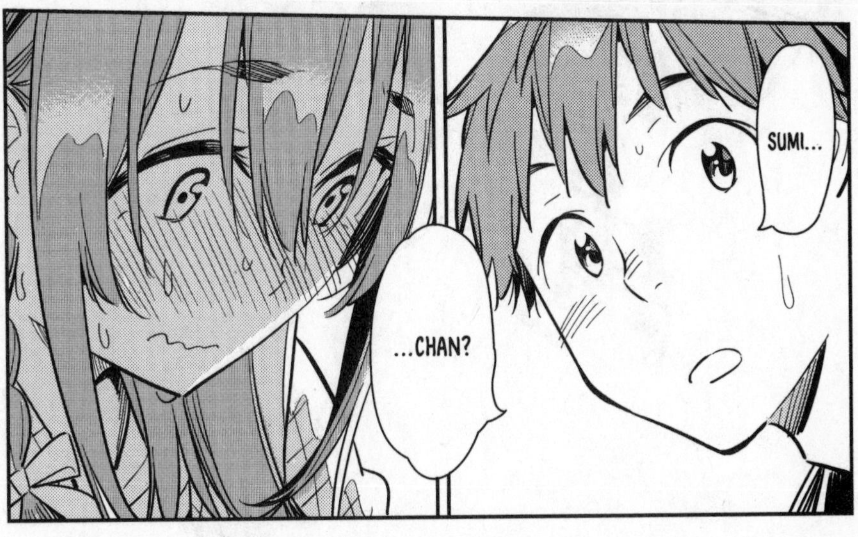
SUMI...
...CHAN?

# RATING 96 MY GIRLFRIEND AND WHAT I'M CAPABLE OF 5

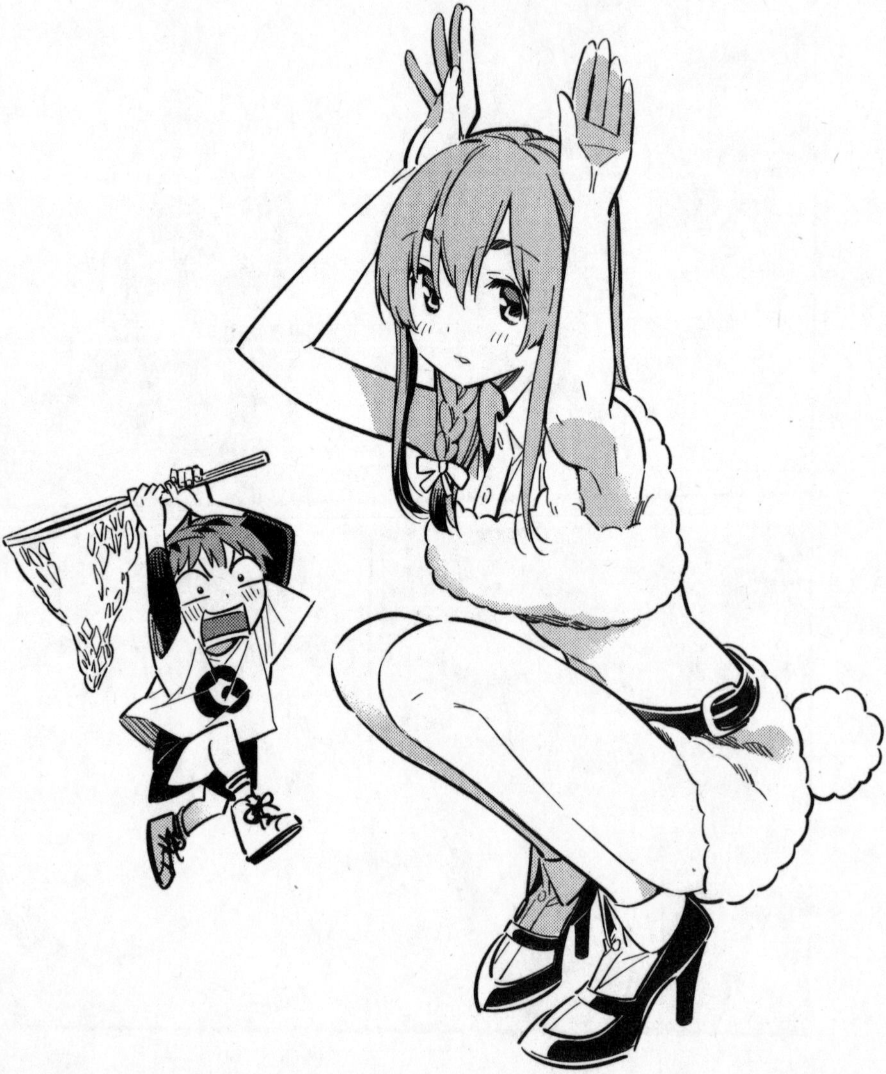

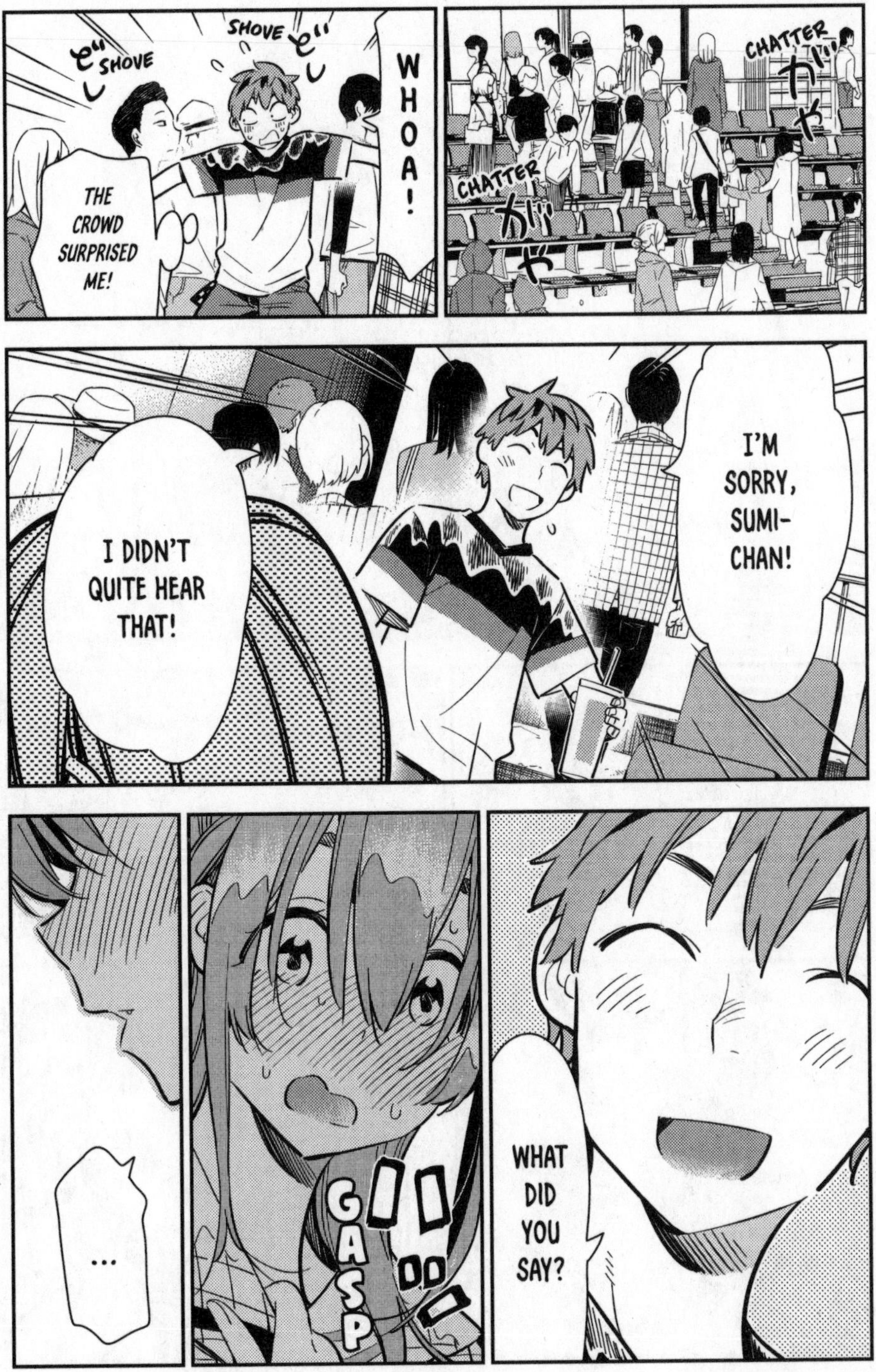
CHATTER
CHATTER
WHOA!
SHOVE
SHOVE
THE CROWD SURPRISED ME!
I'M SORRY, SUMI-CHAN!
I DIDN'T QUITE HEAR THAT!
WHAT DID YOU SAY?
GASP
...

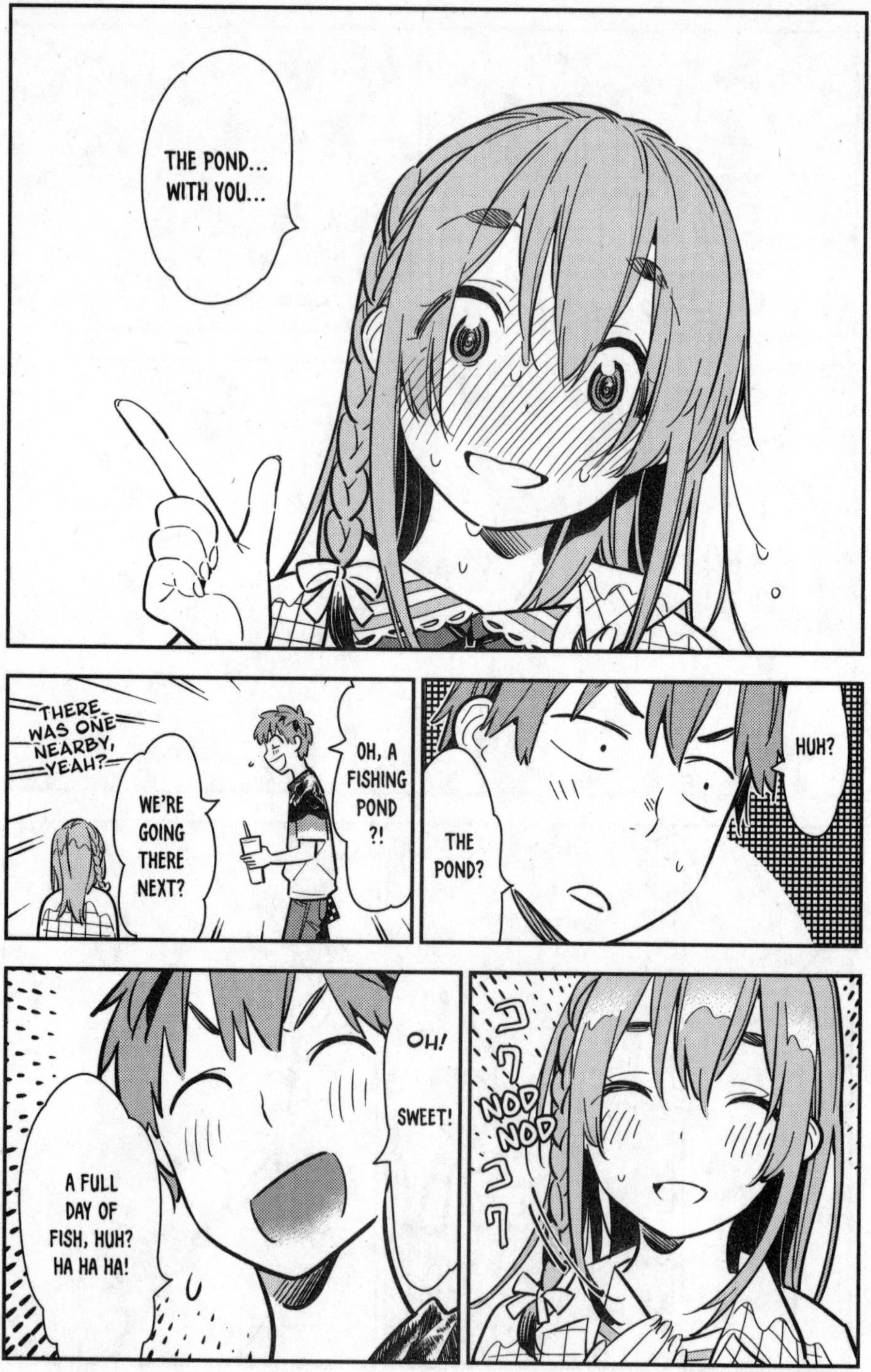
THE POND... WITH YOU...
HUH?
THE POND?
OH, A FISHING POND?!
THERE WAS ONE NEARBY, YEAH?
WE'RE GOING THERE NEXT?
コク
NOD NOD
コク
OH!
SWEET!
A FULL DAY OF FISH, HUH? HA HA HA!

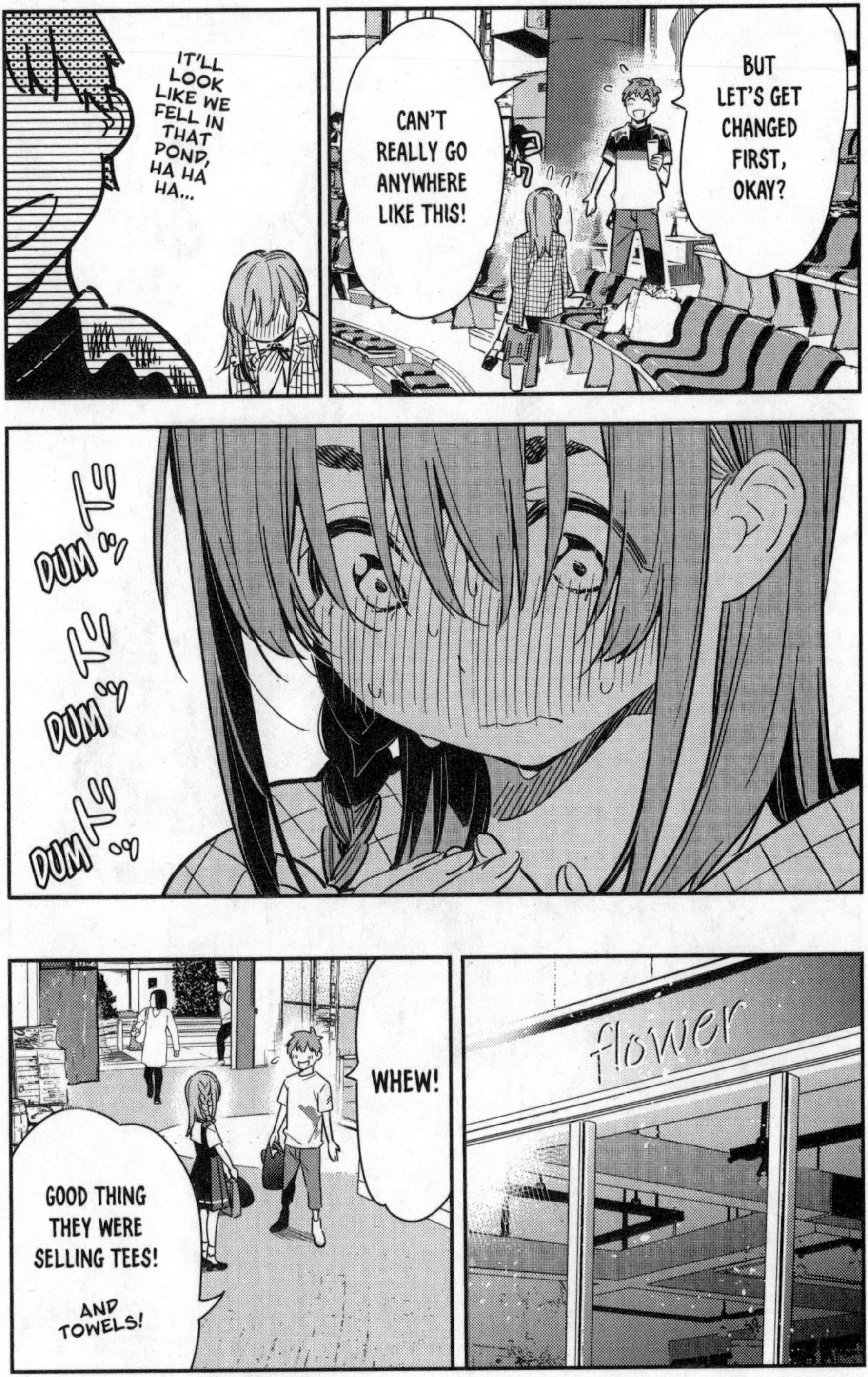
BUT LET'S GET CHANGED FIRST, OKAY?
CAN'T REALLY GO ANYWHERE LIKE THIS!
IT'LL LOOK LIKE WE FELL IN THAT POND, HA HA HA...
ドッ DUM
ドッ DUM
ドッ DUM
flower
WHEW!
GOOD THING THEY WERE SELLING TEES!
AND TOWELS!

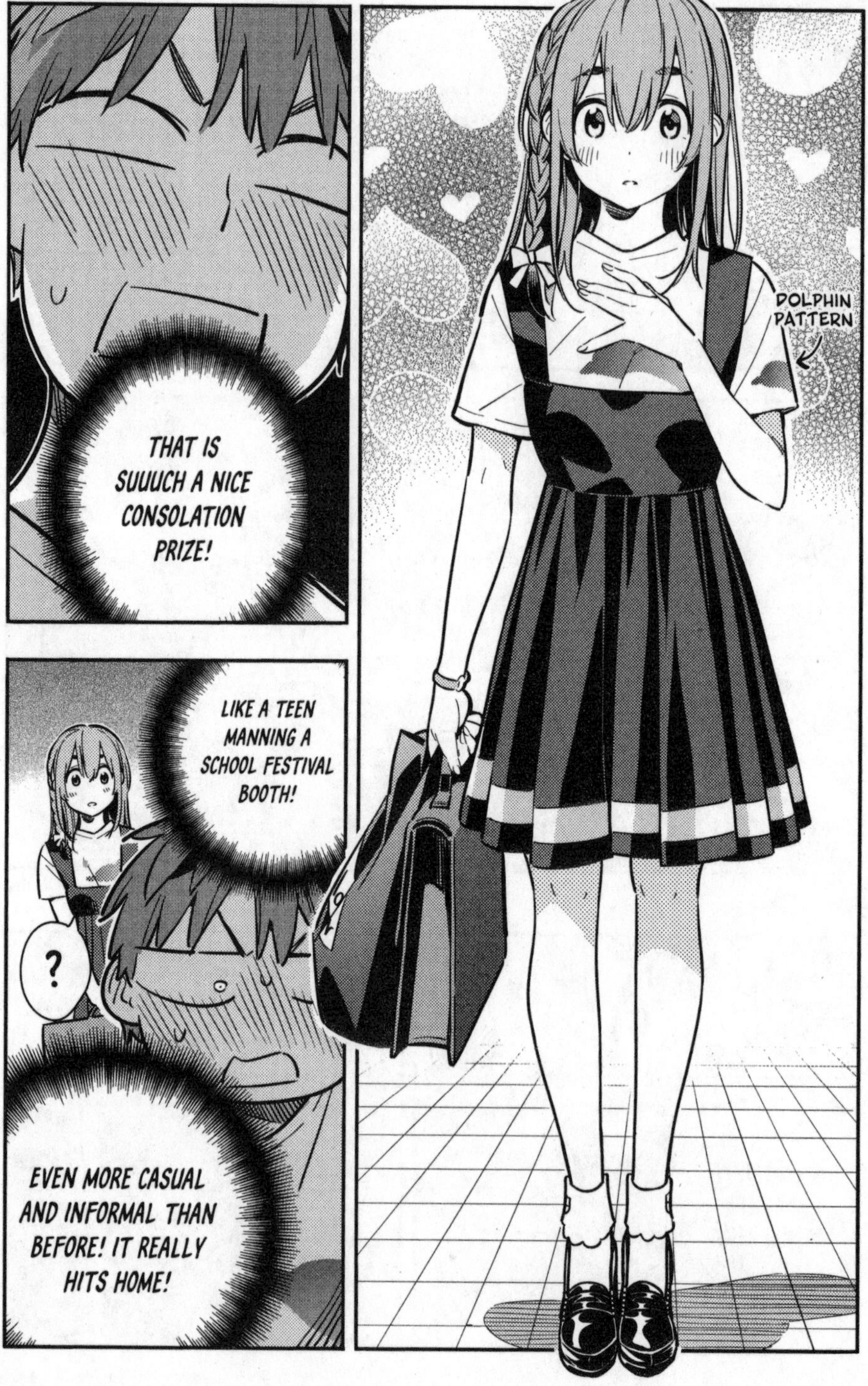

DOLPHIN PATTERN
THAT IS SUUUCH A NICE CONSOLATION PRIZE!
LIKE A TEEN MANNING A SCHOOL FESTIVAL BOOTH!
?
EVEN MORE CASUAL AND INFORMAL THAN BEFORE! IT REALLY HITS HOME!

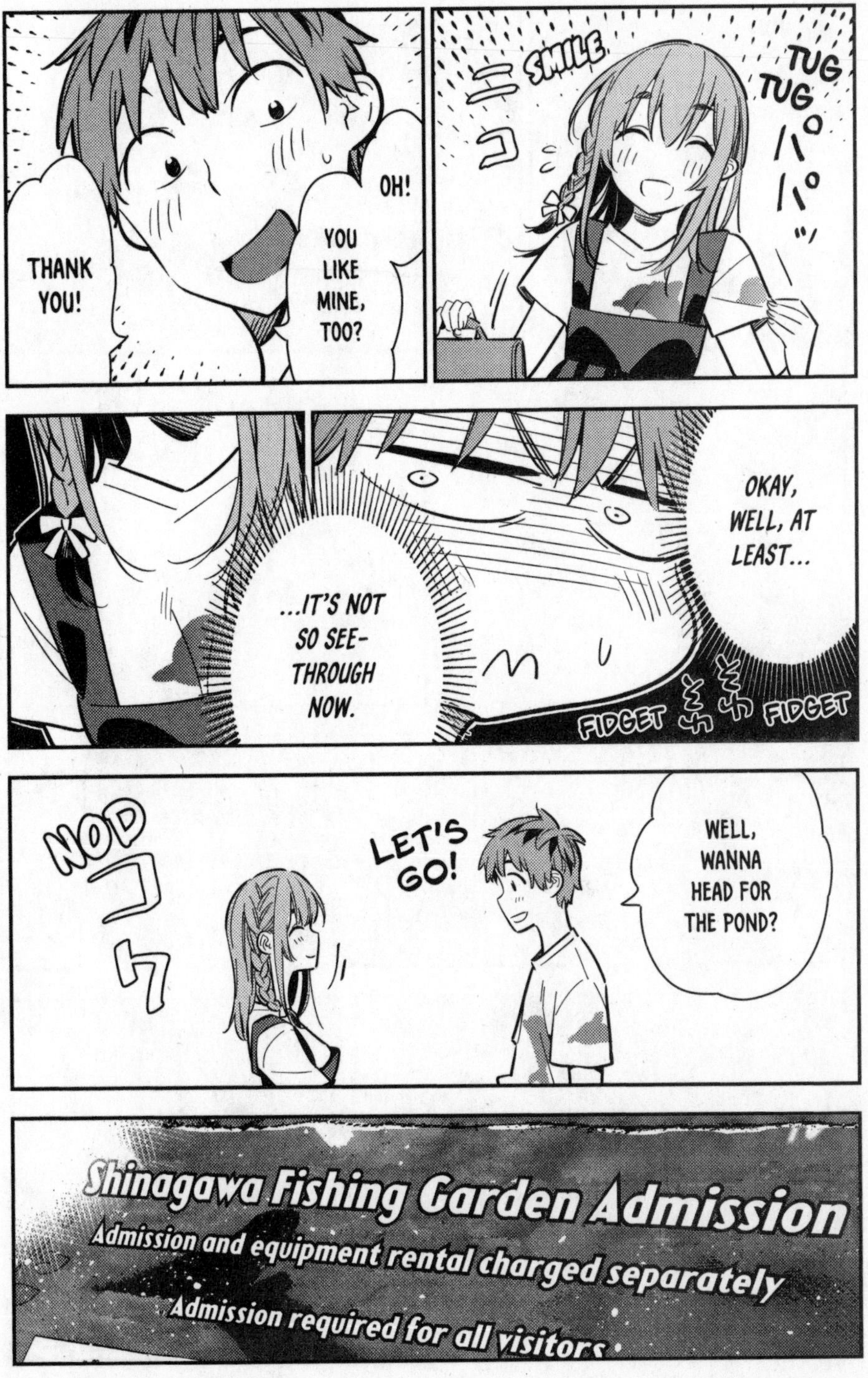
SMILE
ニコ
TUG TUG
パパッ
OH!
YOU LIKE MINE, TOO?
THANK YOU!
OKAY, WELL, AT LEAST...
...IT'S NOT SO SEE-THROUGH NOW.
FIDGET
FIDGET
WELL, WANNA HEAD FOR THE POND?
LET'S GO!
NOD
コク
Shinagawa Fishing Garden Admission
Admission and equipment rental charged separately
Admission required for all visitors

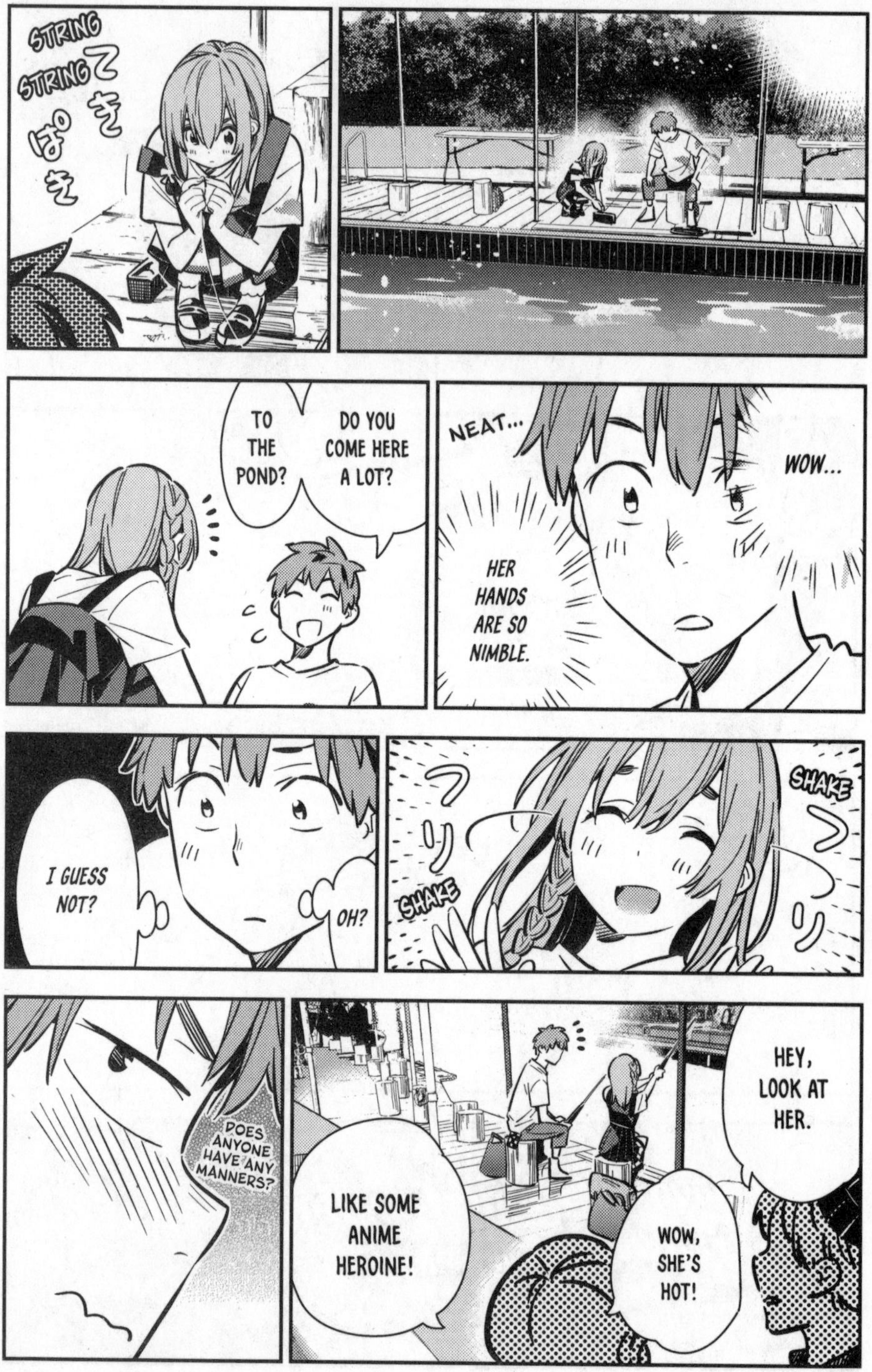
STRING
STRING
てきぱき
NEAT...
WOW...
HER HANDS ARE SO NIMBLE.
DO YOU COME HERE A LOT?
TO THE POND?
SHAKE
フリ
SHAKE
フリ
OH?
I GUESS NOT?
HEY, LOOK AT HER.
WOW, SHE'S HOT!
LIKE SOME ANIME HEROINE!
DOES ANYONE HAVE ANY MANNERS?

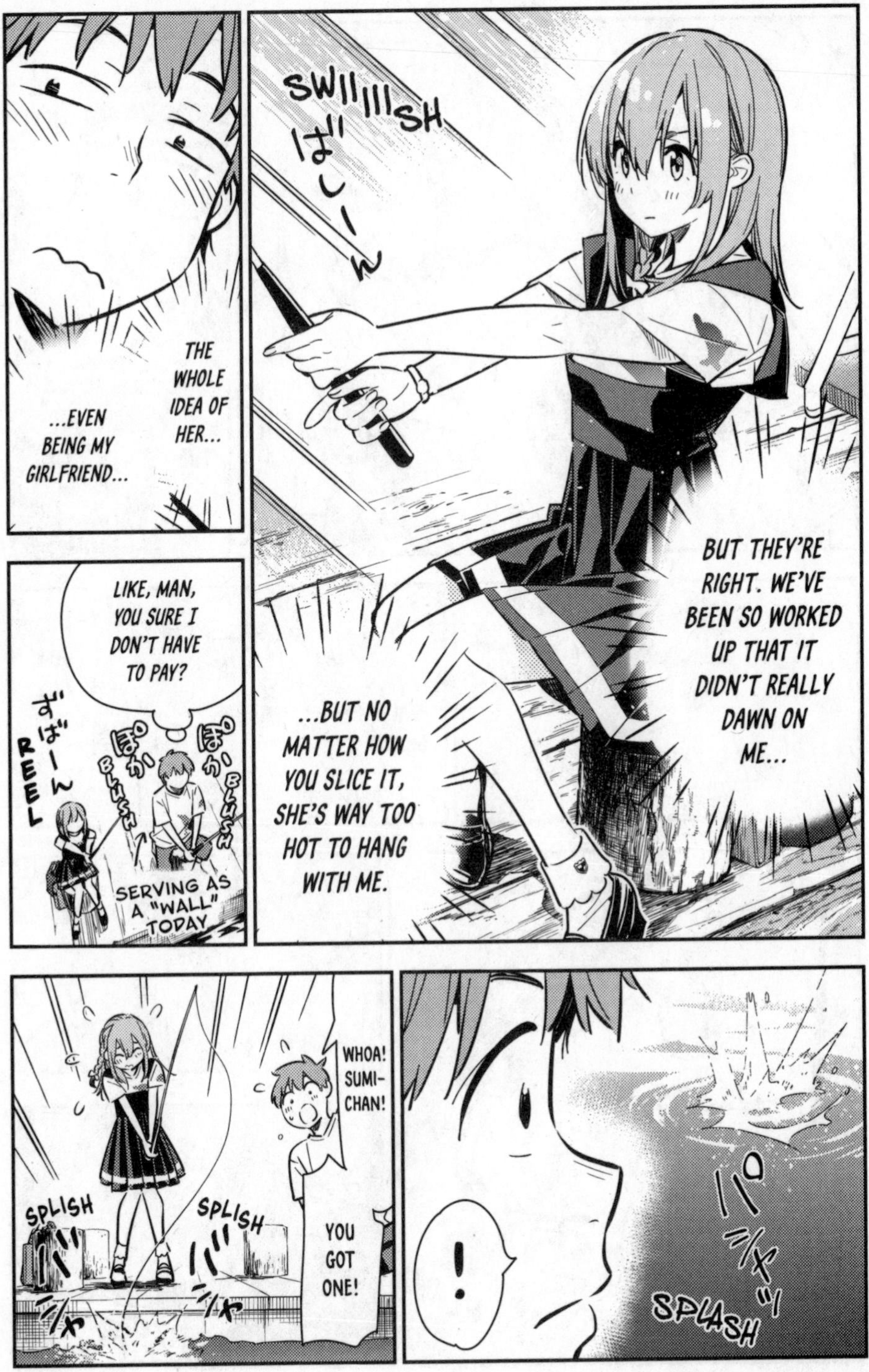
SWIIIIIISH
ばしーん
BUT THEY'RE RIGHT. WE'VE BEEN SO WORKED UP THAT IT DIDN'T REALLY DAWN ON ME...
...BUT NO MATTER HOW YOU SLICE IT, SHE'S WAY TOO HOT TO HANG WITH ME.
THE WHOLE IDEA OF HER...
...EVEN BEING MY GIRLFRIEND...
LIKE, MAN, YOU SURE I DON'T HAVE TO PAY?
ぽか BLUSH
ぽか BLUSH
ずばーん REEL
SERVING AS A "WALL" TODAY
パシャッ
SPLASH
!
WHOA! SUMI-CHAN!
YOU GOT ONE!
バシャ SPLISH
バシャ SPLISH

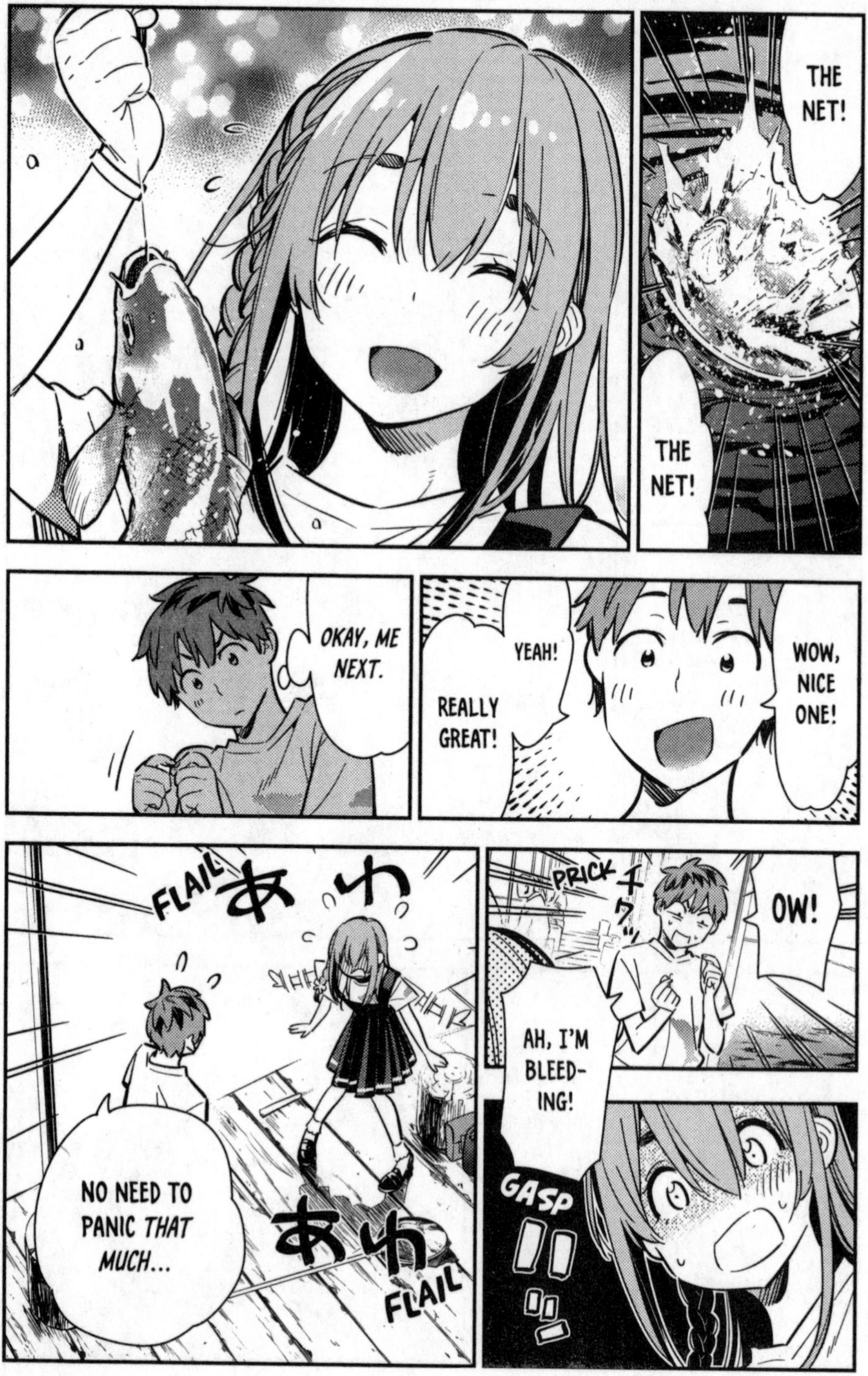
THE NET!
THE NET!
WOW, NICE ONE!
YEAH!
REALLY GREAT!
OKAY, ME NEXT.
OW!
PRICK
チクッ
AH, I'M BLEED-ING!
GASP
FLAIL
あわ
NO NEED TO PANIC *THAT* MUCH...
あわ
FLAIL

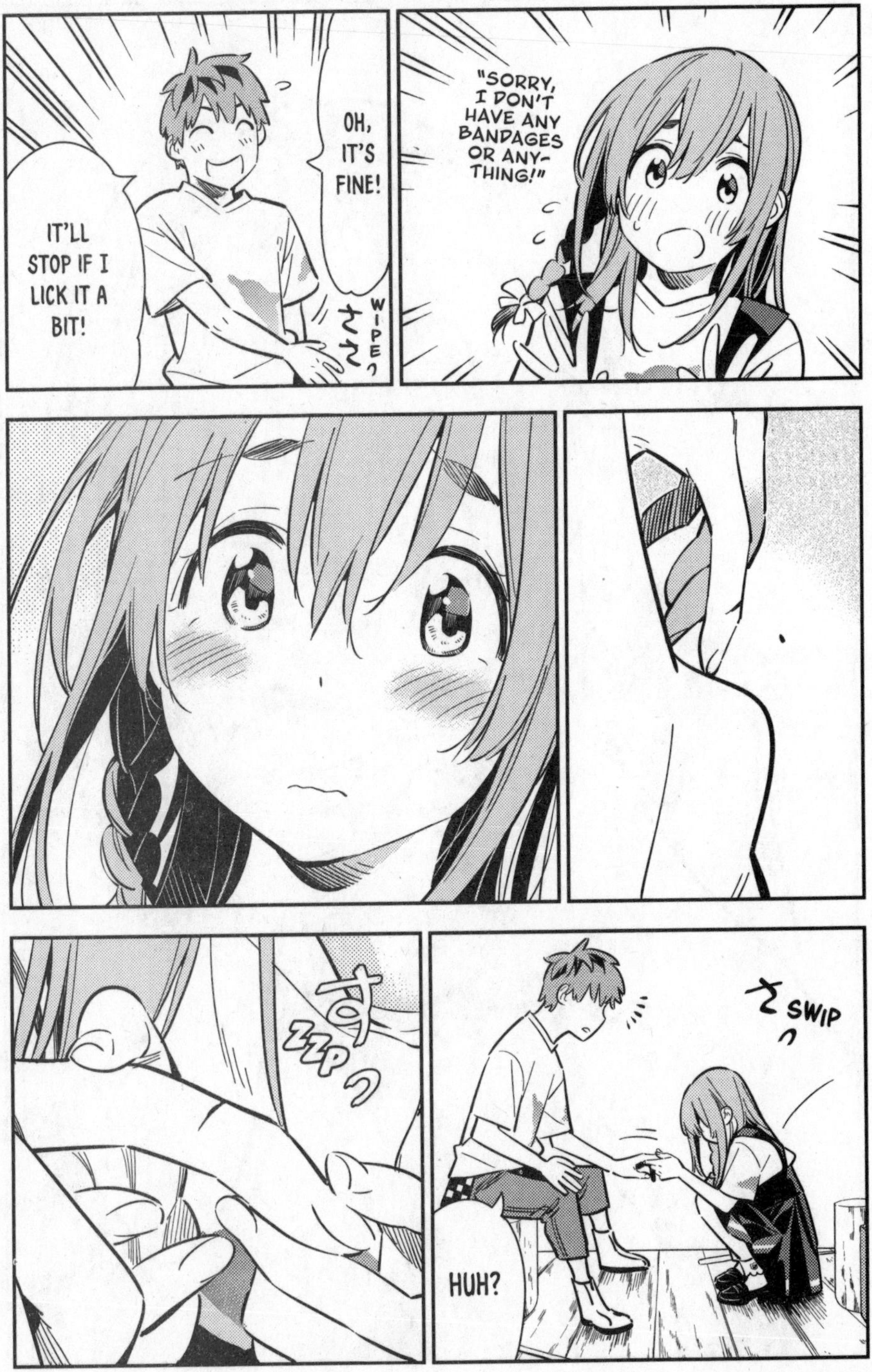
"SORRY, I DON'T HAVE ANY BANDAGES OR ANYTHING!"
OH, IT'S FINE!
WIPE
IT'LL STOP IF I LICK IT A BIT!
SWIP
HUH?
ZZP

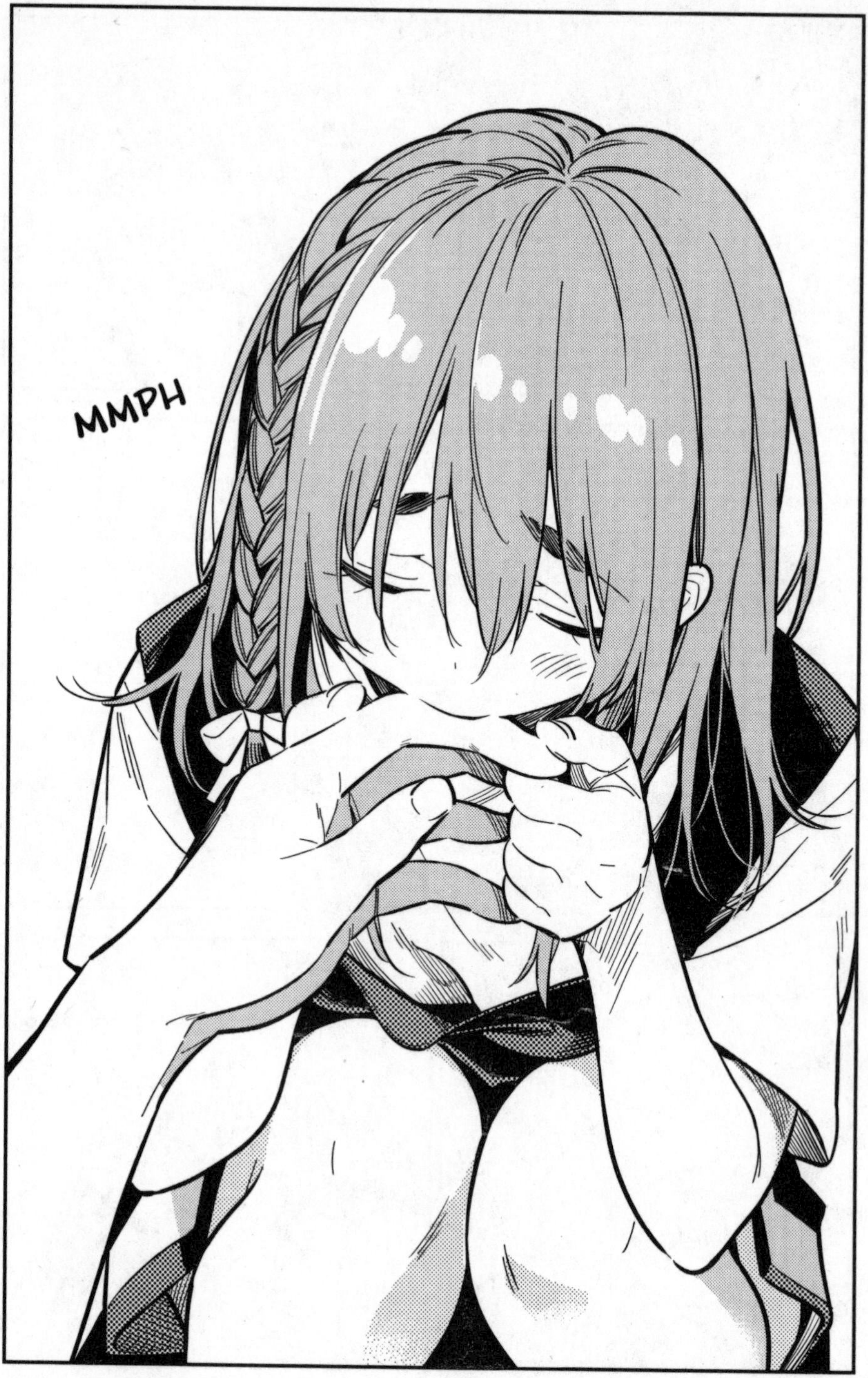
MMPH

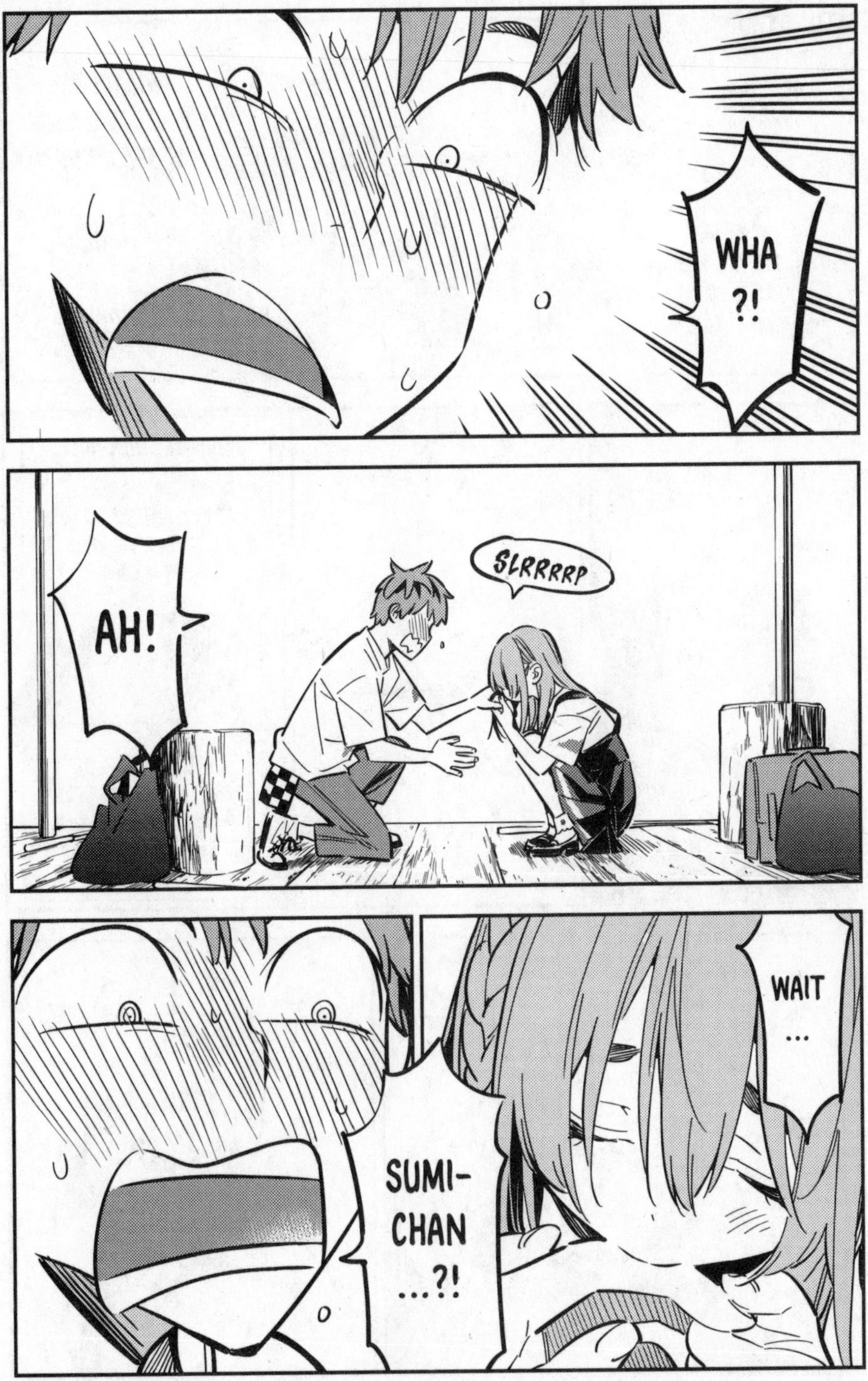
WHA ?!
SLRRRRP
AH!
WAIT ...
SUMI-CHAN ...?!

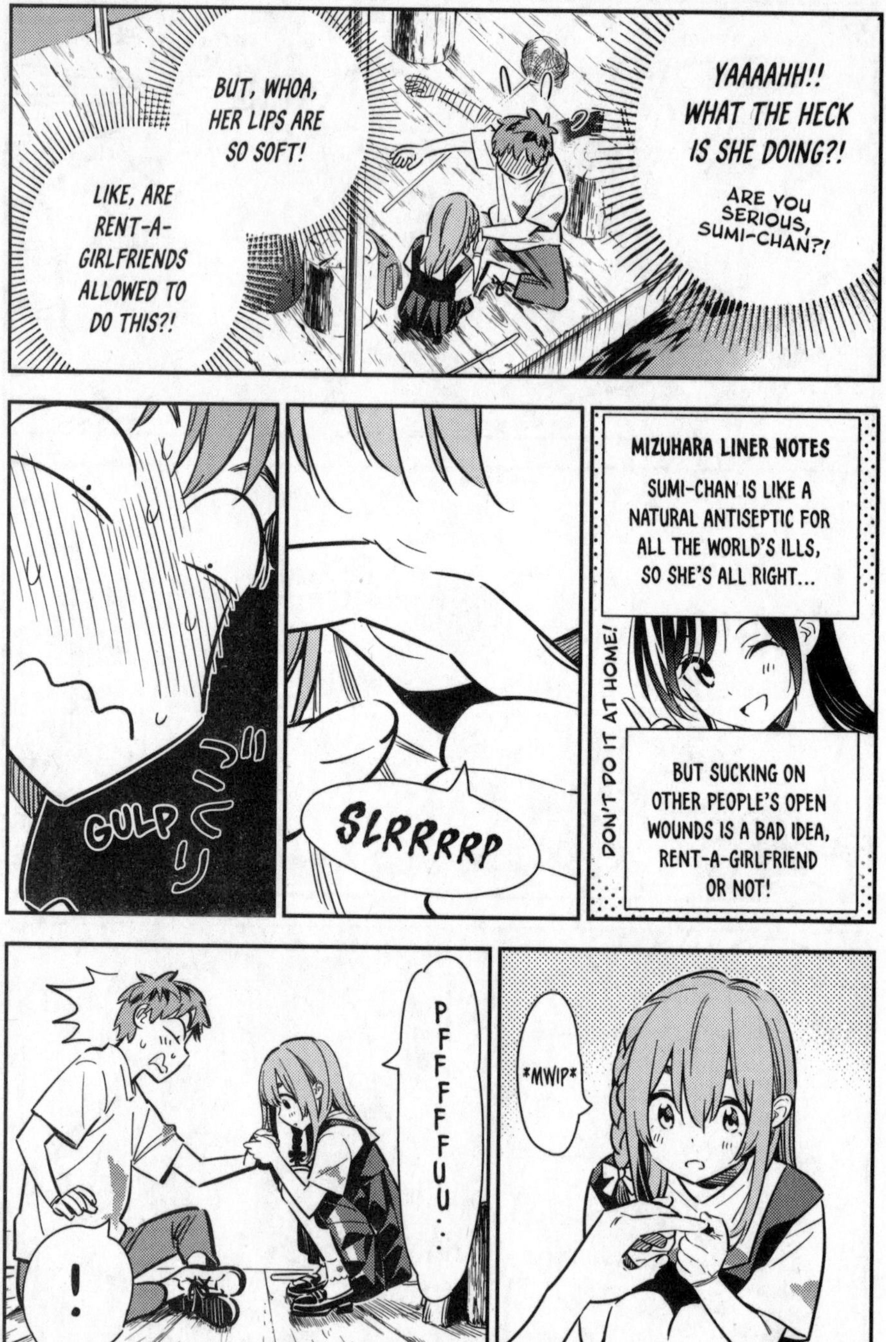

YAAAAHH!! WHAT THE HECK IS SHE DOING?!
ARE YOU SERIOUS, SUMI-CHAN?!
BUT, WHOA, HER LIPS ARE SO SOFT!
LIKE, ARE RENT-A-GIRLFRIENDS ALLOWED TO DO THIS?!
MIZUHARA LINER NOTES
SUMI-CHAN IS LIKE A NATURAL ANTISEPTIC FOR ALL THE WORLD'S ILLS, SO SHE'S ALL RIGHT...
DON'T DO IT AT HOME!
BUT SUCKING ON OTHER PEOPLE'S OPEN WOUNDS IS A BAD IDEA, RENT-A-GIRLFRIEND OR NOT!
SLRRRRP
GULP
*MWIP*
PFFFFFUU...
!

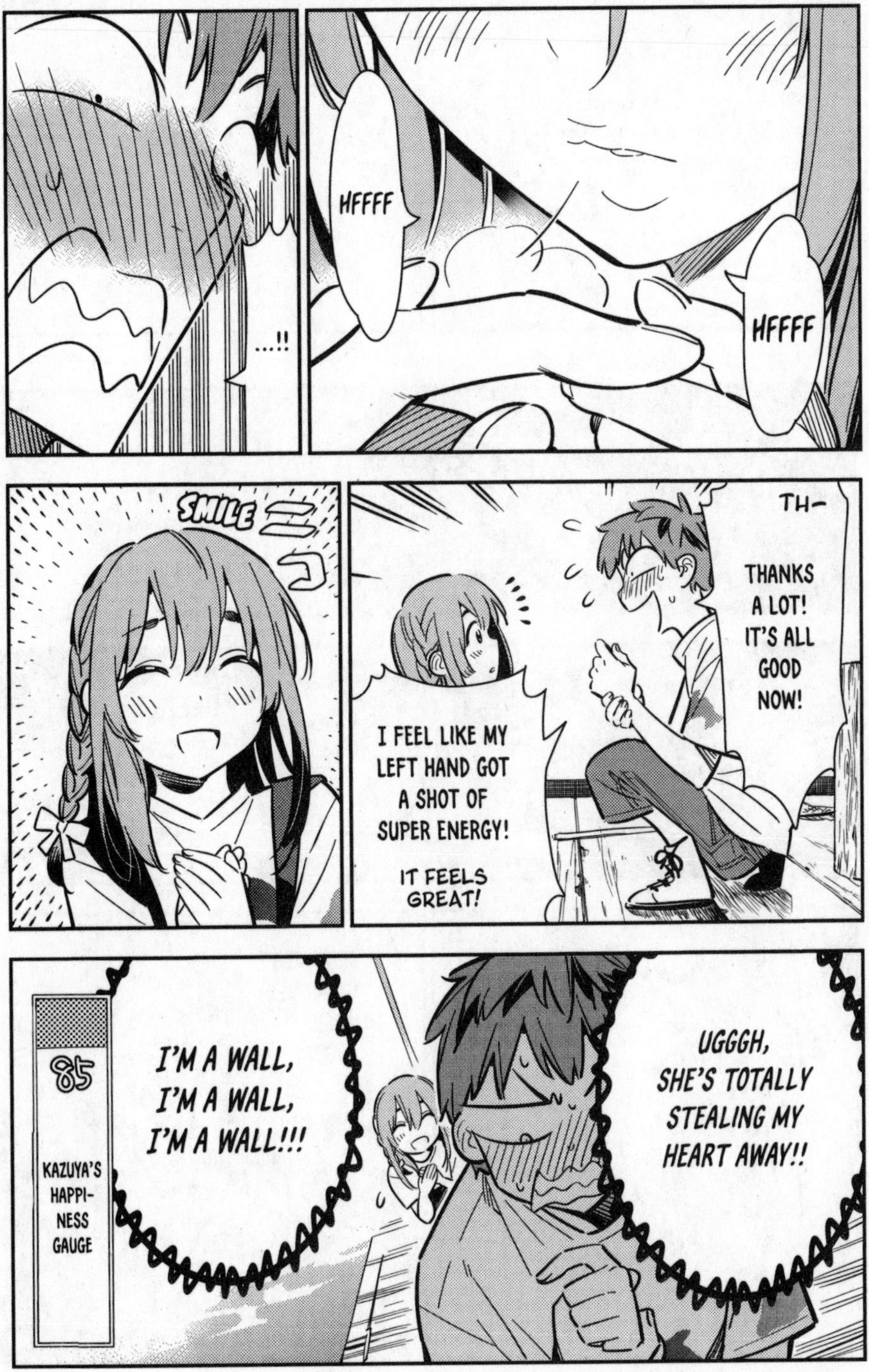
HFFFF
HFFFF
...!!
TH-
THANKS A LOT! IT'S ALL GOOD NOW!
I FEEL LIKE MY LEFT HAND GOT A SHOT OF SUPER ENERGY!
IT FEELS GREAT!
SMILE
UGGGH, SHE'S TOTALLY STEALING MY HEART AWAY!!
I'M A WALL, I'M A WALL, I'M A WALL!!!
85
KAZUYA'S HAPPI-NESS GAUGE

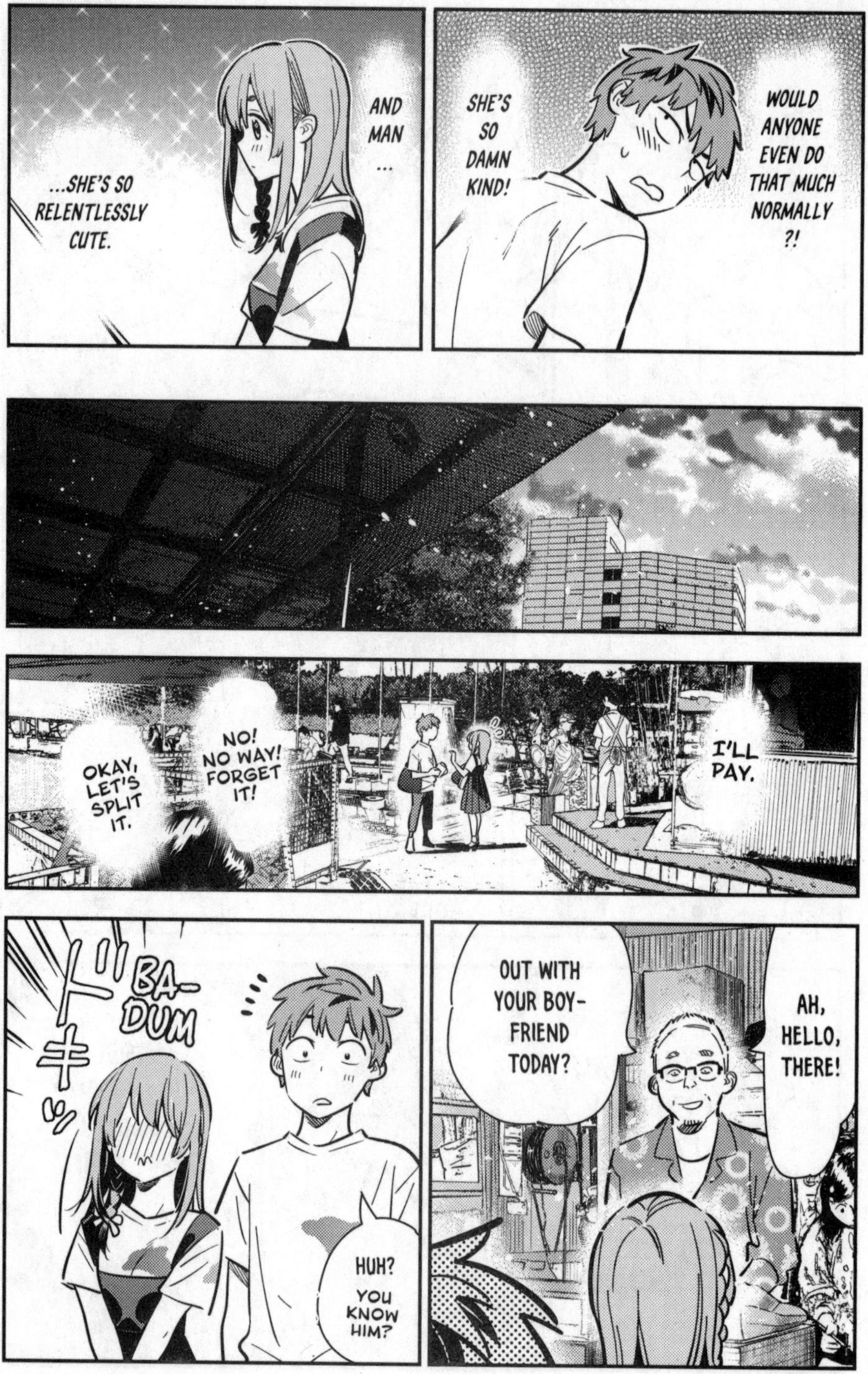
WOULD ANYONE EVEN DO THAT MUCH NORMALLY ?!
SHE'S SO DAMN KIND!
AND MAN ...
...SHE'S SO RELENTLESSLY CUTE.
I'LL PAY.
NO! NO WAY! FORGET IT!
OKAY, LET'S SPLIT IT.
AH, HELLO, THERE!
OUT WITH YOUR BOY-FRIEND TODAY?
ドキッ
BA-DUM
HUH? YOU KNOW HIM?

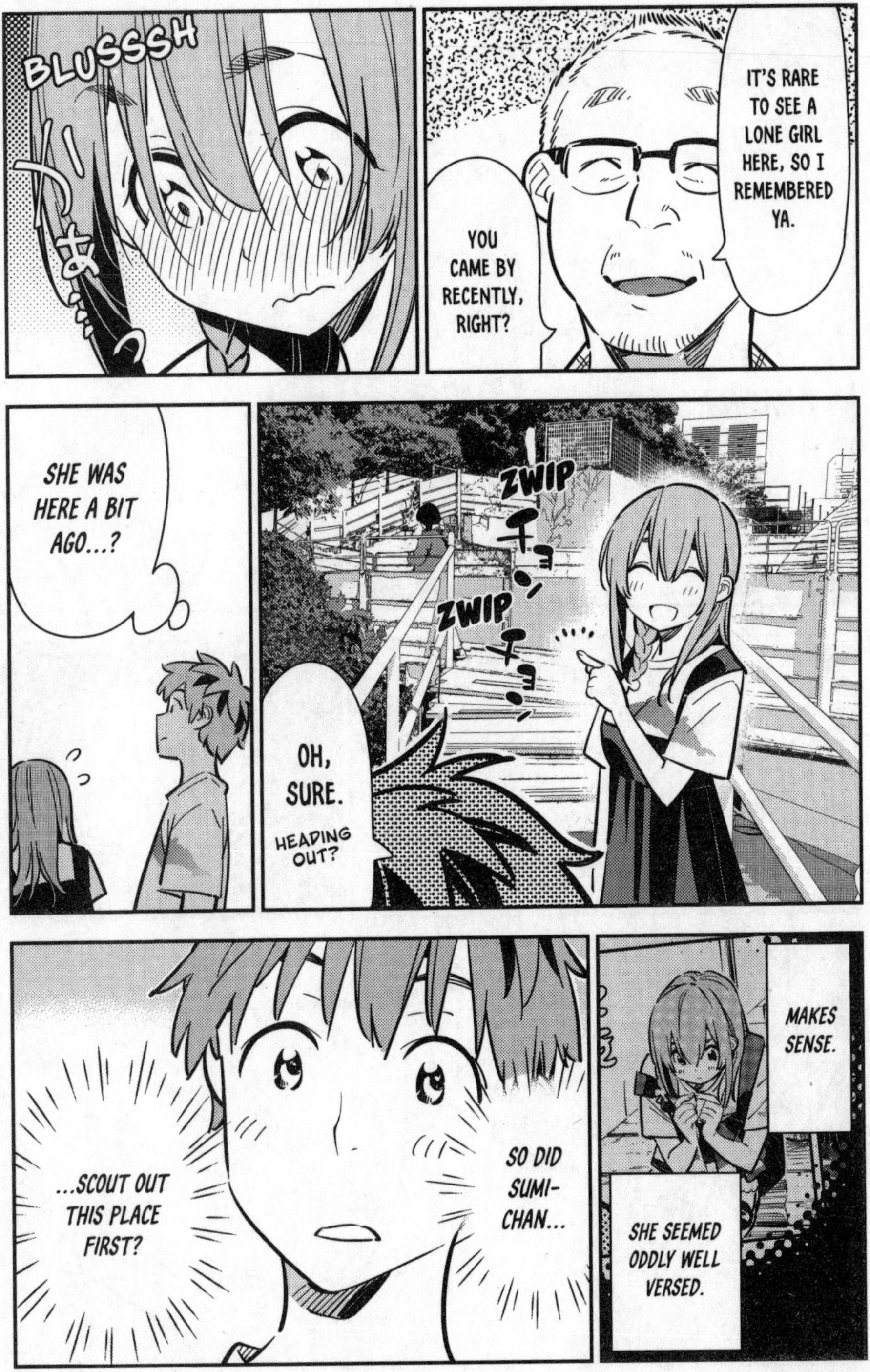
IT'S RARE TO SEE A LONE GIRL HERE, SO I REMEMBERED YA.
YOU CAME BY RECENTLY, RIGHT?
BLUSSSH
ZWIP
ZWIP
OH, SURE.
HEADING OUT?
SHE WAS HERE A BIT AGO...?
MAKES SENSE.
SHE SEEMED ODDLY WELL VERSED.
SO DID SUMI-CHAN...
...SCOUT OUT THIS PLACE FIRST?

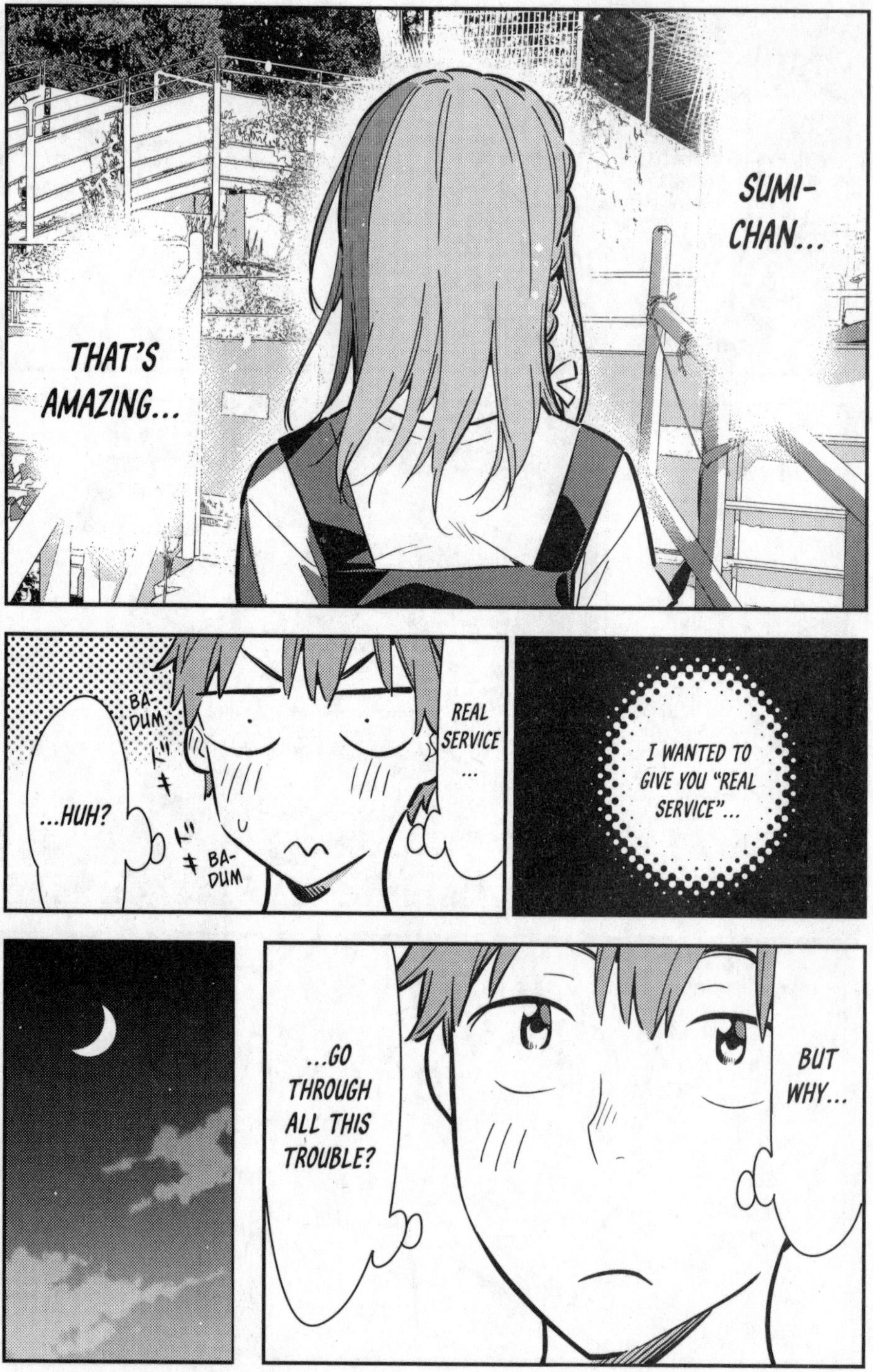
SUMI-CHAN...
THAT'S AMAZING...
I WANTED TO GIVE YOU "REAL SERVICE"...
REAL SERVICE ...
BA-DUM ドキ
...HUH?
ドキ BA-DUM
BUT WHY...
...GO THROUGH ALL THIS TROUBLE?

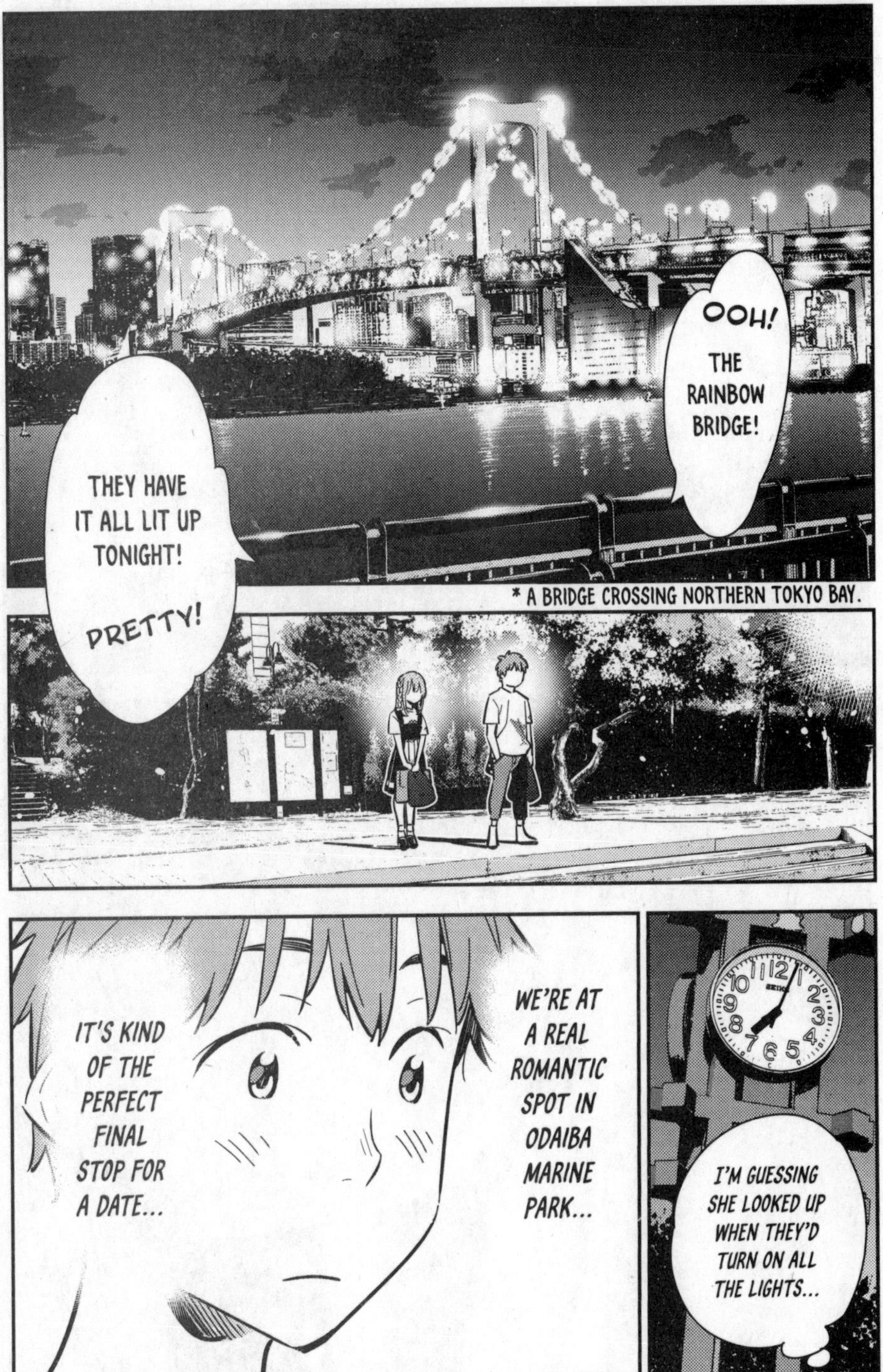
OOH! THE RAINBOW BRIDGE!
THEY HAVE IT ALL LIT UP TONIGHT! PRETTY!
* A BRIDGE CROSSING NORTHERN TOKYO BAY.
I'M GUESSING SHE LOOKED UP WHEN THEY'D TURN ON ALL THE LIGHTS...
WE'RE AT A REAL ROMANTIC SPOT IN ODAIBA MARINE PARK...
IT'S KIND OF THE PERFECT FINAL STOP FOR A DATE...

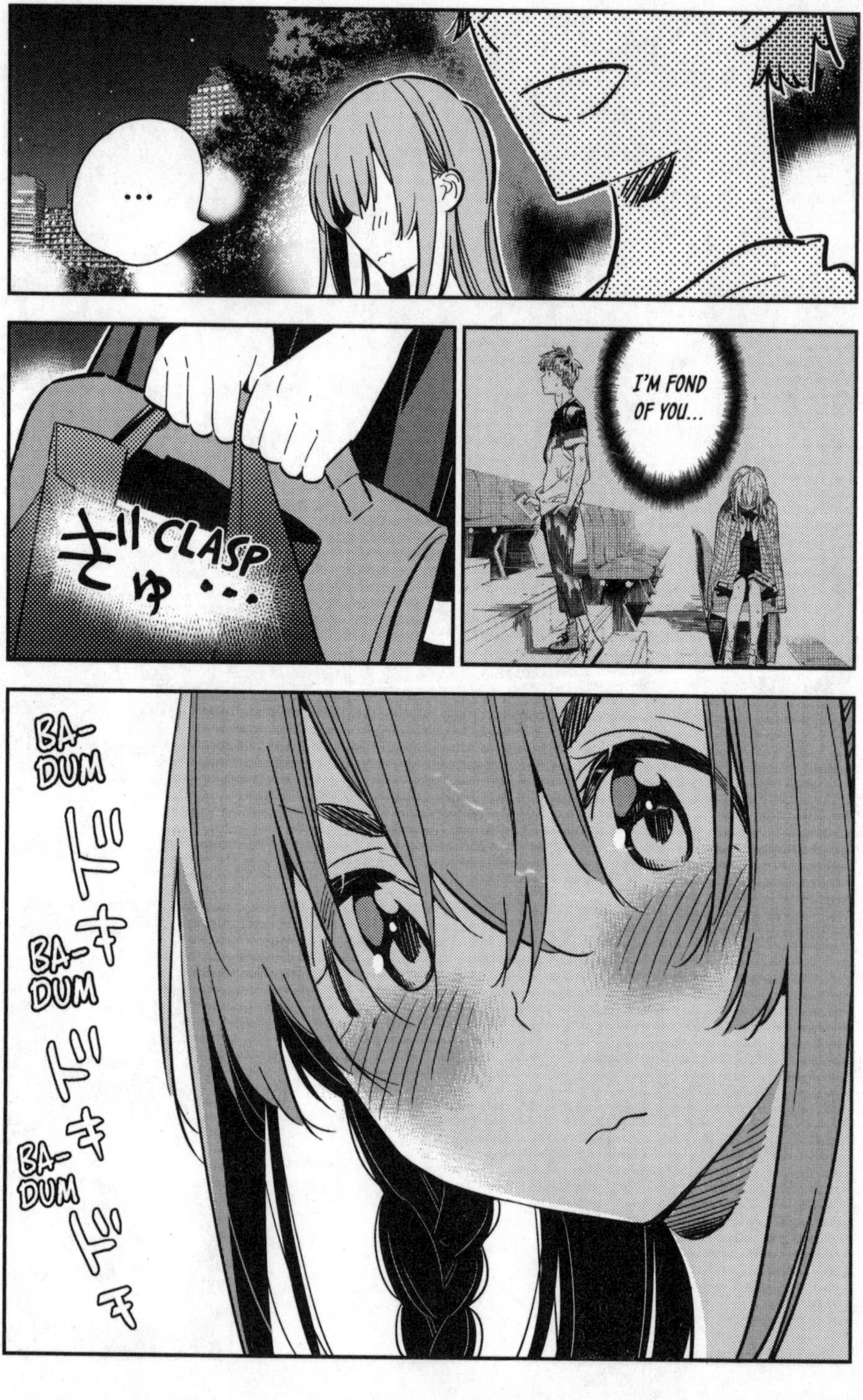
...
I'M FOND OF YOU...
ぎゅ...
CLASP
BA-DUM
BA-DUM
BA-DUM
ドキドキドキ

# RATING 97 MY GIRLFRIEND AND WHAT I'M CAPABLE OF 6

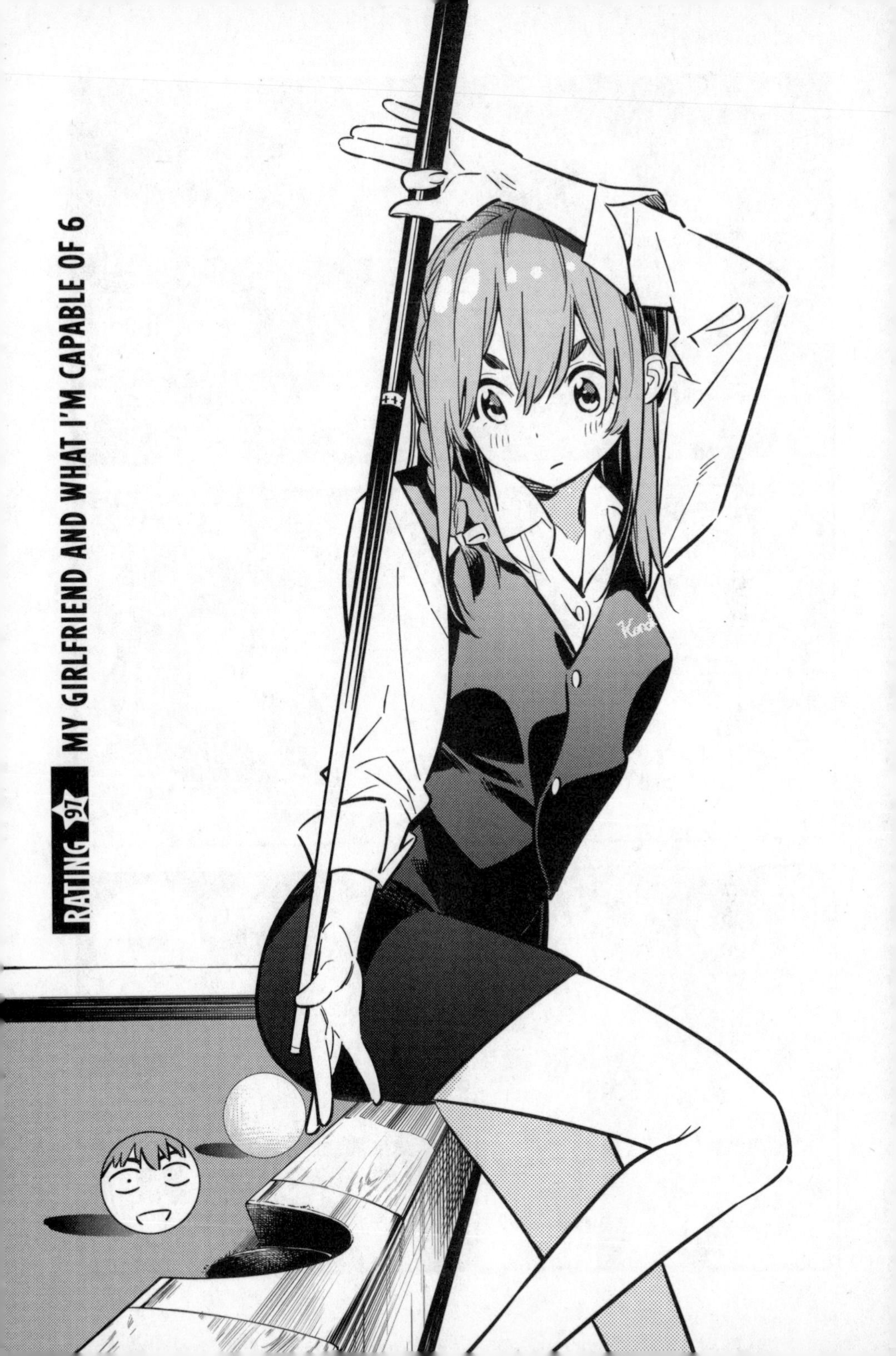

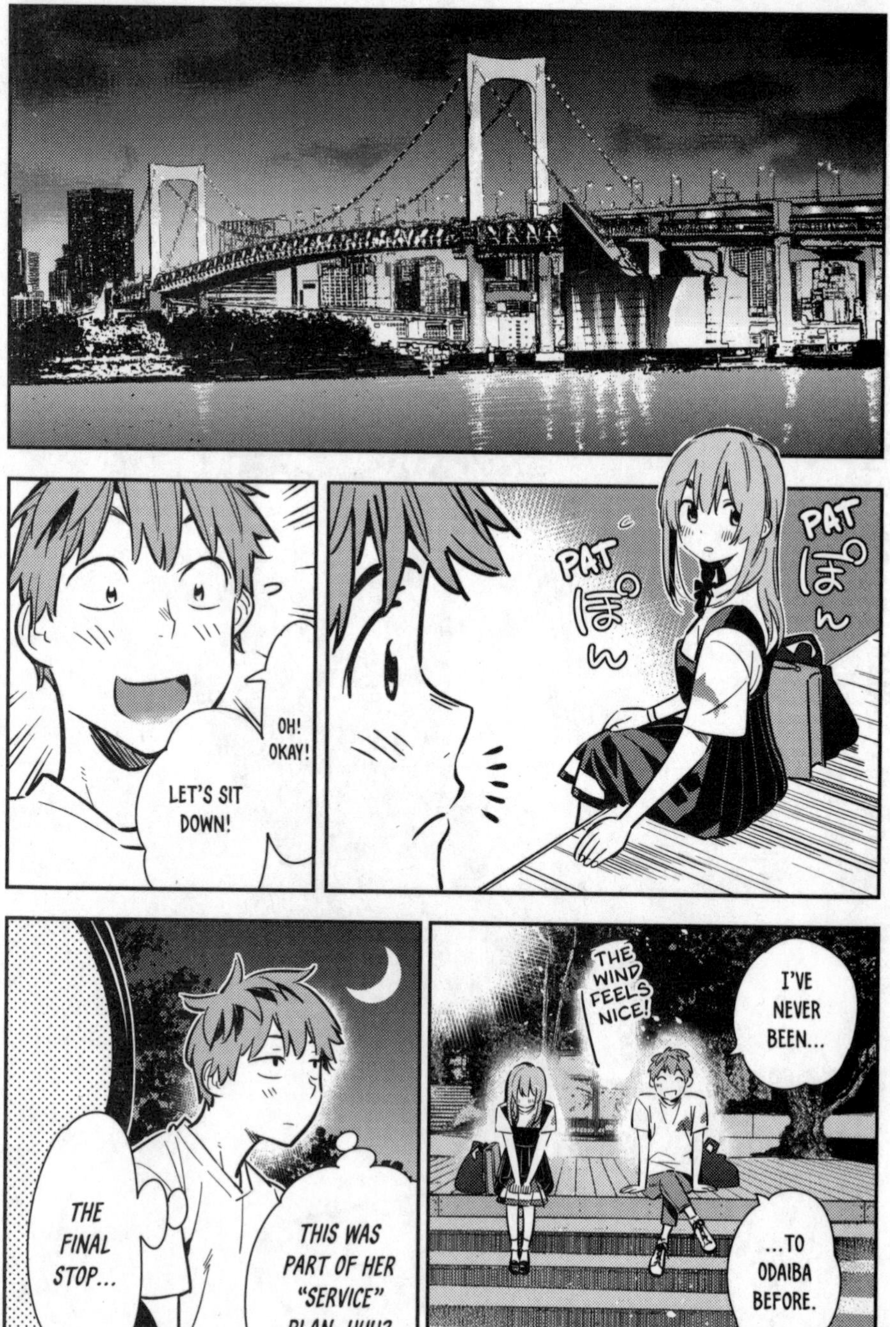
PAT ぽん
PAT ぽん
OH! OKAY!
LET'S SIT DOWN!
I'VE NEVER BEEN...
THE WIND FEELS NICE!
...TO ODAIBA BEFORE.
THIS WAS PART OF HER "SERVICE" PLAN, HUH?
THE FINAL STOP...

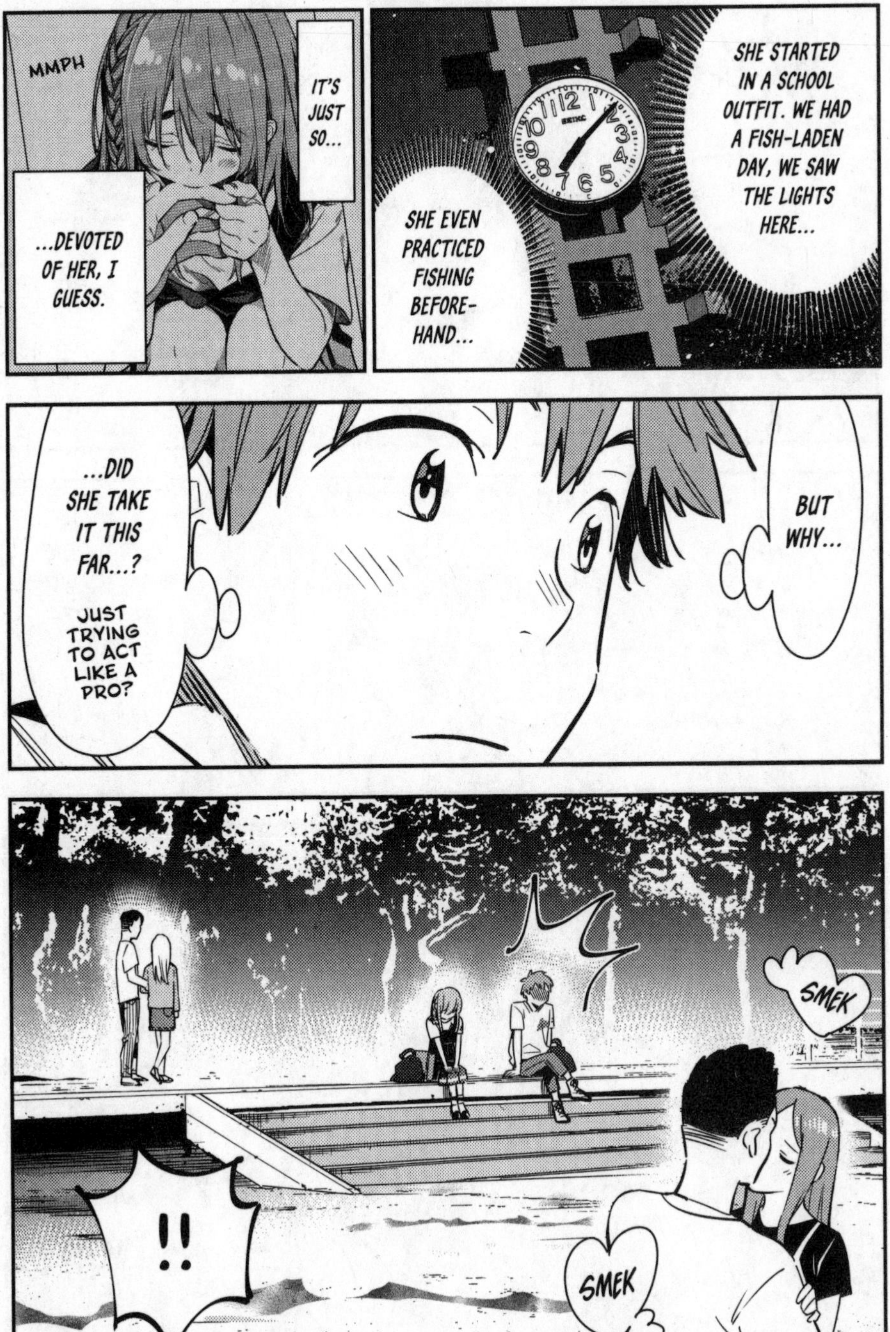
SHE STARTED IN A SCHOOL OUTFIT. WE HAD A FISH-LADEN DAY, WE SAW THE LIGHTS HERE...
SHE EVEN PRACTICED FISHING BEFORE-HAND...
IT'S JUST SO...
...DEVOTED OF HER, I GUESS.
MMPH
BUT WHY...
...DID SHE TAKE IT THIS FAR...?
JUST TRYING TO ACT LIKE A PRO?
SMEK
SMEK
!!

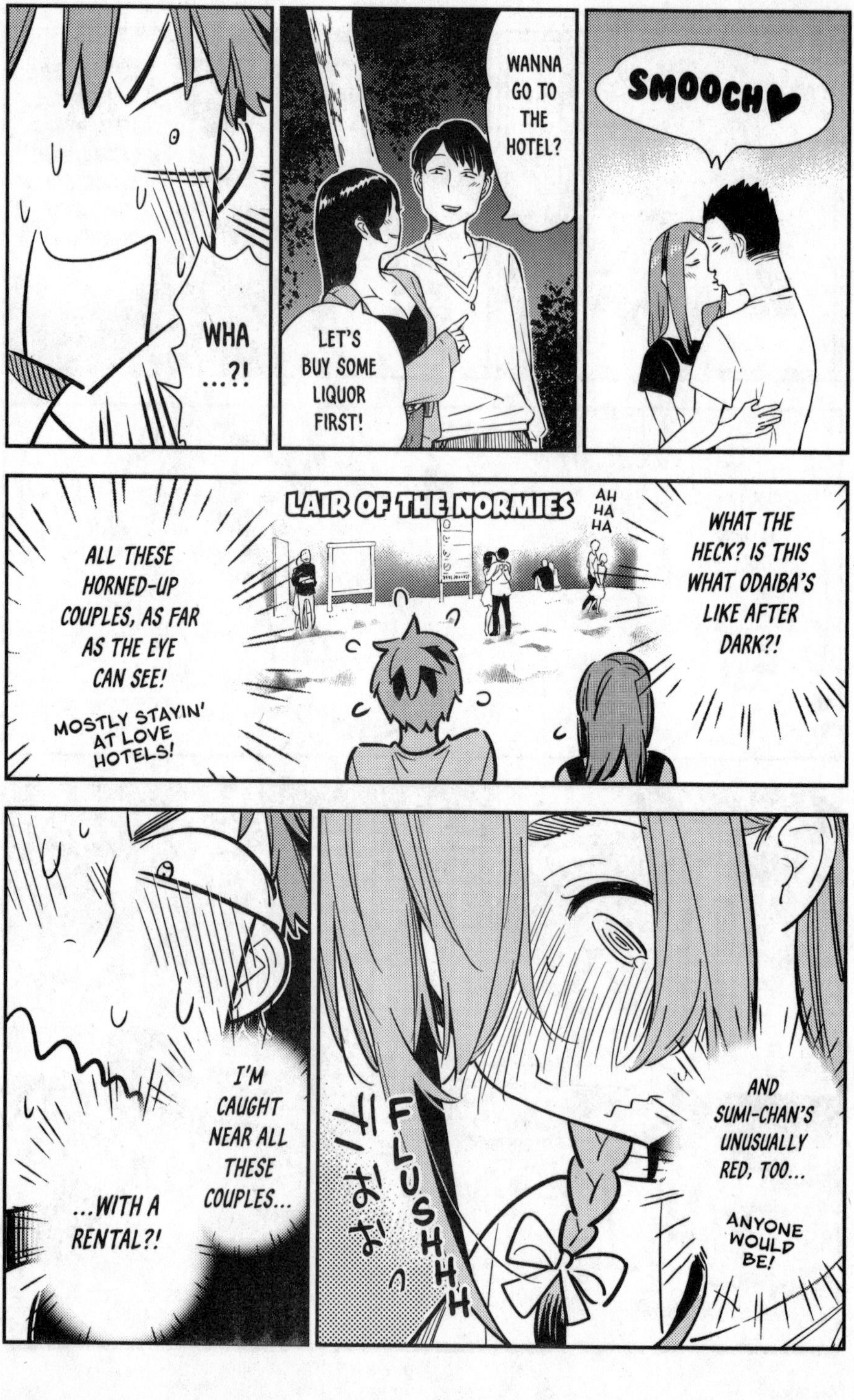
SMOOCH♥
WANNA GO TO THE HOTEL?
LET'S BUY SOME LIQUOR FIRST!
WHA ...?!
AH HA HA
WHAT THE HECK? IS THIS WHAT ODAIBA'S LIKE AFTER DARK?!
LAIR OF THE NORMIES
ALL THESE HORNED-UP COUPLES, AS FAR AS THE EYE CAN SEE!
MOSTLY STAYIN' AT LOVE HOTELS!
AND SUMI-CHAN'S UNUSUALLY RED, TOO...
ANYONE WOULD BE!
FLUSHHH
I'M CAUGHT NEAR ALL THESE COUPLES...
...WITH A RENTAL?!

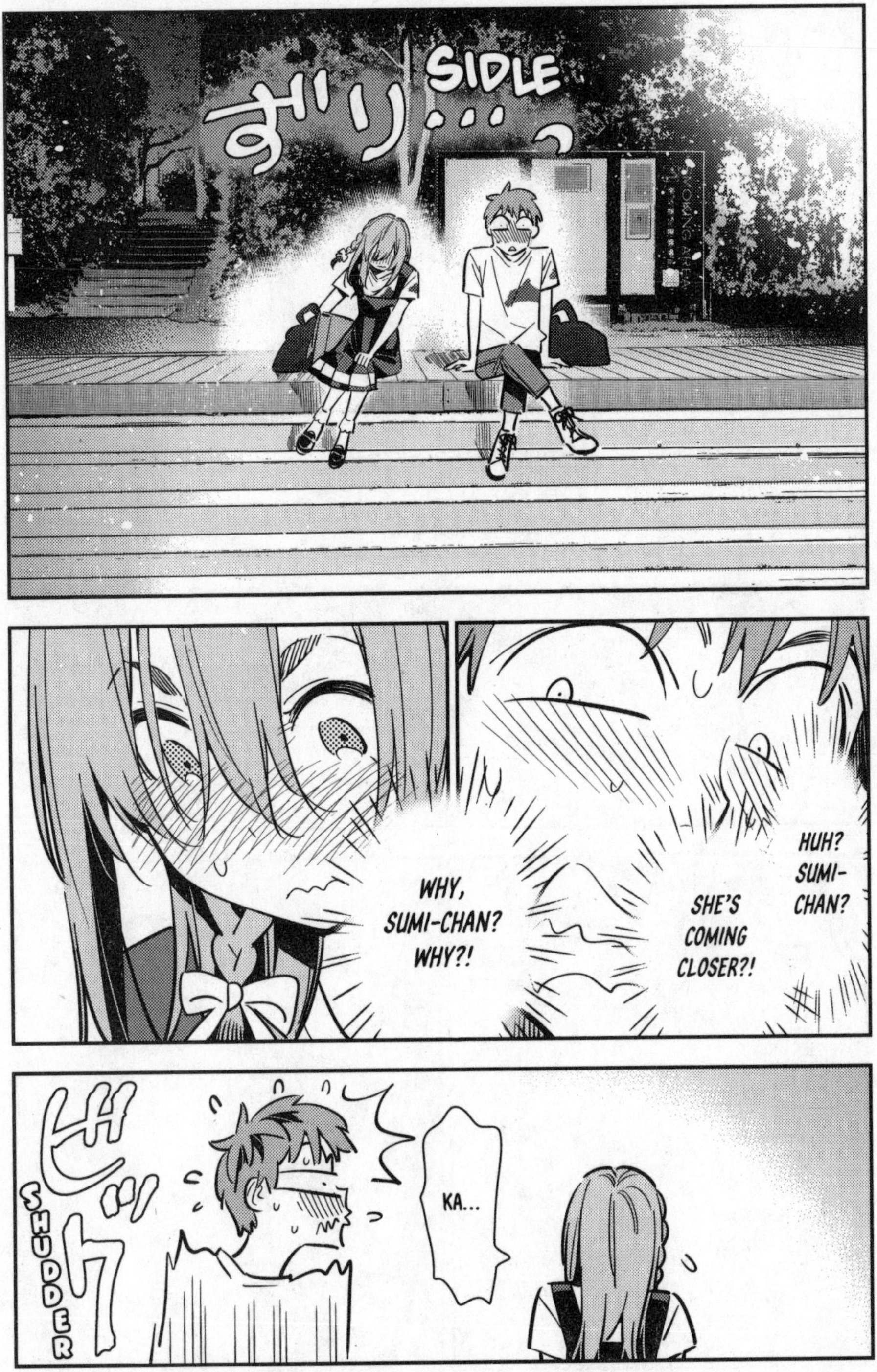

すり…っ
SIDLE
HUH? SUMI-CHAN?
SHE'S COMING CLOSER?!
WHY, SUMI-CHAN? WHY?!
KA...
ビクッ
SHUDDER

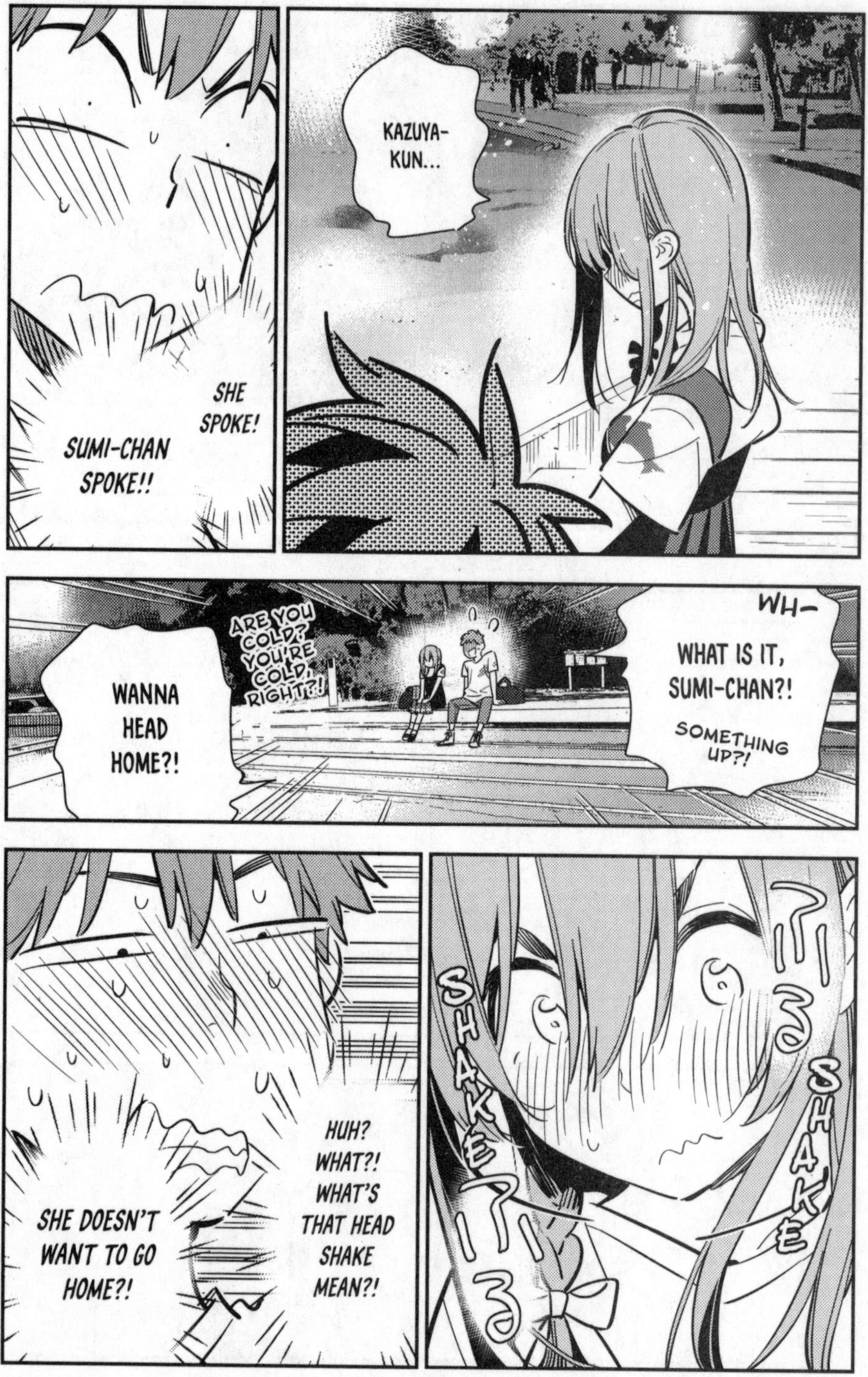
KAZUYA-KUN...
SHE SPOKE!
SUMI-CHAN SPOKE!!
WH- WHAT IS IT, SUMI-CHAN?!
SOMETHING UP?!
ARE YOU COLD? YOU'RE COLD, RIGHT?!
WANNA HEAD HOME?!
SHAKE
SHAKE
HUH? WHAT?! WHAT'S THAT HEAD SHAKE MEAN?!
SHE DOESN'T WANT TO GO HOME?!

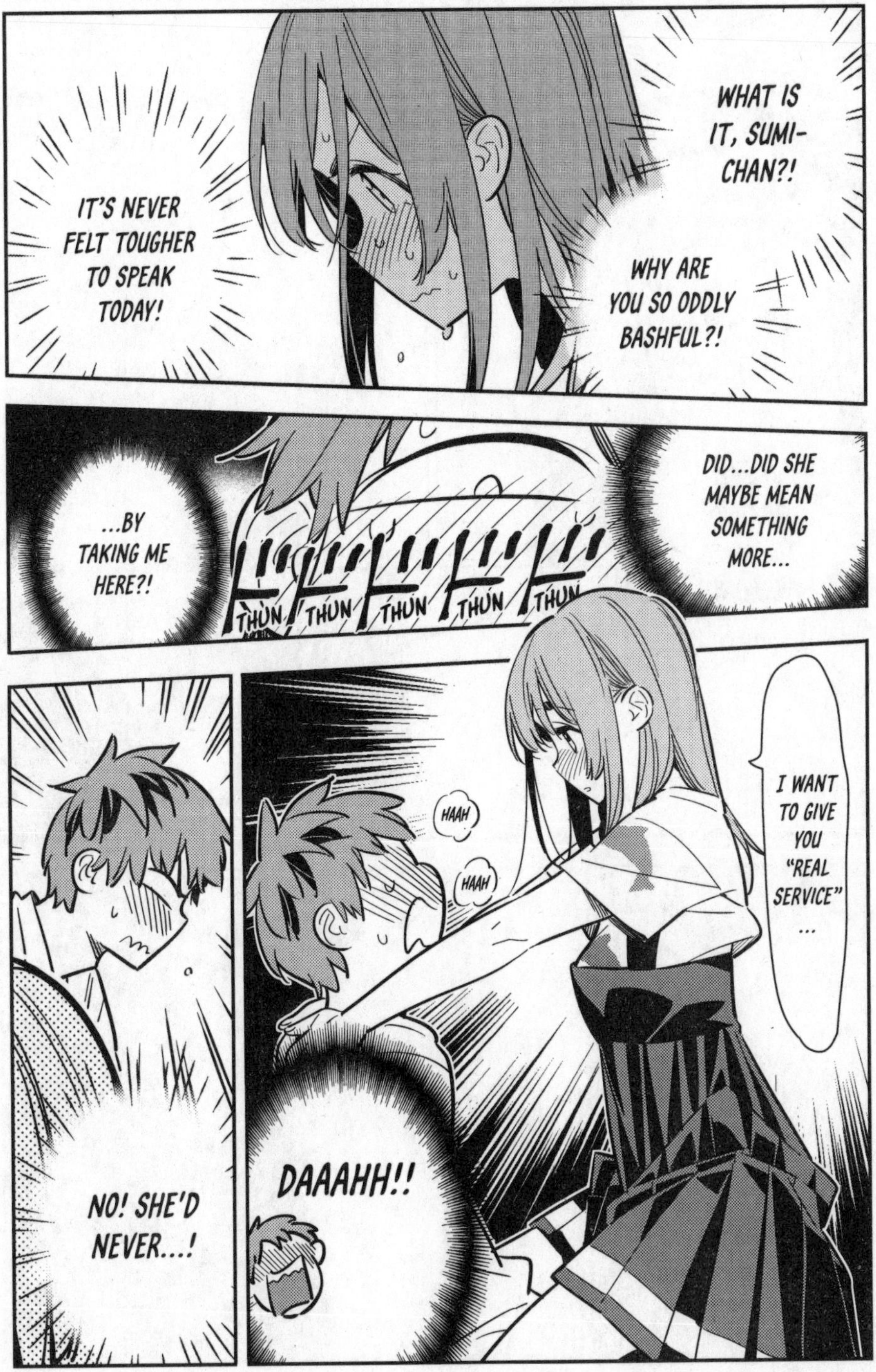
WHAT IS IT, SUMI-CHAN?!
WHY ARE YOU SO ODDLY BASHFUL?!
IT'S NEVER FELT TOUGHER TO SPEAK TODAY!
DID...DID SHE MAYBE MEAN SOMETHING MORE...
THUN THUN THUN THUN THUN
...BY TAKING ME HERE?!
I WANT TO GIVE YOU "REAL SERVICE" ...
HAAH
HAAH
DAAAHH!!
NO! SHE'D NEVER...!

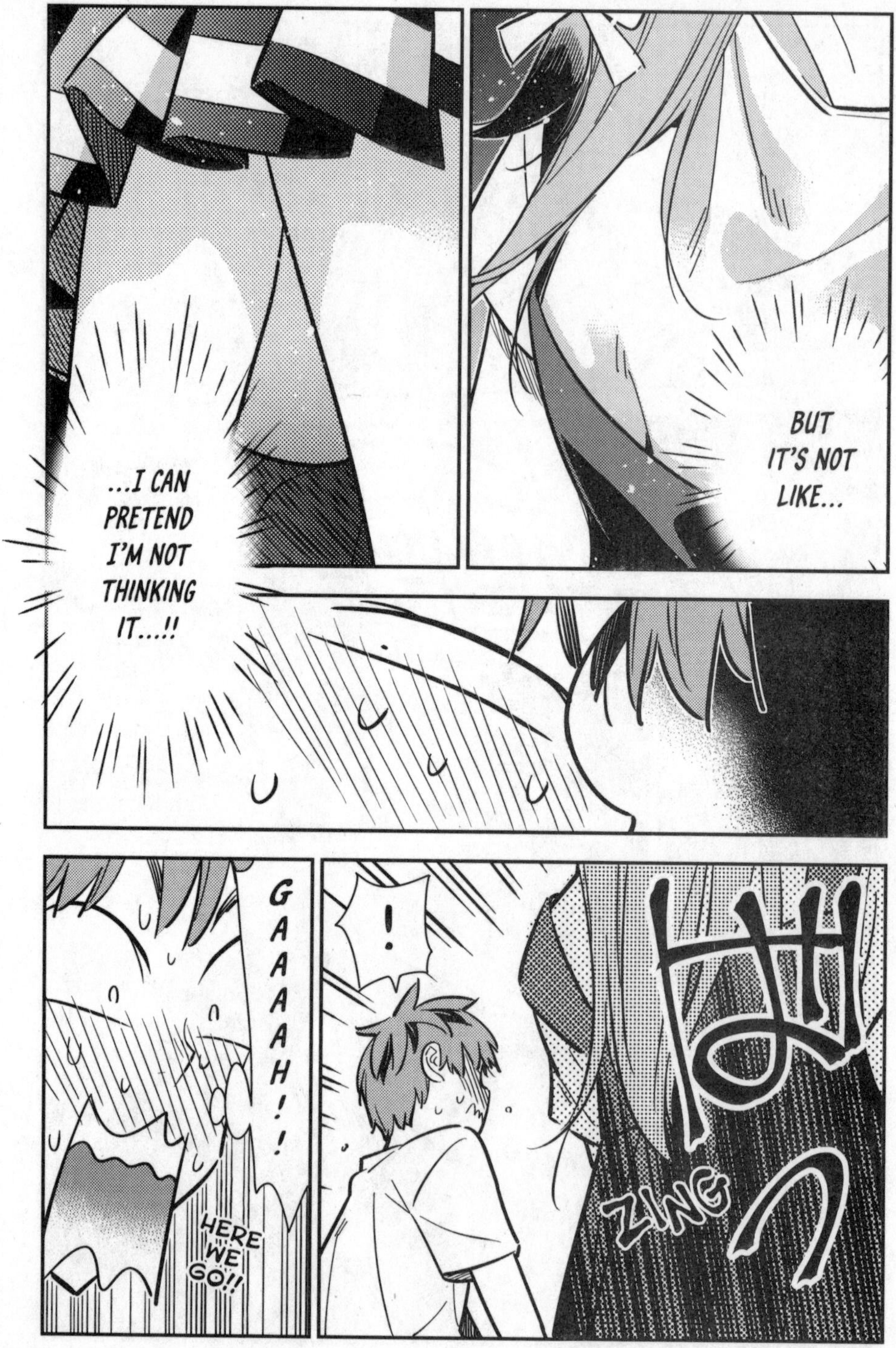
BUT IT'S NOT LIKE...
...I CAN PRETEND I'M NOT THINKING IT...!!
!
ZING
GAAAAAH!!
HERE WE GO!!

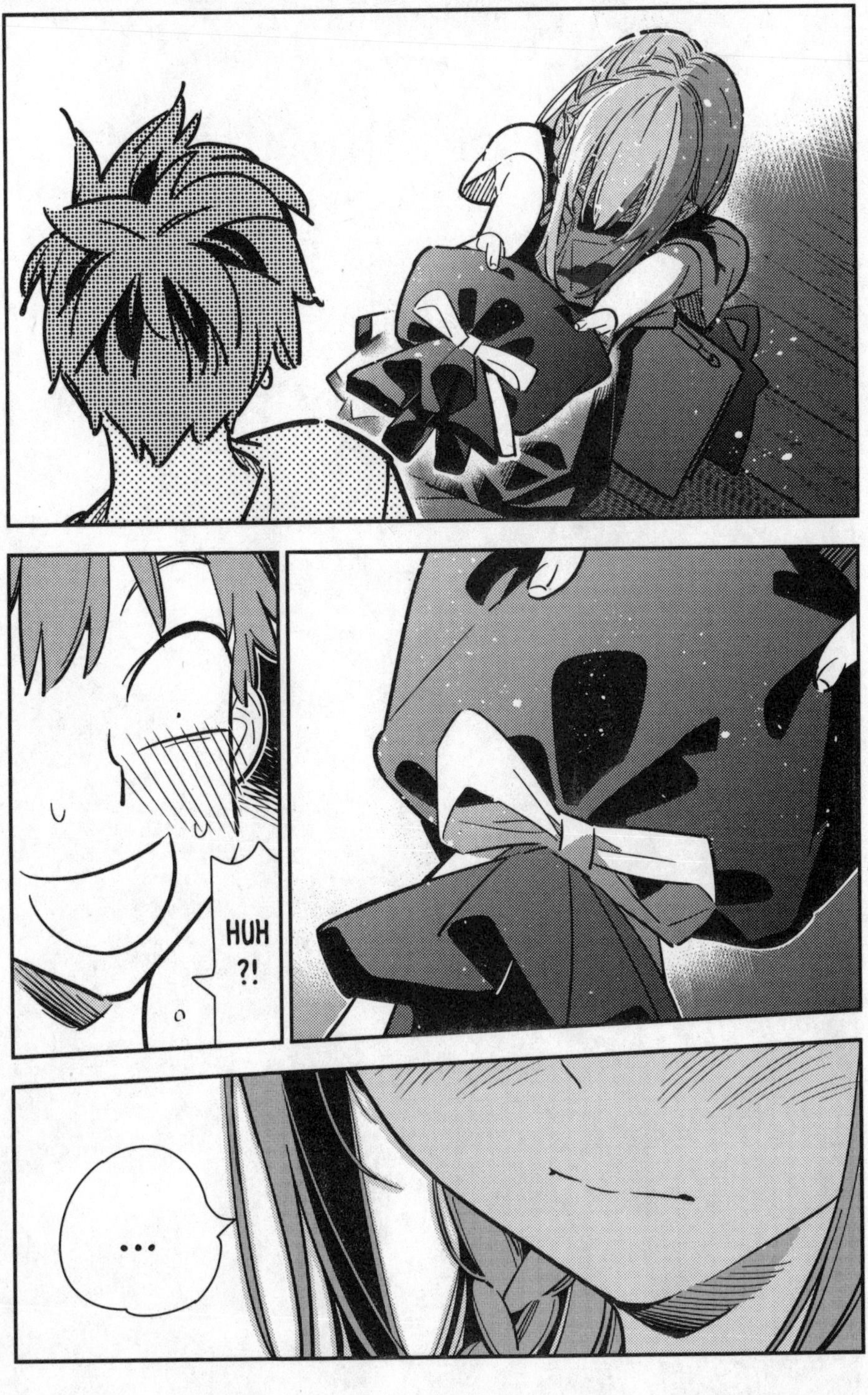
HUH ?!
...

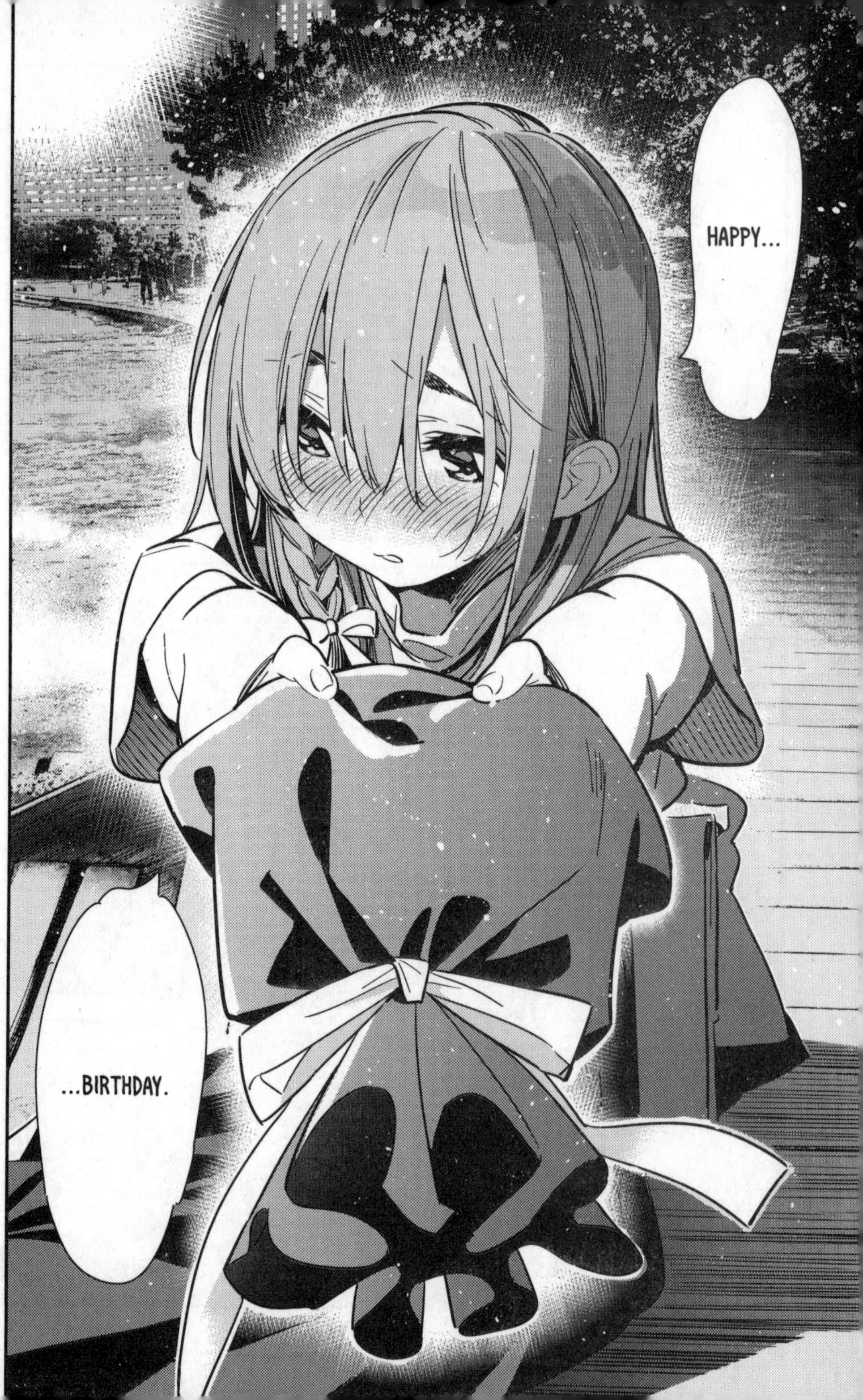
HAPPY...
...BIRTHDAY.

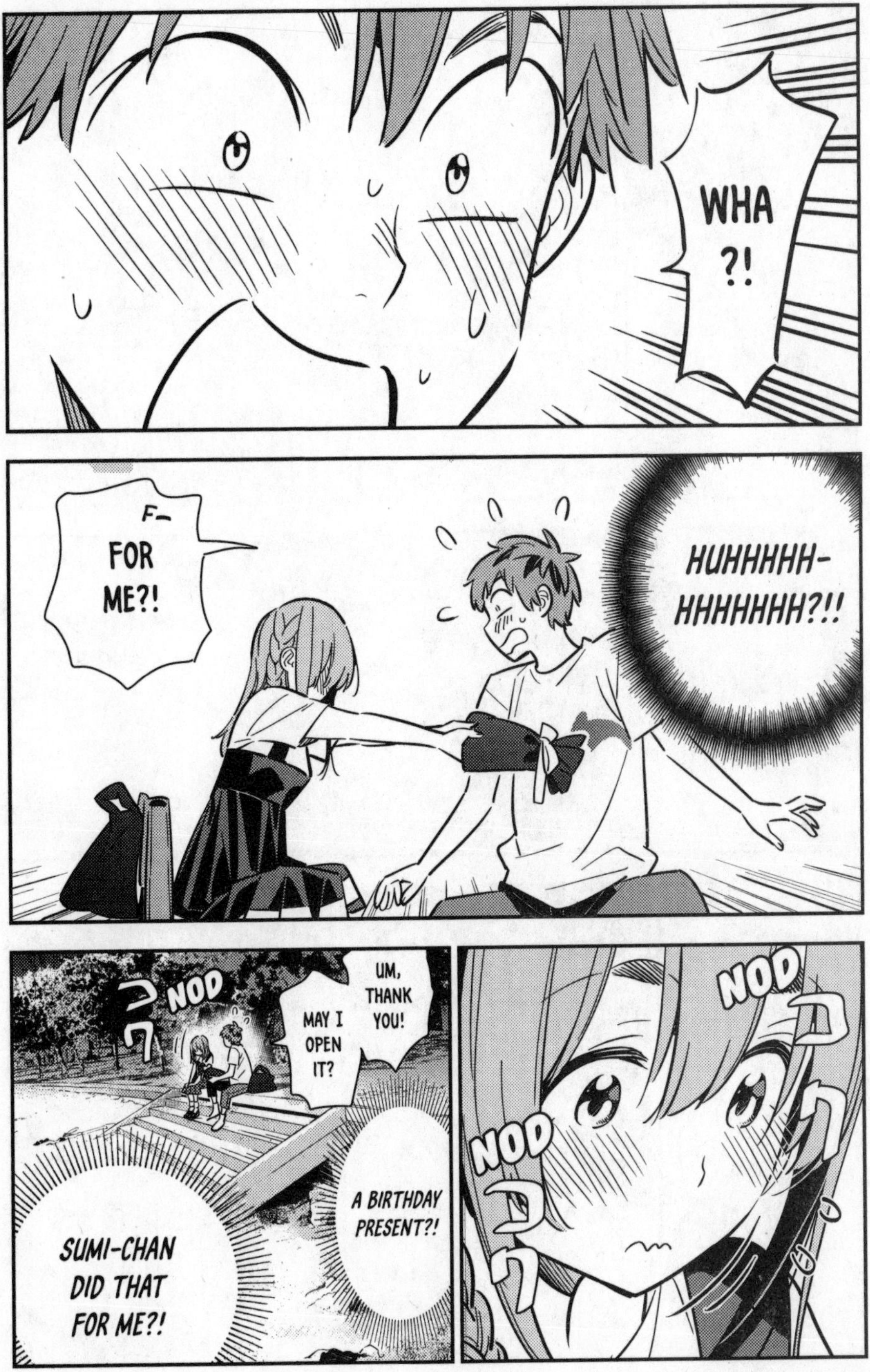
WHA ?!
HUHHHHH-HHHHHHH?!!
F- FOR ME?!
NOD
NOD
UM, THANK YOU!
MAY I OPEN IT?
A BIRTHDAY PRESENT?!
NOD
SUMI-CHAN DID THAT FOR ME?!

SHE REMEM-BERED...

...THE DAY?!

WHEN YOUR...

BIRTH-DAY IS...

IT'S JUNE FIRST!

WHY DO YOU ASK?!

AH... OH!

MY BIRTH-DAY?!

MINE?!

WAIT

TICK

TICK

I HOPE IT'LL LOOK OKAY ON ME!!

WOW, SO STYLISH!

A...

A SUMMER KNIT HAT?

HMM?

CLAP CLAP CLAP

SORRY I HAD THOSE PORN FANTASIES, SUMI-CHAN...

NOD NOD

CLAP CLAP

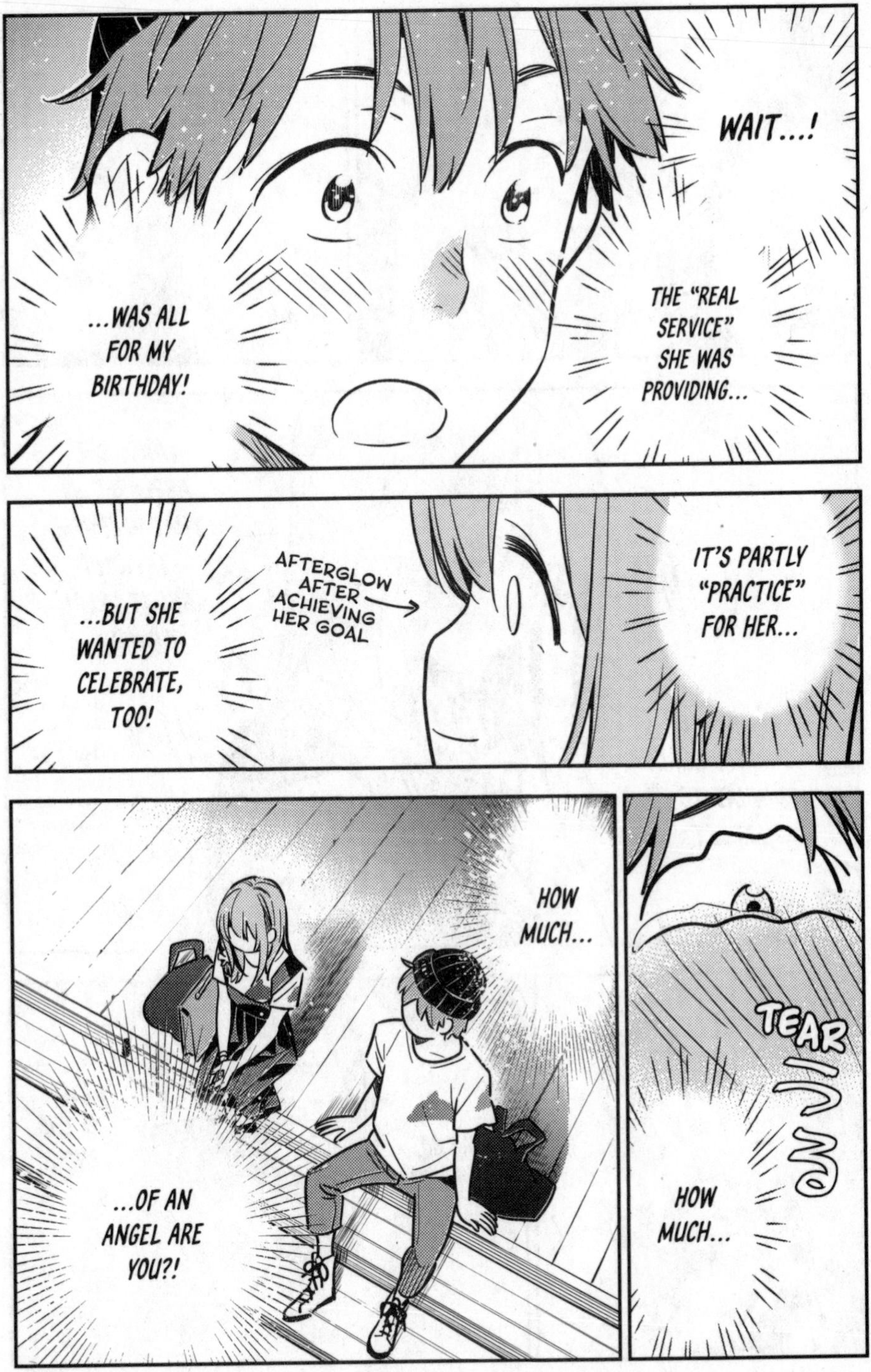
WAIT...!
THE "REAL SERVICE" SHE WAS PROVIDING...
...WAS ALL FOR MY BIRTHDAY!
IT'S PARTLY "PRACTICE" FOR HER...
AFTERGLOW AFTER ACHIEVING HER GOAL
...BUT SHE WANTED TO CELEBRATE, TOO!
TEAR
うる
HOW MUCH...
HOW MUCH...
...OF AN ANGEL ARE YOU?!

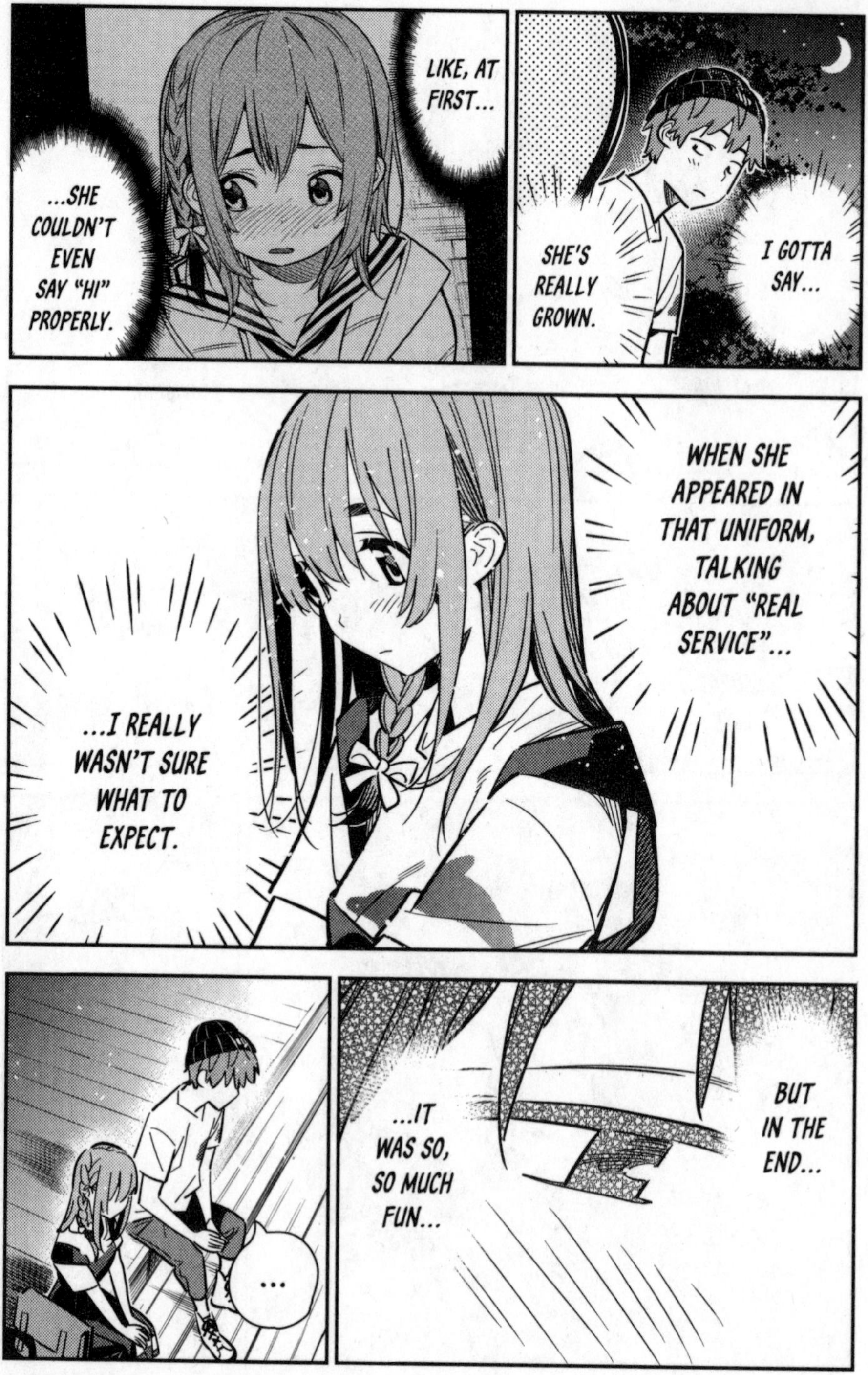
I GOTTA SAY...
SHE'S REALLY GROWN.
LIKE, AT FIRST...
...SHE COULDN'T EVEN SAY "HI" PROPERLY.
WHEN SHE APPEARED IN THAT UNIFORM, TALKING ABOUT "REAL SERVICE"...
...I REALLY WASN'T SURE WHAT TO EXPECT.
BUT IN THE END...
...IT WAS SO, SO MUCH FUN...
...

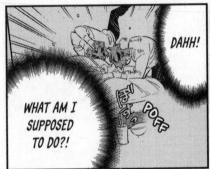

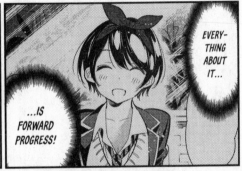

EVERY-THING ABOUT IT...
...IS FORWARD PROGRESS!
DAHH!
WHAT AM I SUPPOSED TO DO?!
POFF
AND ISN'T THAT GOOD ENOUGH?
GUESS I'M THE ONLY ONE...
...NOT MAKING ANY PROGRESS, HUH?

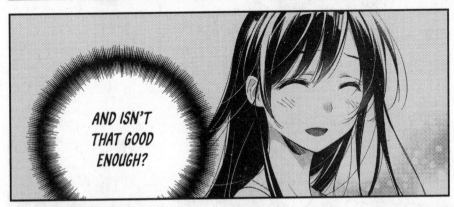

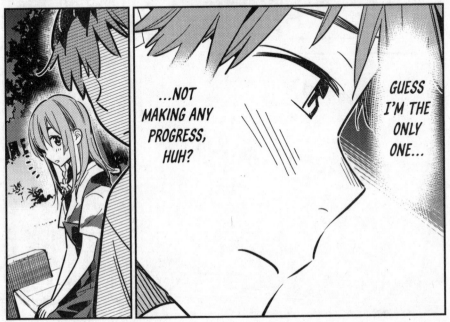

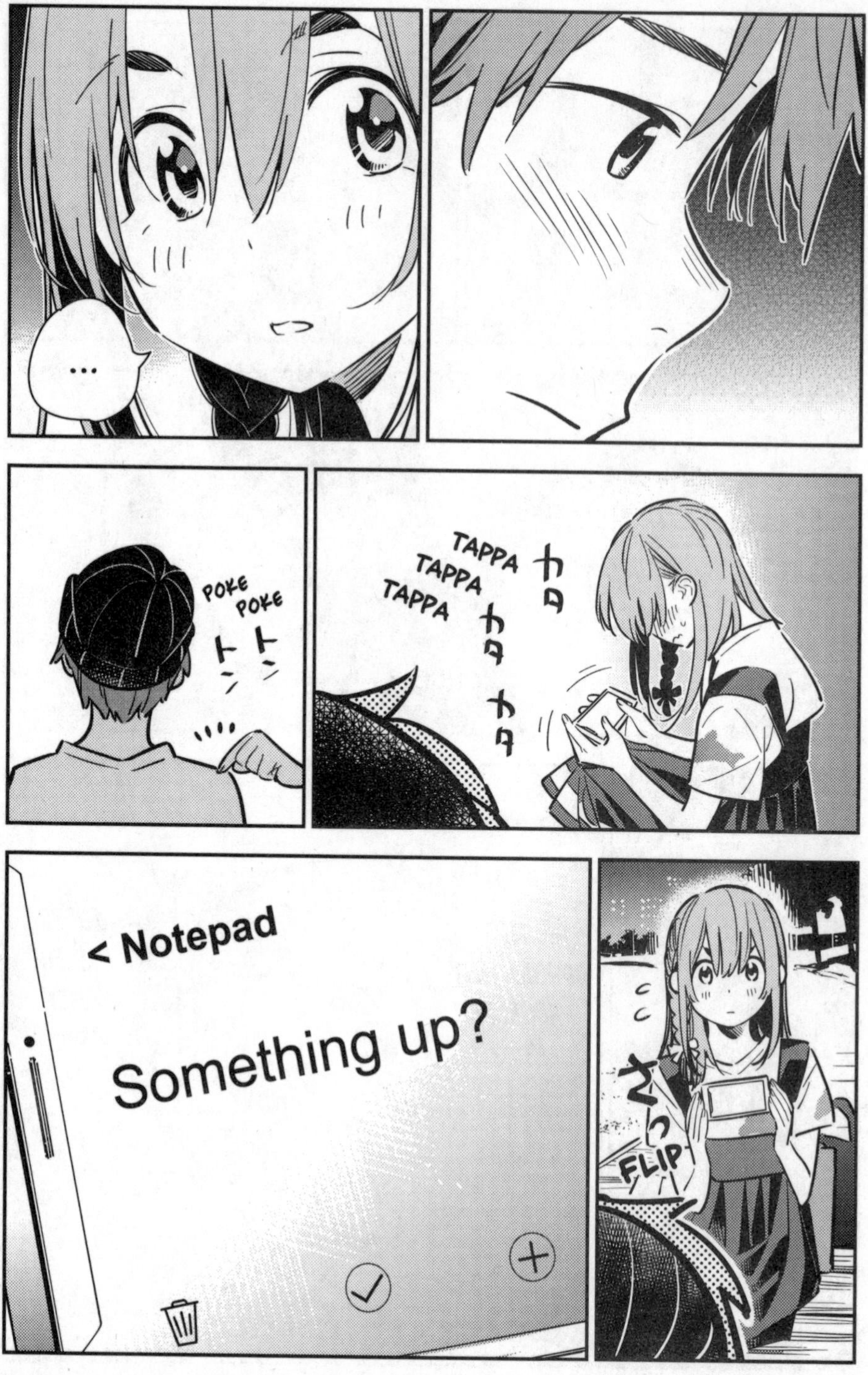
...
TAPPA
TAPPA
TAPPA
カタ
カタ
カタ
POKE
POKE
トン
トン
FLIP
さっ
< Notepad
Something up?

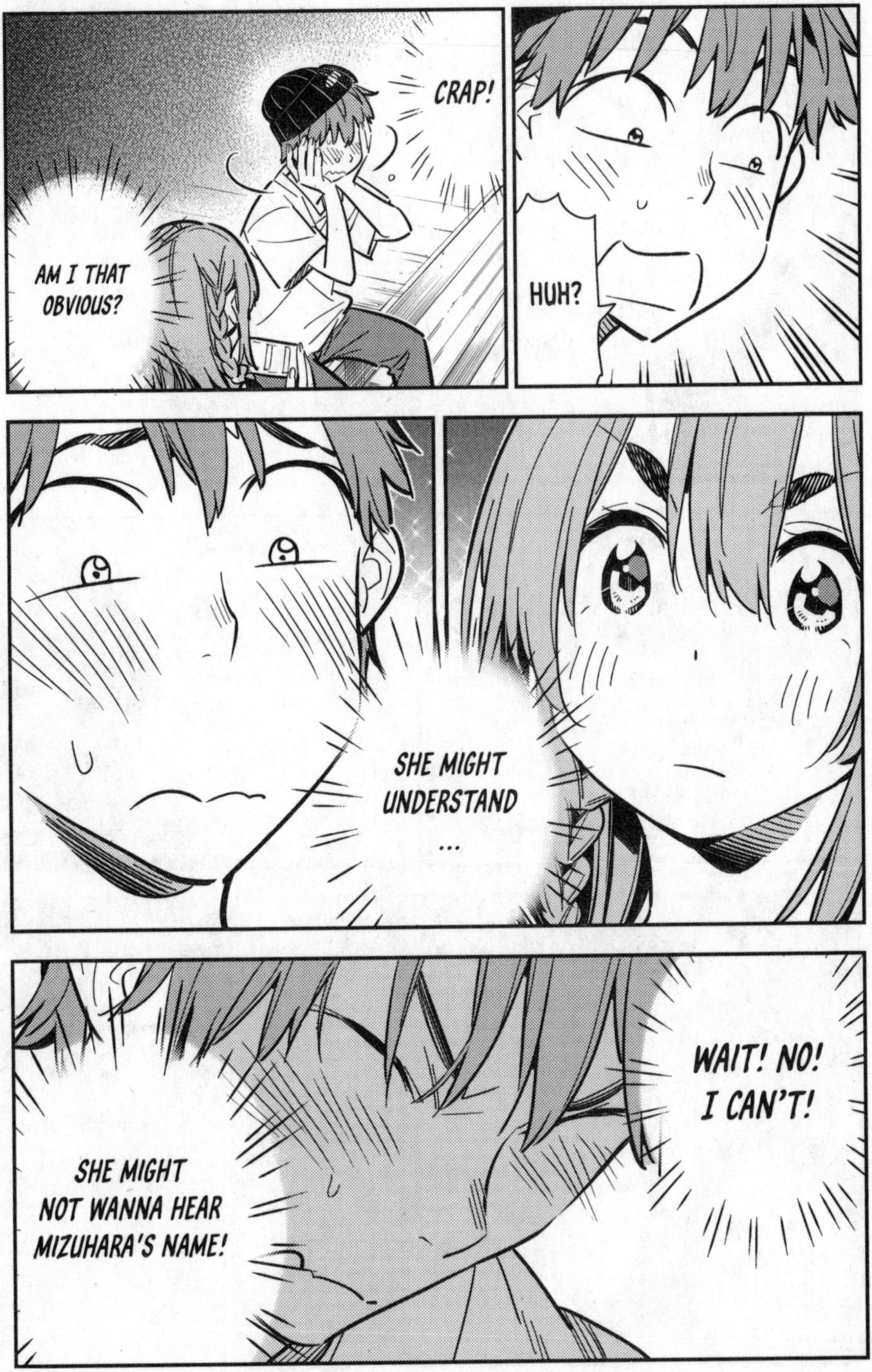
HUH?
CRAP!
AM I THAT OBVIOUS?
SHE MIGHT UNDERSTAND ...
WAIT! NO! I CAN'T!
SHE MIGHT NOT WANNA HEAR MIZUHARA'S NAME!

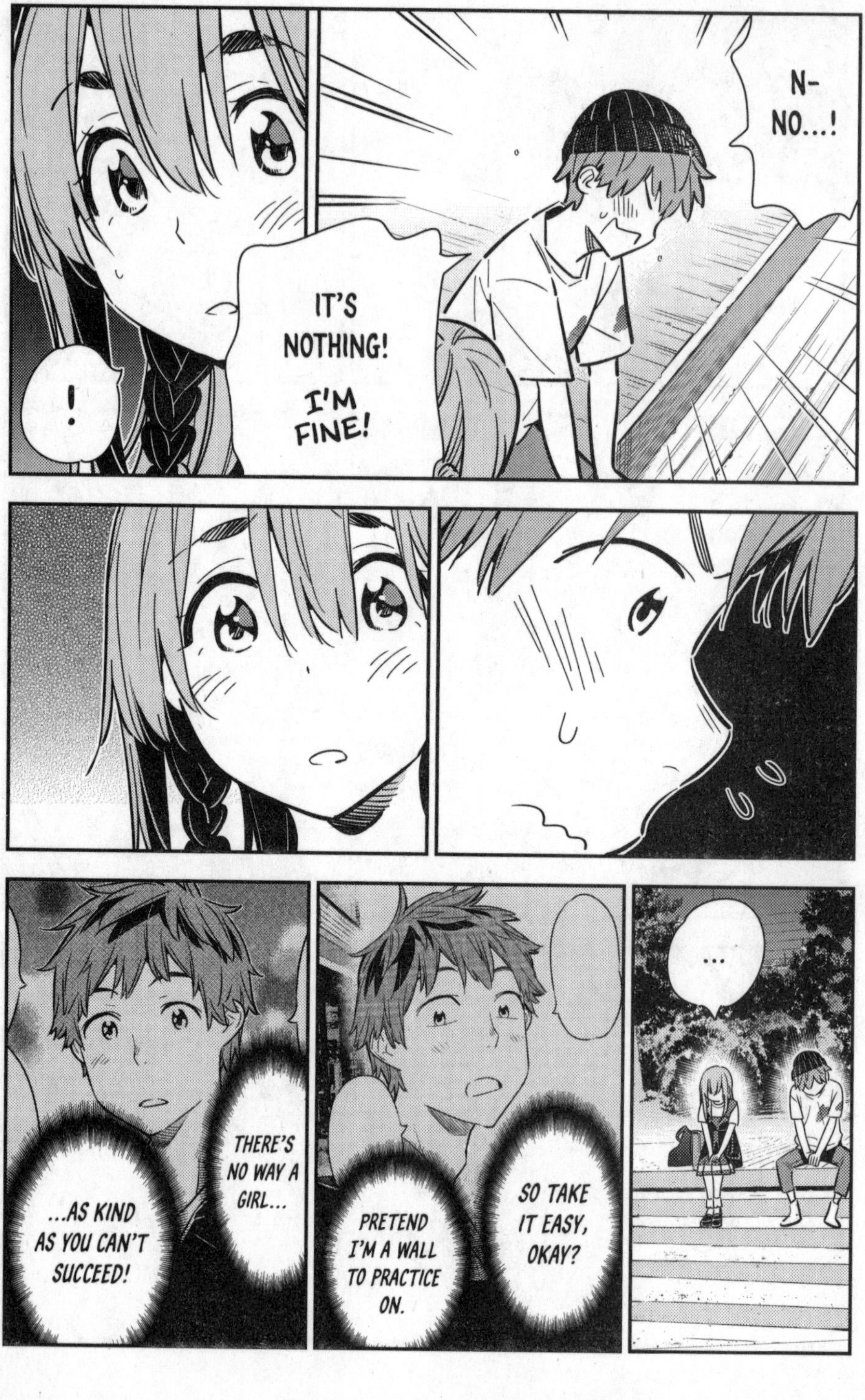
N- NO...!
IT'S NOTHING!
I'M FINE!
!
...
SO TAKE IT EASY, OKAY?
PRETEND I'M A WALL TO PRACTICE ON.
THERE'S NO WAY A GIRL...
...AS KIND AS YOU CAN'T SUCCEED!

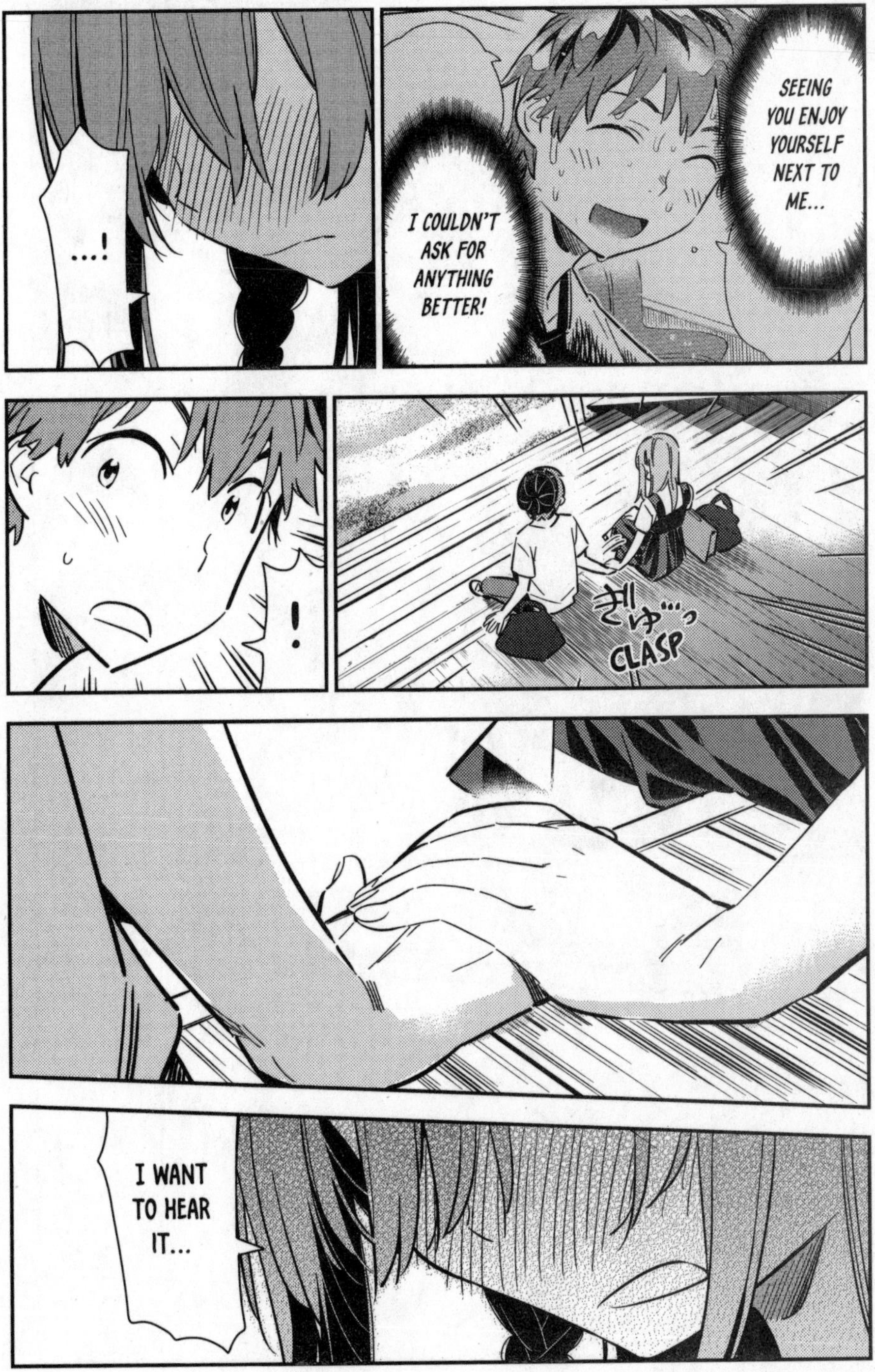
SEEING YOU ENJOY YOURSELF NEXT TO ME...
I COULDN'T ASK FOR ANYTHING BETTER!
...!
ぎゅっ
CLASP
!
I WANT TO HEAR IT...

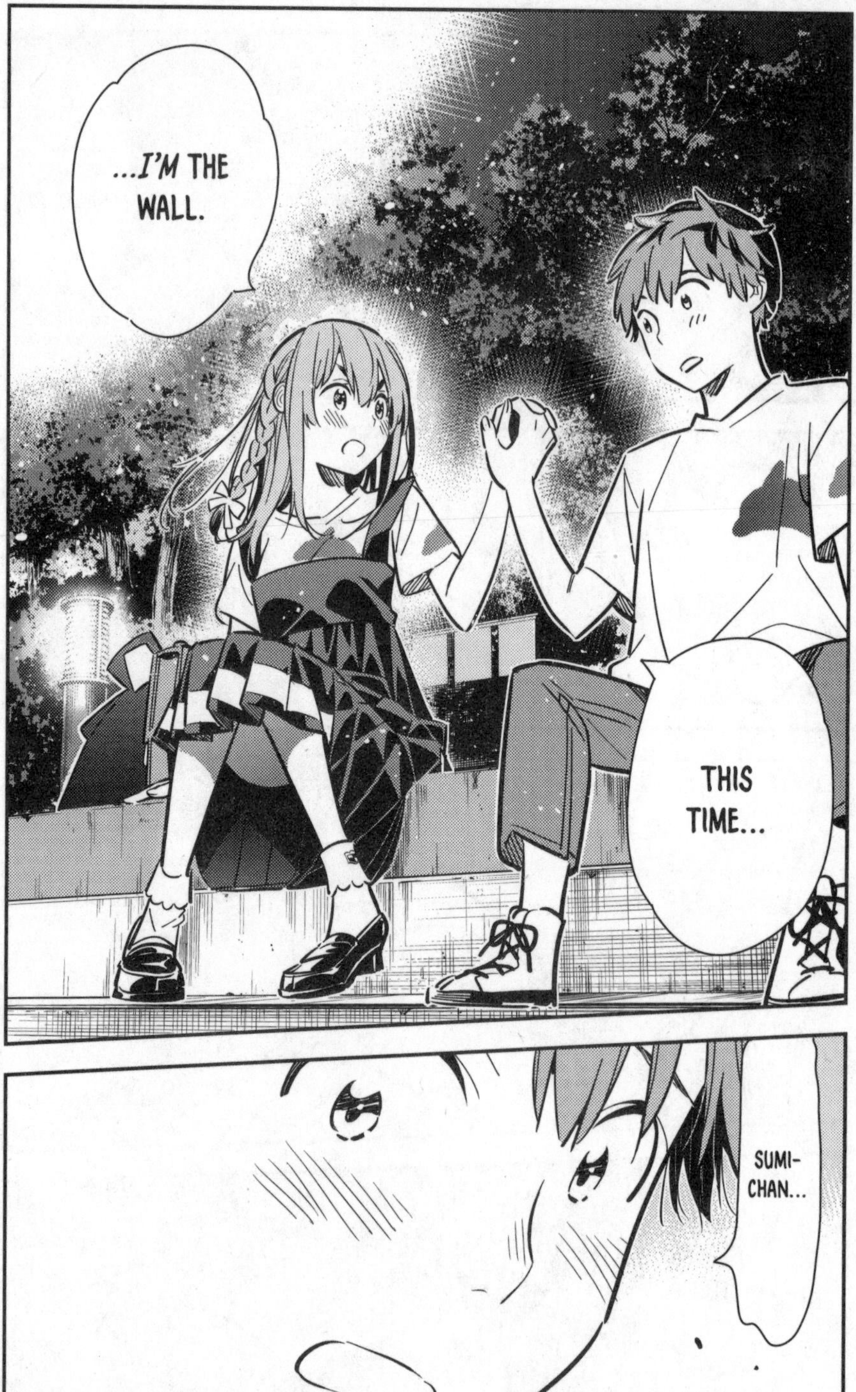
...I'M THE WALL.
THIS TIME...
SUMI-CHAN...

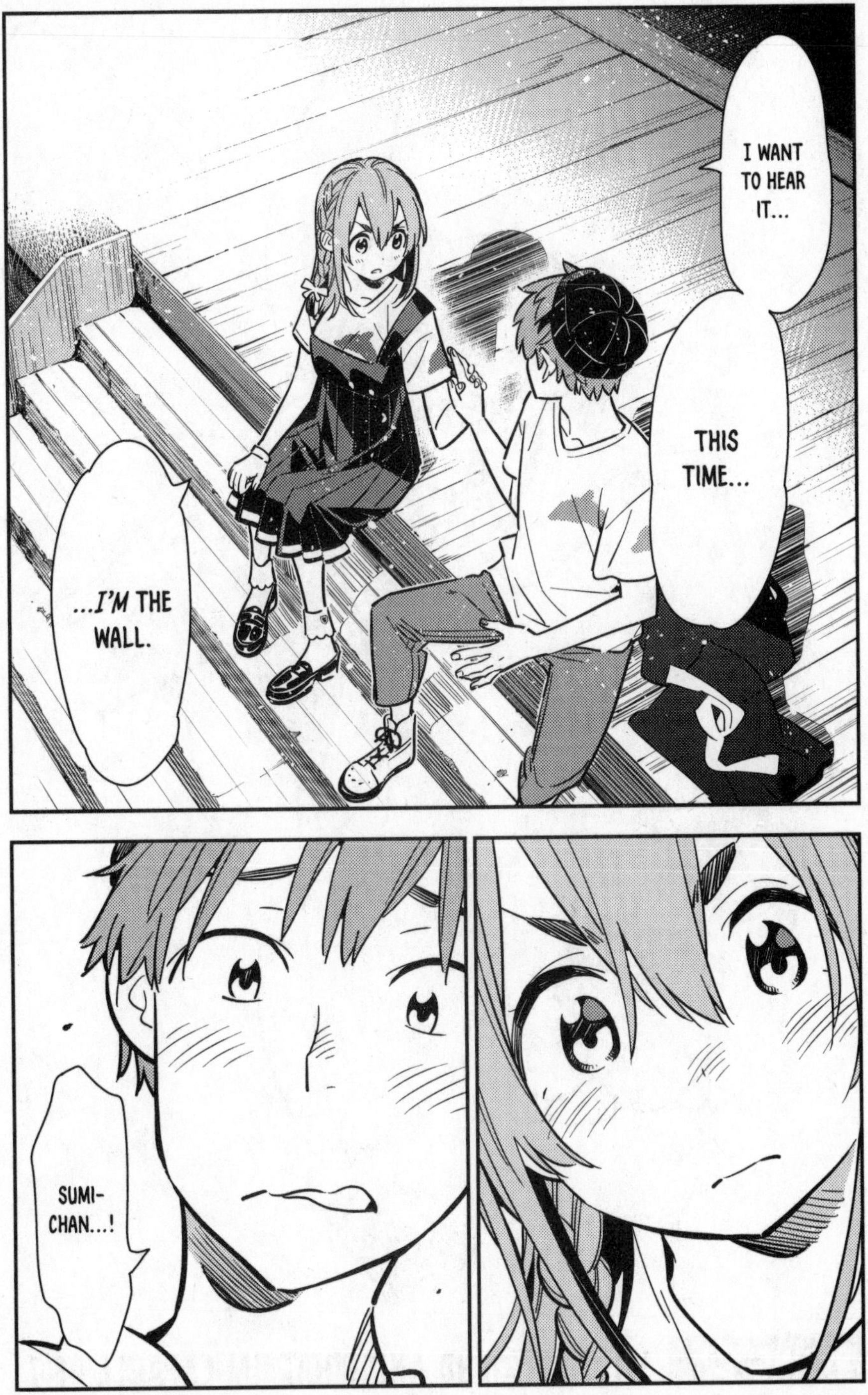
I WANT TO HEAR IT...
THIS TIME...
...*I'M* THE WALL.
SUMI-CHAN...!

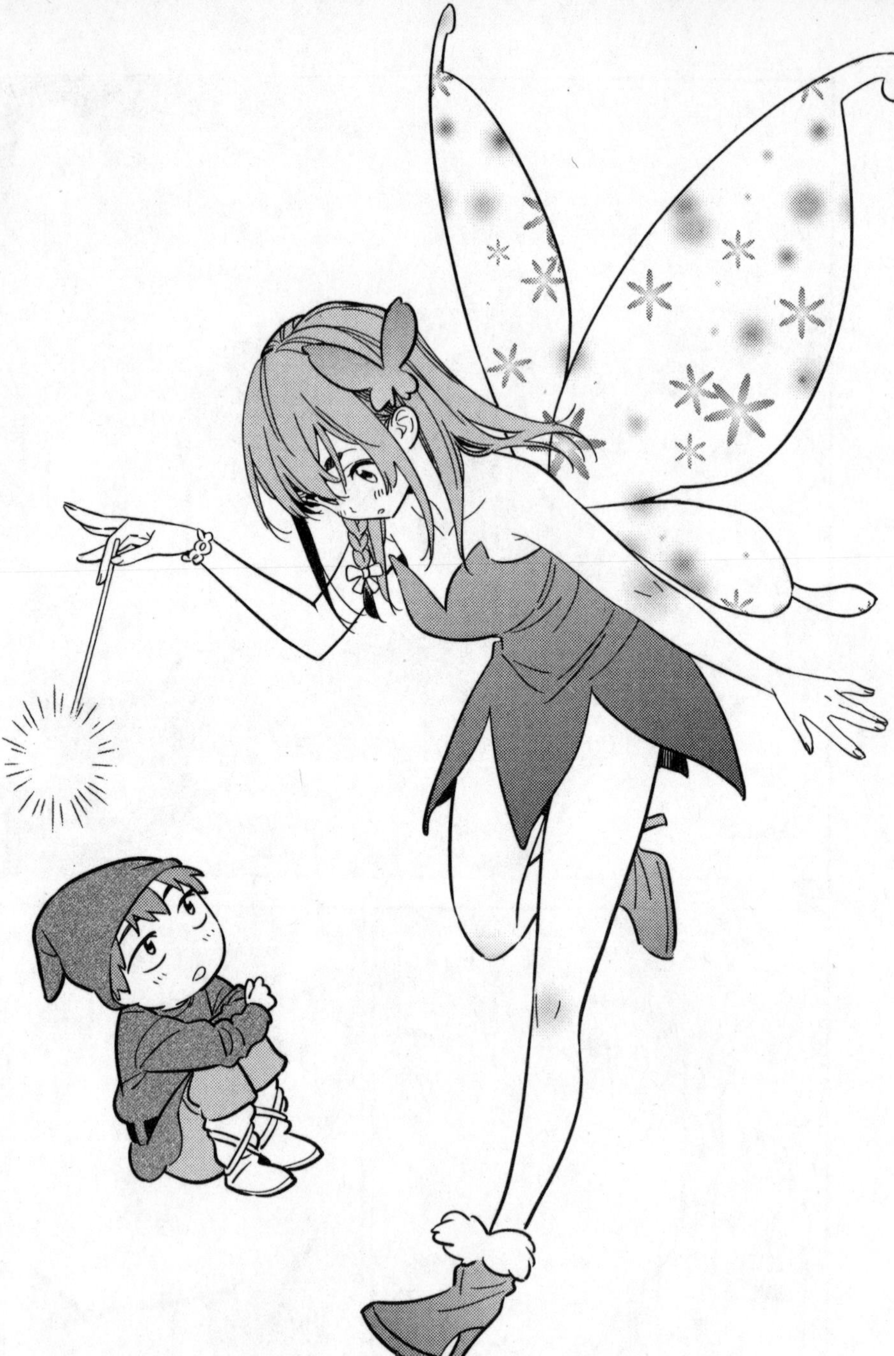

## RATING 98 MY GIRLFRIEND AND WHAT I'M CAPABLE OF 7

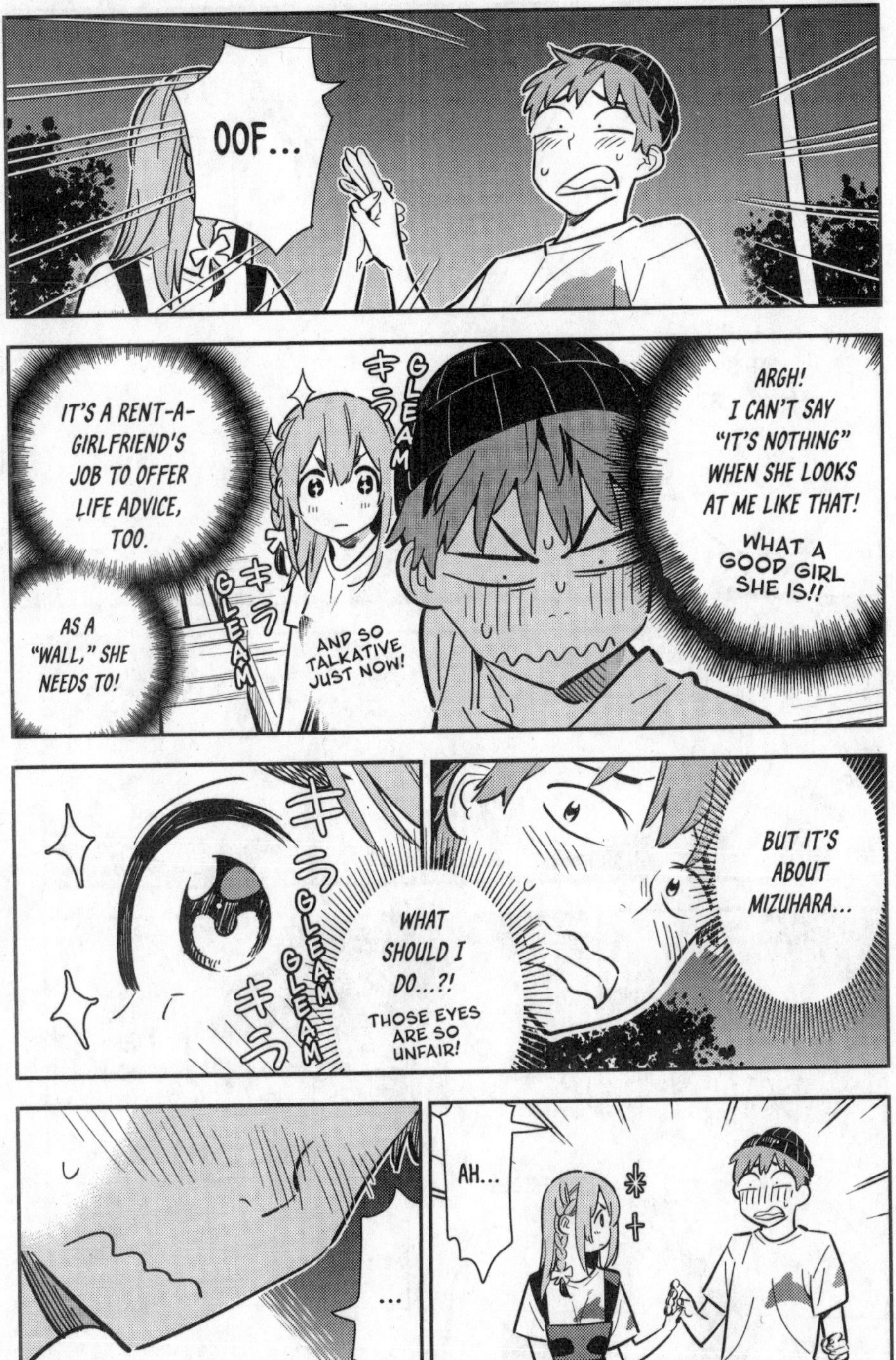
OOF...
ARGH! I CAN'T SAY "IT'S NOTHING" WHEN SHE LOOKS AT ME LIKE THAT!
WHAT A GOOD GIRL SHE IS!!
キラ
GLEAM
IT'S A RENT-A-GIRLFRIEND'S JOB TO OFFER LIFE ADVICE, TOO.
キラ
GLEAM
AND SO TALKATIVE JUST NOW!
AS A "WALL," SHE NEEDS TO!
BUT IT'S ABOUT MIZUHARA...
WHAT SHOULD I DO...?!
THOSE EYES ARE SO UNFAIR!
キラ
GLEAM
キラ
GLEAM
AH...
...

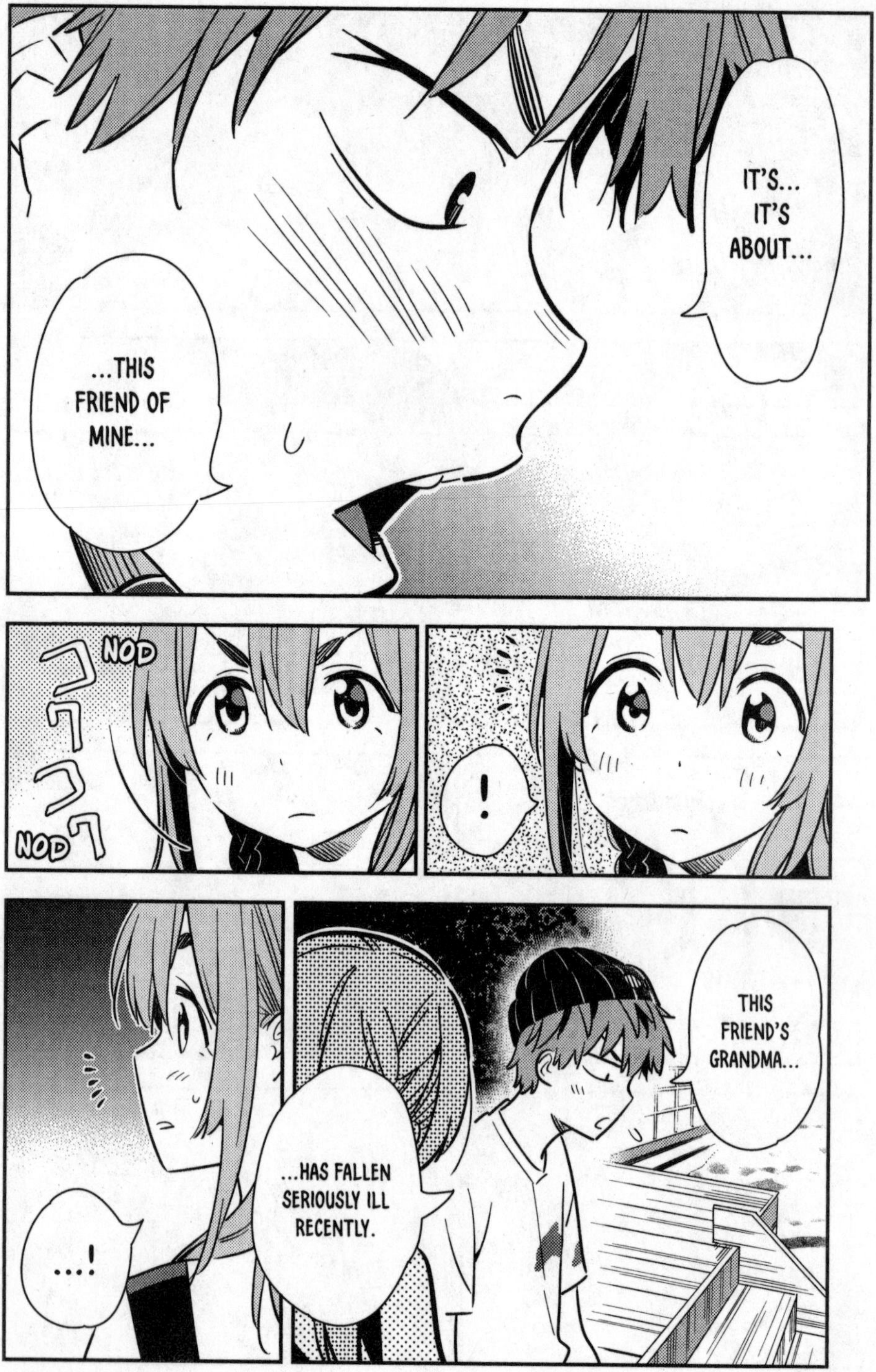
IT'S... IT'S ABOUT...
...THIS FRIEND OF MINE...
!
NOD
NOD
THIS FRIEND'S GRANDMA...
...HAS FALLEN SERIOUSLY ILL RECENTLY.
...!

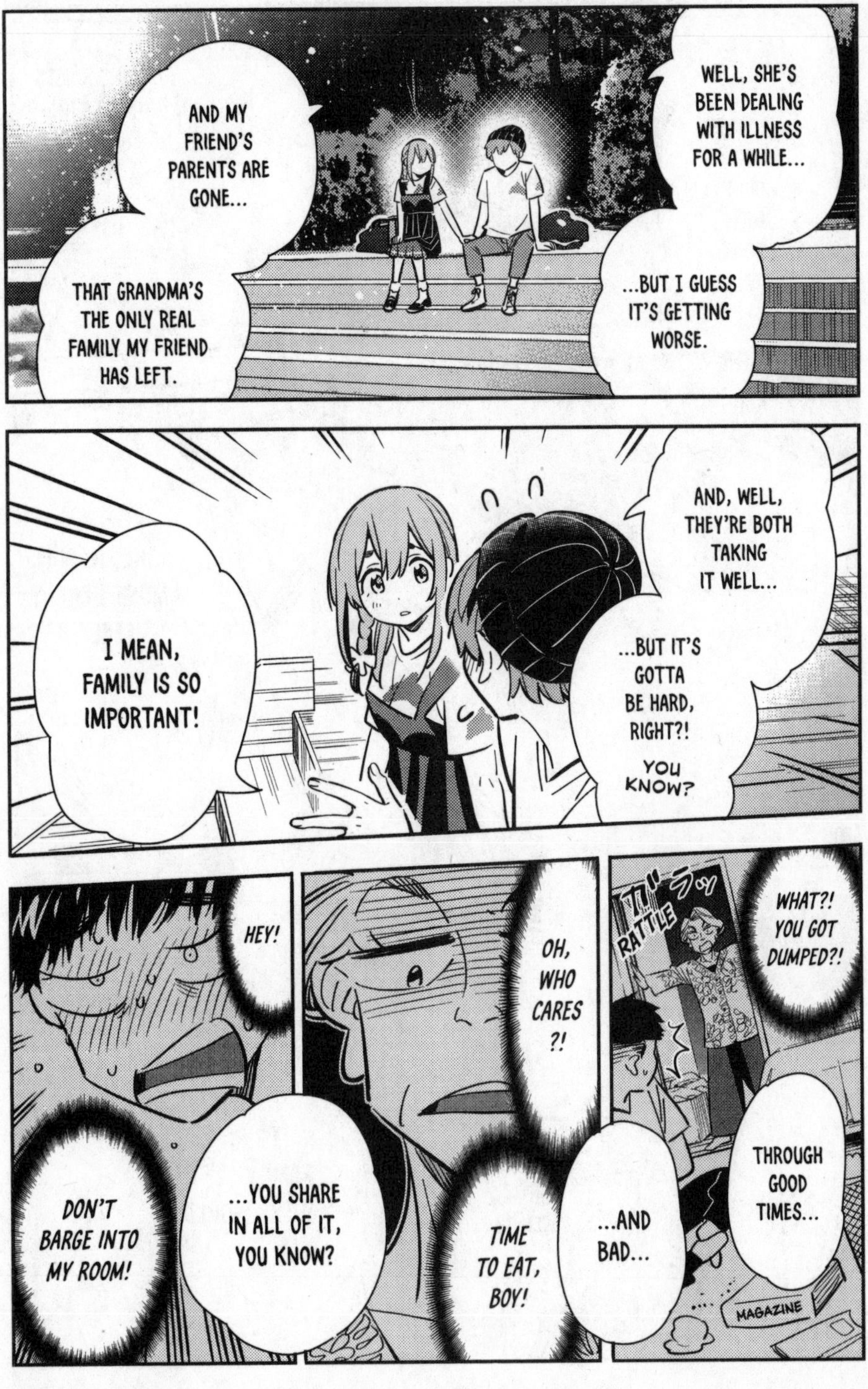
WELL, SHE'S BEEN DEALING WITH ILLNESS FOR A WHILE...
...BUT I GUESS IT'S GETTING WORSE.
AND MY FRIEND'S PARENTS ARE GONE...
THAT GRANDMA'S THE ONLY REAL FAMILY MY FRIEND HAS LEFT.
AND, WELL, THEY'RE BOTH TAKING IT WELL...
...BUT IT'S GOTTA BE HARD, RIGHT?!
YOU KNOW?
I MEAN, FAMILY IS SO IMPORTANT!
RATTLE
WHAT?! YOU GOT DUMPED?!
THROUGH GOOD TIMES...
...AND BAD...
MAGAZINE
OH, WHO CARES?!
TIME TO EAT, BOY!
...YOU SHARE IN ALL OF IT, YOU KNOW?
HEY!
DON'T BARGE INTO MY ROOM!

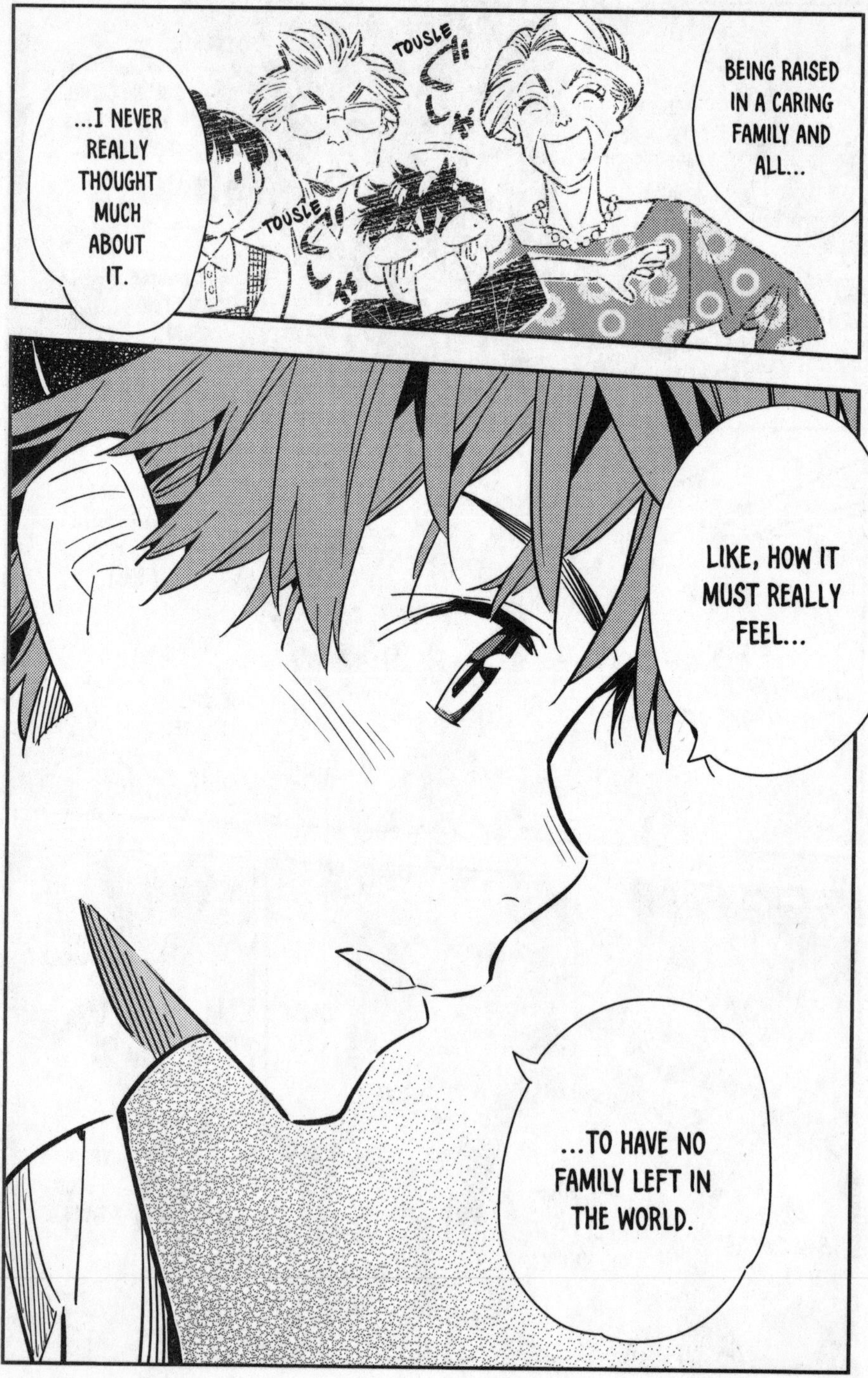
BEING RAISED IN A CARING FAMILY AND ALL...
TOUSLE
TOUSLE
...I NEVER REALLY THOUGHT MUCH ABOUT IT.
LIKE, HOW IT MUST REALLY FEEL...
...TO HAVE NO FAMILY LEFT IN THE WORLD.

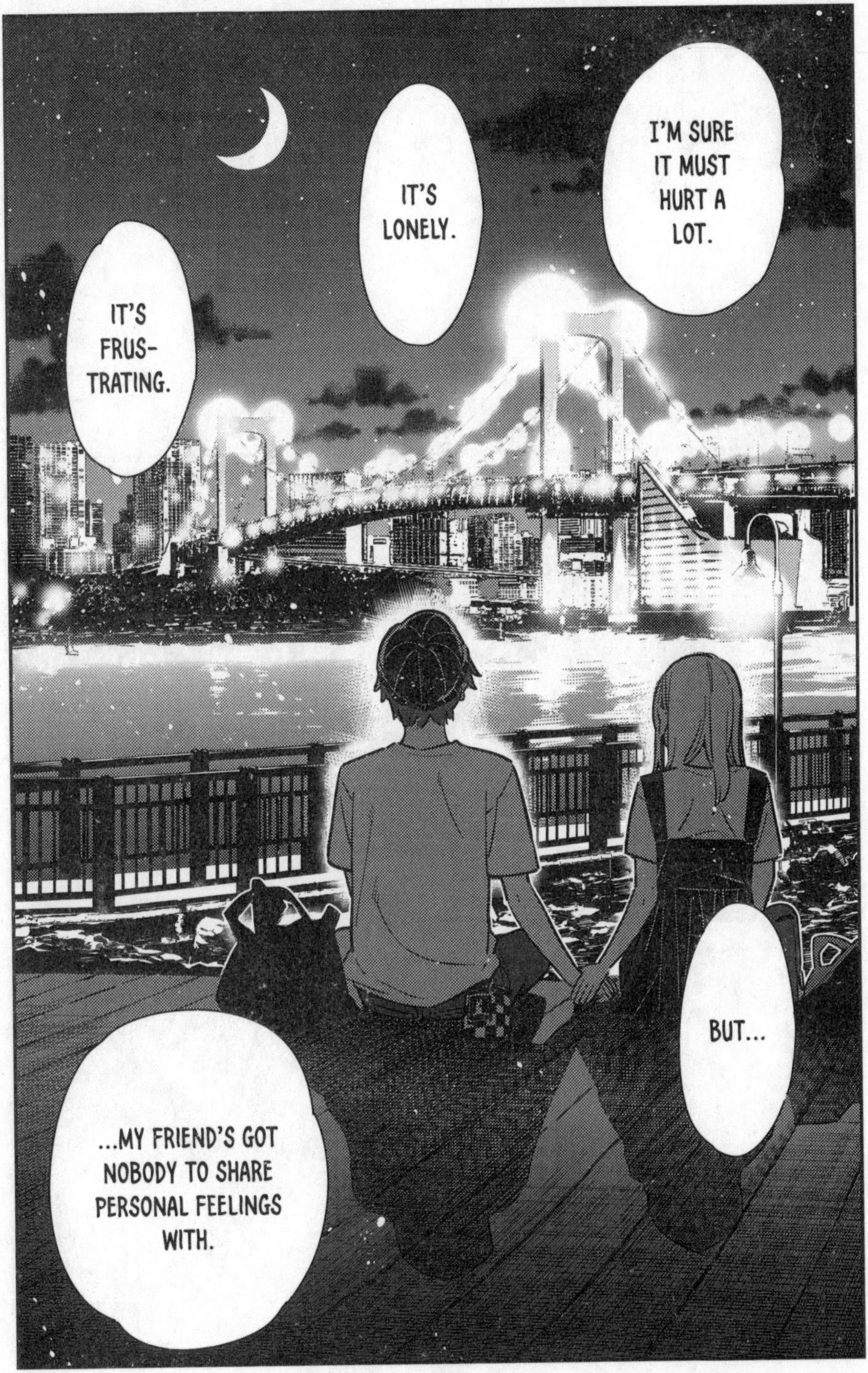
I'M SURE IT MUST HURT A LOT.
IT'S LONELY.
IT'S FRUS- TRATING.
BUT...
...MY FRIEND'S GOT NOBODY TO SHARE PERSONAL FEELINGS WITH.

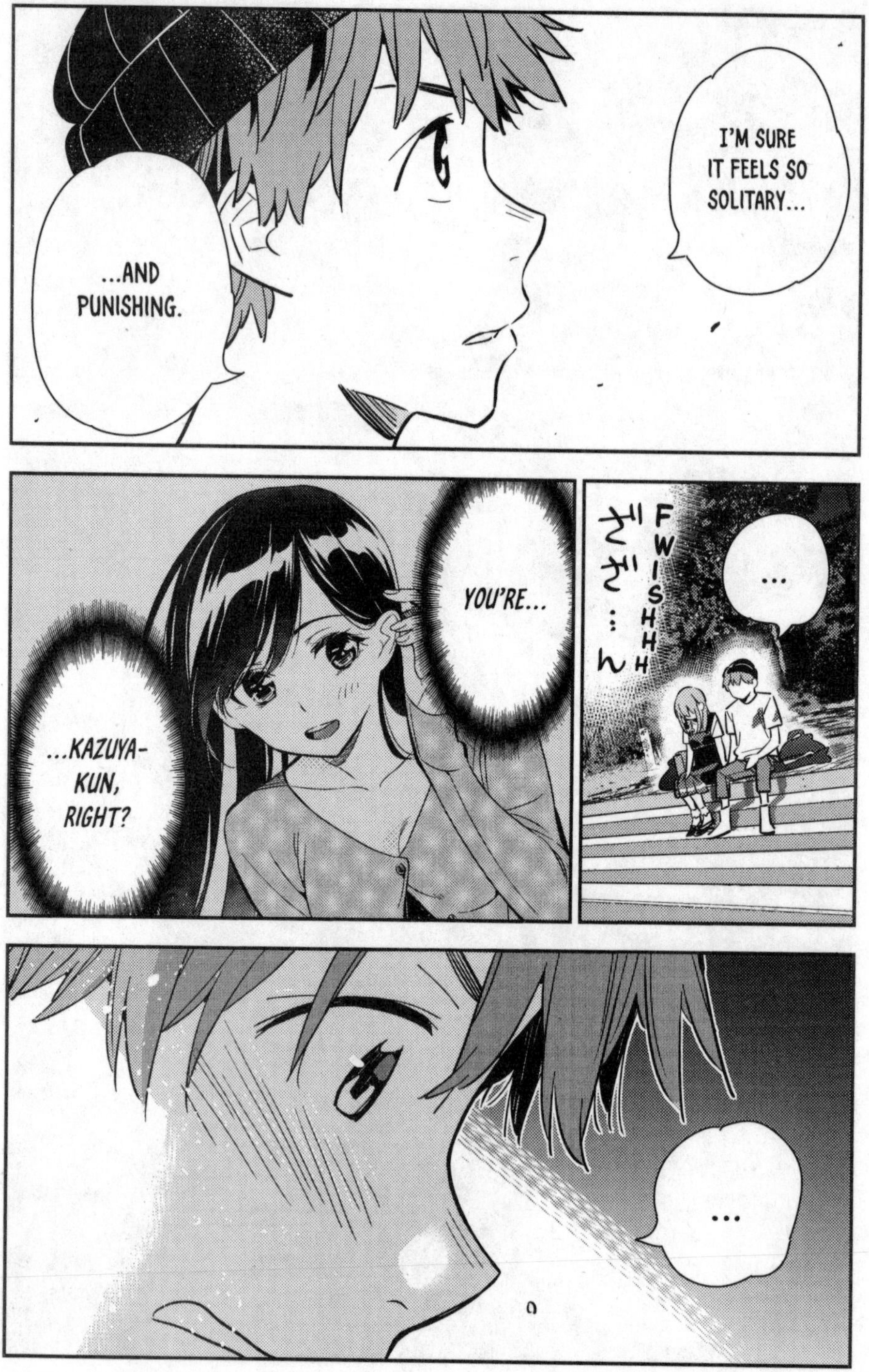

I'M SURE IT FEELS SO SOLITARY...
...AND PUNISHING.
...
FWISHHH
ざざ…ん
YOU'RE...
...KAZUYA-KUN, RIGHT?
...

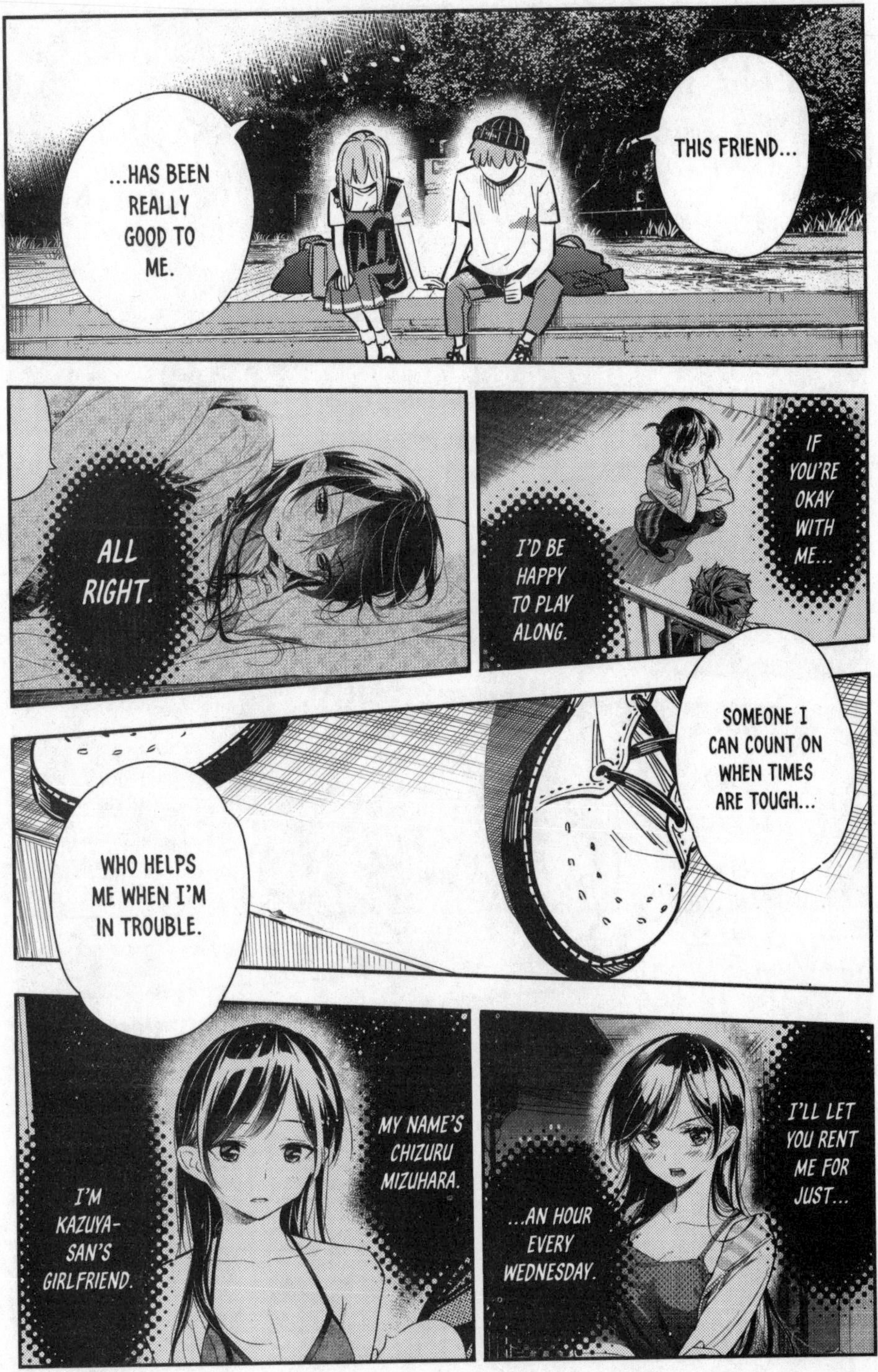
THIS FRIEND...
...HAS BEEN REALLY GOOD TO ME.
IF YOU'RE OKAY WITH ME...
I'D BE HAPPY TO PLAY ALONG.
ALL RIGHT.
SOMEONE I CAN COUNT ON WHEN TIMES ARE TOUGH...
WHO HELPS ME WHEN I'M IN TROUBLE.
I'LL LET YOU RENT ME FOR JUST...
...AN HOUR EVERY WEDNESDAY.
MY NAME'S CHIZURU MIZUHARA.
I'M KAZUYA-SAN'S GIRLFRIEND.

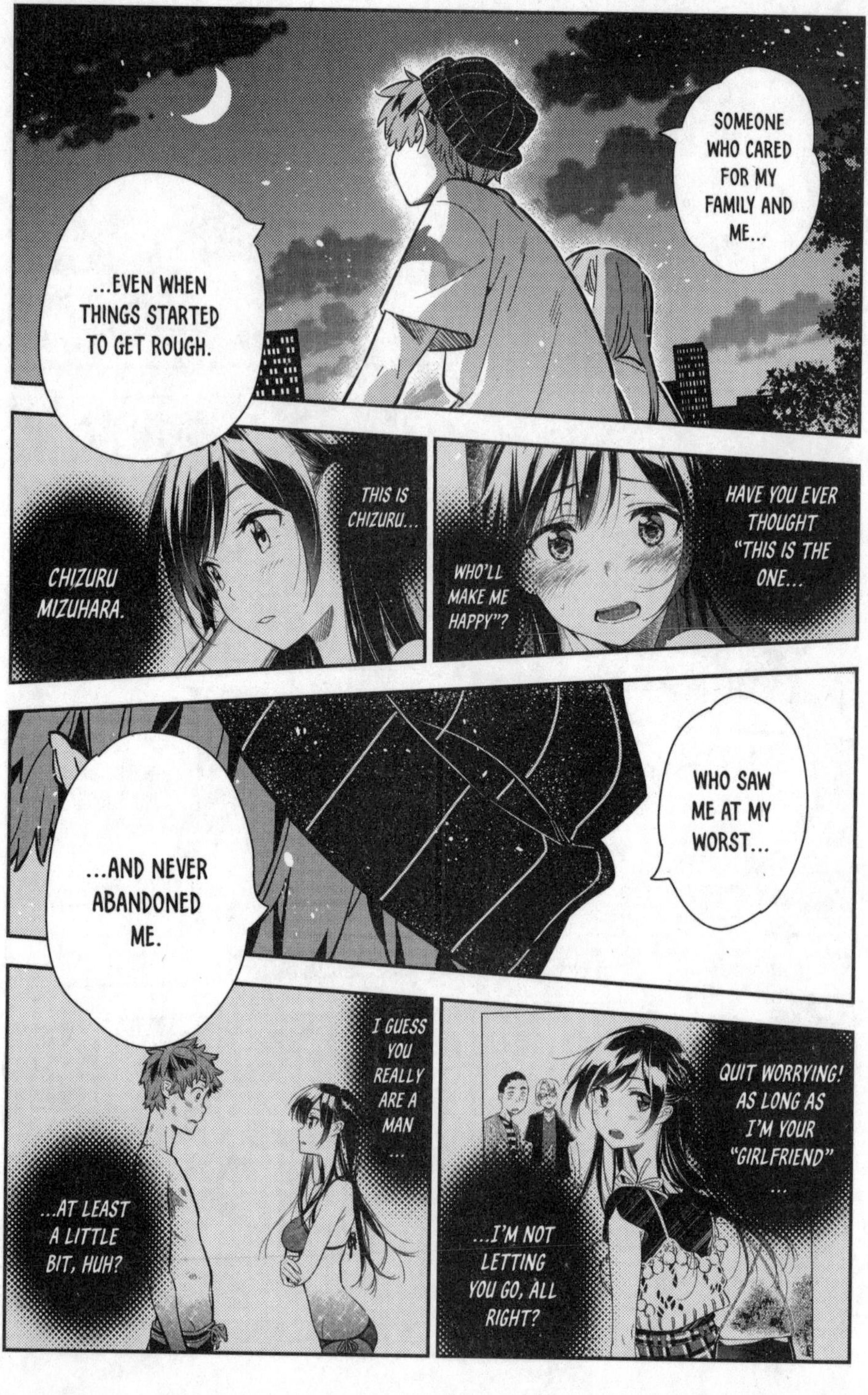
SOMEONE WHO CARED FOR MY FAMILY AND ME...
...EVEN WHEN THINGS STARTED TO GET ROUGH.
HAVE YOU EVER THOUGHT "THIS IS THE ONE...
WHO'LL MAKE ME HAPPY"?
THIS IS CHIZURU...
CHIZURU MIZUHARA.
WHO SAW ME AT MY WORST...
...AND NEVER ABANDONED ME.
QUIT WORRYING! AS LONG AS I'M YOUR "GIRLFRIEND"...
...I'M NOT LETTING YOU GO, ALL RIGHT?
I GUESS YOU REALLY ARE A MAN...
...AT LEAST A LITTLE BIT, HUH?

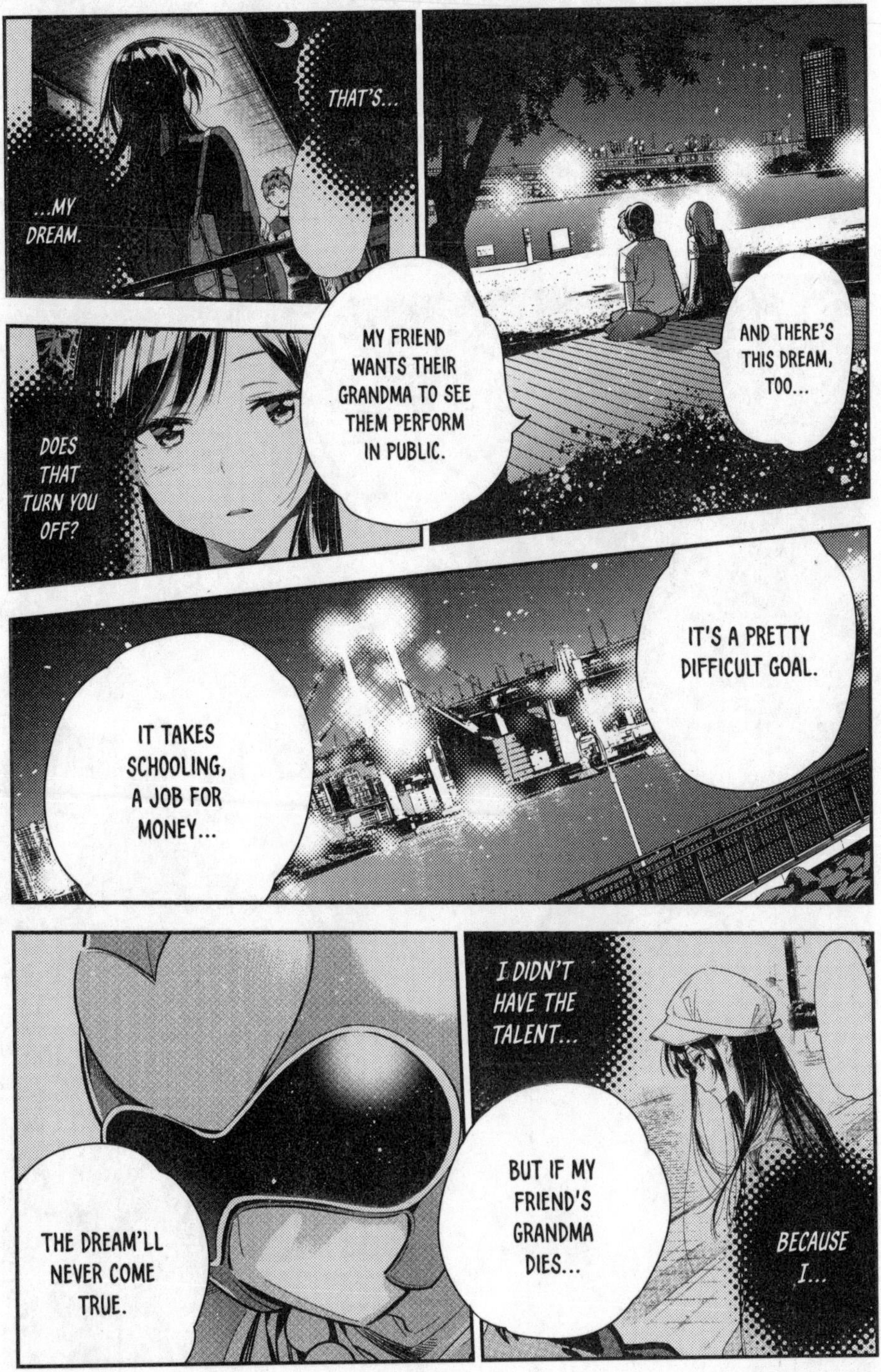
AND THERE'S THIS DREAM, TOO...
MY FRIEND WANTS THEIR GRANDMA TO SEE THEM PERFORM IN PUBLIC.
THAT'S...
...MY DREAM.
DOES THAT TURN YOU OFF?
IT'S A PRETTY DIFFICULT GOAL.
IT TAKES SCHOOLING, A JOB FOR MONEY...
I DIDN'T HAVE THE TALENT...
BECAUSE I...
BUT IF MY FRIEND'S GRANDMA DIES...
THE DREAM'LL NEVER COME TRUE.

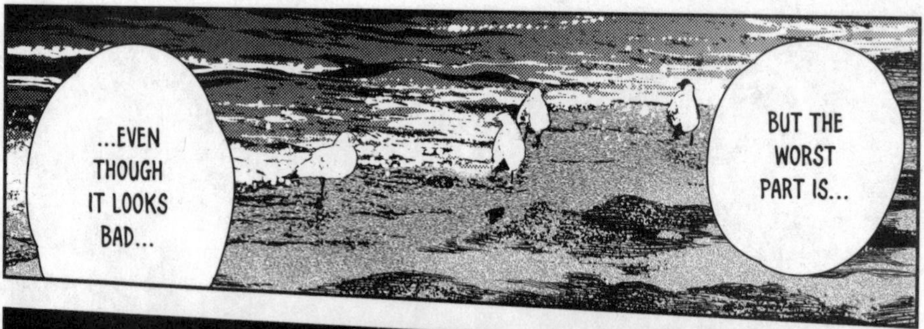
BUT THE WORST PART IS...
...EVEN THOUGH IT LOOKS BAD...

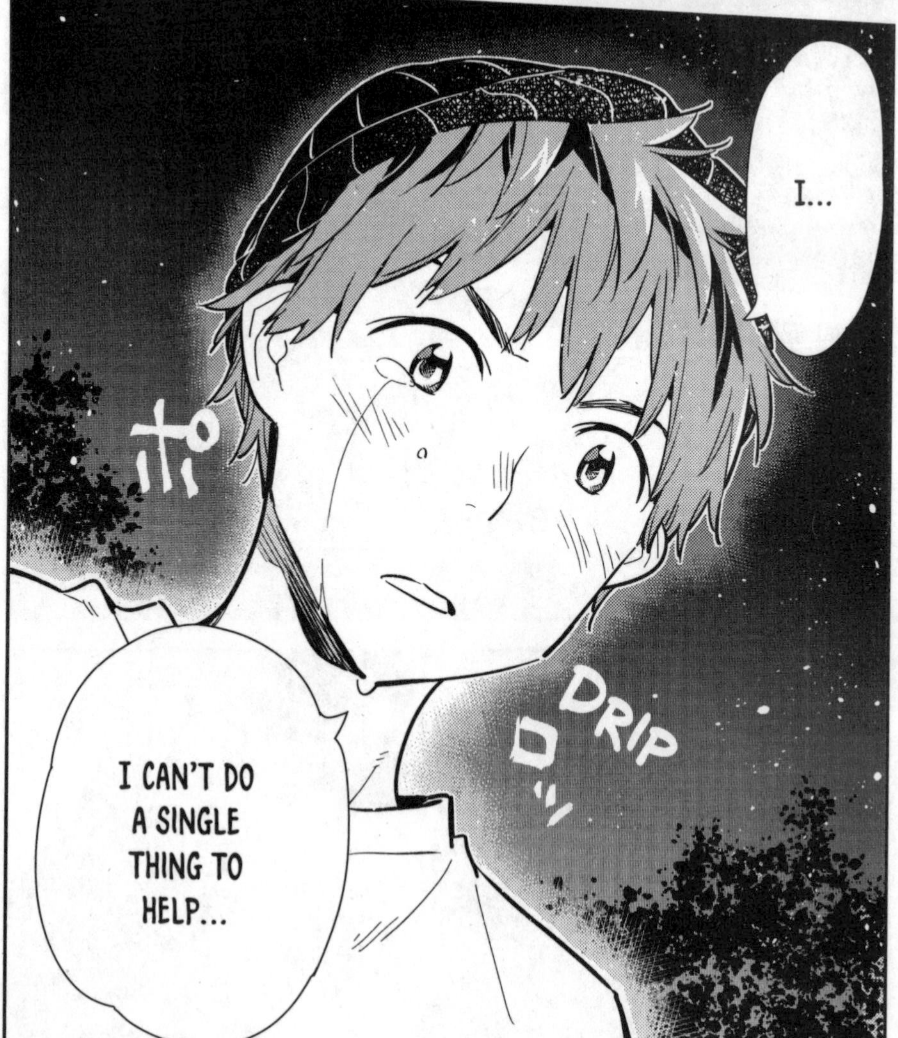
I...
DRIP
I CAN'T DO A SINGLE THING TO HELP...

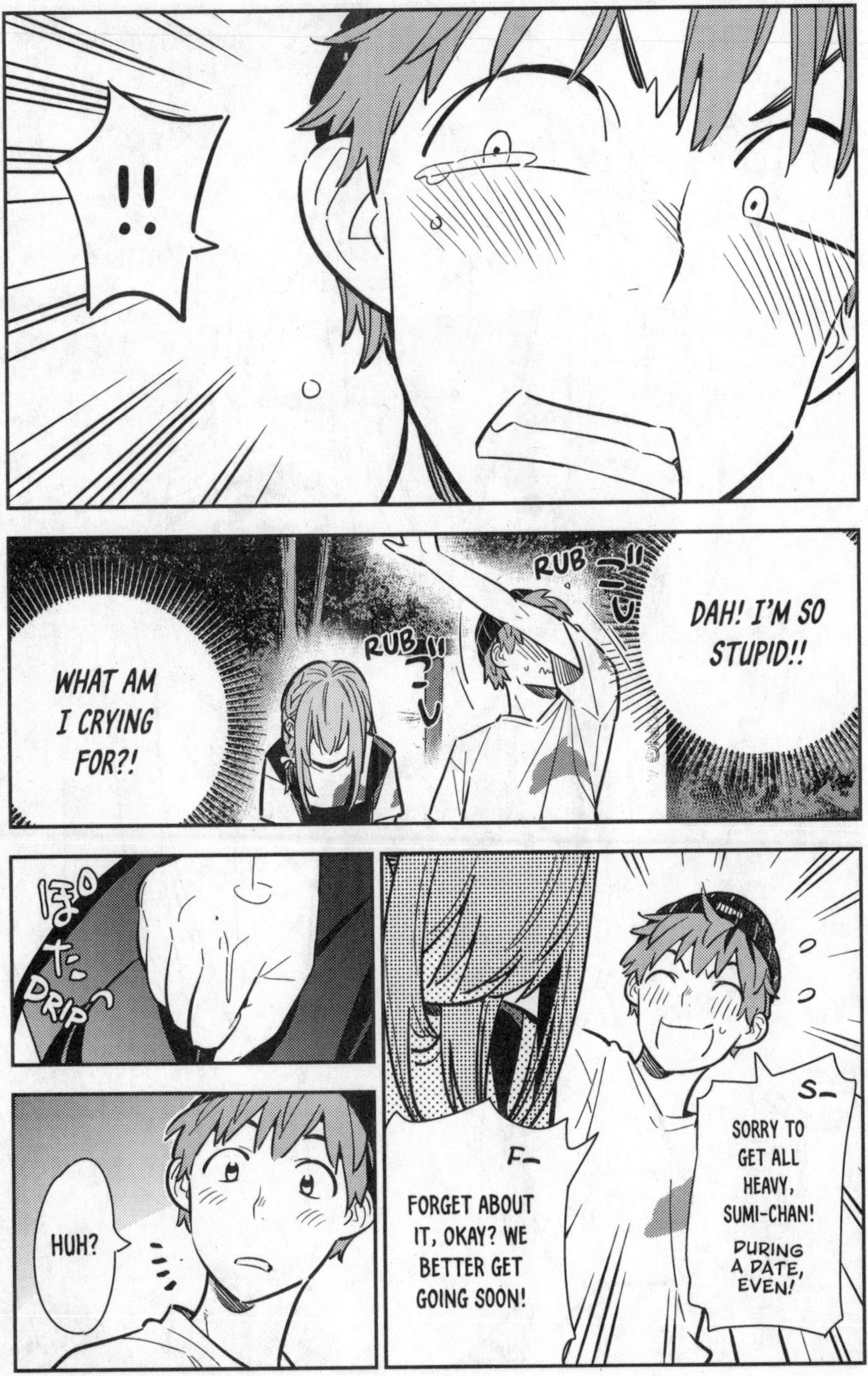
!!
DAH! I'M SO STUPID!!
RUB
RUB
WHAT AM I CRYING FOR?!
S—
SORRY TO GET ALL HEAVY, SUMI-CHAN!
DURING A DATE, EVEN!
F—
FORGET ABOUT IT, OKAY? WE BETTER GET GOING SOON!
DRIP
HUH?

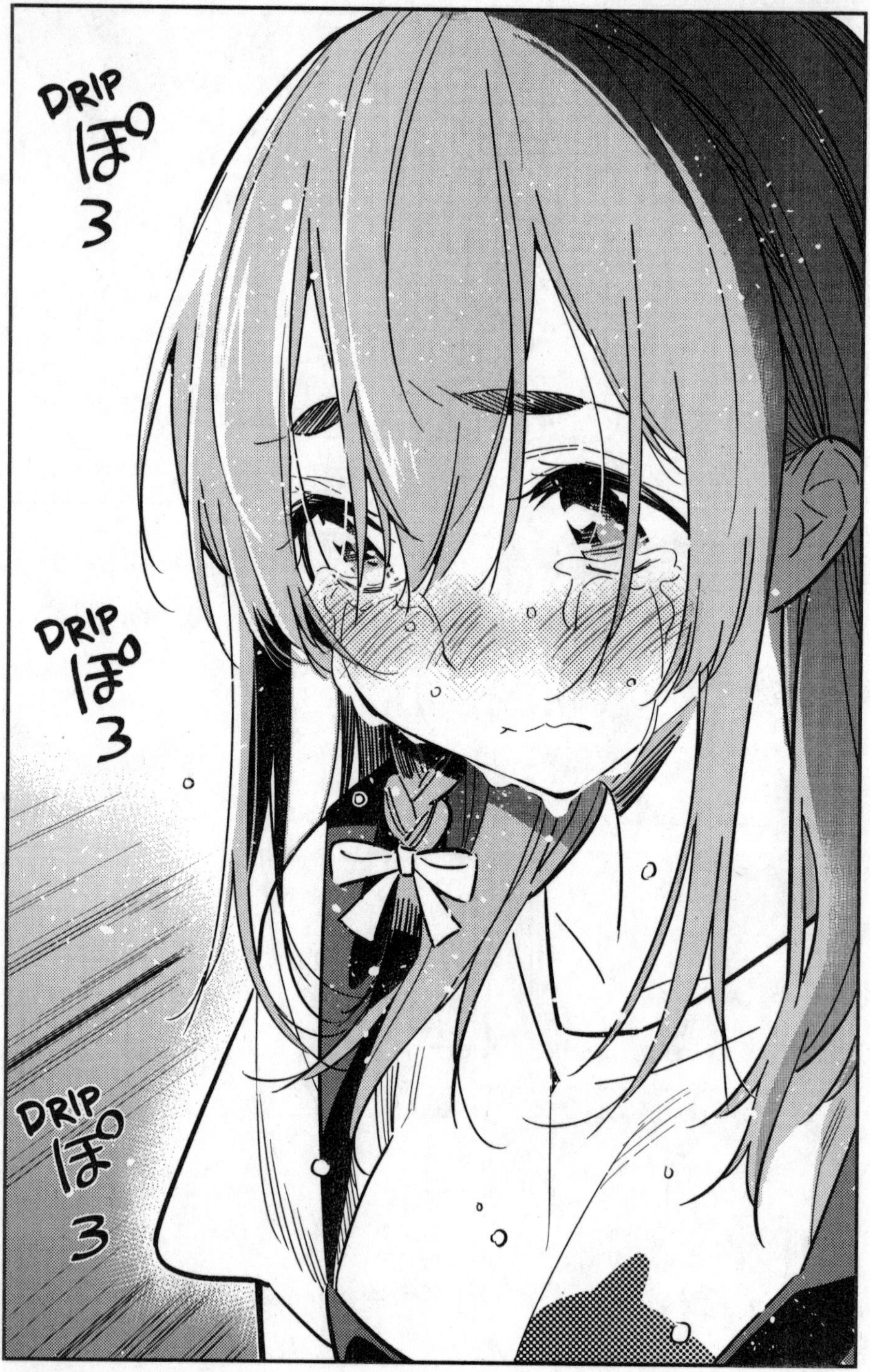
DRIP
ぽろ
DRIP
ぽろ
DRIP
ぽろ

HUH
?!

DID I SAY SOMETHING BAD...?!

SWEAT

SWEAT

I, I'M SORRY! YOU OKAY?!

SUMI-CHAN...!

....!

SHAKE

SHAKE

...YOU FEEL... KAZUYA-KUN...!

I... I KNOW HOW...

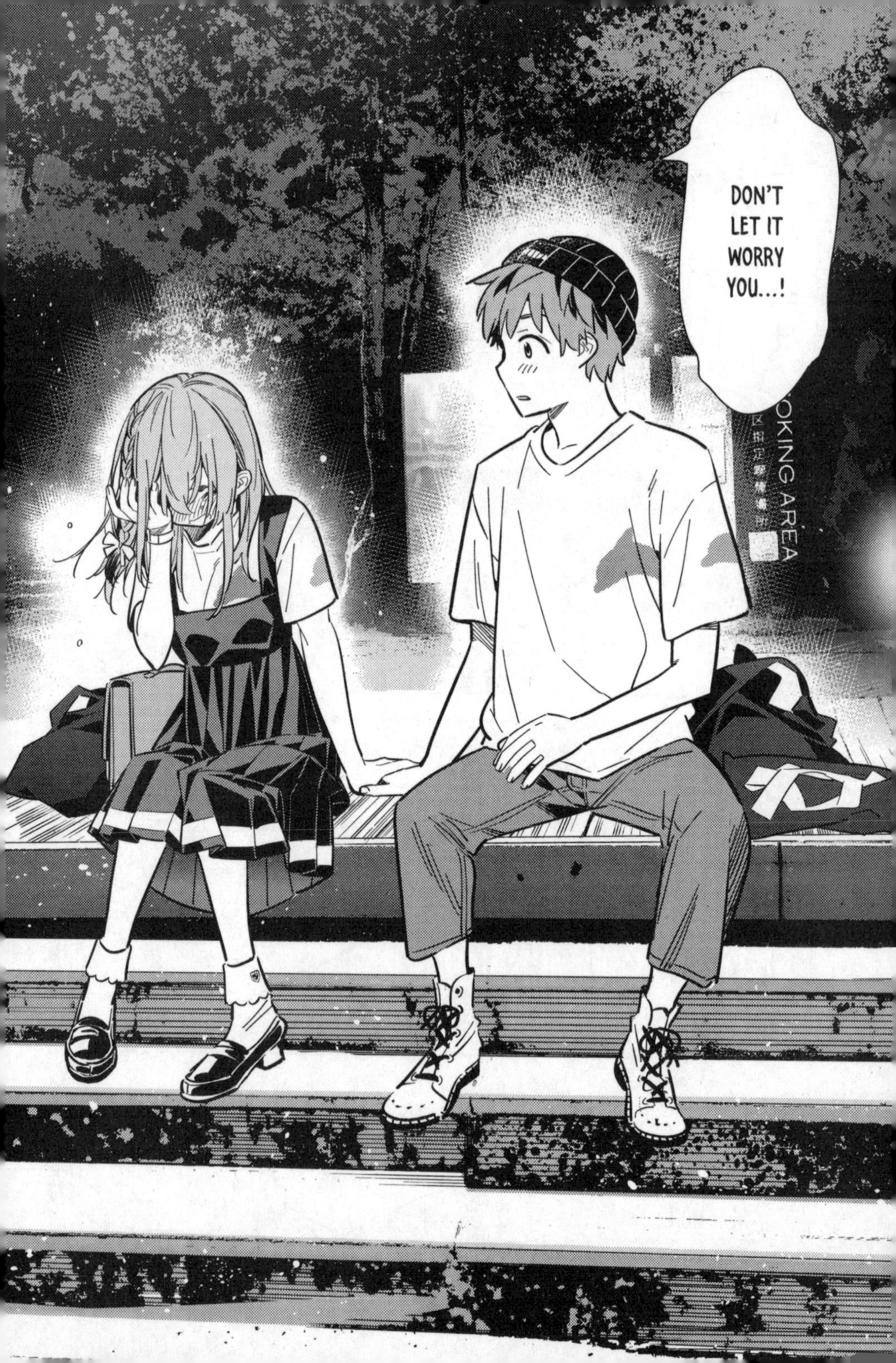
DON'T LET IT WORRY YOU...!

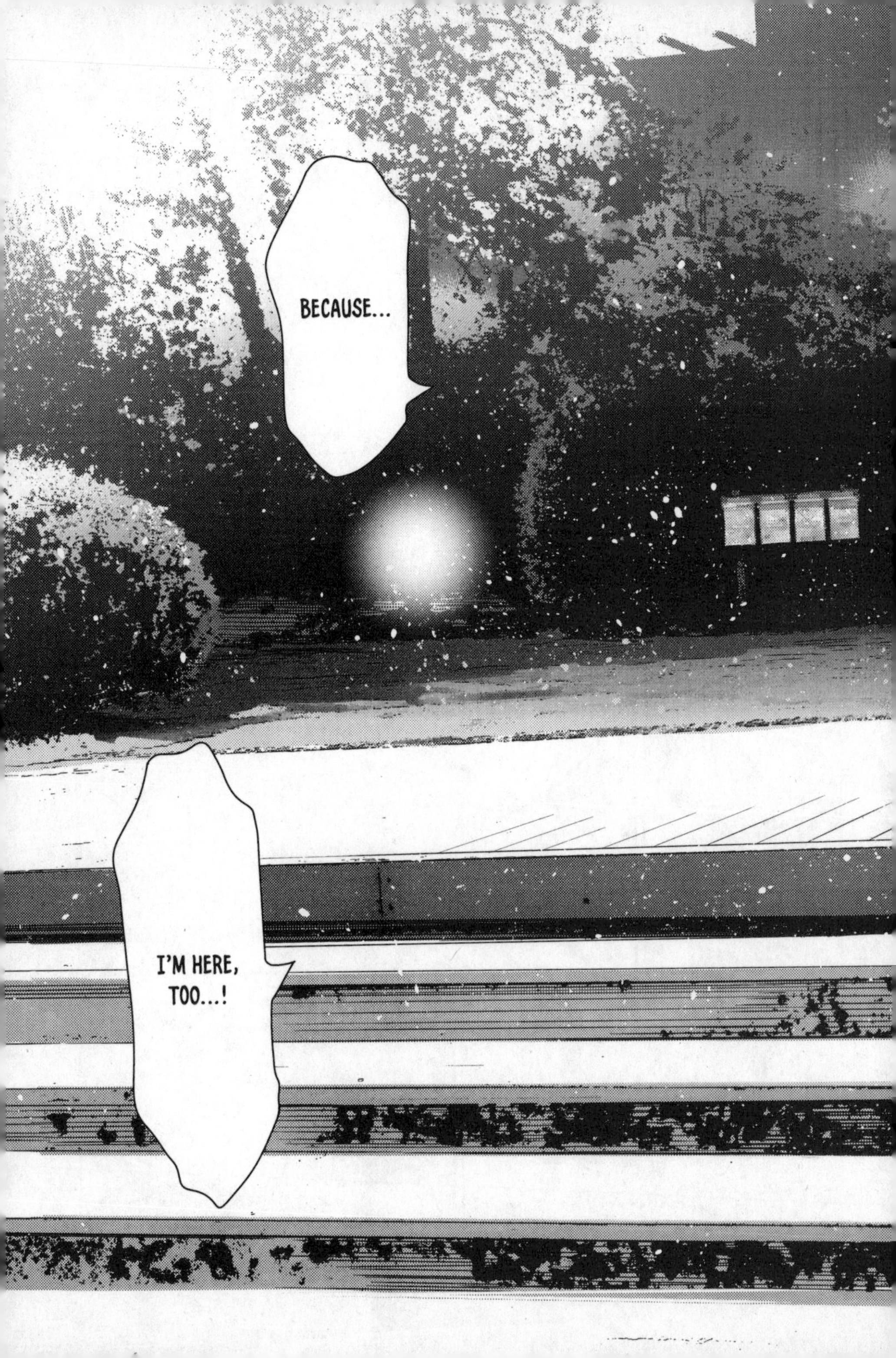
BECAUSE...
I'M HERE, TOO...!

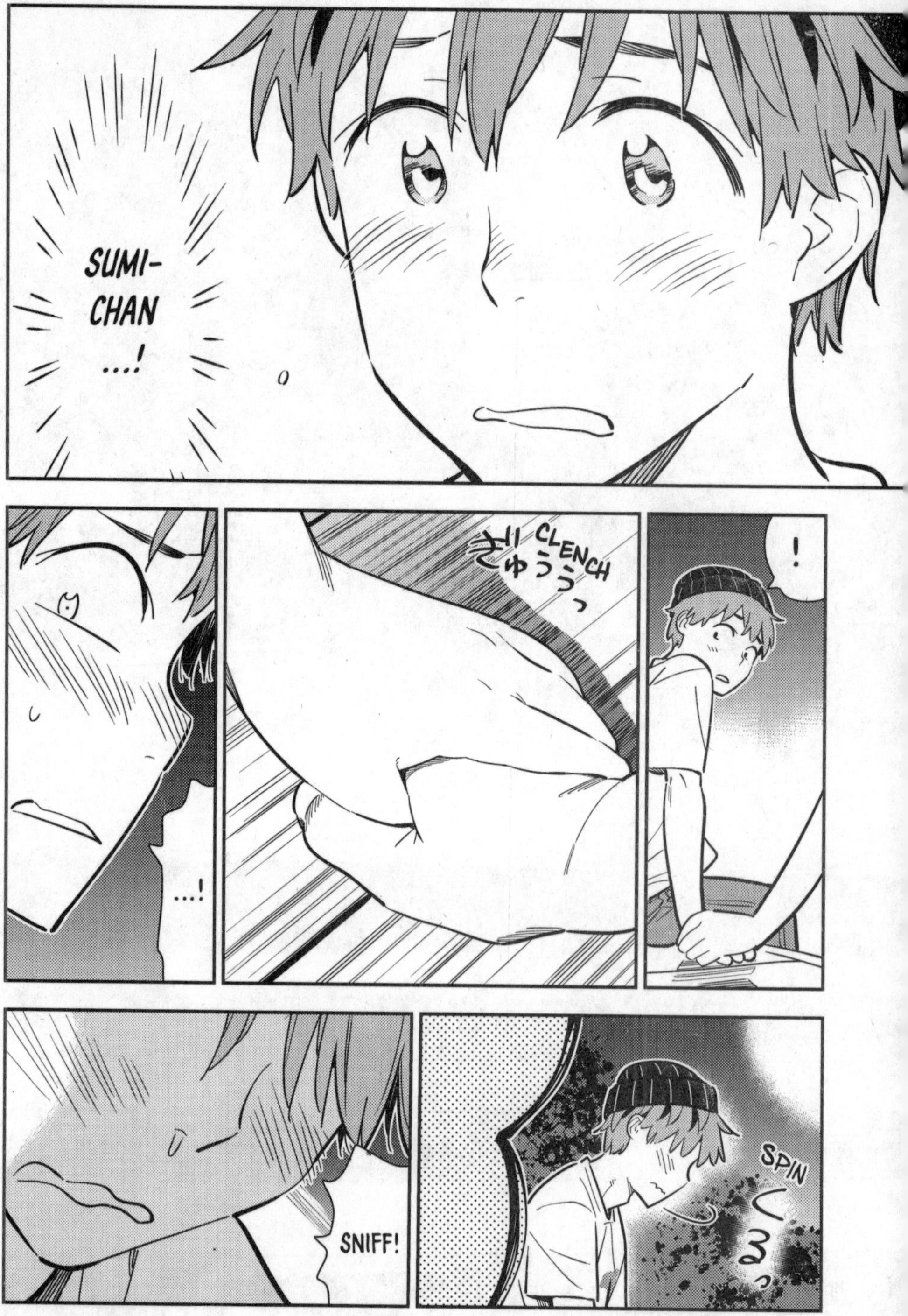
SUMI-CHAN ...!
!
CLENCH
ぎゅううっ
...!
SPIN
くるっ
SNIFF!

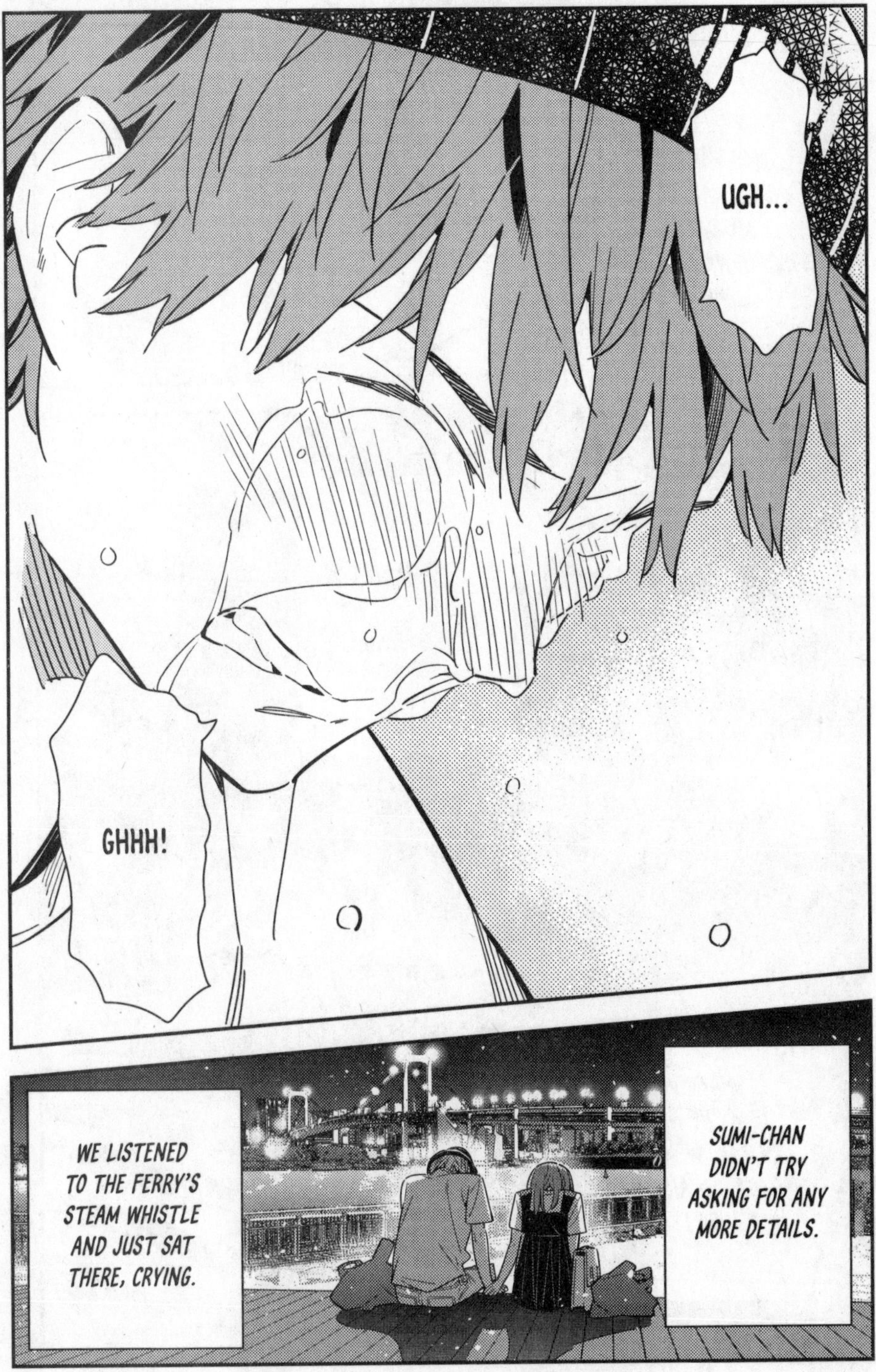
UGH...
GHHH!
SUMI-CHAN DIDN'T TRY ASKING FOR ANY MORE DETAILS.
WE LISTENED TO THE FERRY'S STEAM WHISTLE AND JUST SAT THERE, CRYING.

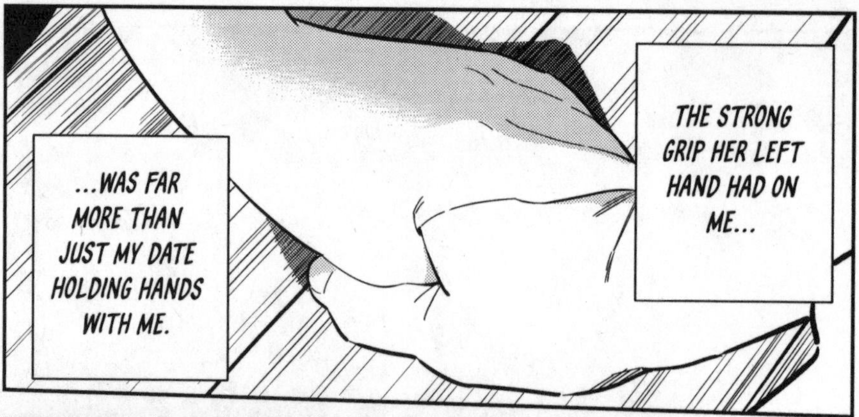
THE STRONG GRIP HER LEFT HAND HAD ON ME...
...WAS FAR MORE THAN JUST MY DATE HOLDING HANDS WITH ME.
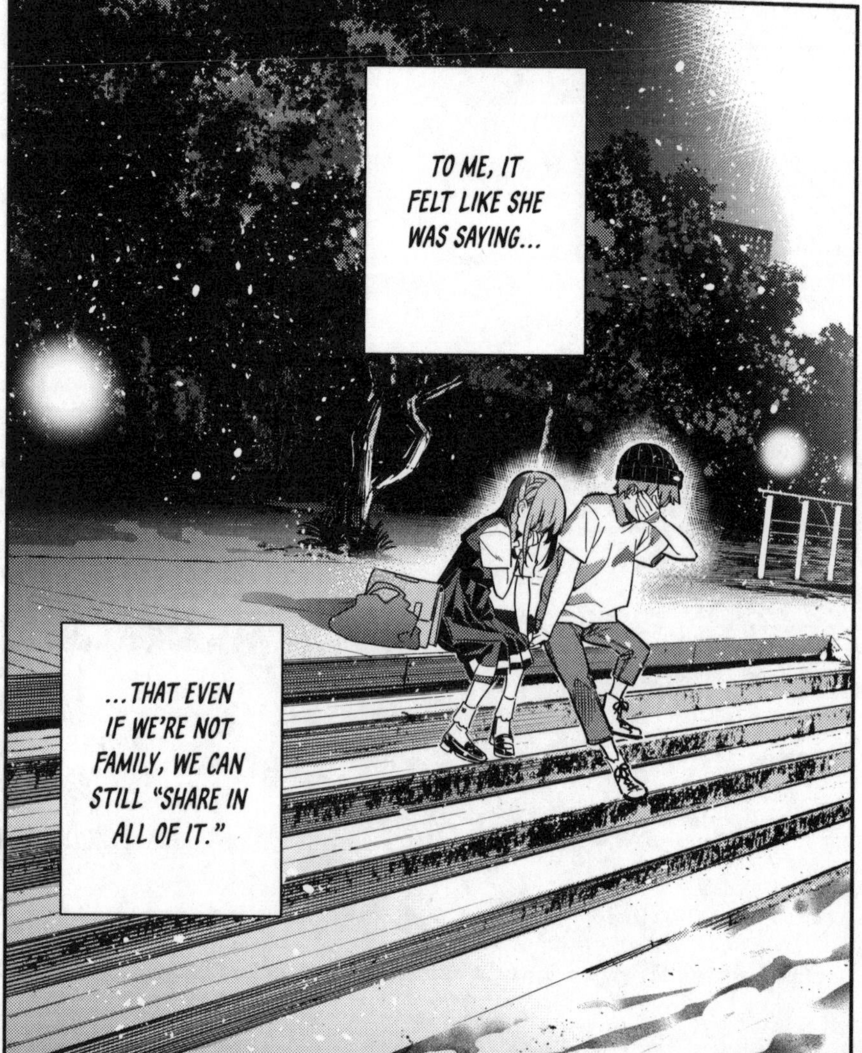
TO ME, IT FELT LIKE SHE WAS SAYING...
...THAT EVEN IF WE'RE NOT FAMILY, WE CAN STILL "SHARE IN ALL OF IT."

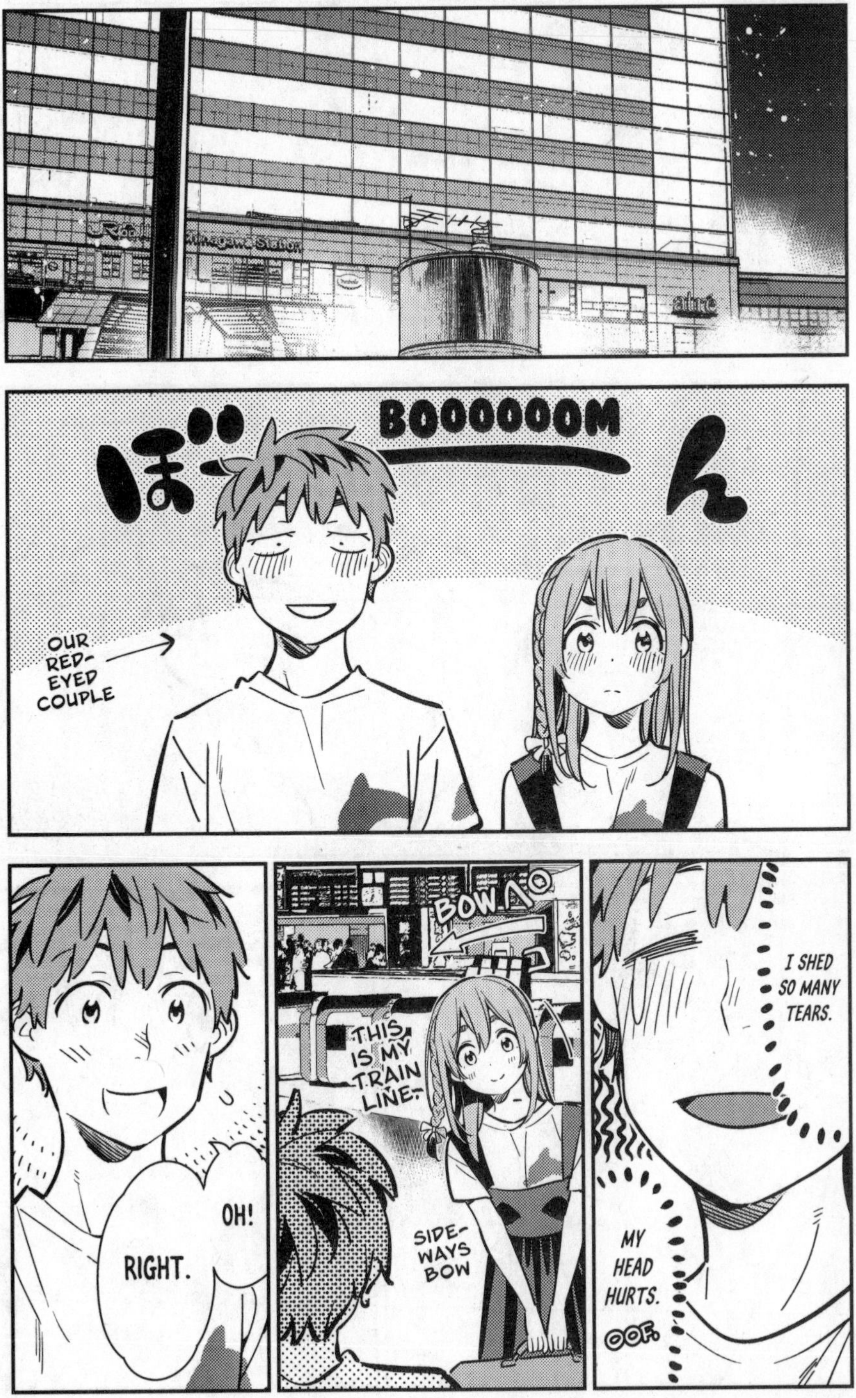
BOOOOOOM
ぼーん
OUR RED-EYED COUPLE
I SHED SO MANY TEARS.
MY HEAD HURTS.
OOF.
BOW
THIS IS MY TRAIN LINE.
SIDEWAYS BOW
OH!
RIGHT.

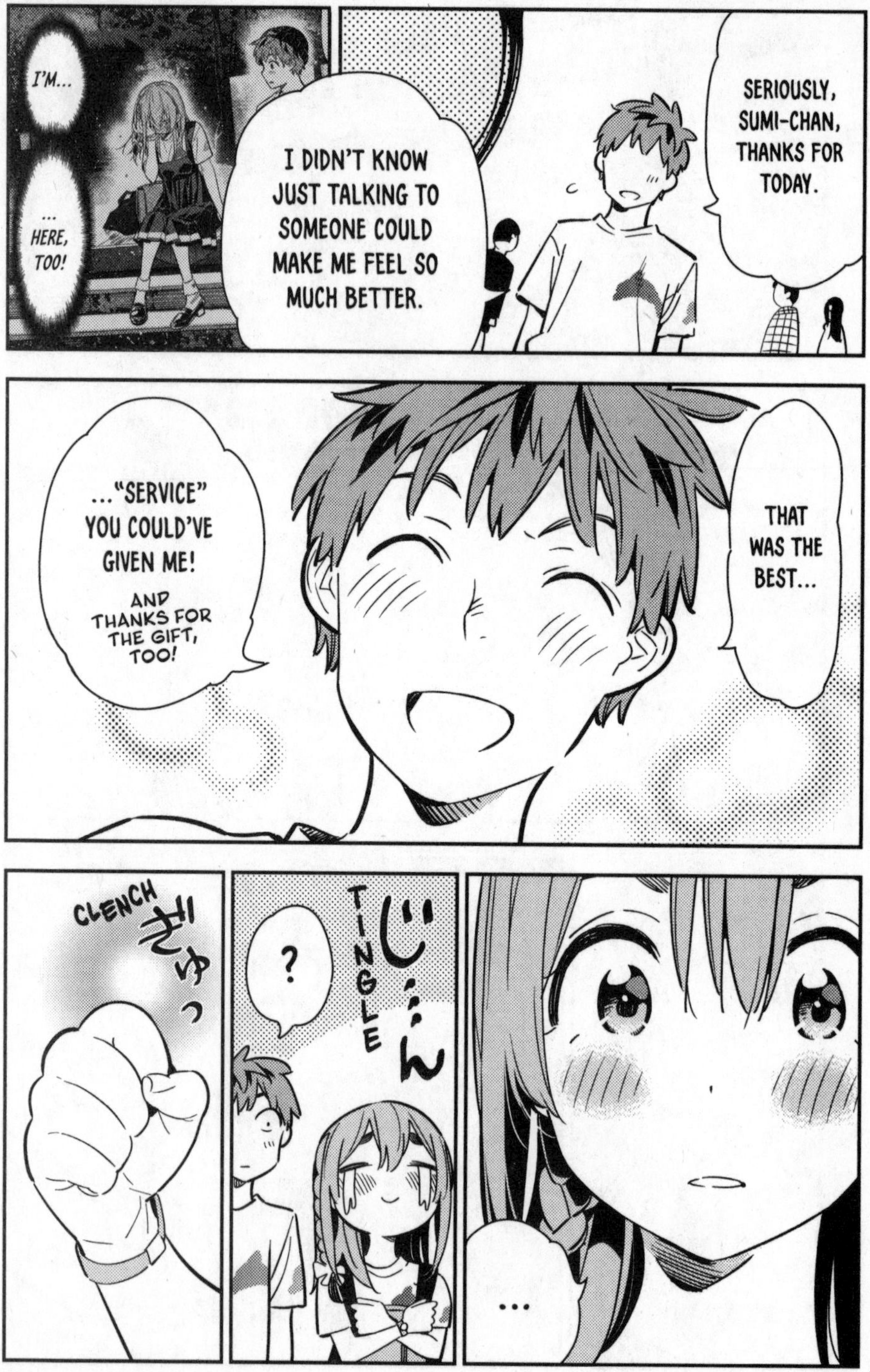
SERIOUSLY, SUMI-CHAN, THANKS FOR TODAY.
I DIDN'T KNOW JUST TALKING TO SOMEONE COULD MAKE ME FEEL SO MUCH BETTER.
I'M...
... HERE, TOO!
THAT WAS THE BEST...
..."SERVICE" YOU COULD'VE GIVEN ME!
AND THANKS FOR THE GIFT, TOO!
...
?
じーん
TINGLE
ぎゅっ
CLENCH

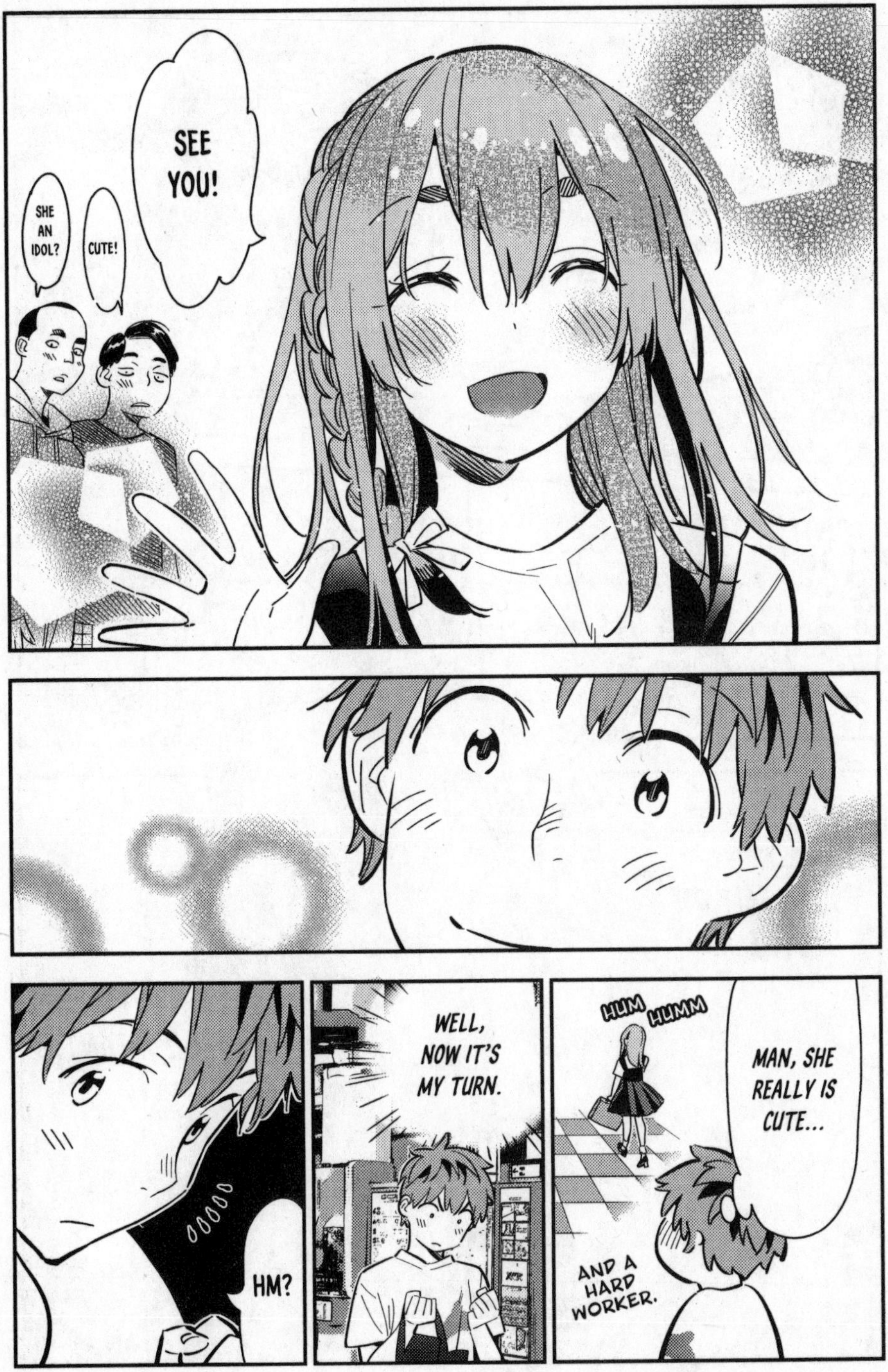
SEE YOU!
CUTE!
SHE AN IDOL?
HUM HUMM
MAN, SHE REALLY IS CUTE...
AND A HARD WORKER.
WELL, NOW IT'S MY TURN.
HM?

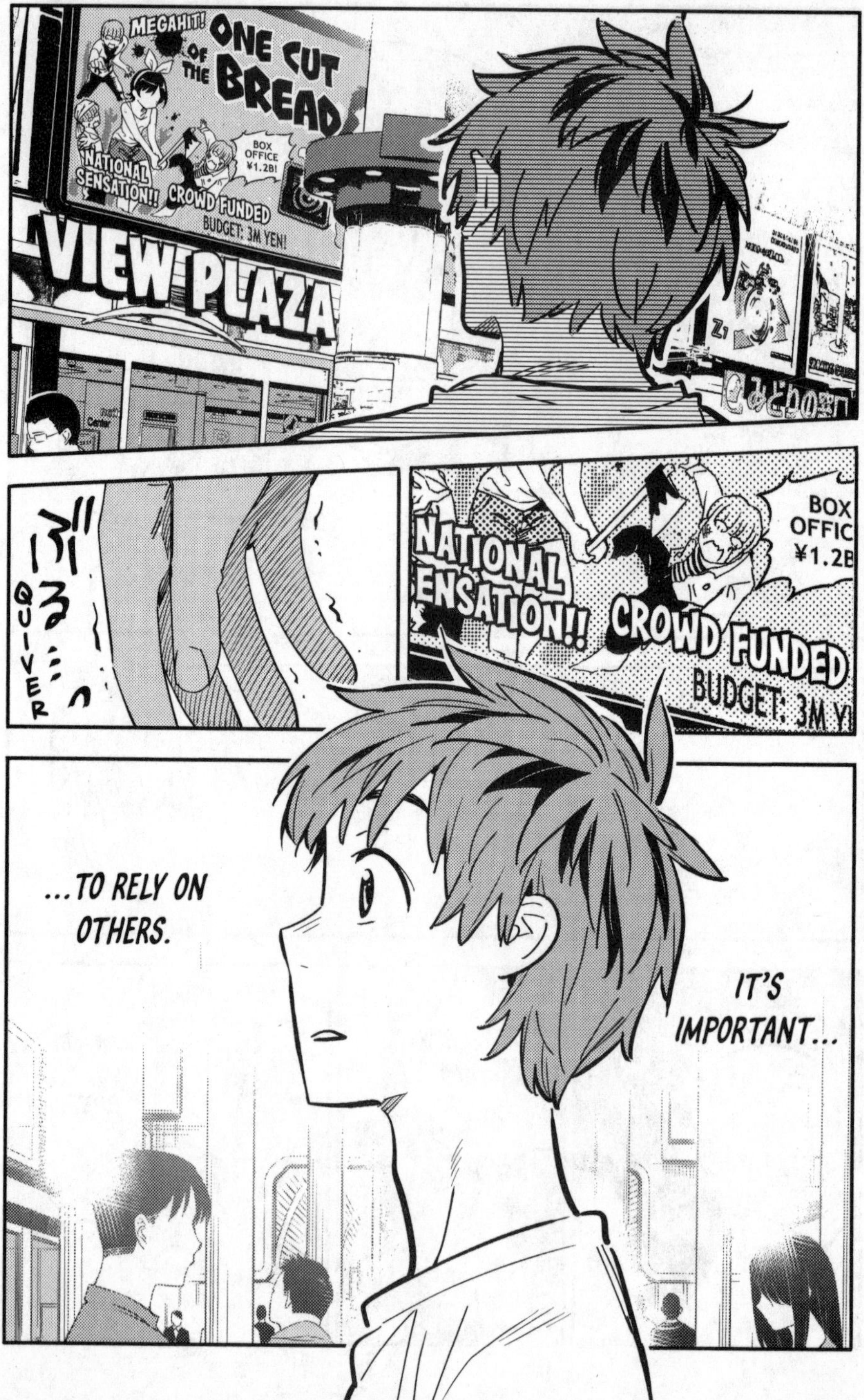
MEGAHIT!
ONE CUT OF THE BREAD
BOX OFFICE ¥1.2B!
NATIONAL SENSATION!!
CROWD FUNDED BUDGET: 3M YEN!
VIEW PLAZA
BOX OFFIC ¥1.2B
NATIONAL ENSATION!!
CROWD FUNDED
BUDGET: 3M YI
ぶるっ
QUIVER
IT'S IMPORTANT...
...TO RELY ON OTHERS.

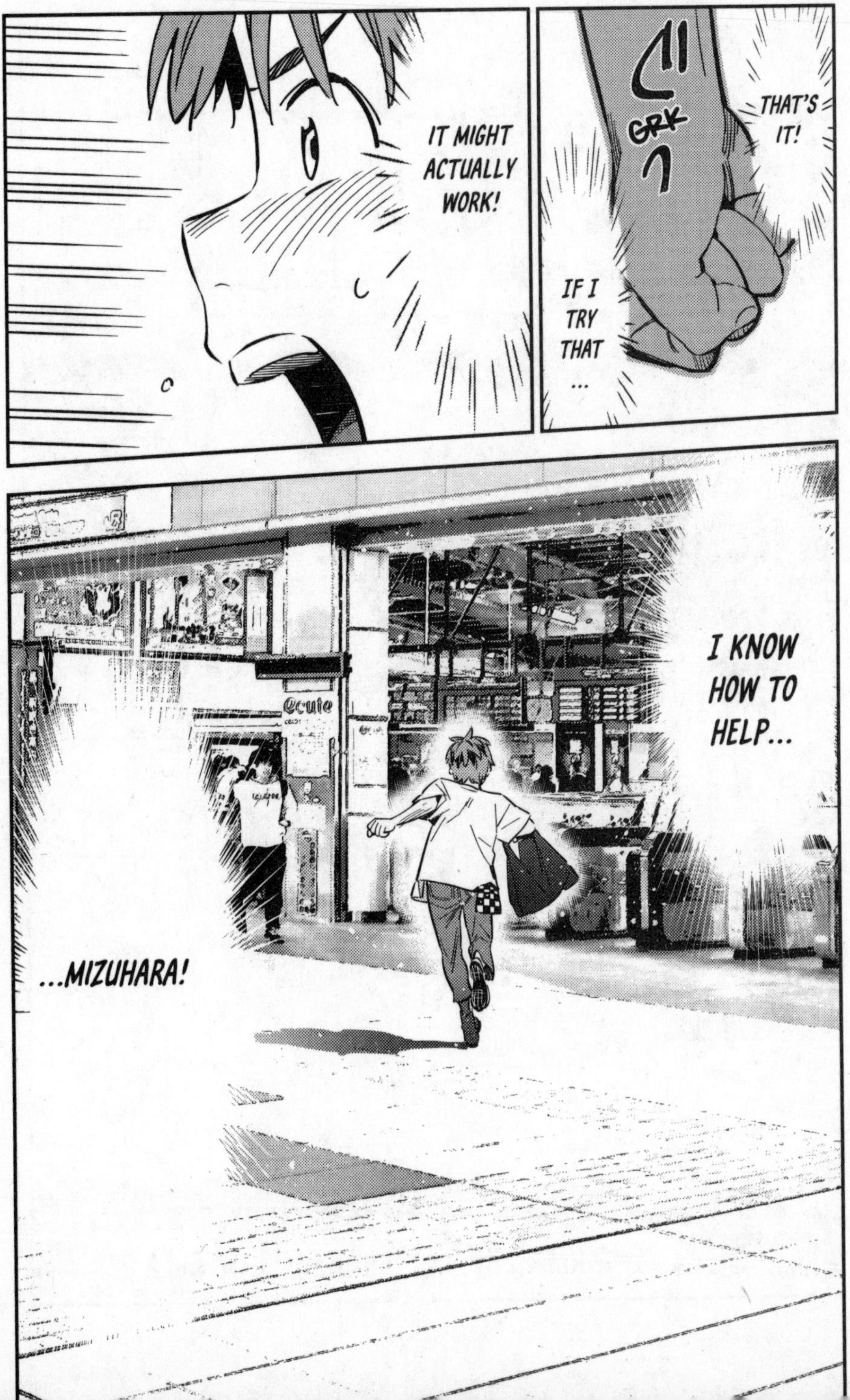
THAT'S IT!
GRK
IF I TRY THAT ...
IT MIGHT ACTUALLY WORK!
I KNOW HOW TO HELP...
...MIZUHARA!

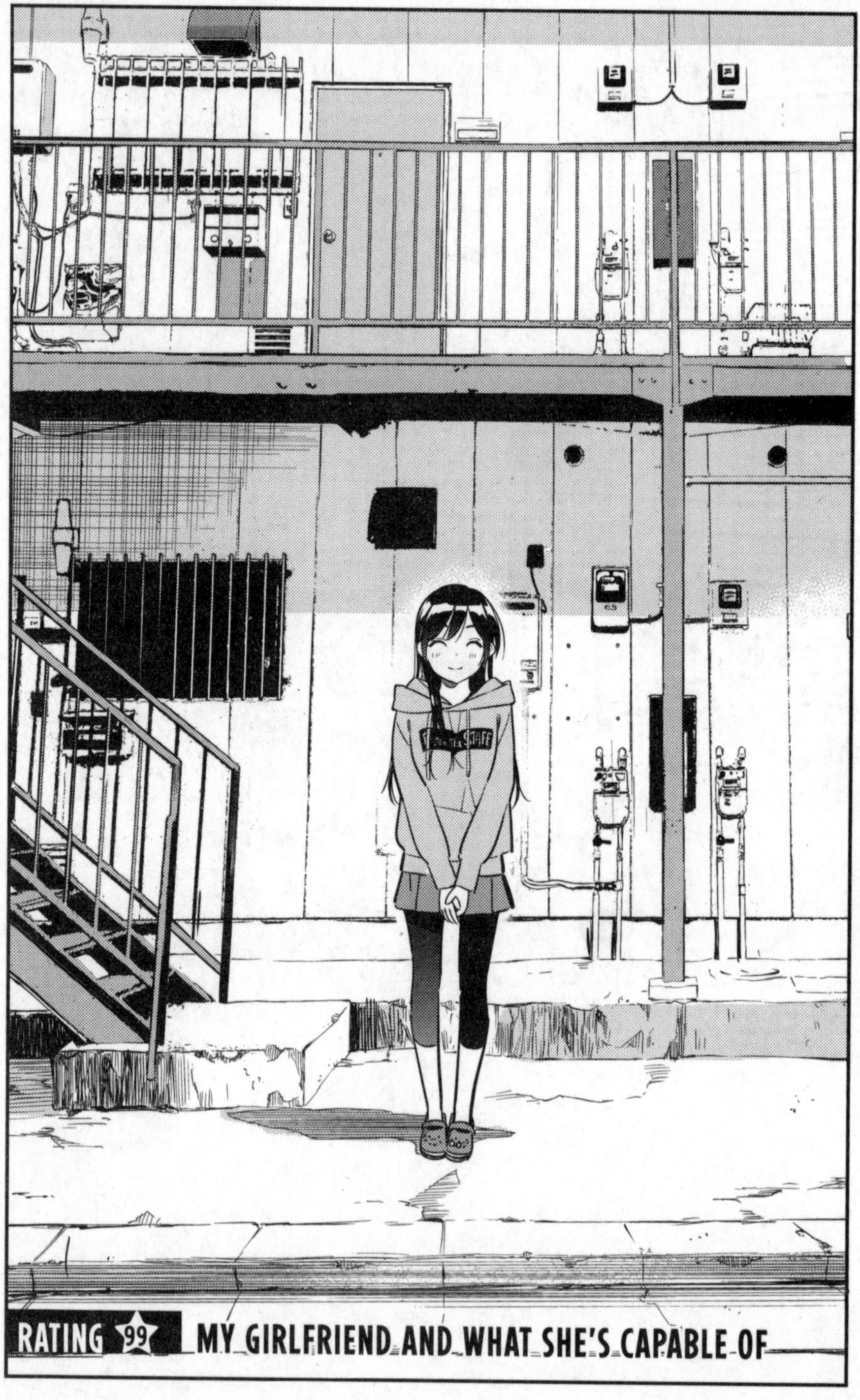

# RATING 99 MY GIRLFRIEND AND WHAT SHE'S CAPABLE OF

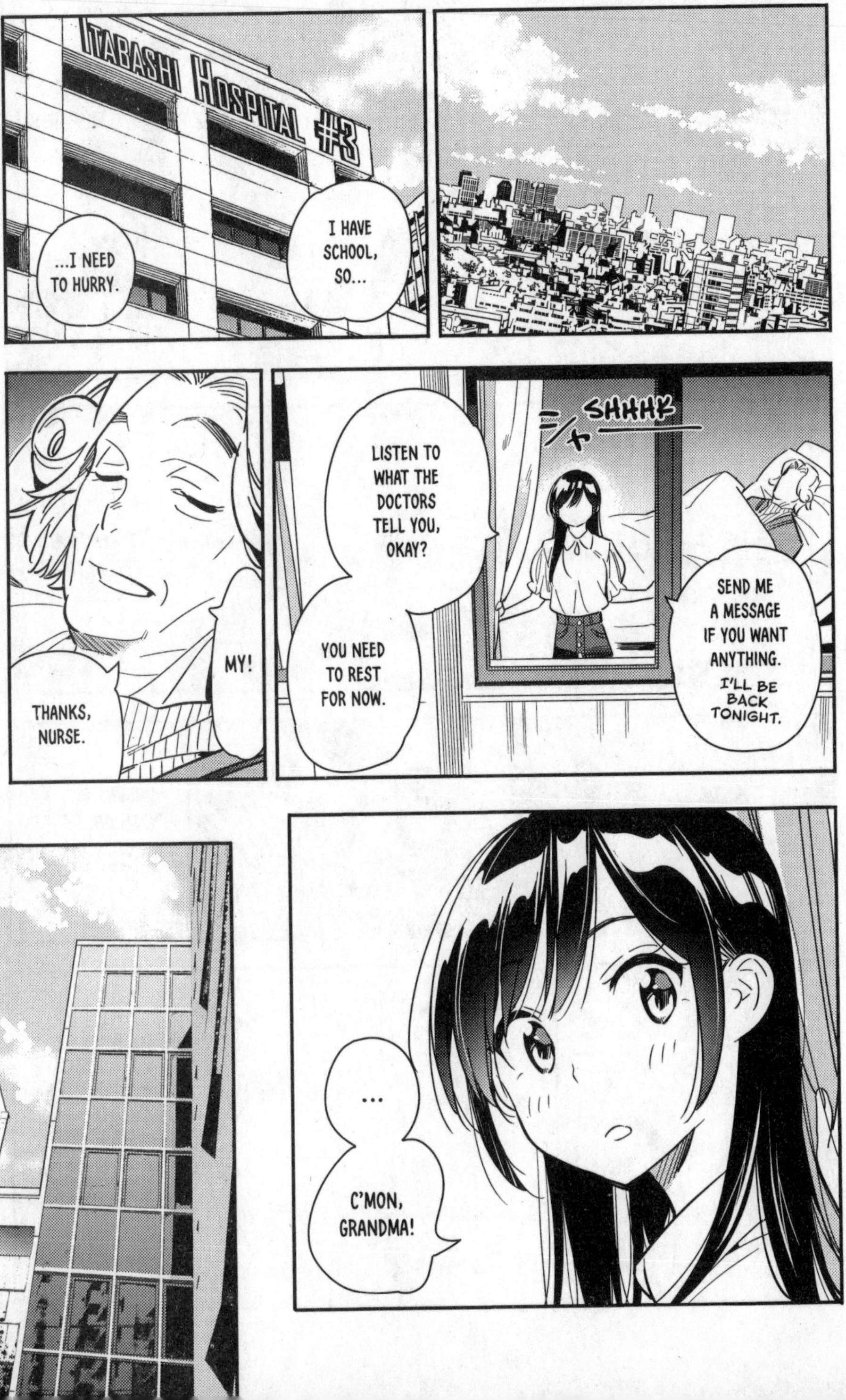
ITABASHI HOSPITAL #3
I HAVE SCHOOL, SO...
...I NEED TO HURRY.
SHHHK
SEND ME A MESSAGE IF YOU WANT ANYTHING. I'LL BE BACK TONIGHT.
LISTEN TO WHAT THE DOCTORS TELL YOU, OKAY?
YOU NEED TO REST FOR NOW.
MY!
THANKS, NURSE.
...
C'MON, GRANDMA!

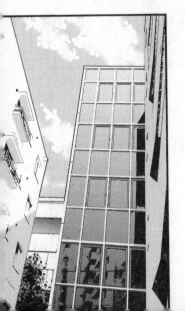

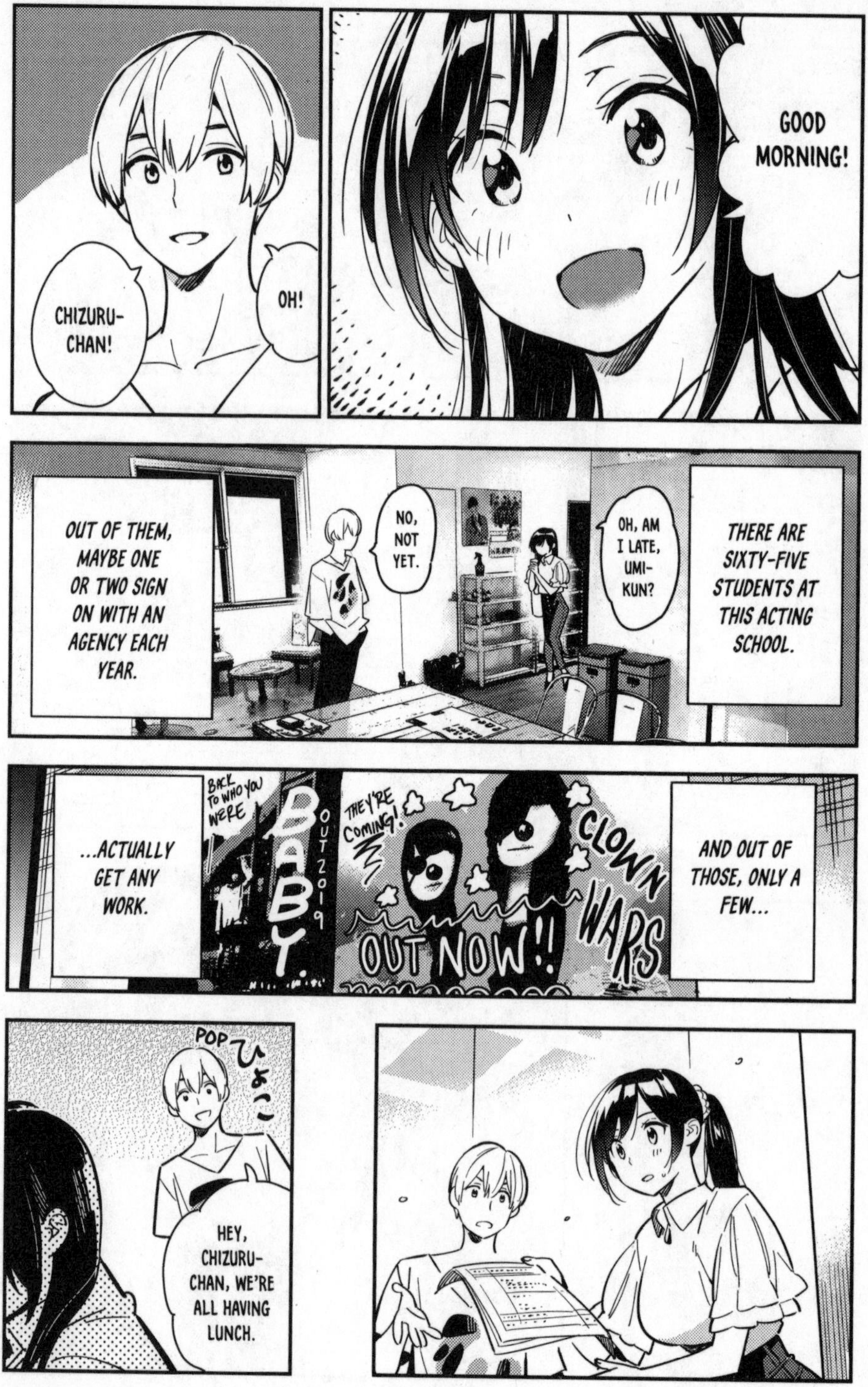
GOOD MORNING!
OH!
CHIZURU-CHAN!
THERE ARE SIXTY-FIVE STUDENTS AT THIS ACTING SCHOOL.
OH, AM I LATE, UMI-KUN?
NO, NOT YET.
OUT OF THEM, MAYBE ONE OR TWO SIGN ON WITH AN AGENCY EACH YEAR.
AND OUT OF THOSE, ONLY A FEW...
CLOWN WARS
THEY'RE COMING!
OUT NOW!!
OUT 2019
BABY.
BACK TO WHO YOU WERE
...ACTUALLY GET ANY WORK.
POP ひょこ
HEY, CHIZURU-CHAN, WE'RE ALL HAVING LUNCH.

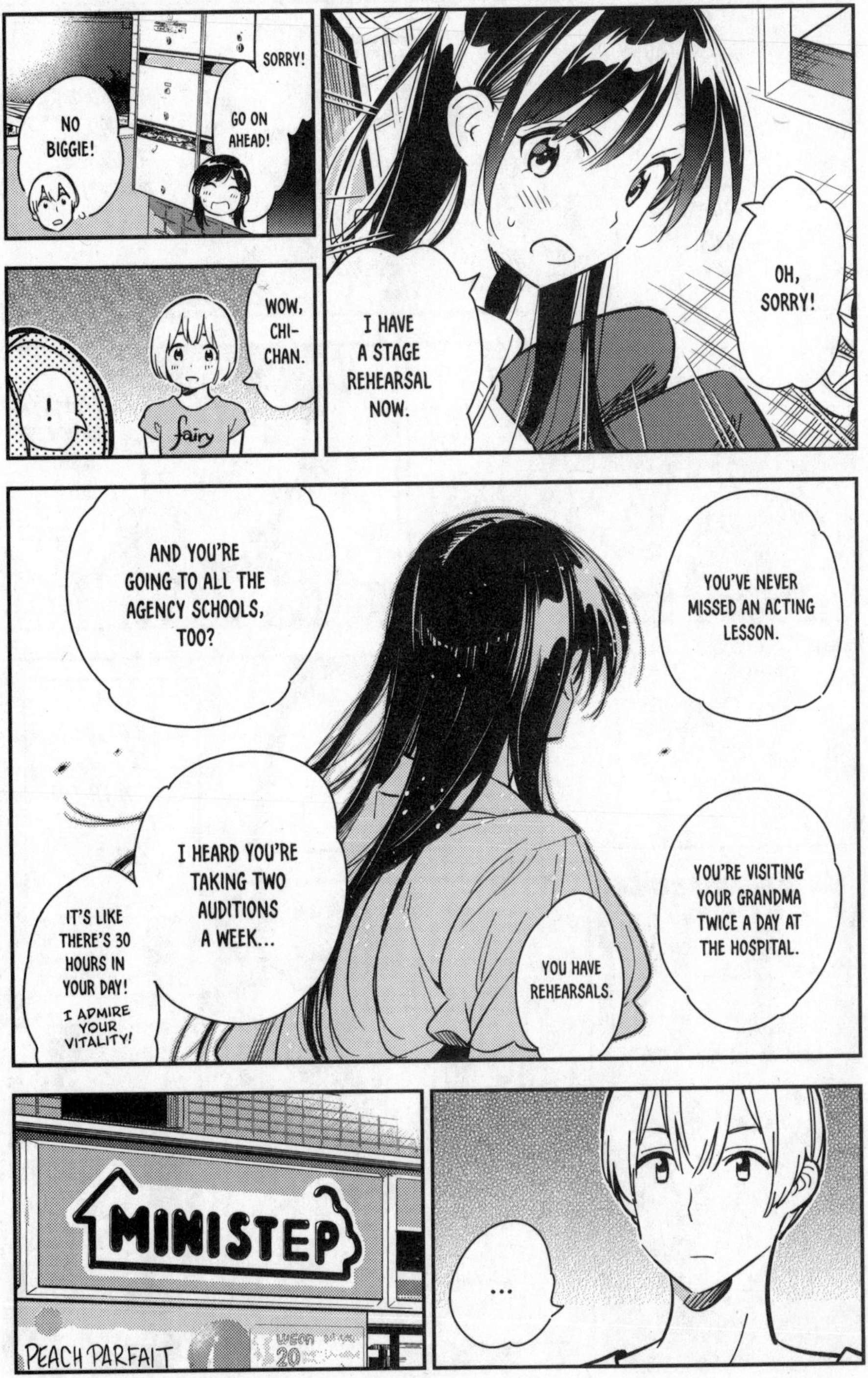
OH, SORRY!
I HAVE A STAGE REHEARSAL NOW.
SORRY!
GO ON AHEAD!
NO BIGGIE!
WOW, CHI-CHAN.
!
YOU'VE NEVER MISSED AN ACTING LESSON.
AND YOU'RE GOING TO ALL THE AGENCY SCHOOLS, TOO?
YOU'RE VISITING YOUR GRANDMA TWICE A DAY AT THE HOSPITAL.
YOU HAVE REHEARSALS.
I HEARD YOU'RE TAKING TWO AUDITIONS A WEEK...
IT'S LIKE THERE'S 30 HOURS IN YOUR DAY!
I ADMIRE YOUR VITALITY!
...
MINISTEP
PEACH PARFAIT

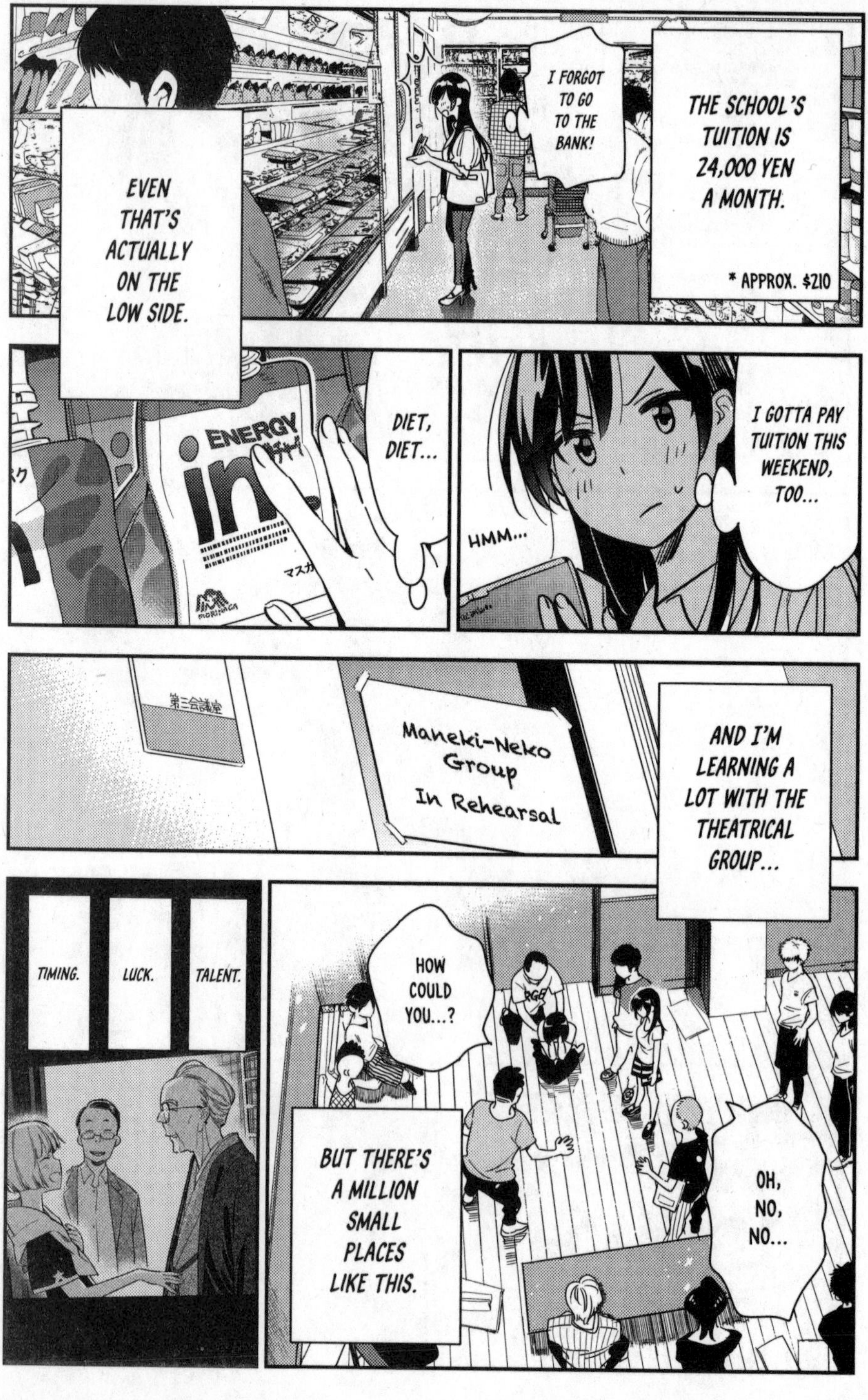
THE SCHOOL'S TUITION IS 24,000 YEN A MONTH.
* APPROX. $210
I FORGOT TO GO TO THE BANK!
EVEN THAT'S ACTUALLY ON THE LOW SIDE.
I GOTTA PAY TUITION THIS WEEKEND, TOO...
HMM...
DIET, DIET...
ENERGY
in
第三会議室
Maneki-Neko Group
In Rehearsal
AND I'M LEARNING A LOT WITH THE THEATRICAL GROUP...
HOW COULD YOU...?
OH, NO, NO...
BUT THERE'S A MILLION SMALL PLACES LIKE THIS.
TALENT.
LUCK.
TIMING.

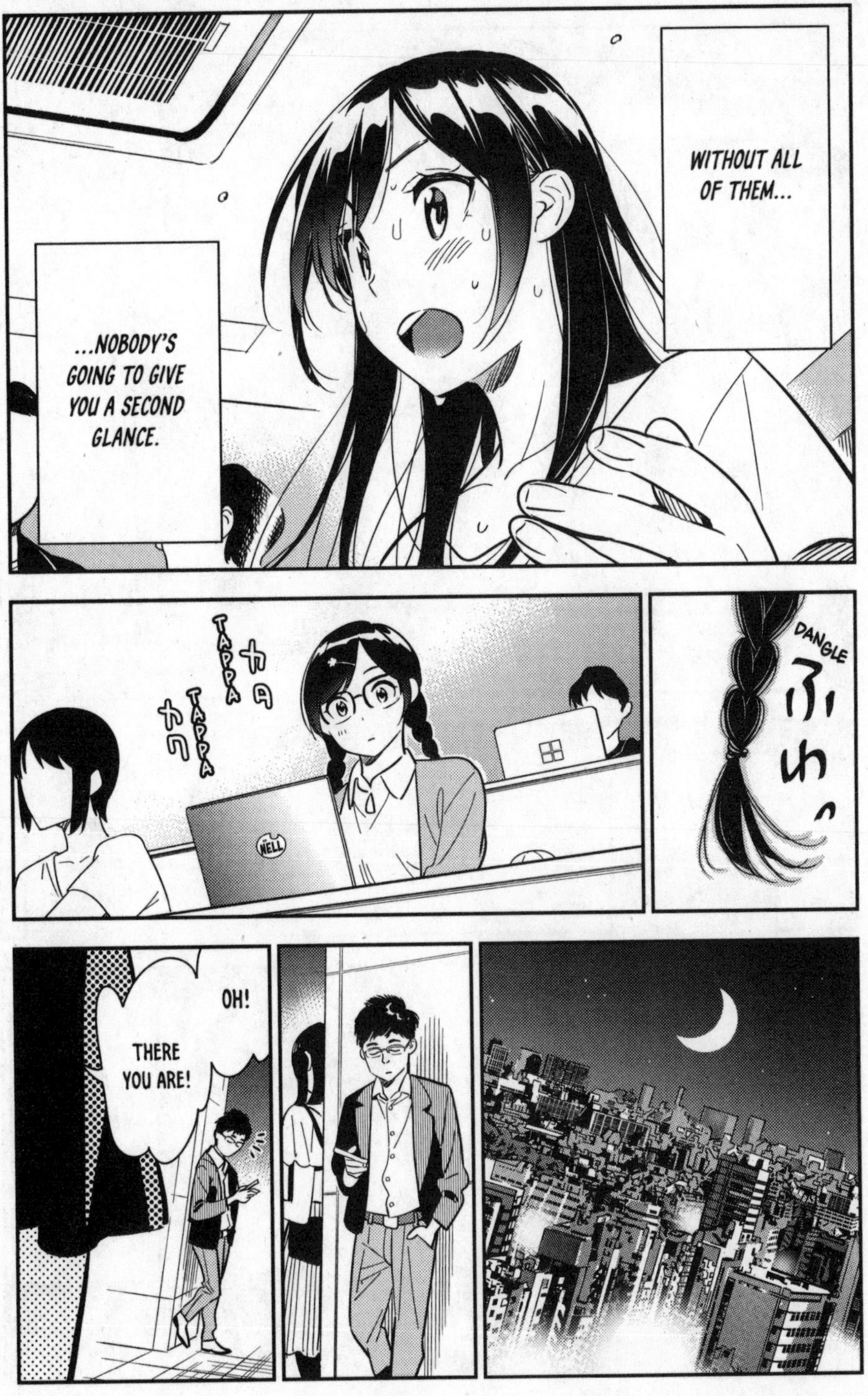

WITHOUT ALL OF THEM...
...NOBODY'S GOING TO GIVE YOU A SECOND GLANCE.
DANGLE
TAPPA
TAPPA
OH!
THERE YOU ARE!

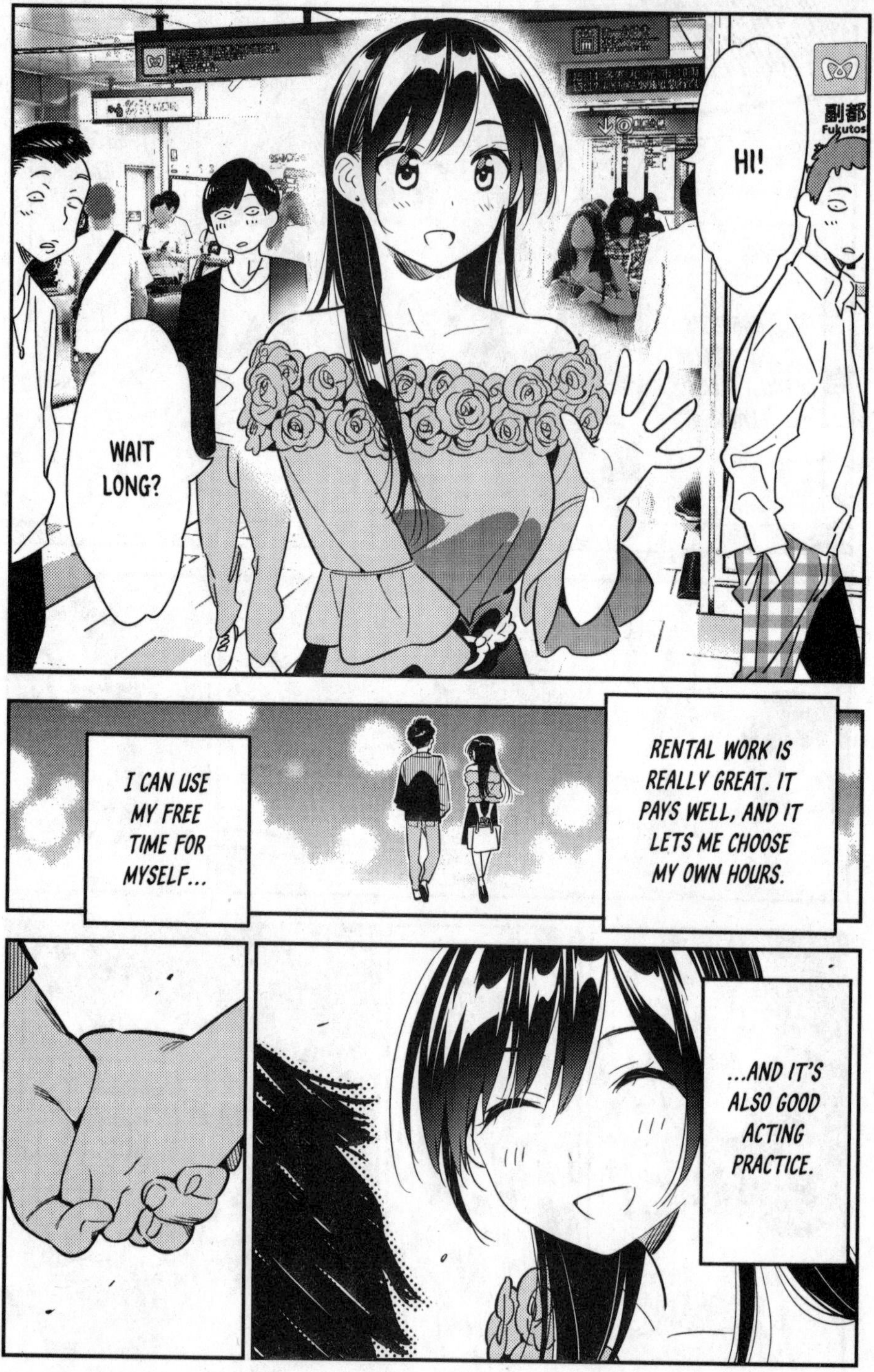
HI!
WAIT LONG?
RENTAL WORK IS REALLY GREAT. IT PAYS WELL, AND IT LETS ME CHOOSE MY OWN HOURS.
I CAN USE MY FREE TIME FOR MYSELF...
...AND IT'S ALSO GOOD ACTING PRACTICE.

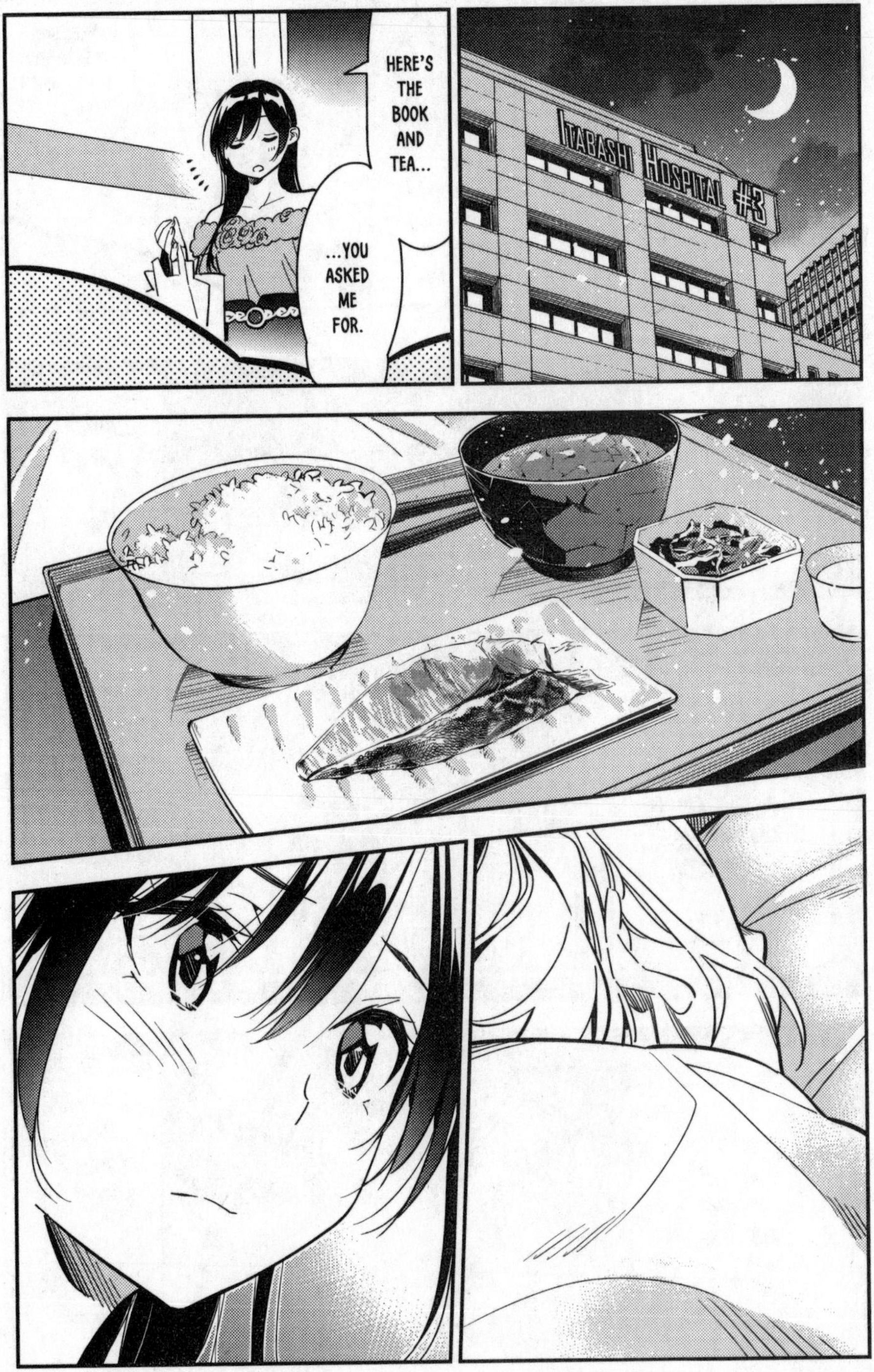
ITABASHI HOSPITAL #3
HERE'S THE BOOK AND TEA...
...YOU ASKED ME FOR.

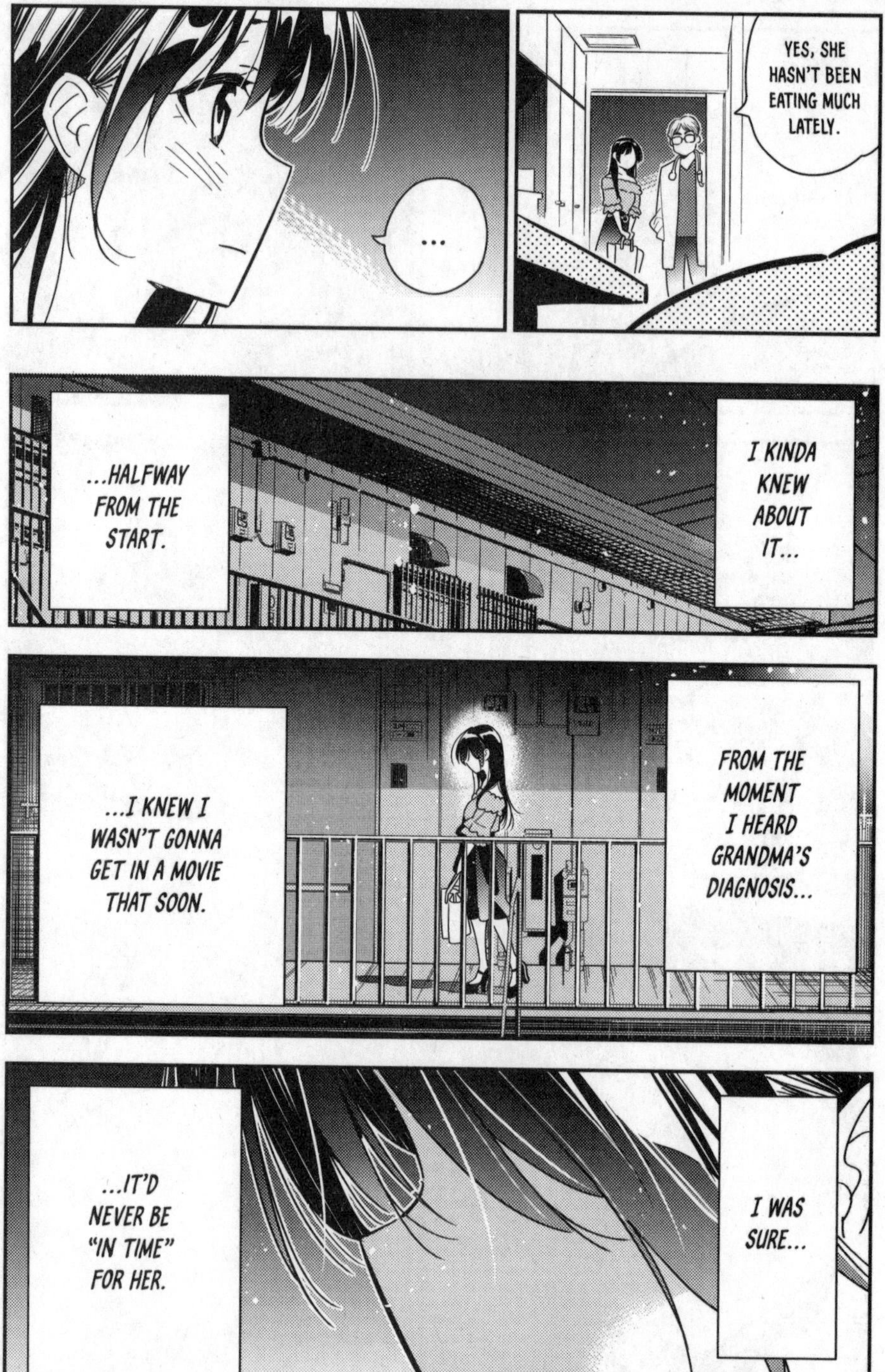
YES, SHE HASN'T BEEN EATING MUCH LATELY.
...
I KINDA KNEW ABOUT IT...
...HALFWAY FROM THE START.
FROM THE MOMENT I HEARD GRANDMA'S DIAGNOSIS...
...I KNEW I WASN'T GONNA GET IN A MOVIE THAT SOON.
I WAS SURE...
...IT'D NEVER BE "IN TIME" FOR HER.

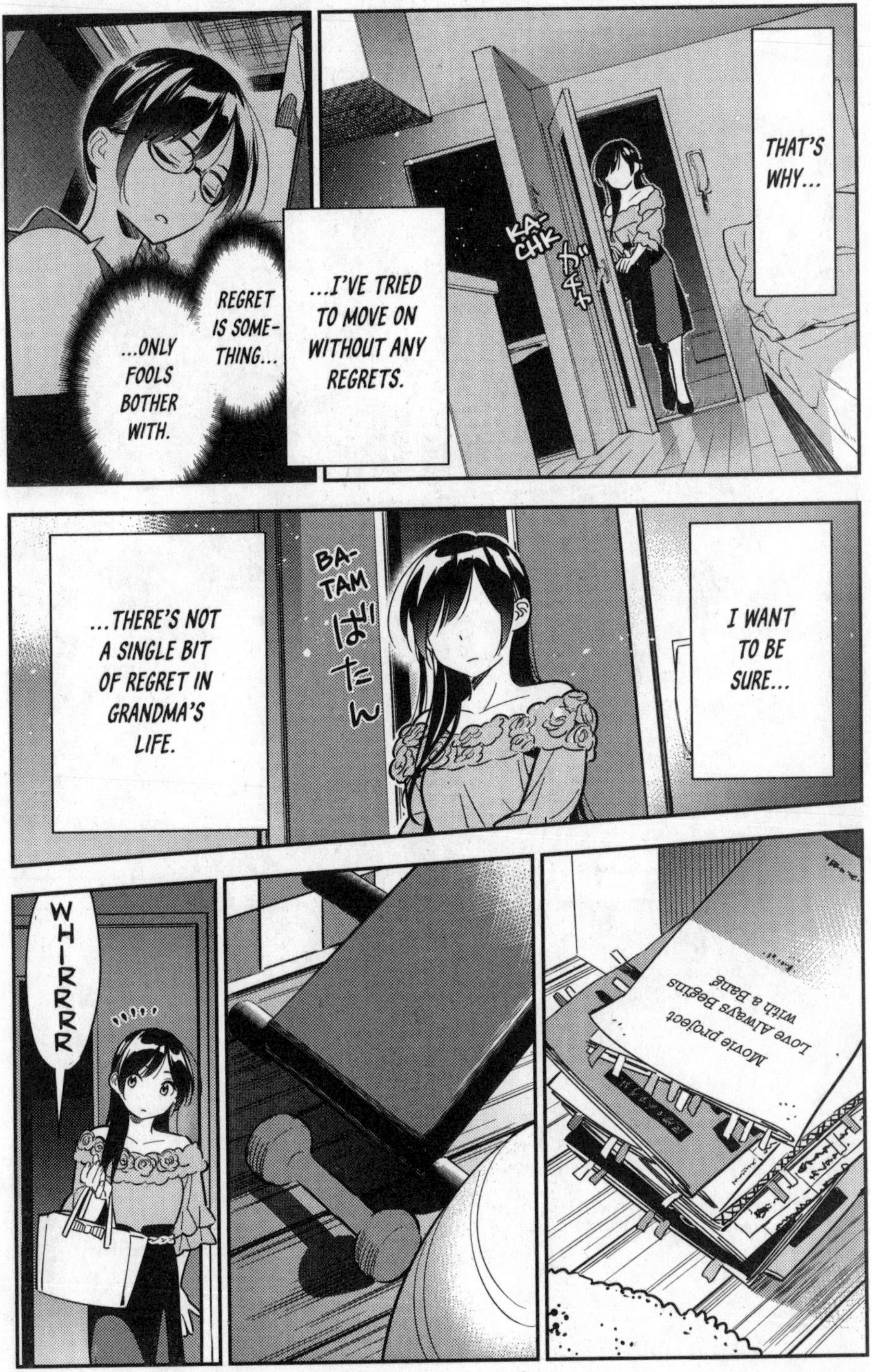
THAT'S WHY...
KA-CHK ガチャ
...I'VE TRIED TO MOVE ON WITHOUT ANY REGRETS.
REGRET IS SOME-THING...
...ONLY FOOLS BOTHER WITH.
I WANT TO BE SURE...
BA-TAM ばたん
...THERE'S NOT A SINGLE BIT OF REGRET IN GRANDMA'S LIFE.
Movie project
Love Always Begins
with a Bang
WHIRRRR

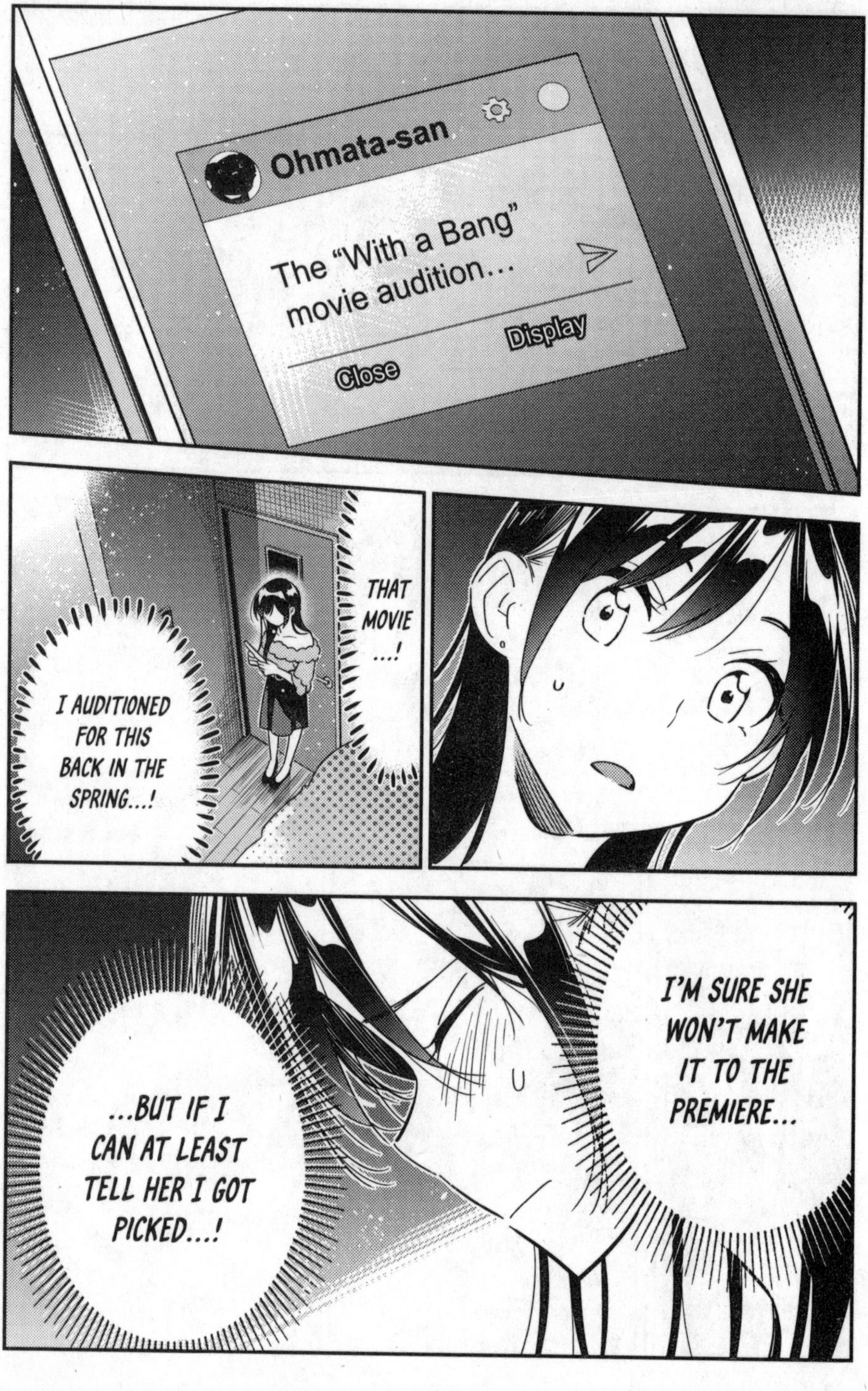
Ohmata-san
The "With a Bang" movie audition...
Display
Close
THAT MOVIE ...!
I AUDITIONED FOR THIS BACK IN THE SPRING...!
I'M SURE SHE WON'T MAKE IT TO THE PREMIERE...
...BUT IF I CAN AT LEAST TELL HER I GOT PICKED...!

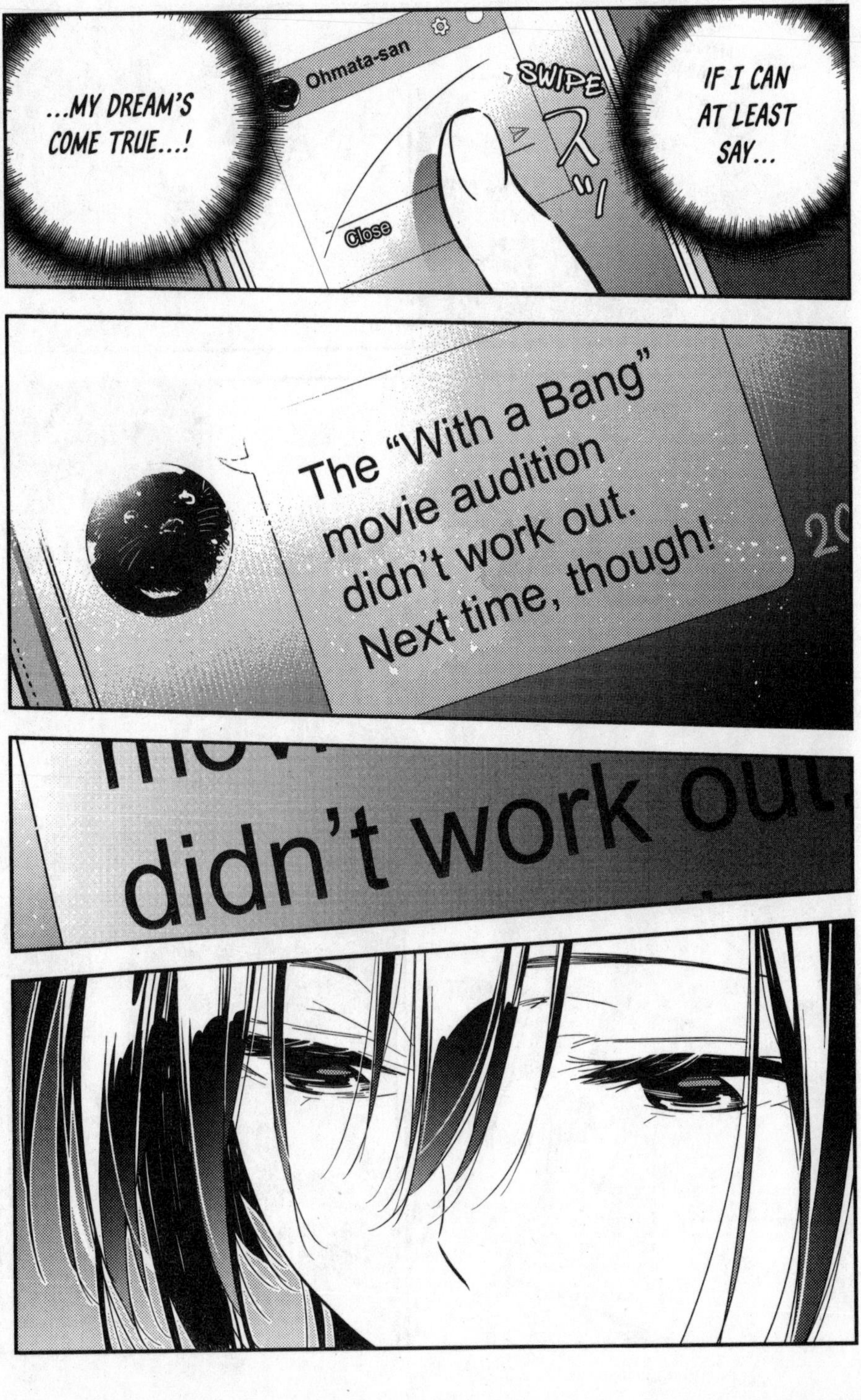
IF I CAN AT LEAST SAY...
...MY DREAM'S COME TRUE...!
Ohmata-san
SWIPE
Close
The "With a Bang" movie audition didn't work out. Next time, though!
didn't work out.

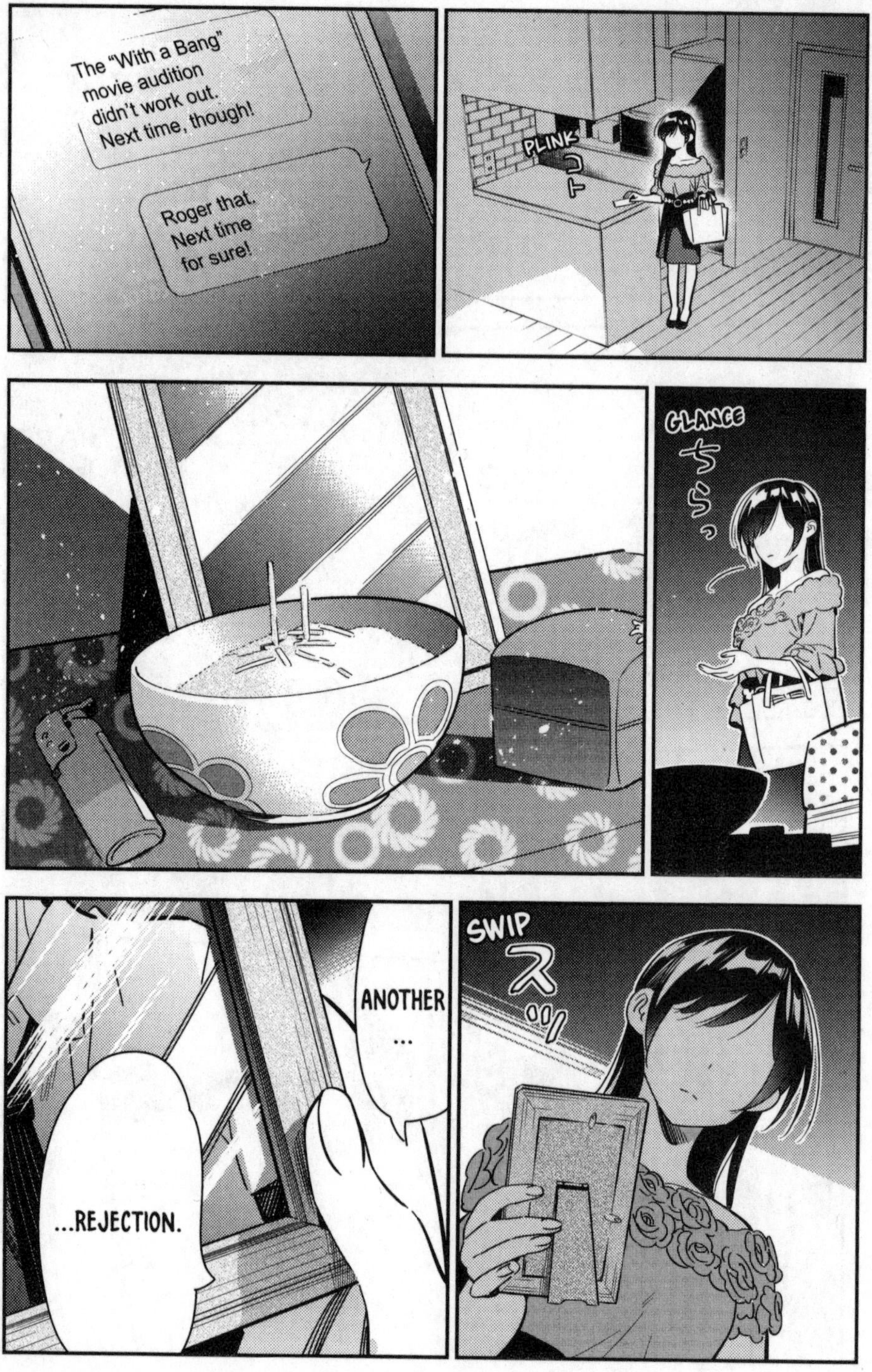

PLINK
コト
The "With a Bang" movie audition didn't work out. Next time, though!
Roger that. Next time for sure!
GLANCE
ちらっ
SWIP
スッ
ANOTHER ...
...REJECTION.

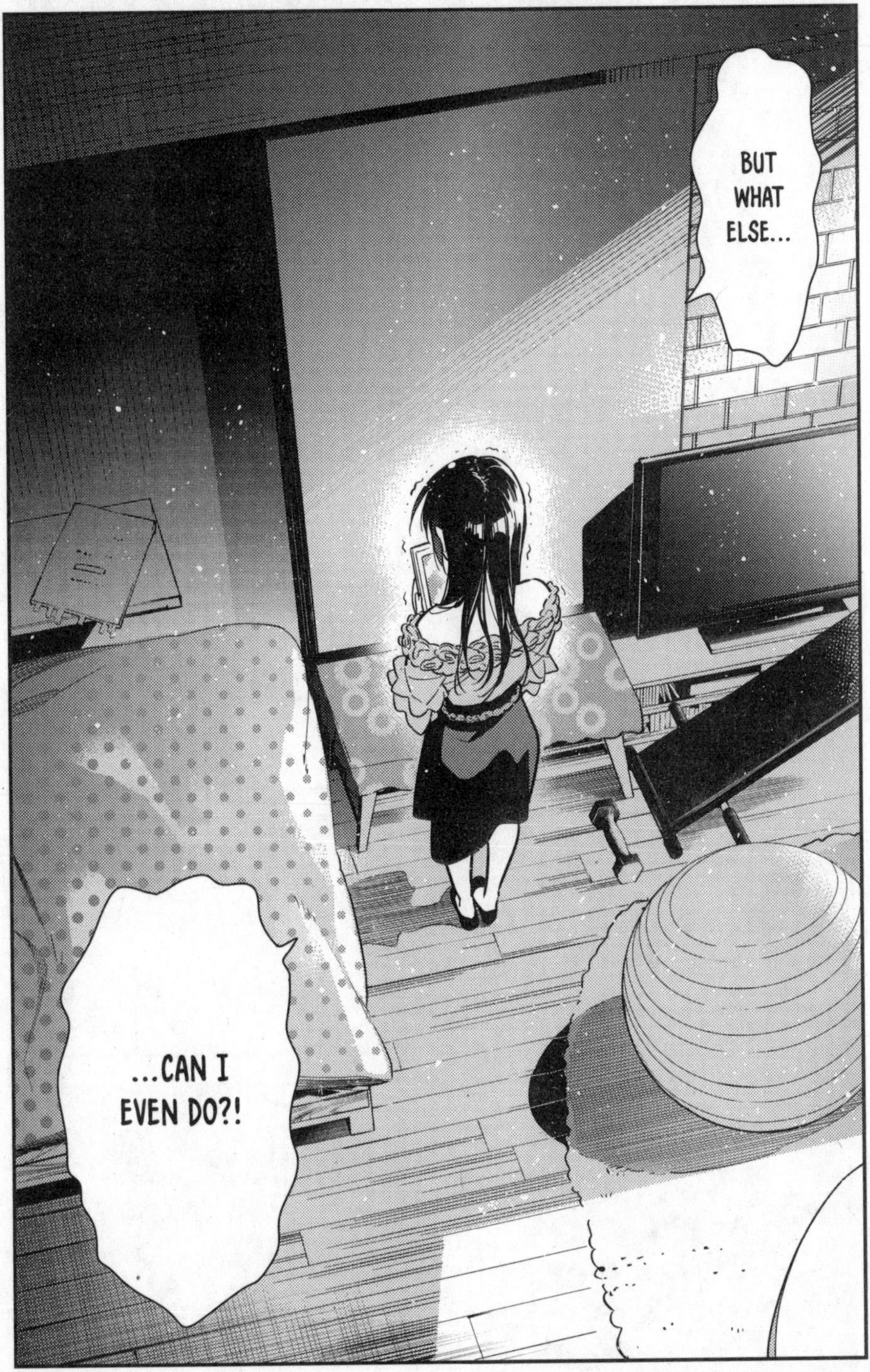
BUT WHAT ELSE...
...CAN I EVEN DO?!

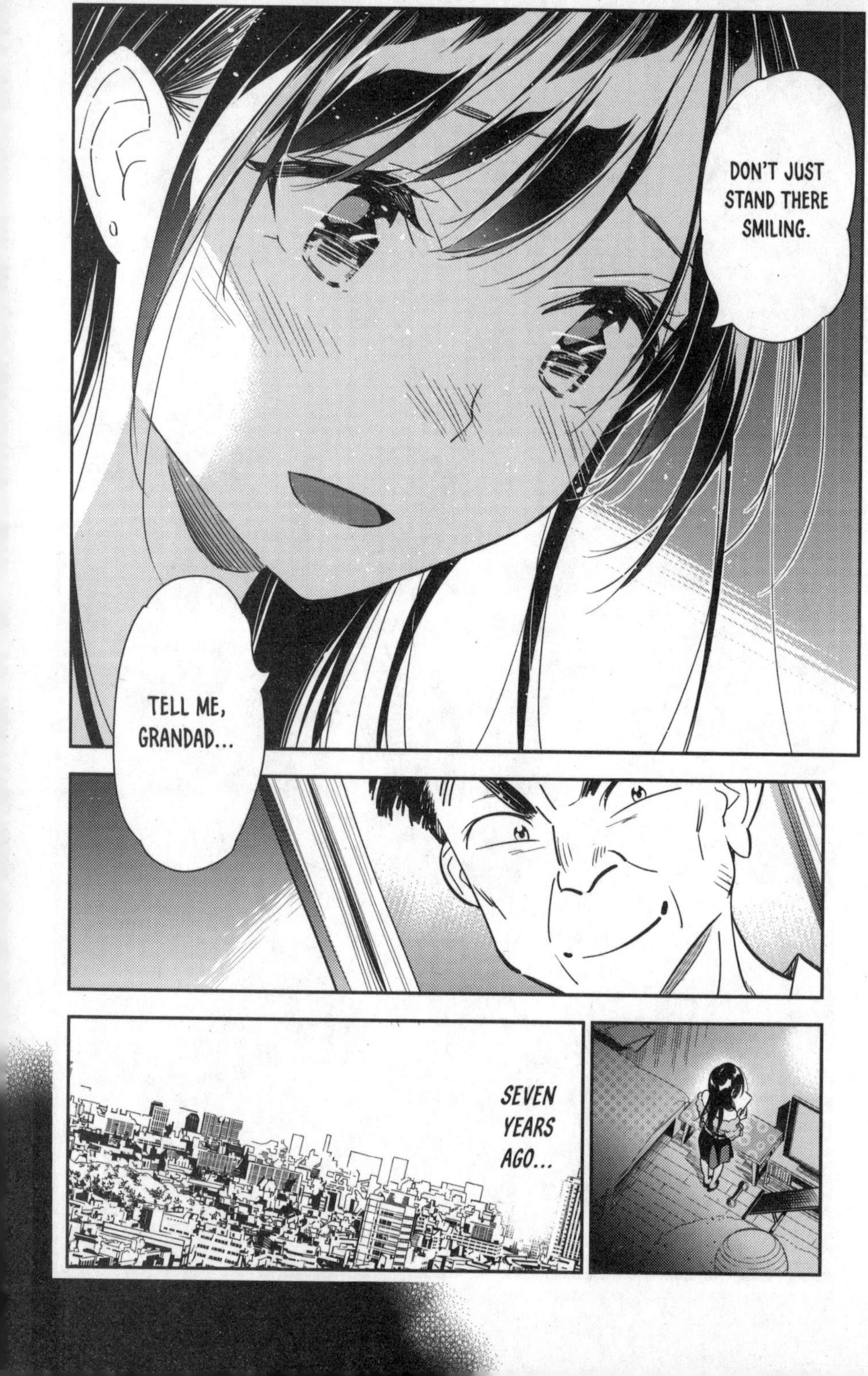
DON'T JUST STAND THERE SMILING.
TELL ME, GRANDAD...
SEVEN YEARS AGO...

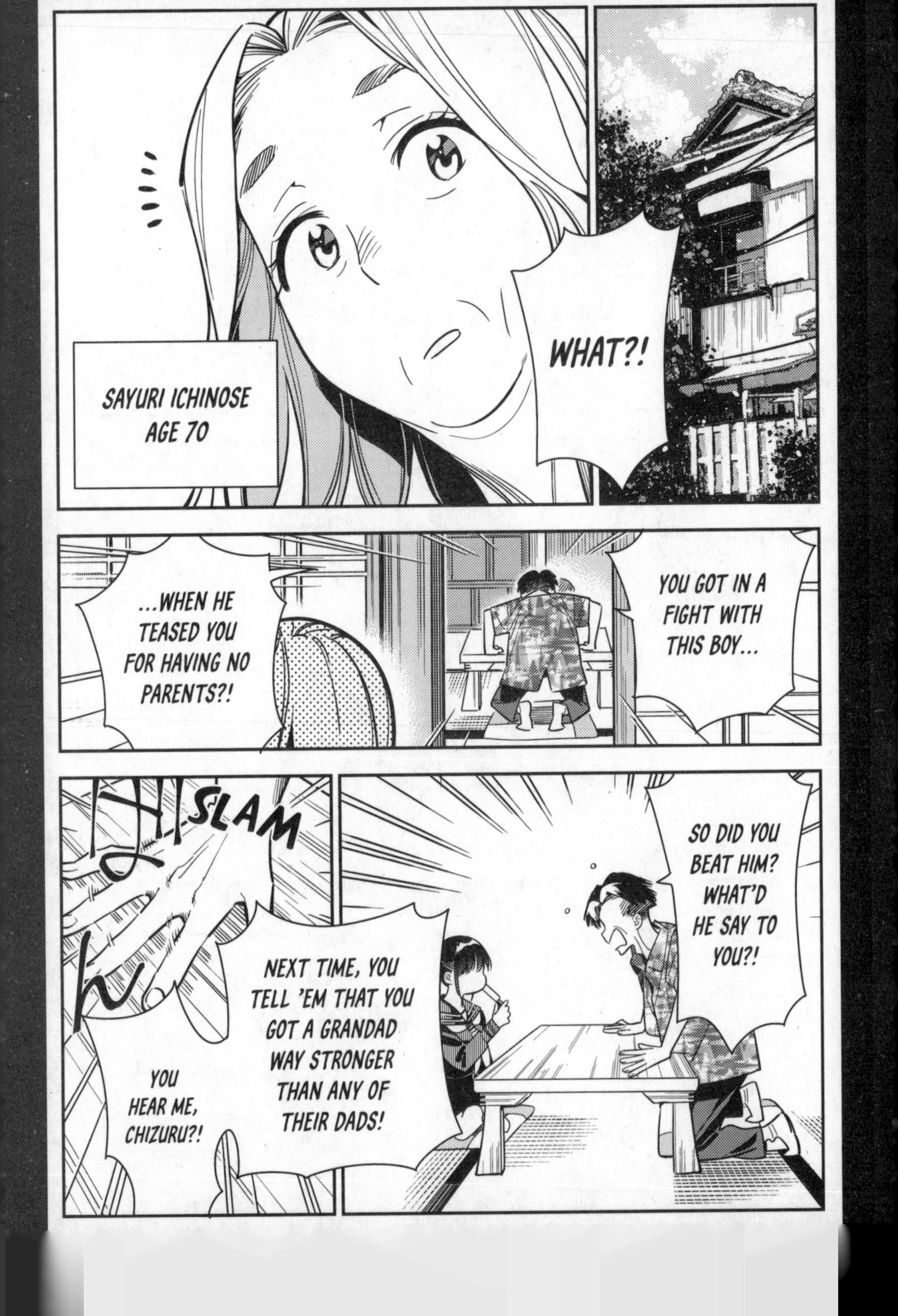
WHAT?!
SAYURI ICHINOSE AGE 70
YOU GOT IN A FIGHT WITH THIS BOY...
...WHEN HE TEASED YOU FOR HAVING NO PARENTS?!
SO DID YOU BEAT HIM? WHAT'D HE SAY TO YOU?!
SLAM
NEXT TIME, YOU TELL 'EM THAT YOU GOT A GRANDAD WAY STRONGER THAN ANY OF THEIR DADS!
YOU HEAR ME, CHIZURU?!

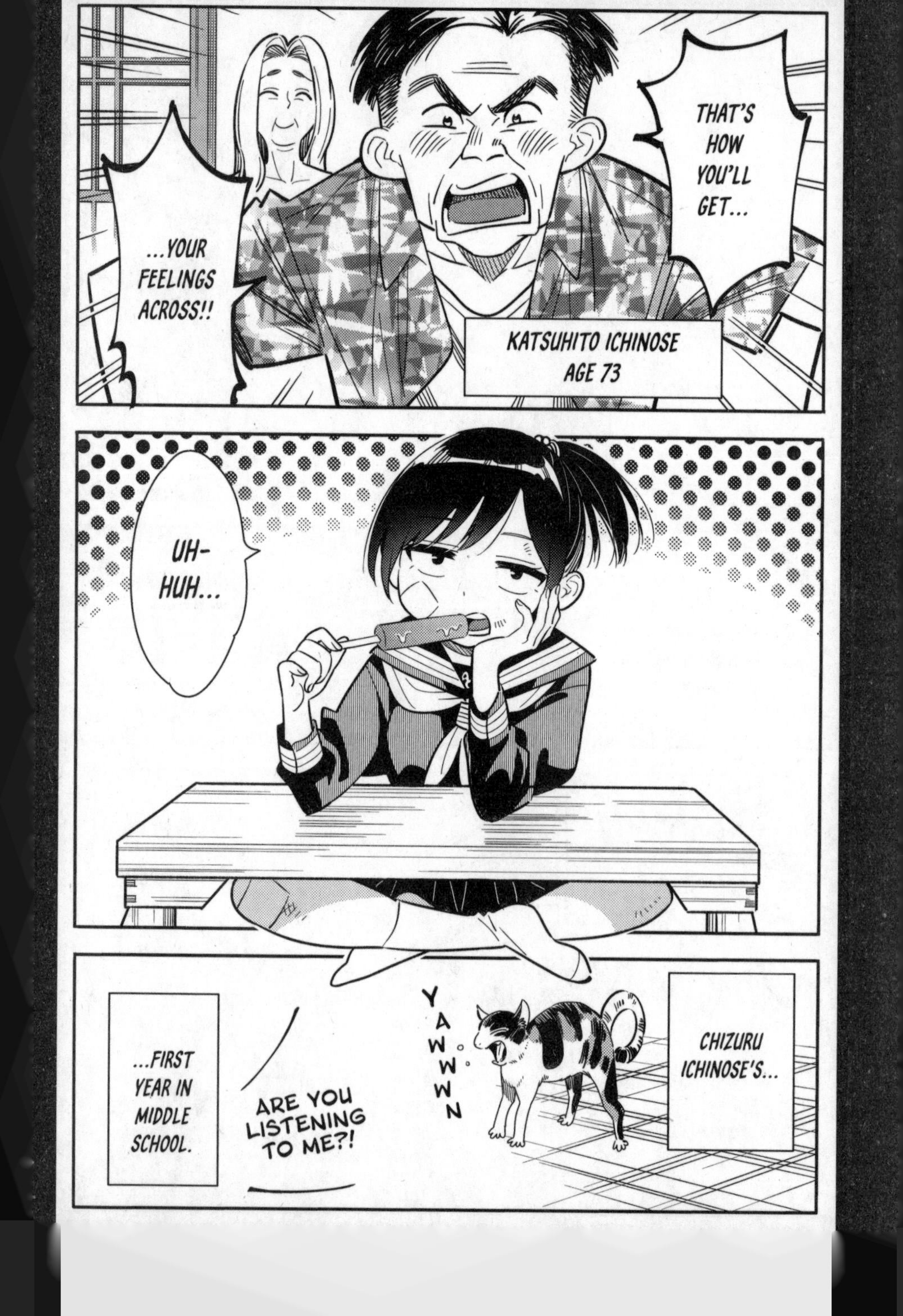
THAT'S HOW YOU'LL GET...
KATSUHITO ICHINOSE AGE 73
...YOUR FEELINGS ACROSS!!
UH-HUH...
CHIZURU ICHINOSE'S...
YAWWWN
ARE YOU LISTENING TO ME?!
...FIRST YEAR IN MIDDLE SCHOOL.

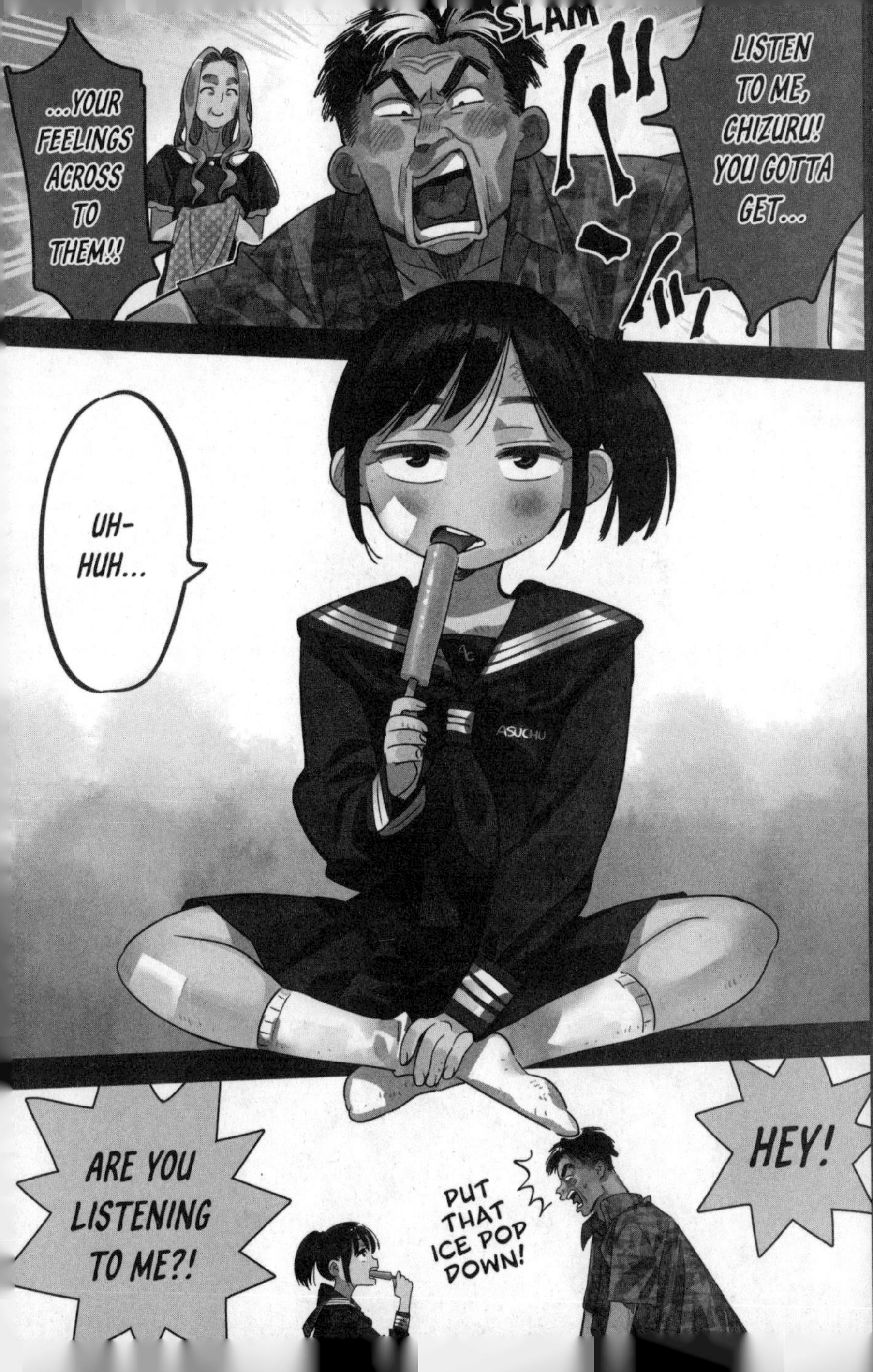
SLAM
LISTEN TO ME, CHIZURU! YOU GOTTA GET...
...YOUR FEELINGS ACROSS TO THEM!!
UH-HUH...
ASUCHU
HEY!
PUT THAT ICE POP DOWN!
ARE YOU LISTENING TO ME?!

# RATING 100 MY "GIRLFRIEND," CHIZURU MIZUHARA 2

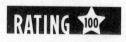

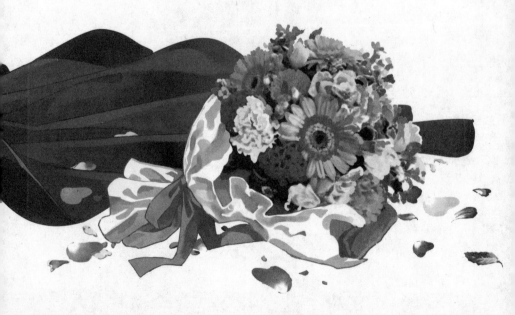

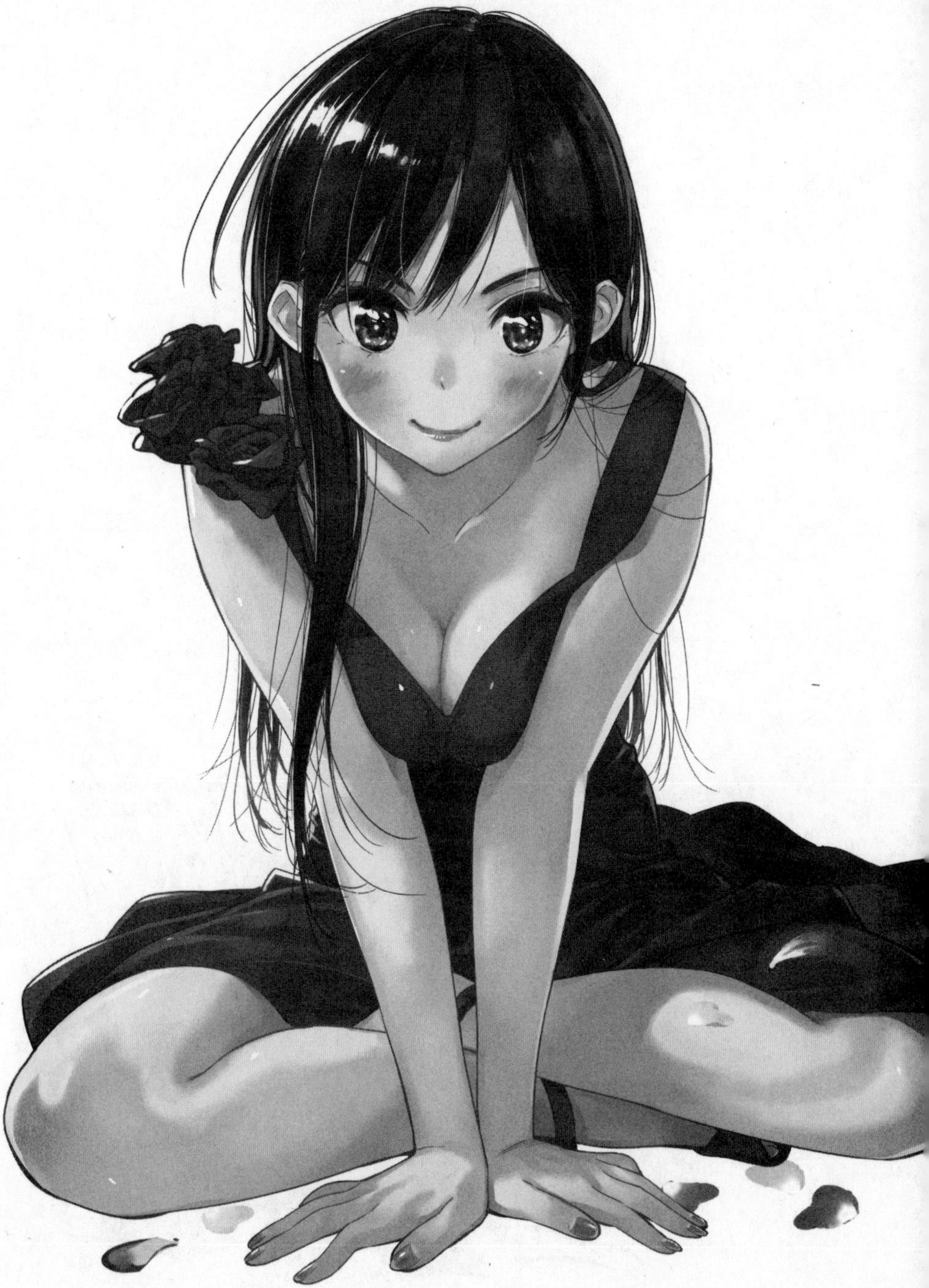

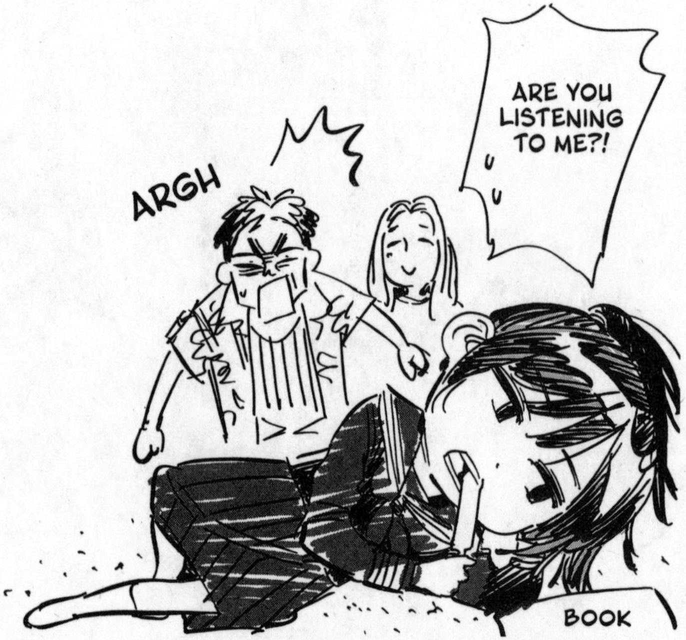
ARE YOU LISTENING TO ME?!
ARGH
BOOK

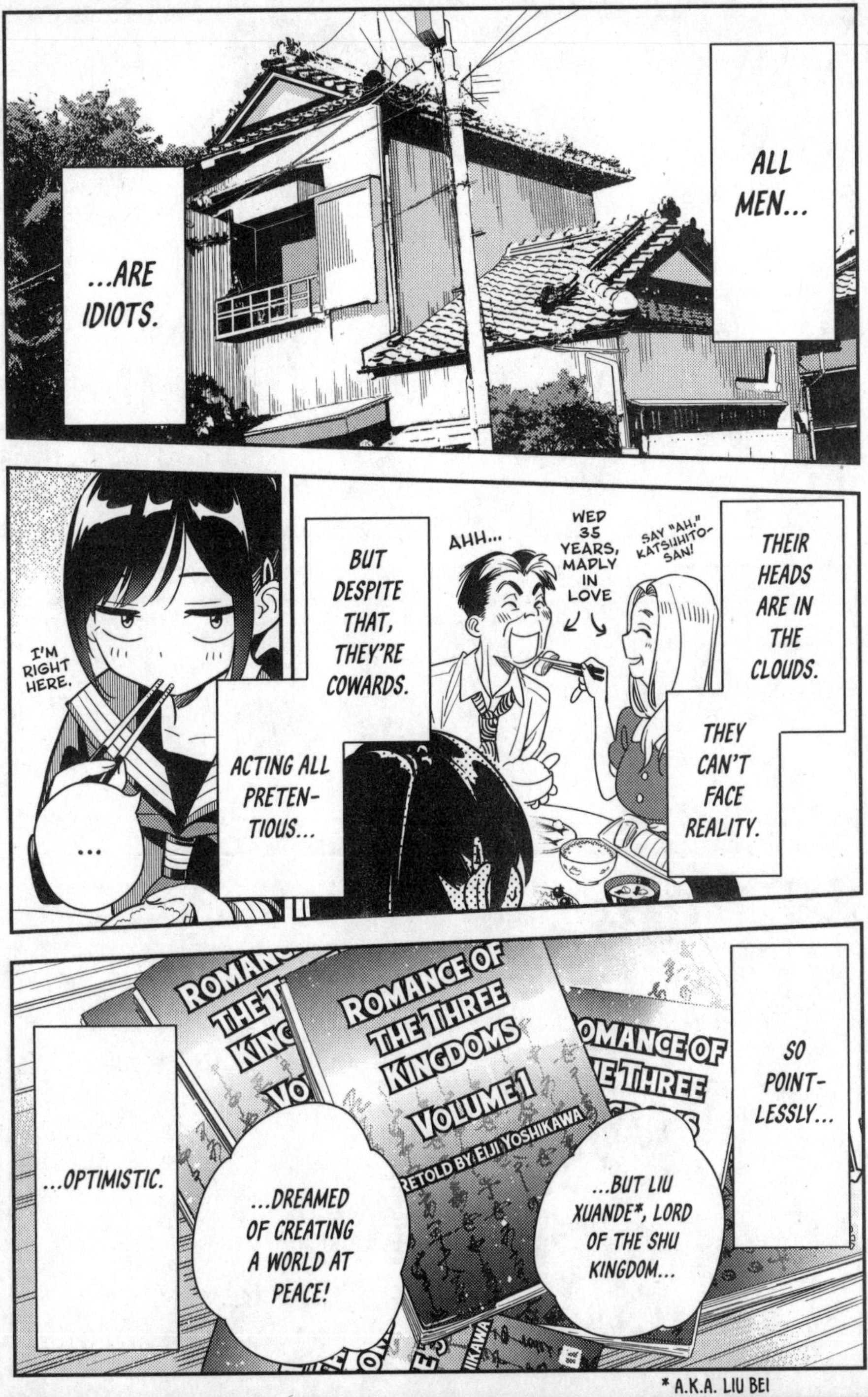
ALL MEN...
...ARE IDIOTS.
THEIR HEADS ARE IN THE CLOUDS.
THEY CAN'T FACE REALITY.
SAY "AH," KATSUHITO-SAN!
WED 35 YEARS, MADLY IN LOVE
AHH...
BUT DESPITE THAT, THEY'RE COWARDS.
ACTING ALL PRETEN-TIOUS...
I'M RIGHT HERE.
...
SO POINT-LESSLY...
...BUT LIU XUANDE*, LORD OF THE SHU KINGDOM...
ROMANCE OF THE THREE KINGDOMS VOLUME 1
RETOLD BY EIJI YOSHIKAWA
...DREAMED OF CREATING A WORLD AT PEACE!
...OPTIMISTIC.

* A.K.A. LIU BEI

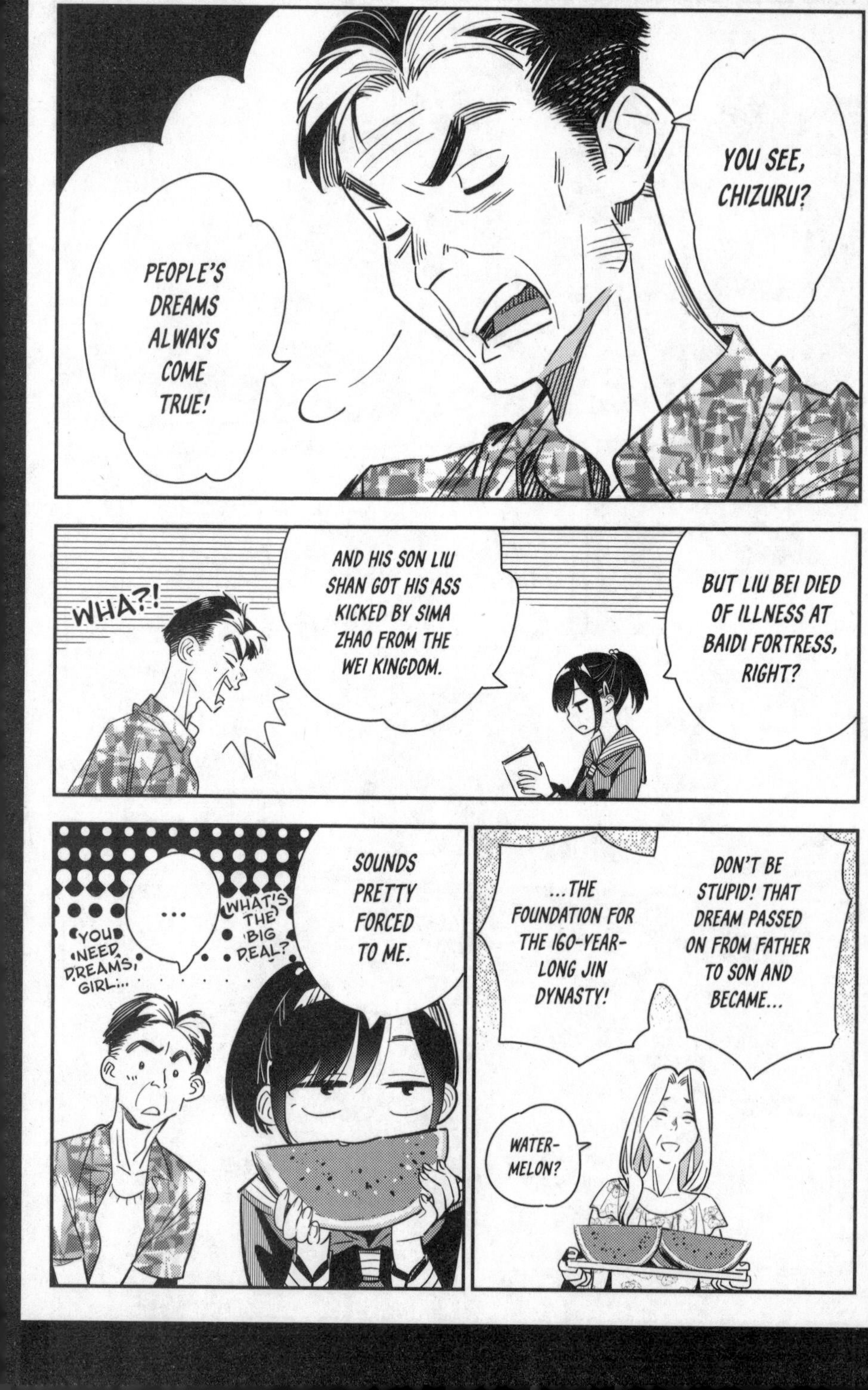
YOU SEE, CHIZURU?
PEOPLE'S DREAMS ALWAYS COME TRUE!
BUT LIU BEI DIED OF ILLNESS AT BAIDI FORTRESS, RIGHT?
AND HIS SON LIU SHAN GOT HIS ASS KICKED BY SIMA ZHAO FROM THE WEI KINGDOM.
WHA?!
DON'T BE STUPID! THAT DREAM PASSED ON FROM FATHER TO SON AND BECAME…
…THE FOUNDATION FOR THE 160-YEAR-LONG JIN DYNASTY!
WATER-MELON?
SOUNDS PRETTY FORCED TO ME.
WHAT'S THE BIG DEAL?
…
YOU NEED DREAMS, GIRL…

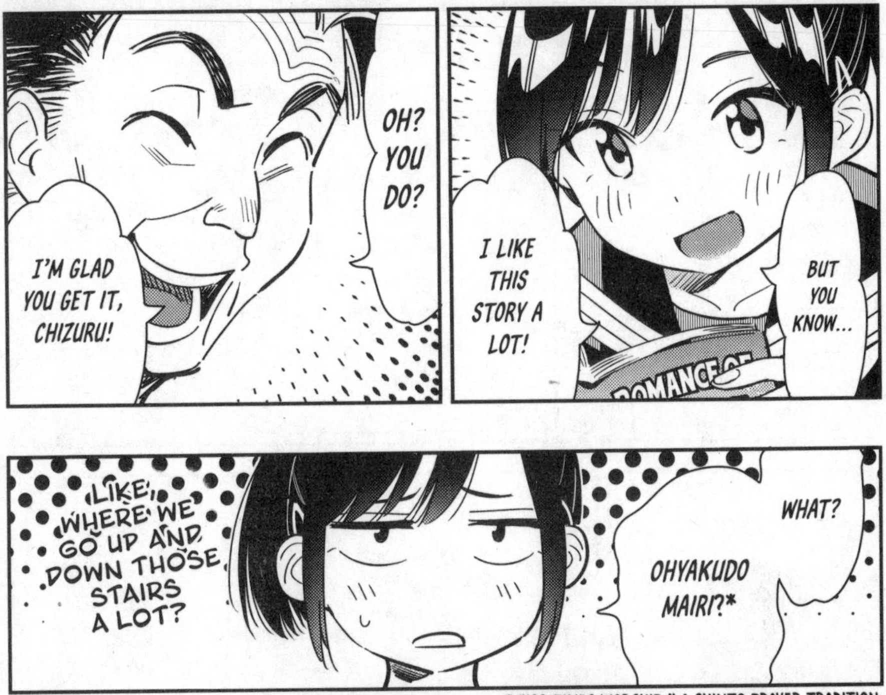
I LIKE THIS STORY A LOT!
BUT YOU KNOW...
OH? YOU DO?
I'M GLAD YOU GET IT, CHIZURU!
WHAT?
OHYAKUDO MAIRI?*
LIKE, WHERE WE GO UP AND DOWN THOSE STAIRS A LOT?

* "100 TIMES WORSHIP," A SHINTO PRAYER TRADITION.

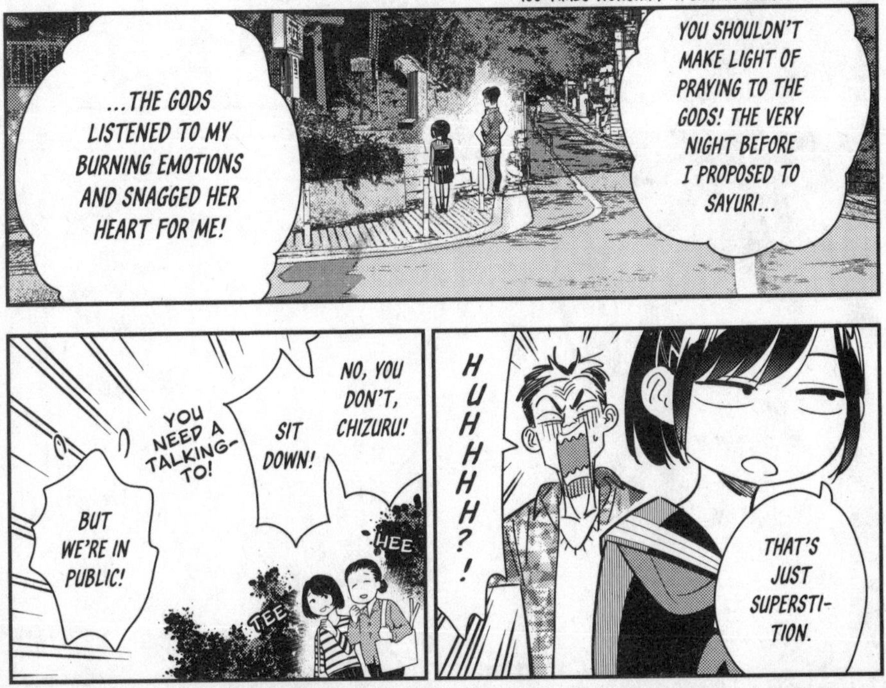
YOU SHOULDN'T MAKE LIGHT OF PRAYING TO THE GODS! THE VERY NIGHT BEFORE I PROPOSED TO SAYURI...
...THE GODS LISTENED TO MY BURNING EMOTIONS AND SNAGGED HER HEART FOR ME!
THAT'S JUST SUPERSTITION.
HUHHHHH?!
NO, YOU DON'T, CHIZURU!
SIT DOWN!
YOU NEED A TALKING-TO!
HEE
BUT WE'RE IN PUBLIC!
TEE

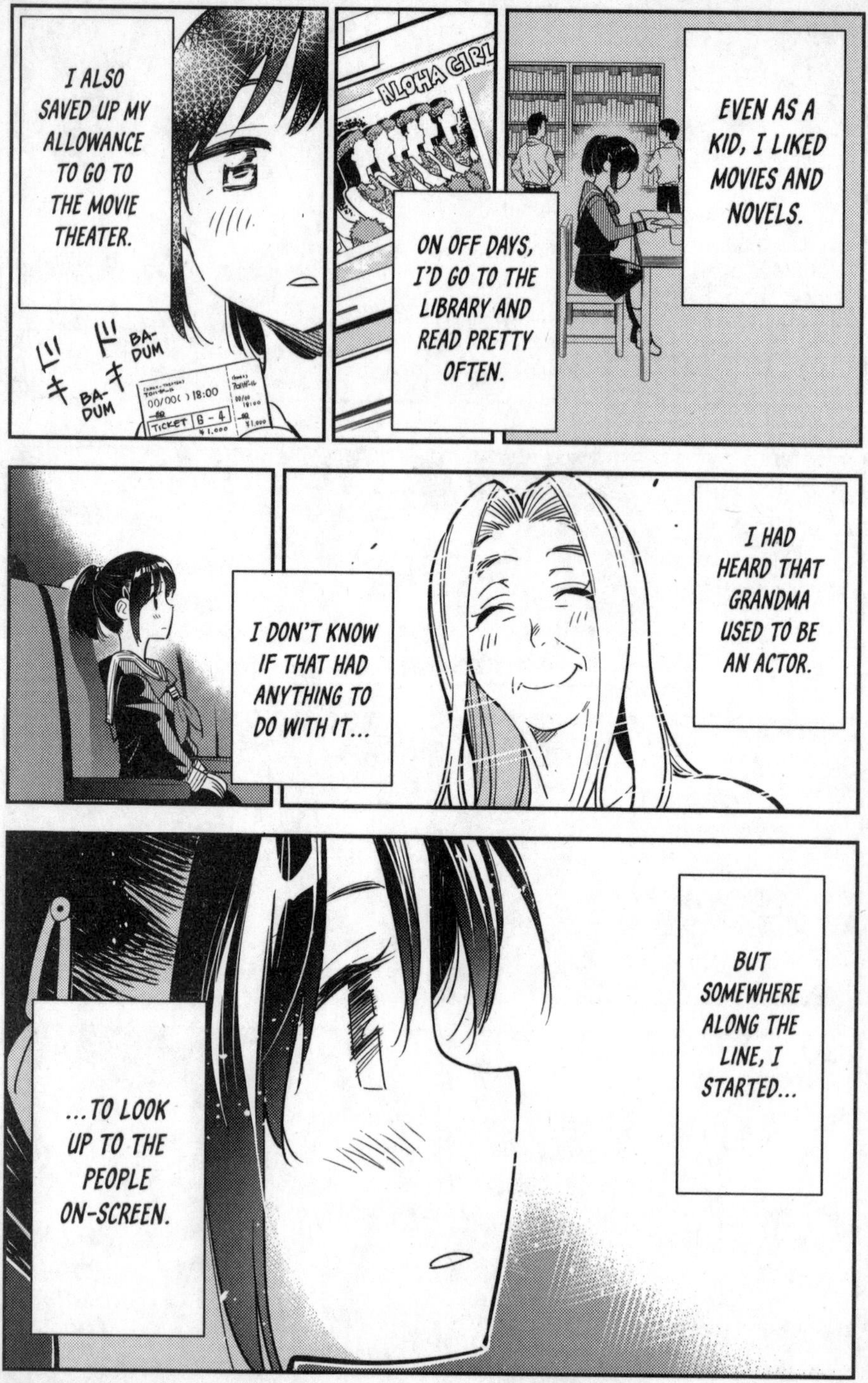
EVEN AS A KID, I LIKED MOVIES AND NOVELS.
ALOHA GIRL
ON OFF DAYS, I'D GO TO THE LIBRARY AND READ PRETTY OFTEN.
I ALSO SAVED UP MY ALLOWANCE TO GO TO THE MOVIE THEATER.
ドキ
BA-DUM
ドキ
BA-DUM
18:00
TICKET G-4
¥1,000
I HAD HEARD THAT GRANDMA USED TO BE AN ACTOR.
I DON'T KNOW IF THAT HAD ANYTHING TO DO WITH IT...
BUT SOMEWHERE ALONG THE LINE, I STARTED...
...TO LOOK UP TO THE PEOPLE ON-SCREEN.

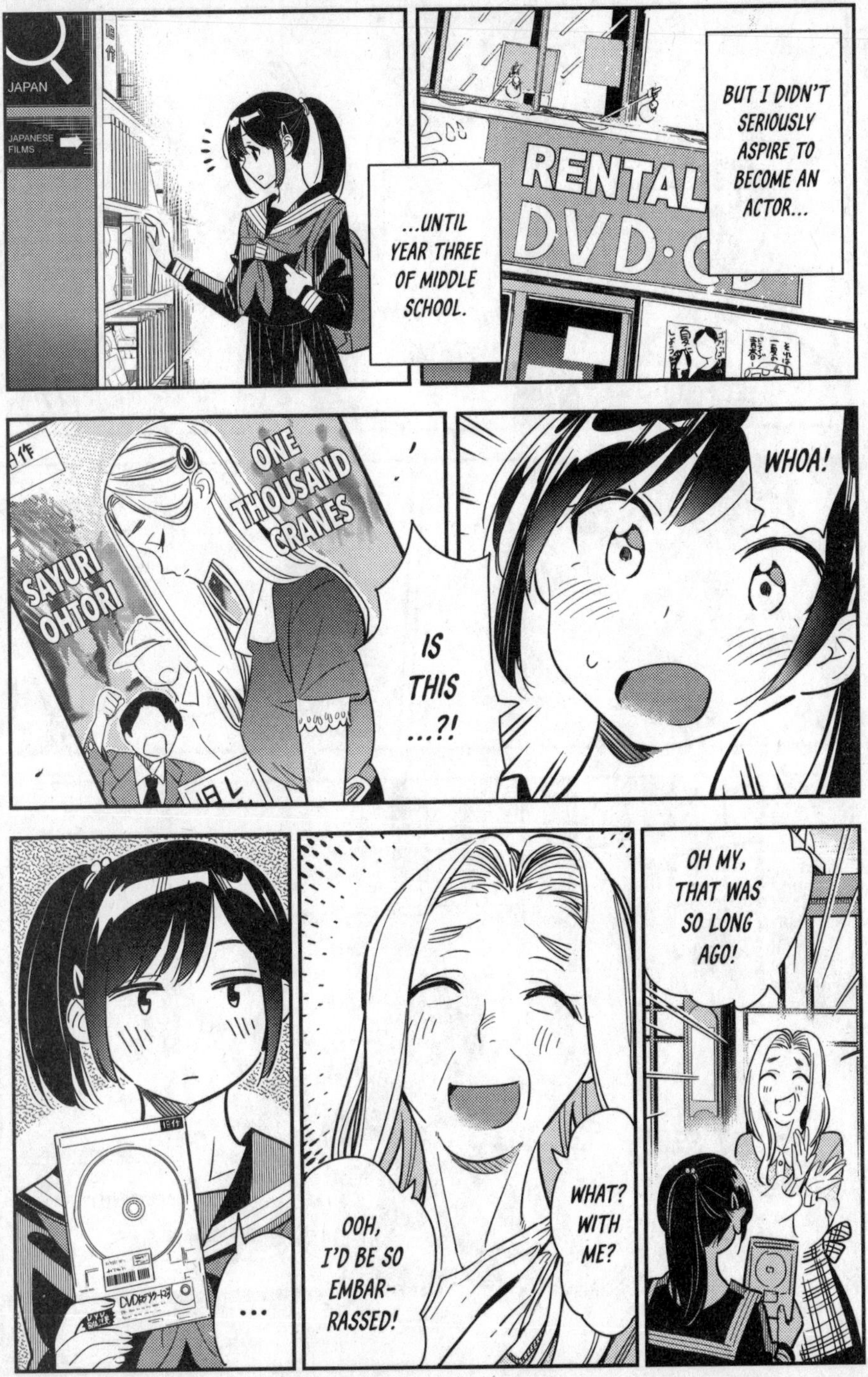
RENTAL
DVD·CD
BUT I DIDN'T SERIOUSLY ASPIRE TO BECOME AN ACTOR...
...UNTIL YEAR THREE OF MIDDLE SCHOOL.
JAPAN
JAPANESE FILMS
WHOA!
IS THIS ...?!
ONE THOUSAND CRANES
SAYURI OHTORI
OH MY, THAT WAS SO LONG AGO!
WHAT? WITH ME?
OOH, I'D BE SO EMBAR-RASSED!
...

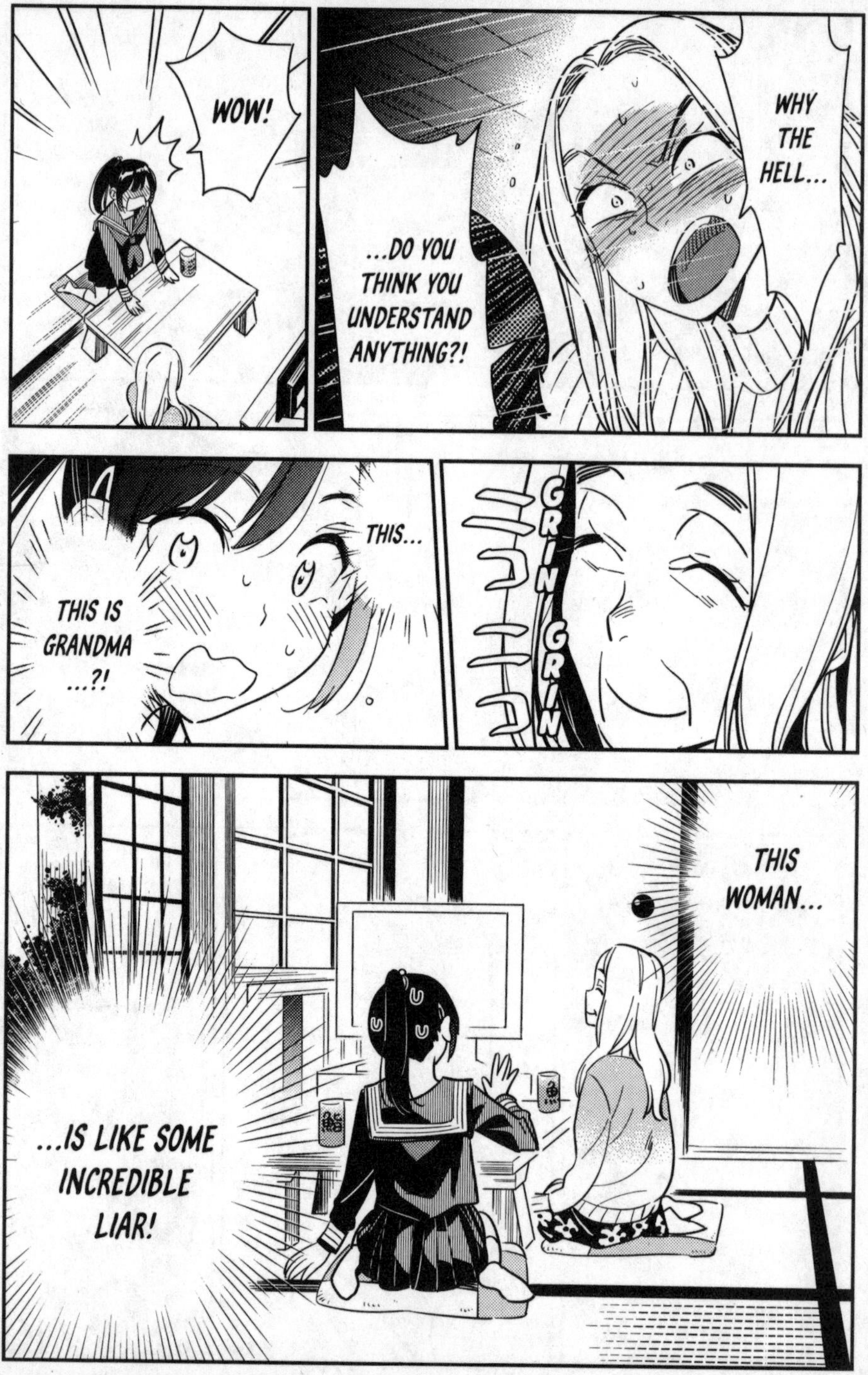
WHY THE HELL...
...DO YOU THINK YOU UNDERSTAND ANYTHING?!
WOW!
GRIN GRIN
THIS...
THIS IS GRANDMA ...?!
THIS WOMAN...
...IS LIKE SOME INCREDIBLE LIAR!

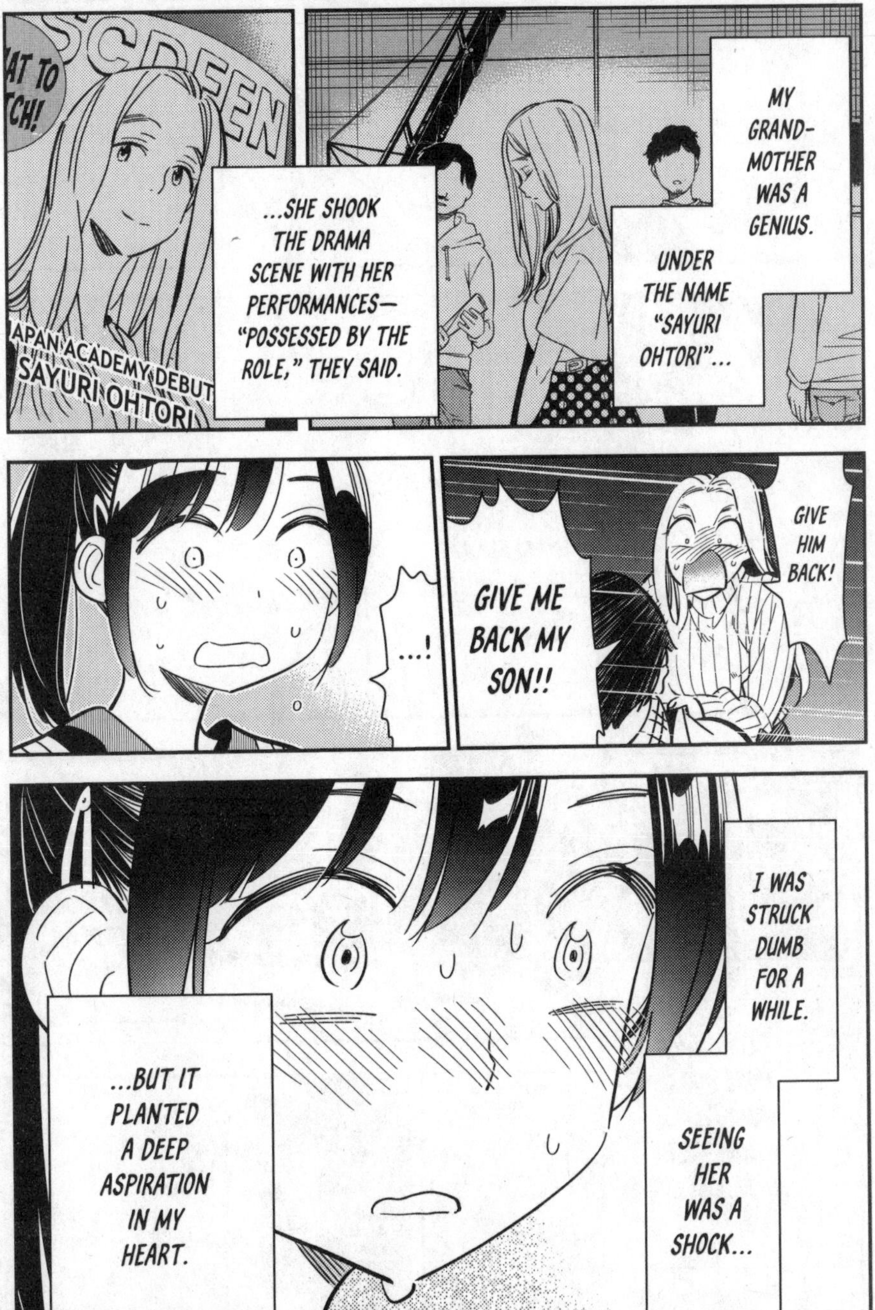
MY GRANDMOTHER WAS A GENIUS.
UNDER THE NAME "SAYURI OHTORI"...
...SHE SHOOK THE DRAMA SCENE WITH HER PERFORMANCES—"POSSESSED BY THE ROLE," THEY SAID.
SCREEN
ACADEMY DEBUT
SAYURI OHTORI
GIVE HIM BACK!
GIVE ME BACK MY SON!!
...!
I WAS STRUCK DUMB FOR A WHILE.
SEEING HER WAS A SHOCK...
...BUT IT PLANTED A DEEP ASPIRATION IN MY HEART.

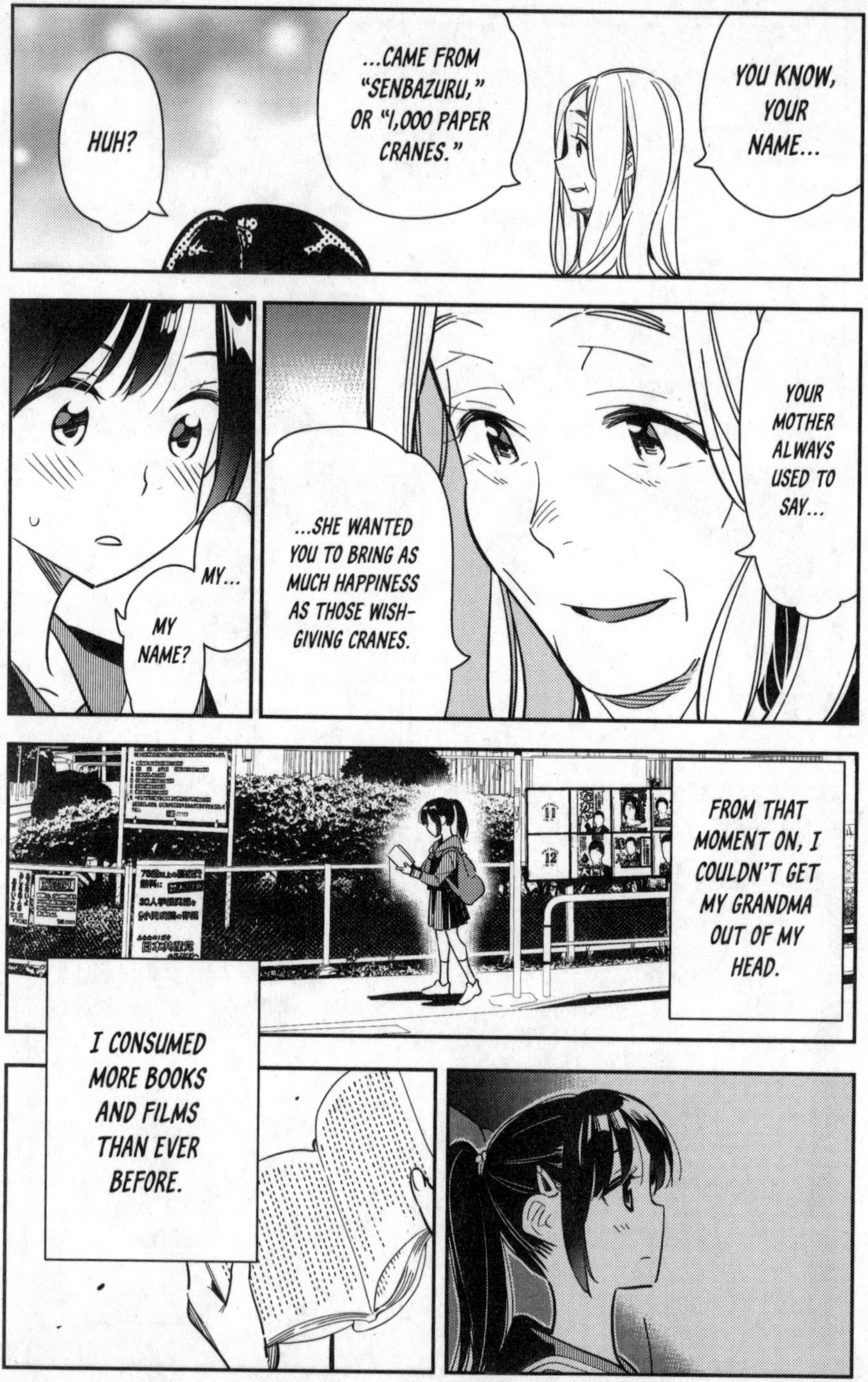
YOU KNOW, YOUR NAME...
...CAME FROM "SENBAZURU," OR "1,000 PAPER CRANES."
HUH?
YOUR MOTHER ALWAYS USED TO SAY...
...SHE WANTED YOU TO BRING AS MUCH HAPPINESS AS THOSE WISH-GIVING CRANES.
MY...
MY NAME?
FROM THAT MOMENT ON, I COULDN'T GET MY GRANDMA OUT OF MY HEAD.
I CONSUMED MORE BOOKS AND FILMS THAN EVER BEFORE.

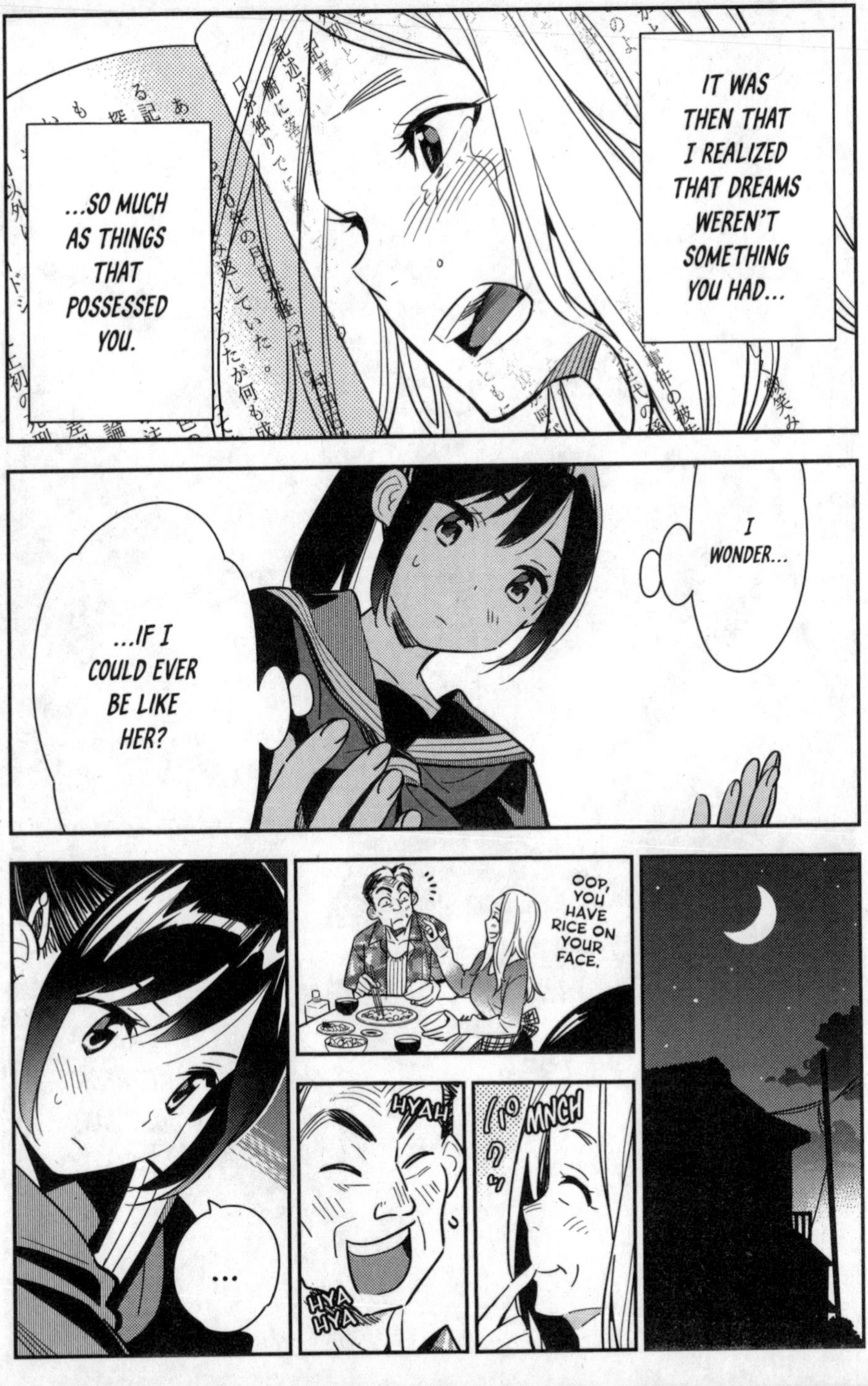

IT WAS THEN THAT I REALIZED THAT DREAMS WEREN'T SOMETHING YOU HAD...
...SO MUCH AS THINGS THAT POSSESSED YOU.
I WONDER...
...IF I COULD EVER BE LIKE HER?
OOP, YOU HAVE RICE ON YOUR FACE.
パクッ
MNCH
HYAH
HYA HYA
...

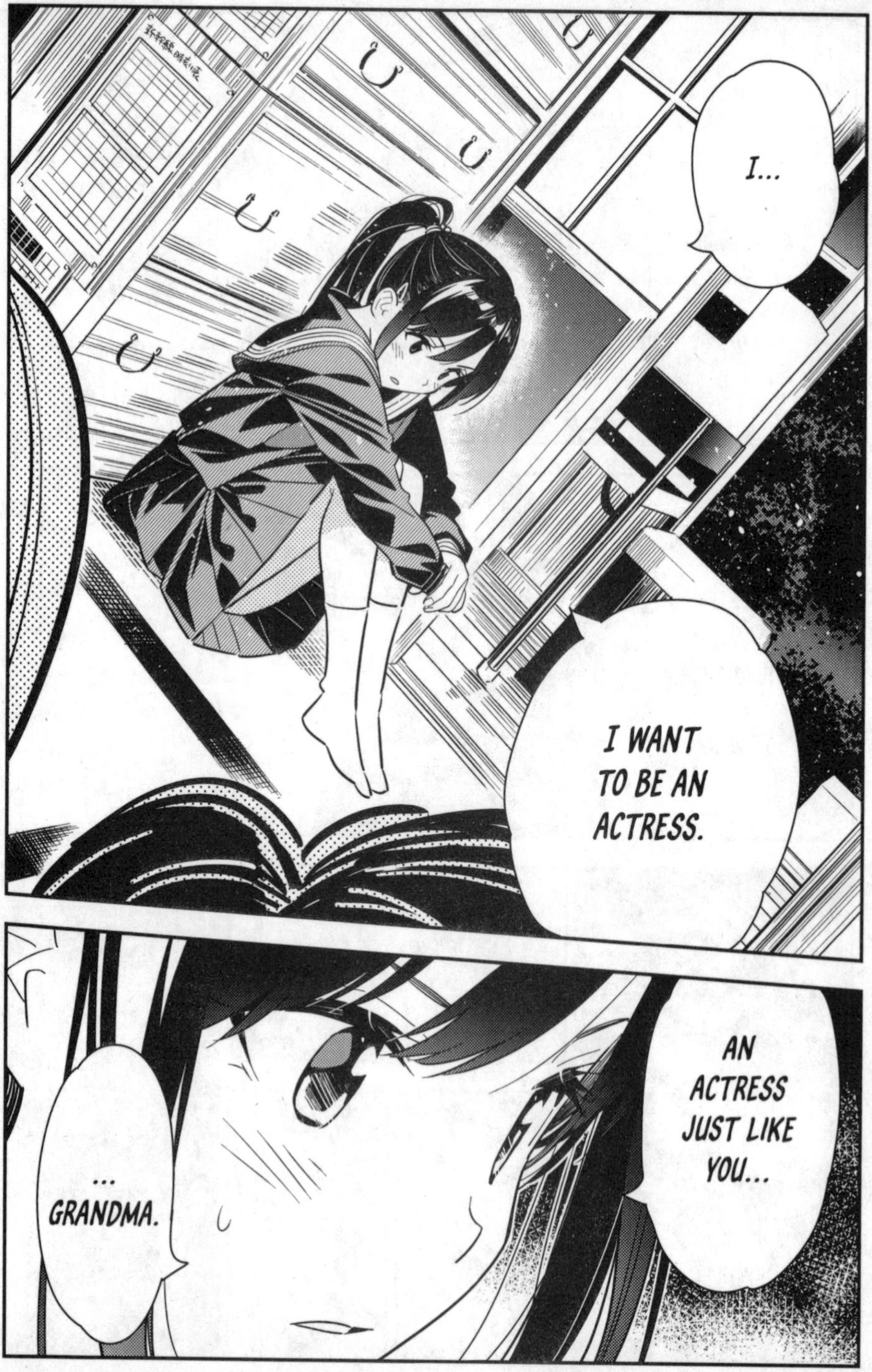
I...
I WANT TO BE AN ACTRESS.
AN ACTRESS JUST LIKE YOU...
... GRANDMA.

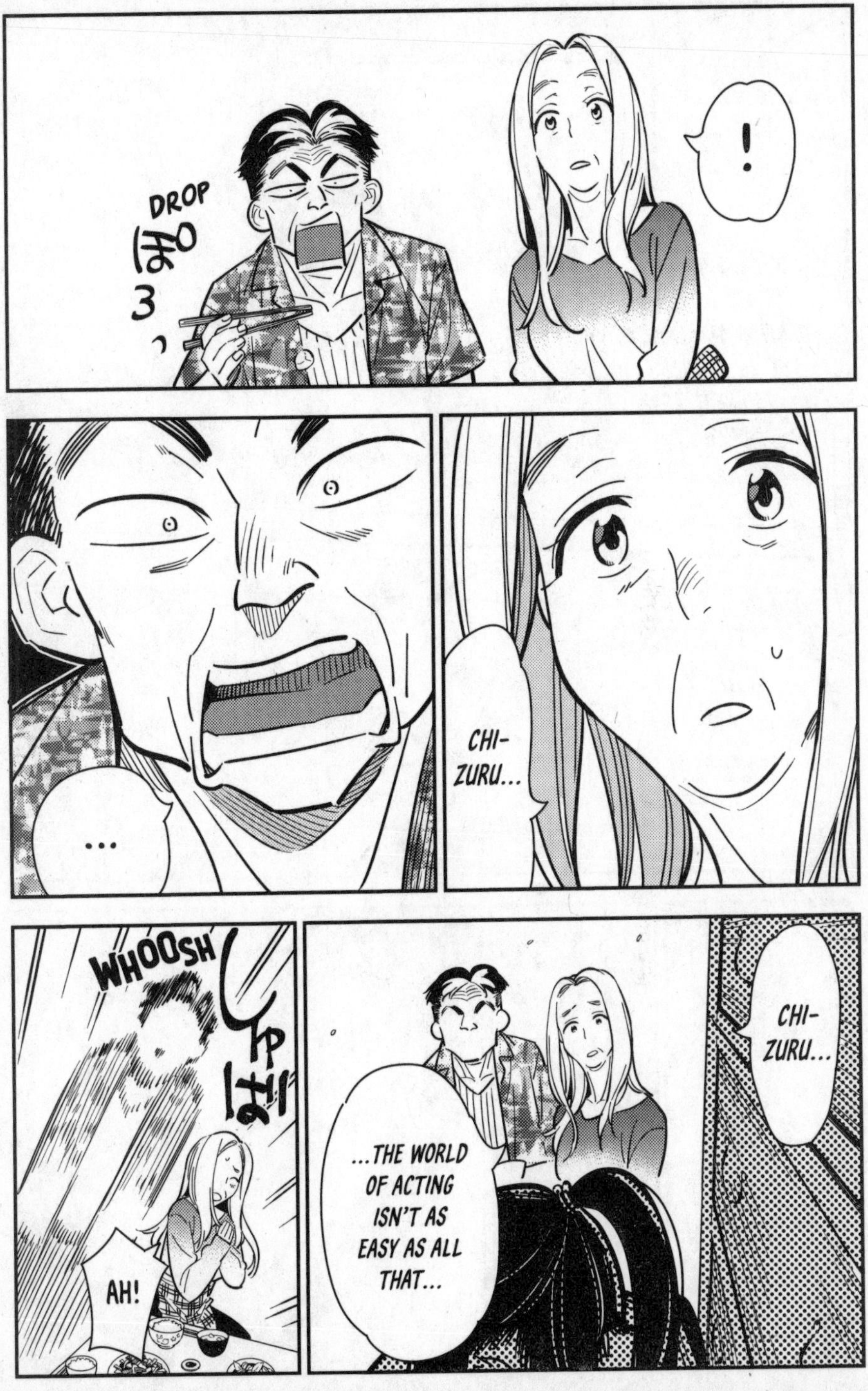
!
DROP
ぽろっ
CHI-ZURU...
...
CHI-ZURU...
...THE WORLD OF ACTING ISN'T AS EASY AS ALL THAT...
WHOOSH
しゅば
AH!

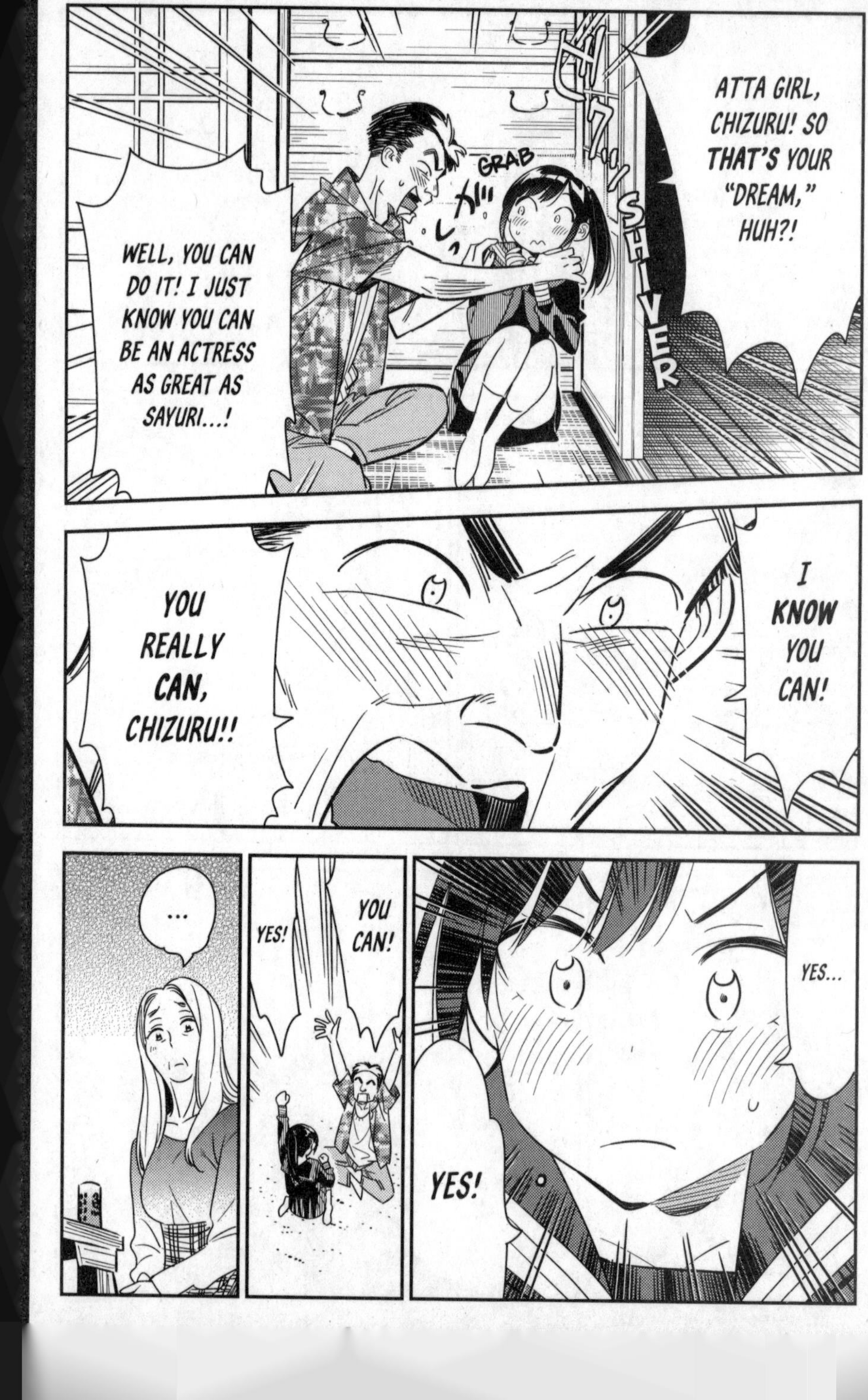
ATTA GIRL, CHIZURU! SO THAT'S YOUR "DREAM," HUH?!
SHIVER
GRAB
WELL, YOU CAN DO IT! I JUST KNOW YOU CAN BE AN ACTRESS AS GREAT AS SAYURI...!
I KNOW YOU CAN!
YOU REALLY CAN, CHIZURU!!
YES...
YES!
YOU CAN!
YES!
...

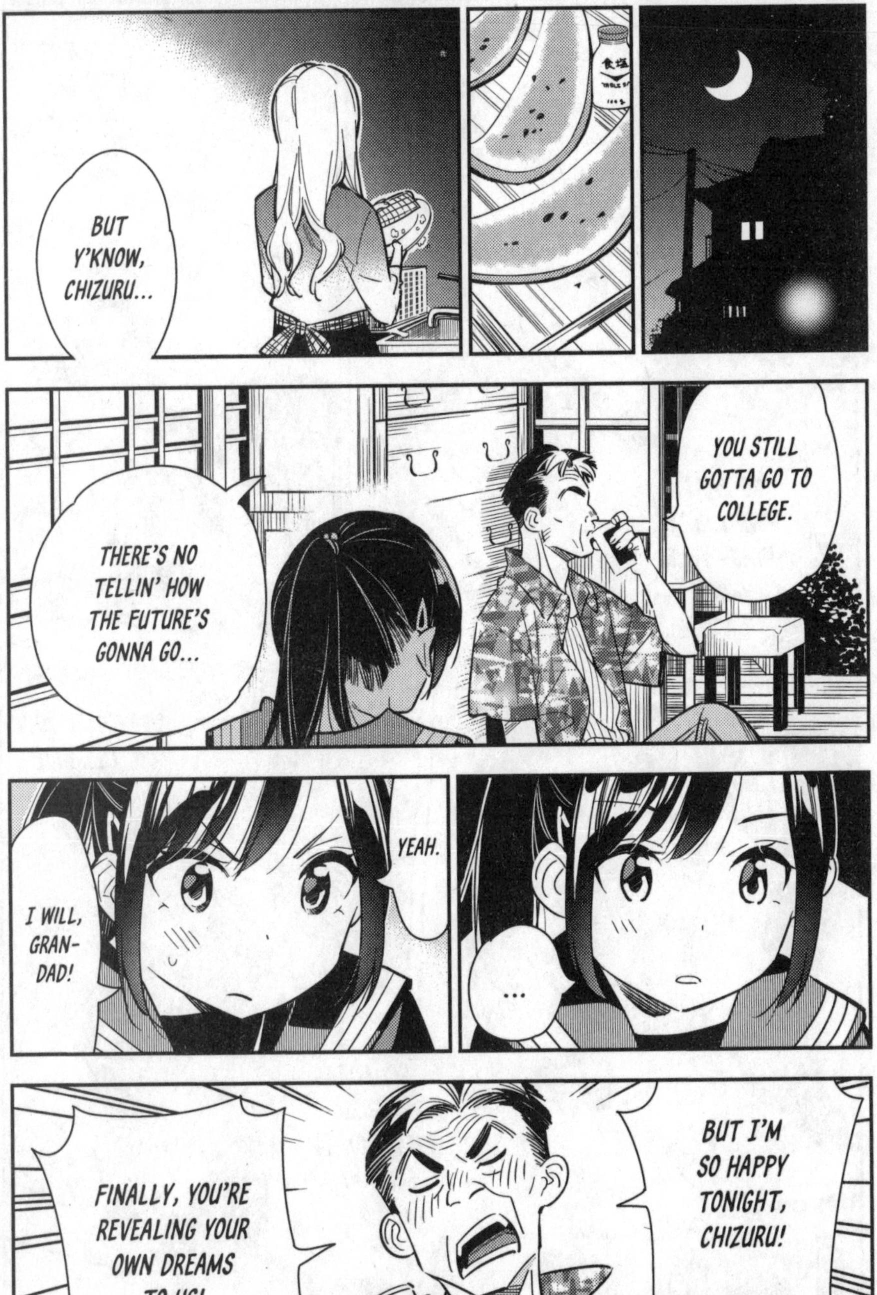
BUT Y'KNOW, CHIZURU...
YOU STILL GOTTA GO TO COLLEGE.
THERE'S NO TELLIN' HOW THE FUTURE'S GONNA GO...
...
YEAH.
I WILL, GRAN-DAD!
BUT I'M SO HAPPY TONIGHT, CHIZURU!
FINALLY, YOU'RE REVEALING YOUR OWN DREAMS TO US!

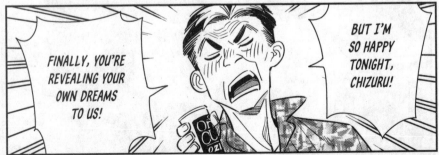

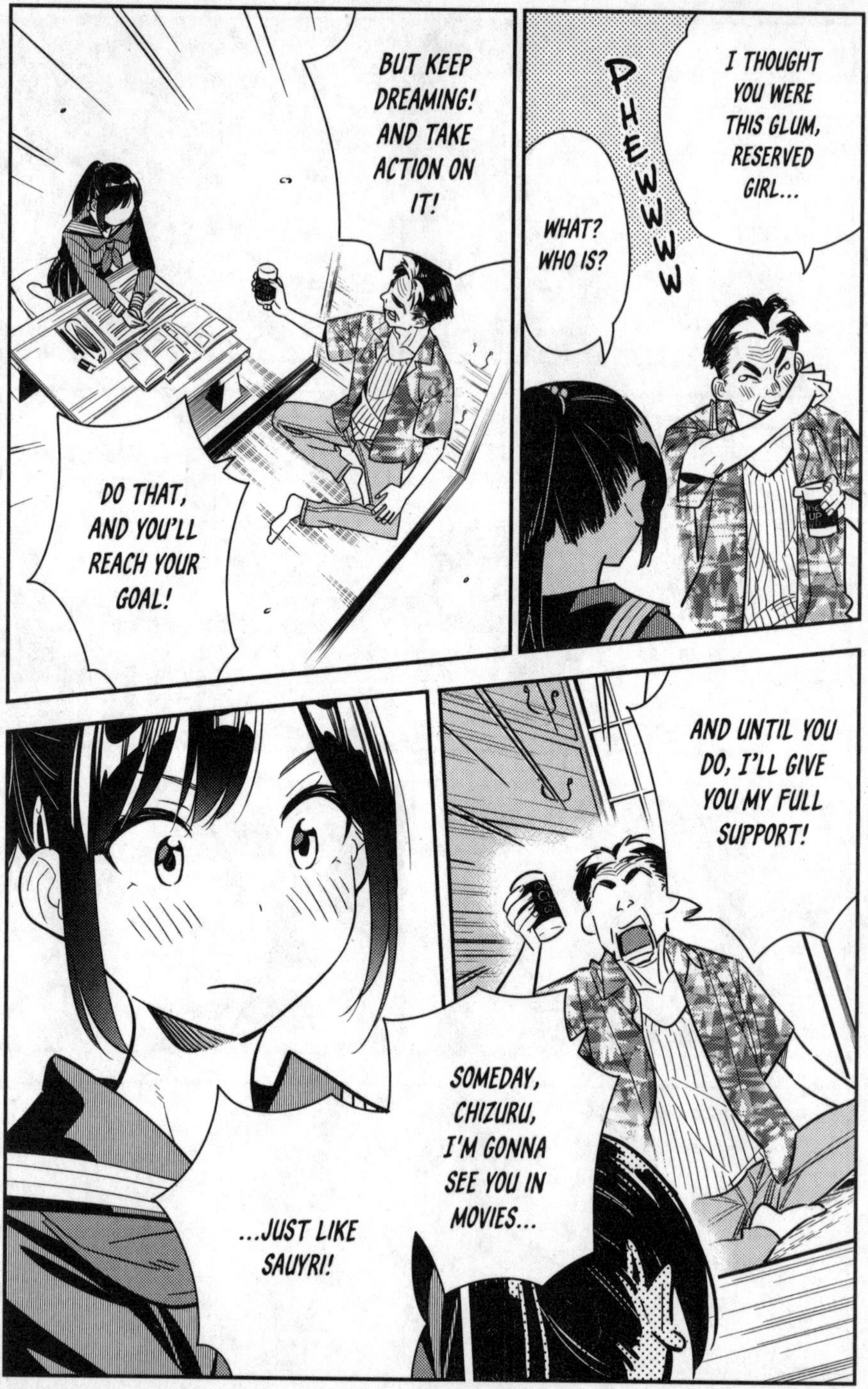
I THOUGHT YOU WERE THIS GLUM, RESERVED GIRL...
PHEWWWW
WHAT? WHO IS?
BUT KEEP DREAMING! AND TAKE ACTION ON IT!
DO THAT, AND YOU'LL REACH YOUR GOAL!
AND UNTIL YOU DO, I'LL GIVE YOU MY FULL SUPPORT!
SOMEDAY, CHIZURU, I'M GONNA SEE YOU IN MOVIES...
...JUST LIKE SAUYRI!

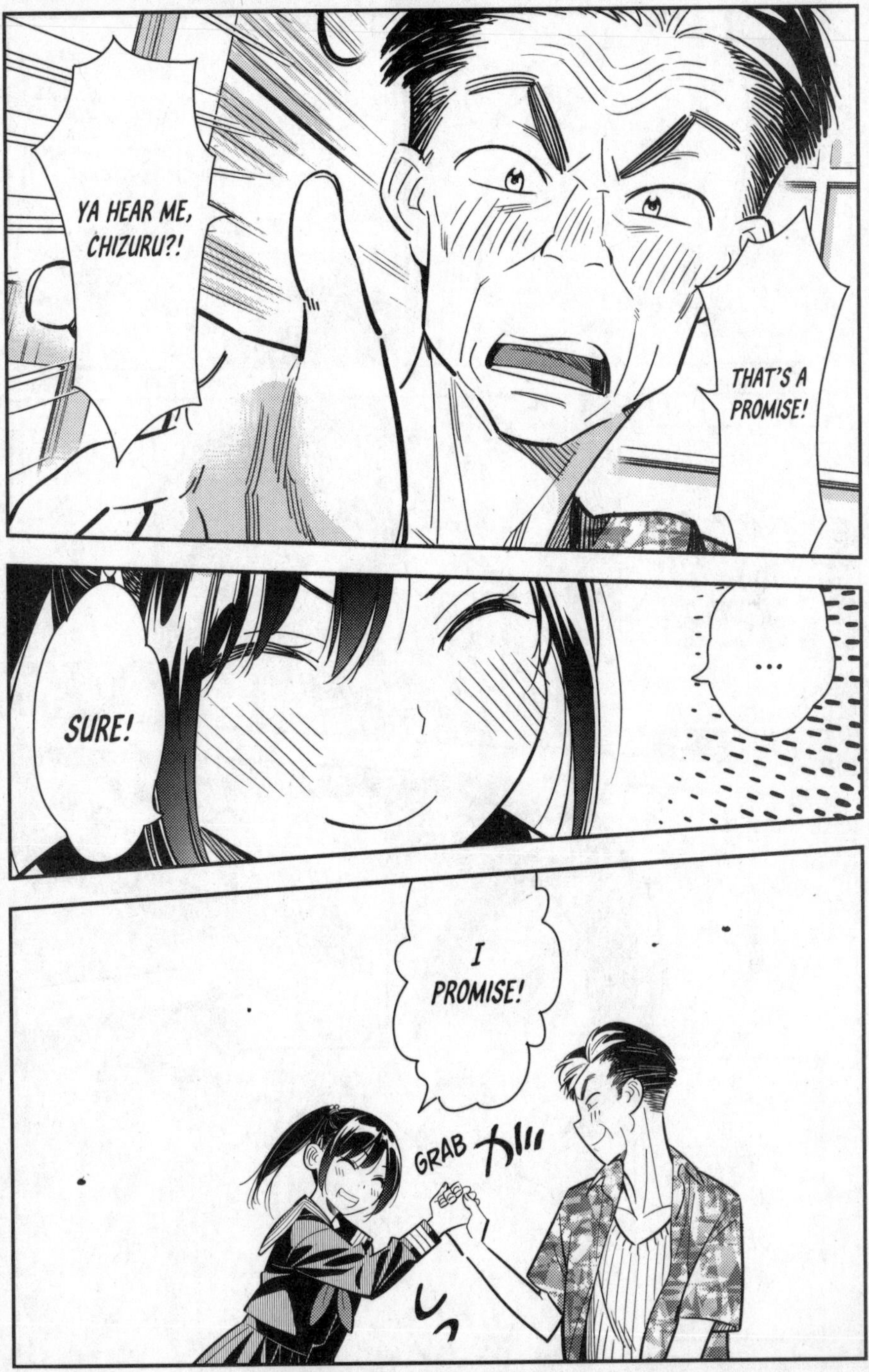
YA HEAR ME, CHIZURU?!
THAT'S A PROMISE!
...
SURE!
I PROMISE!
GRAB
カッ
しっ

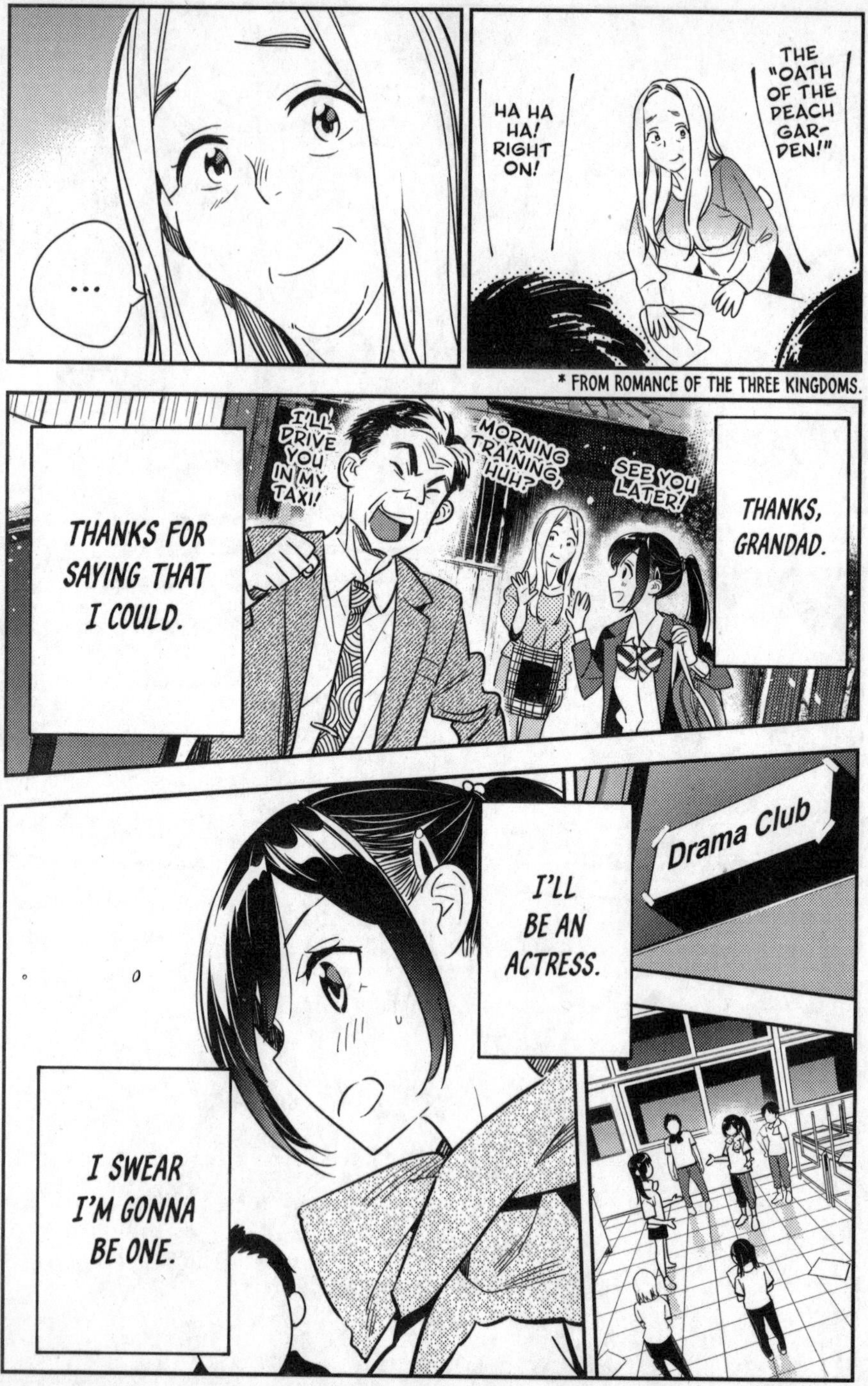
THE "OATH OF THE PEACH GARDEN!"*
HA HA HA! RIGHT ON!
...
THANKS, GRANDAD.
SEE YOU LATER!
MORNING TRAINING, HUH?
I'LL DRIVE YOU IN MY TAXI!
THANKS FOR SAYING THAT I COULD.
Drama Club
I'LL BE AN ACTRESS.
I SWEAR I'M GONNA BE ONE.

* FROM ROMANCE OF THE THREE KINGDOMS.

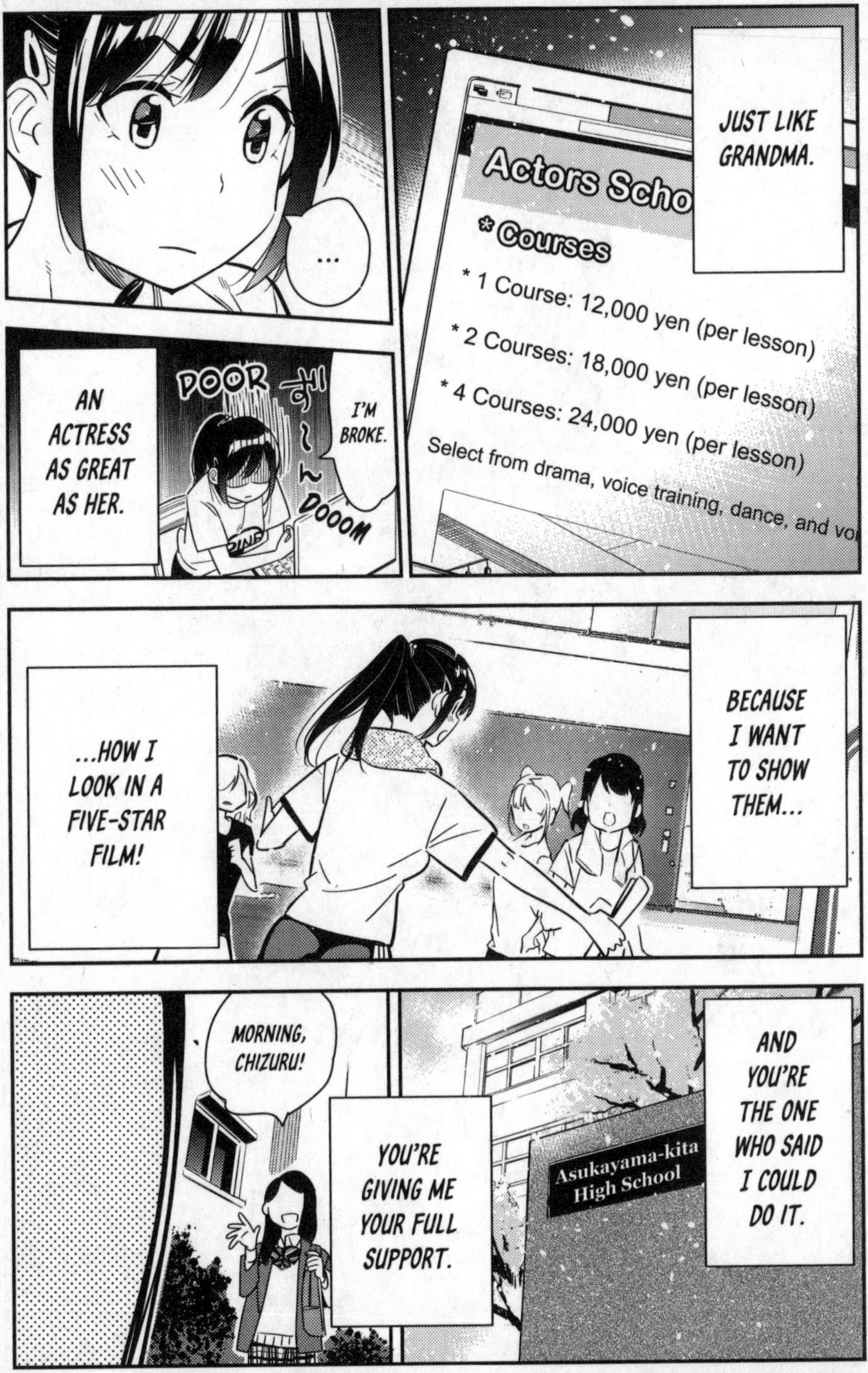
JUST LIKE GRANDMA.
Actors Scho
* Courses
* 1 Course: 12,000 yen (per lesson)
* 2 Courses: 18,000 yen (per lesson)
* 4 Courses: 24,000 yen (per lesson)
Select from drama, voice training, dance, and vo
...
I'M BROKE.
POOR
DOOOM
AN ACTRESS AS GREAT AS HER.
BECAUSE I WANT TO SHOW THEM...
...HOW I LOOK IN A FIVE-STAR FILM!
AND YOU'RE THE ONE WHO SAID I COULD DO IT.
Asukayama-kita High School
YOU'RE GIVING ME YOUR FULL SUPPORT.
MORNING, CHIZURU!

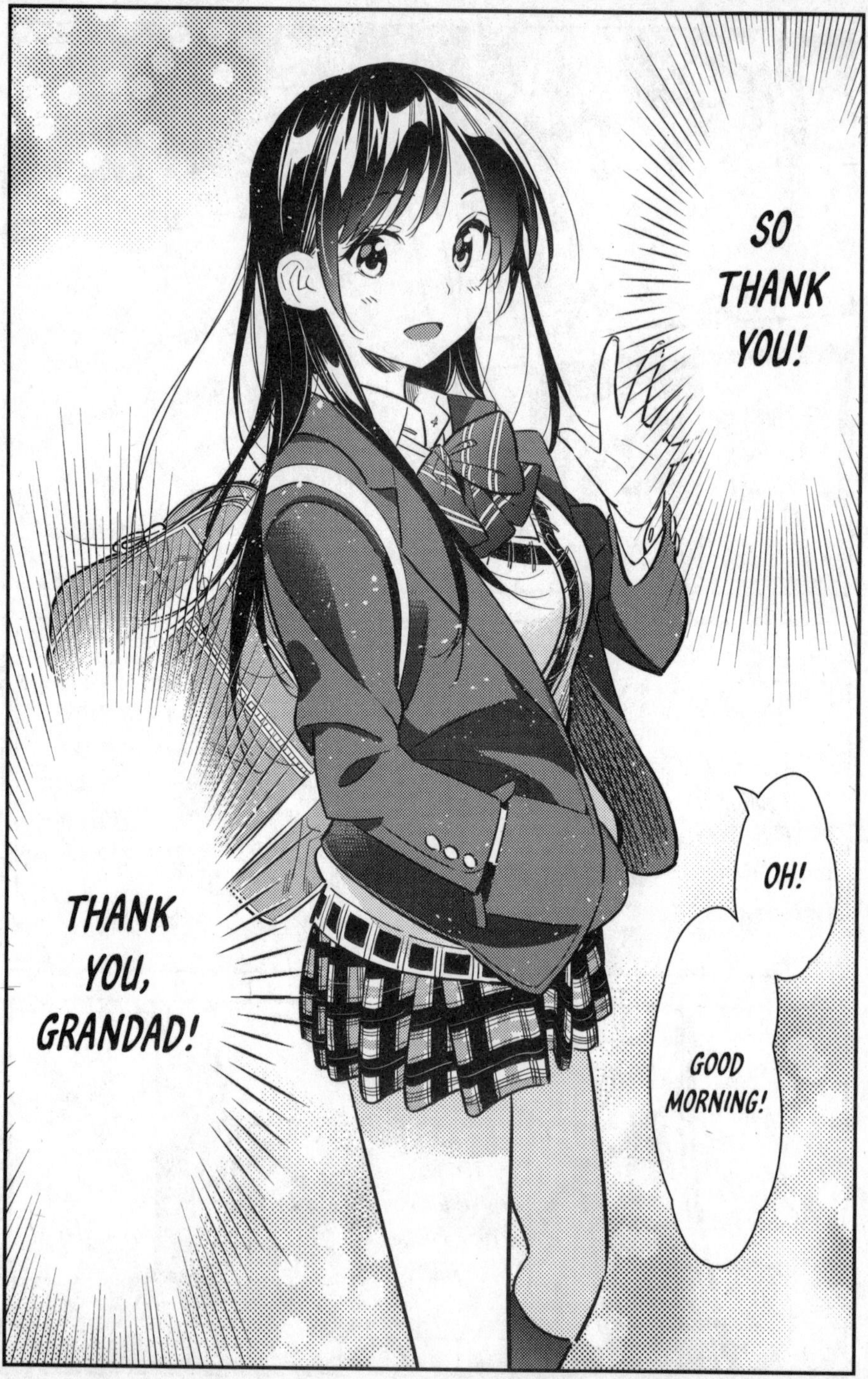
SO THANK YOU!
OH!
GOOD MORNING!
THANK YOU, GRANDAD!

OOOOO

FLASH

SWWWM...

CRANE TAXI

KA-CHK

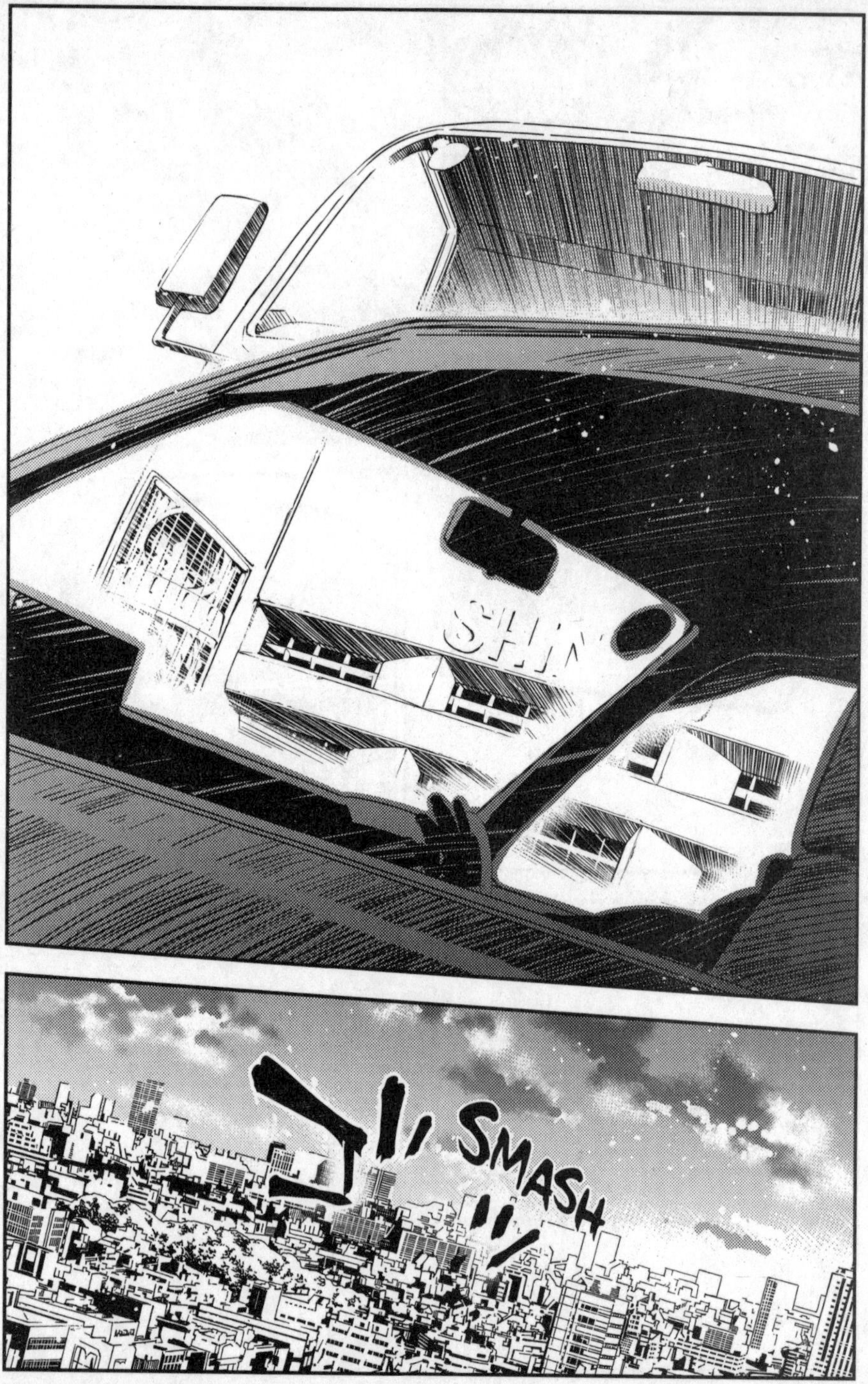
SMASH

## RATING 101 MY "GIRLFRIEND," CHIZURU MIZUHARA-3

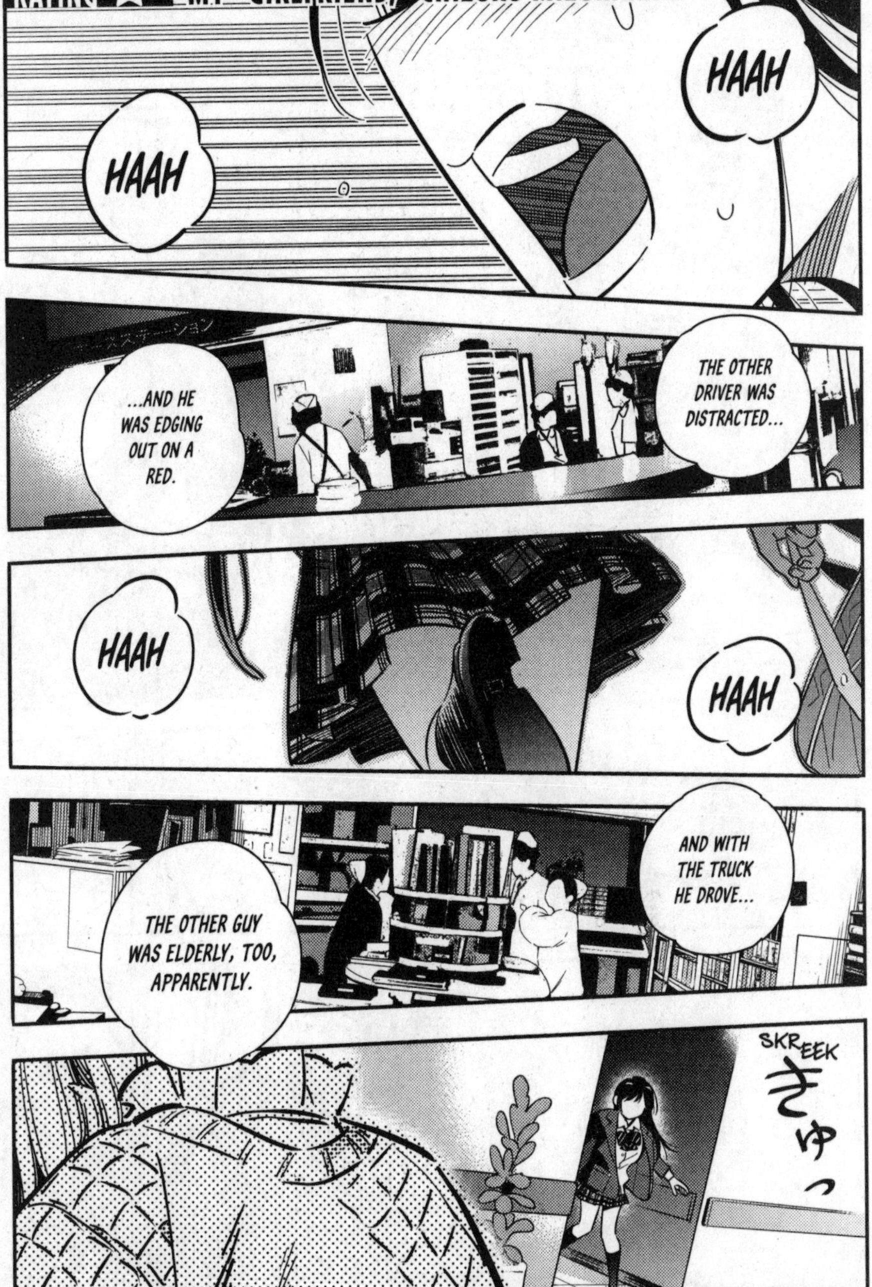
HAAH
HAAH
THE OTHER DRIVER WAS DISTRACTED...
...AND HE WAS EDGING OUT ON A RED.
HAAH
HAAH
AND WITH THE TRUCK HE DROVE...
THE OTHER GUY WAS ELDERLY, TOO, APPARENTLY.
SKREEK
きゅっ

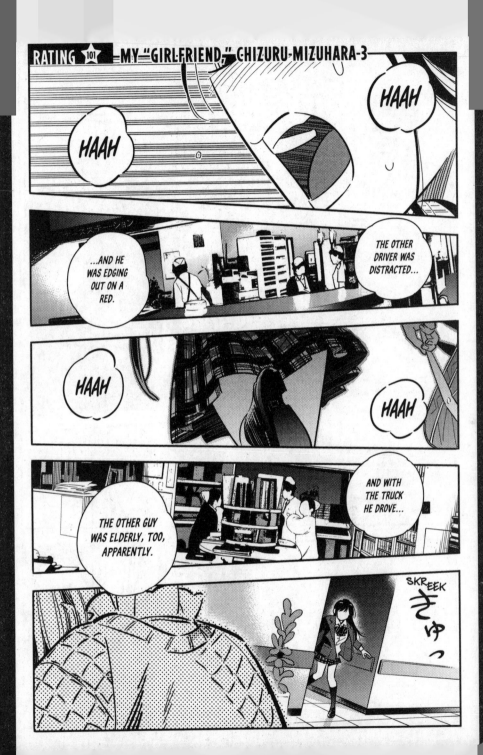

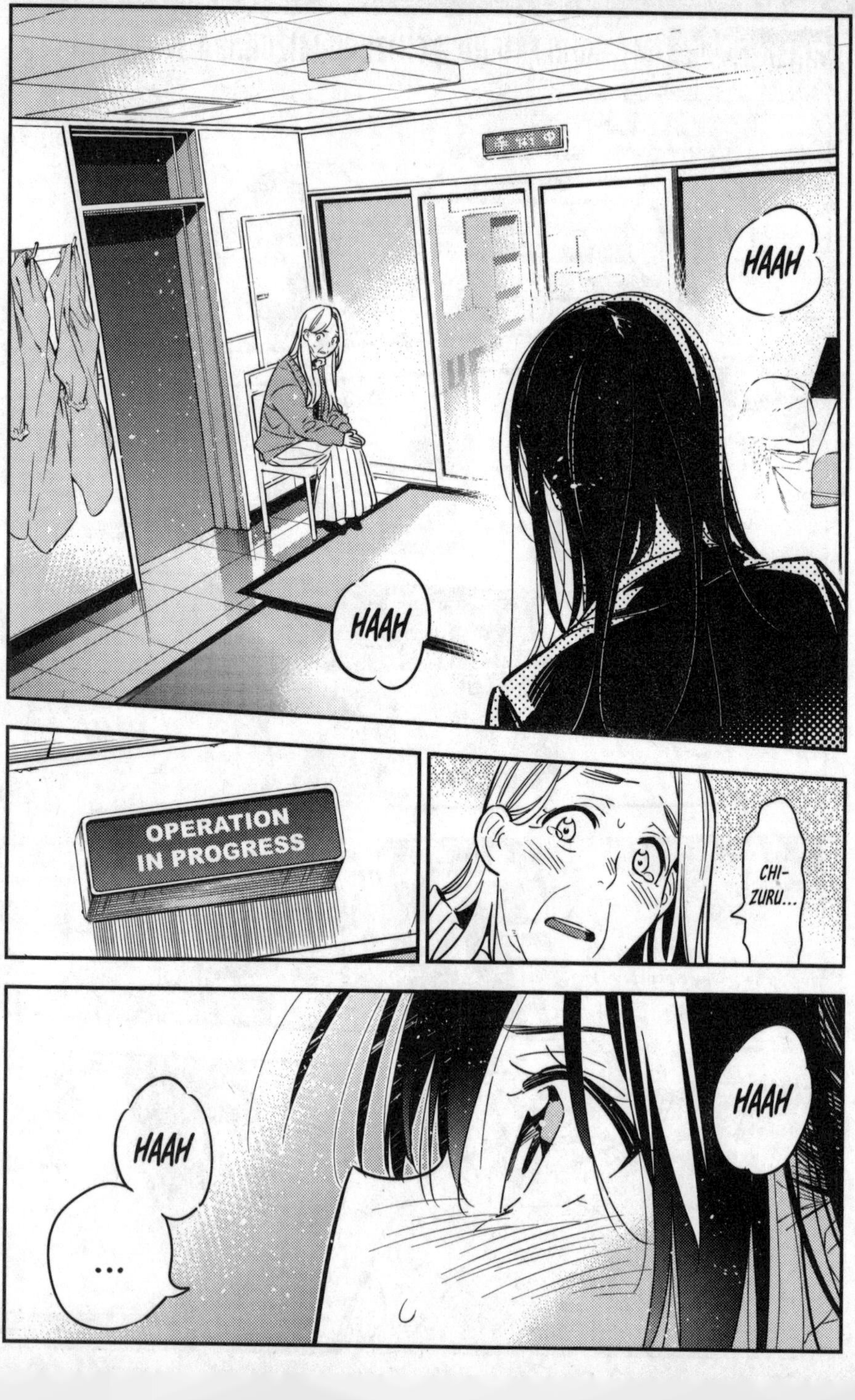
HAAH
HAAH
CHI-ZURU...
OPERATION IN PROGRESS
HAAH
HAAH
...

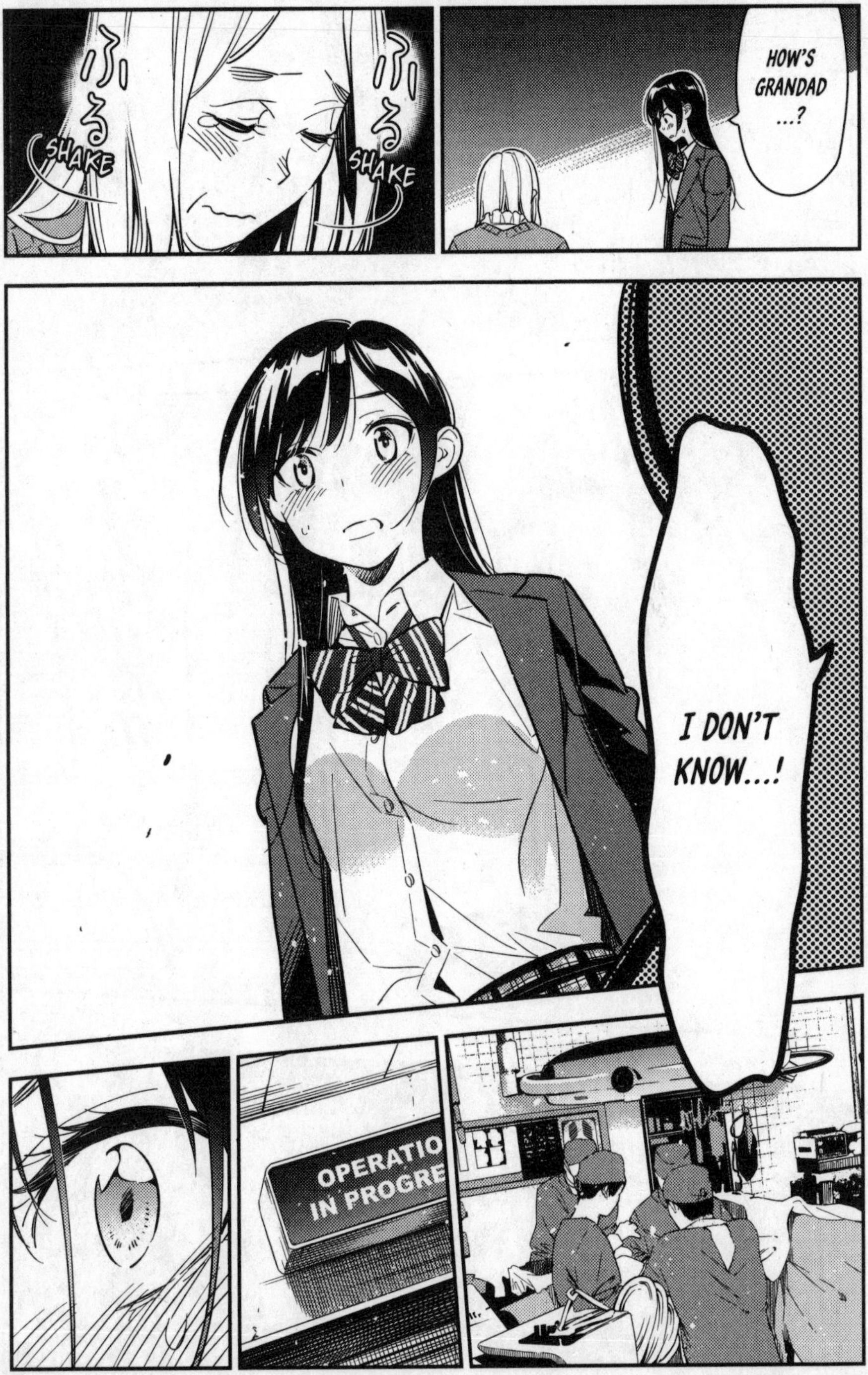
HOW'S GRANDAD ...?
ふる
SHAKE
ふる
SHAKE
I DON'T KNOW...!
OPERATIO
IN PROGRE

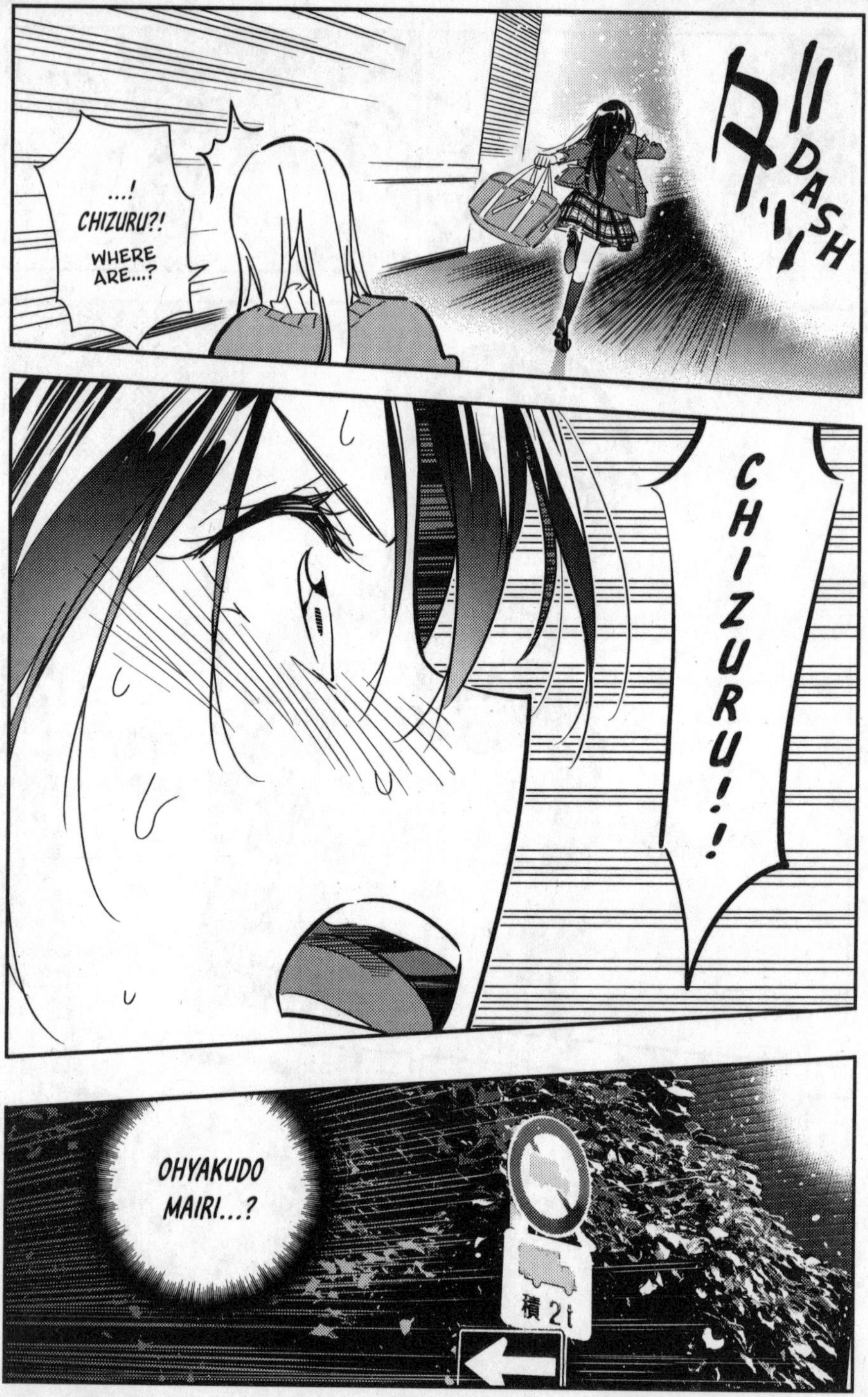
DASH
...! CHIZURU?! WHERE ARE...?
CHIZURU!!!
OHYAKUDO MAIRI...?
積 2t

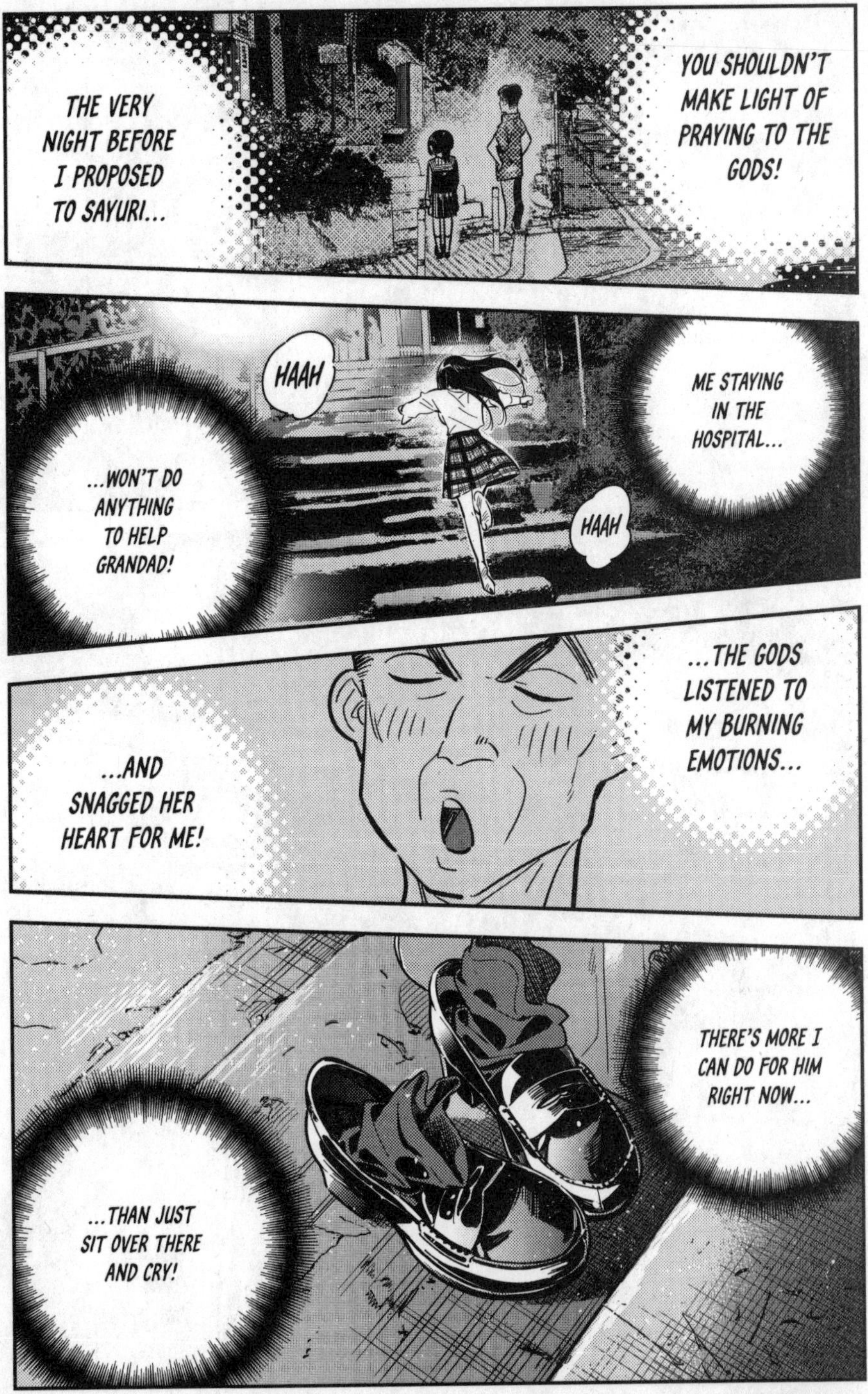
YOU SHOULDN'T MAKE LIGHT OF PRAYING TO THE GODS!
THE VERY NIGHT BEFORE I PROPOSED TO SAYURI...
ME STAYING IN THE HOSPITAL...
HAAH
HAAH
...WON'T DO ANYTHING TO HELP GRANDAD!
...THE GODS LISTENED TO MY BURNING EMOTIONS...
...AND SNAGGED HER HEART FOR ME!
THERE'S MORE I CAN DO FOR HIM RIGHT NOW...
...THAN JUST SIT OVER THERE AND CRY!

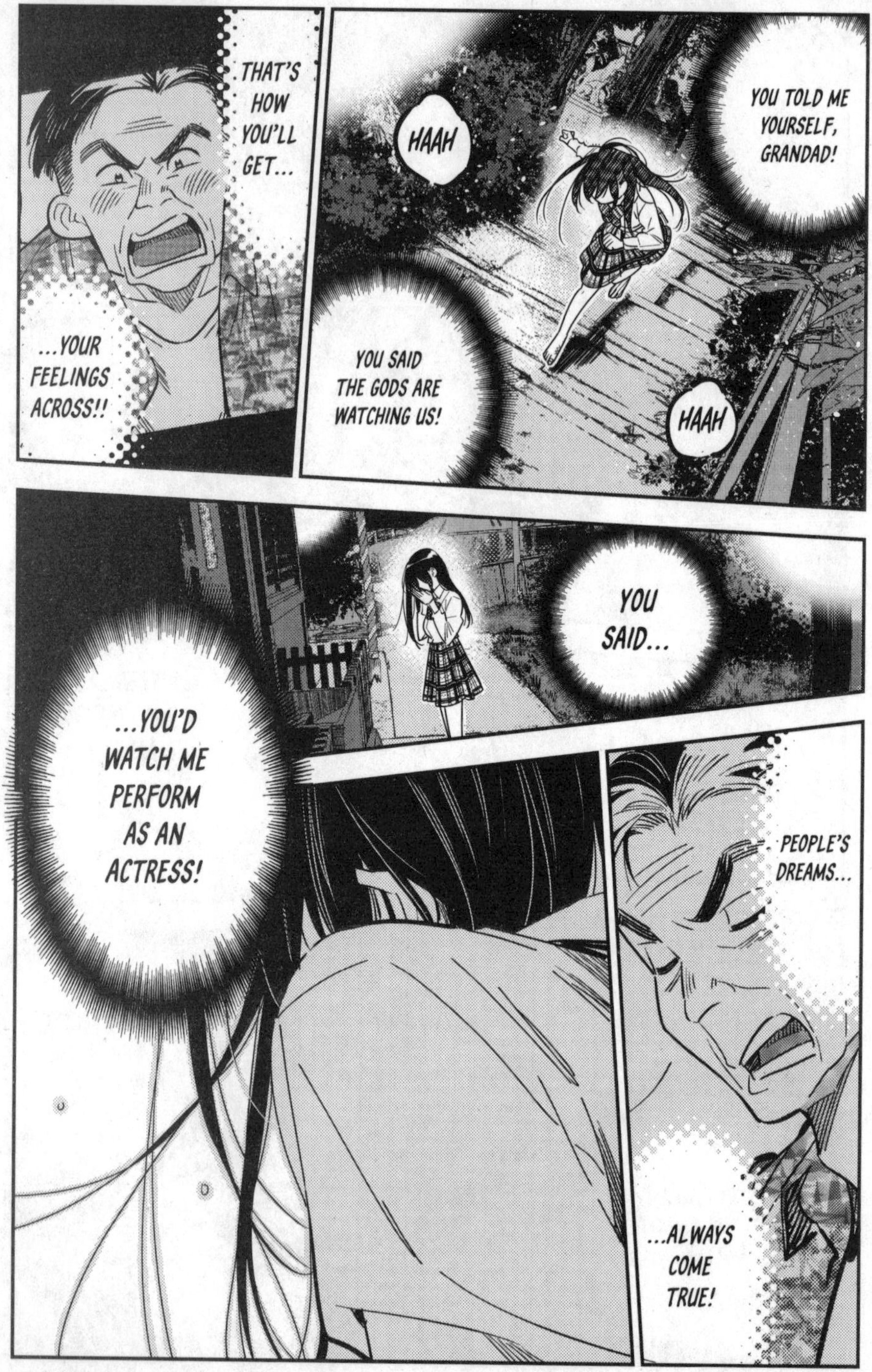
YOU TOLD ME YOURSELF, GRANDAD!
HAAH
HAAH
YOU SAID THE GODS ARE WATCHING US!
THAT'S HOW YOU'LL GET...
...YOUR FEELINGS ACROSS!!
YOU SAID...
...YOU'D WATCH ME PERFORM AS AN ACTRESS!
PEOPLE'S DREAMS...
...ALWAYS COME TRUE!

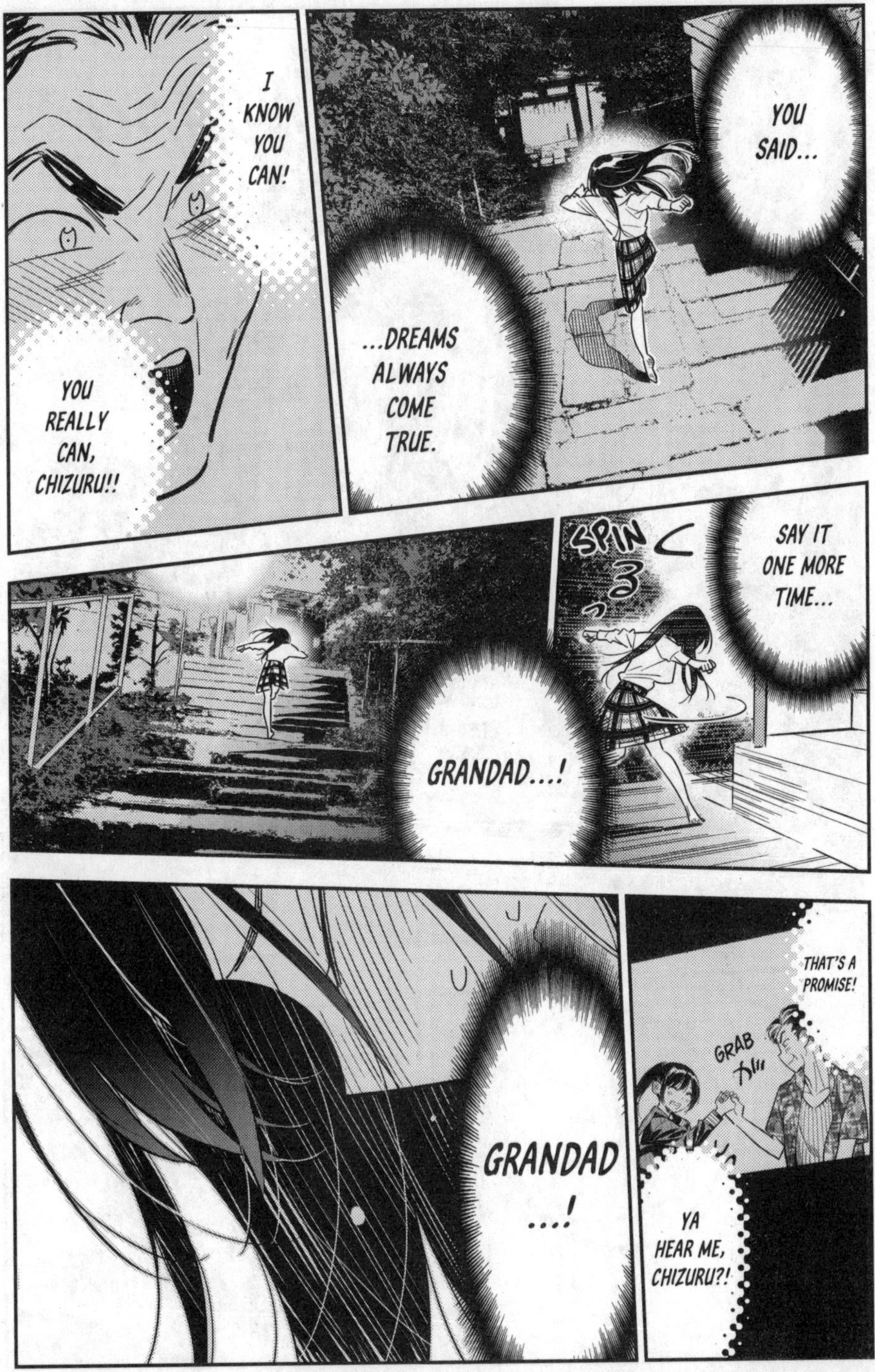
YOU SAID...
...DREAMS ALWAYS COME TRUE.
I KNOW YOU CAN!
YOU REALLY CAN, CHIZURU!!
SAY IT ONE MORE TIME...
SPIN
GRANDAD...!
THAT'S A PROMISE!
GRAB
YA HEAR ME, CHIZURU?!
GRANDAD ...!

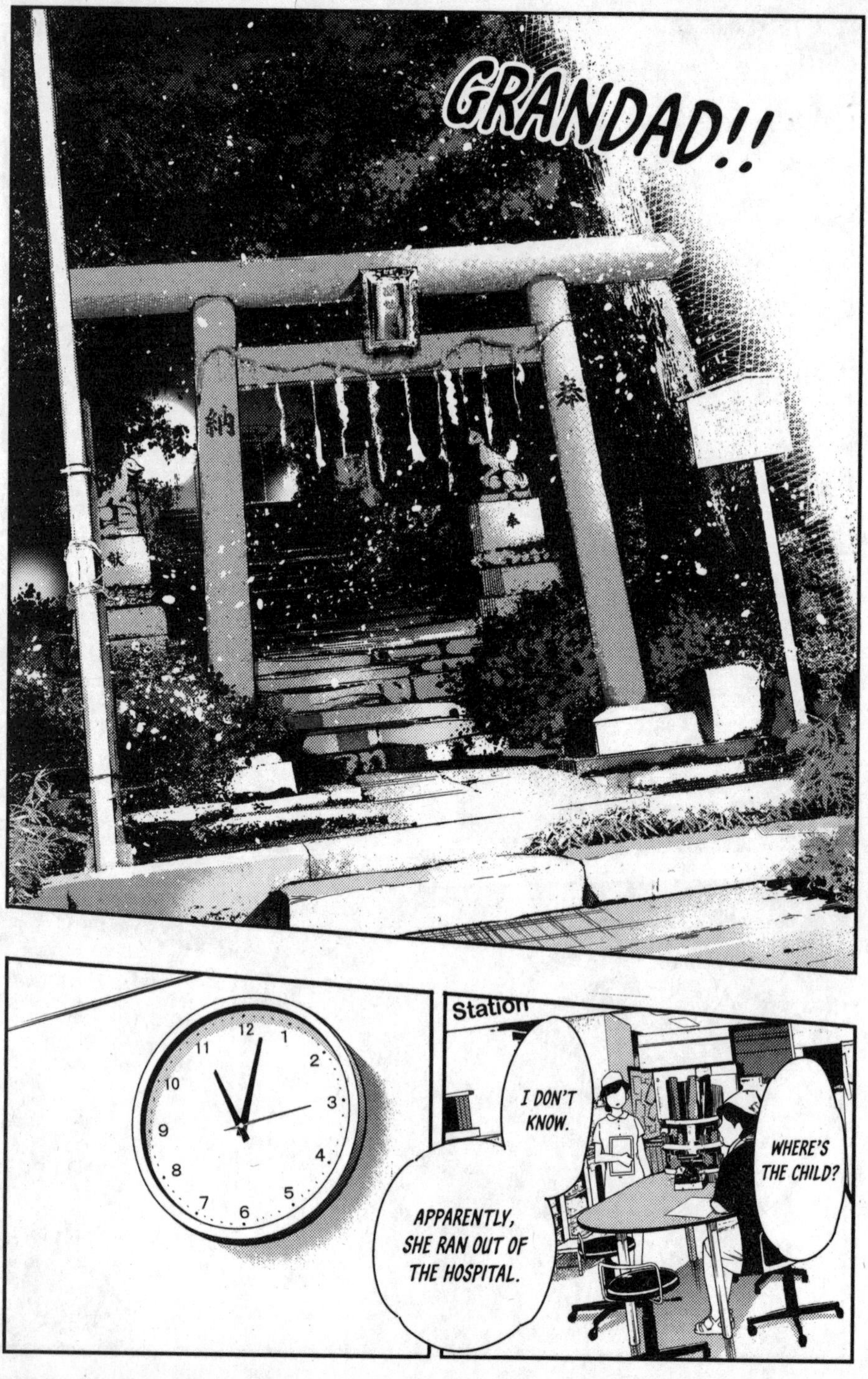
GRANDAD!!
Station
WHERE'S THE CHILD?
I DON'T KNOW.
APPARENTLY, SHE RAN OUT OF THE HOSPITAL.

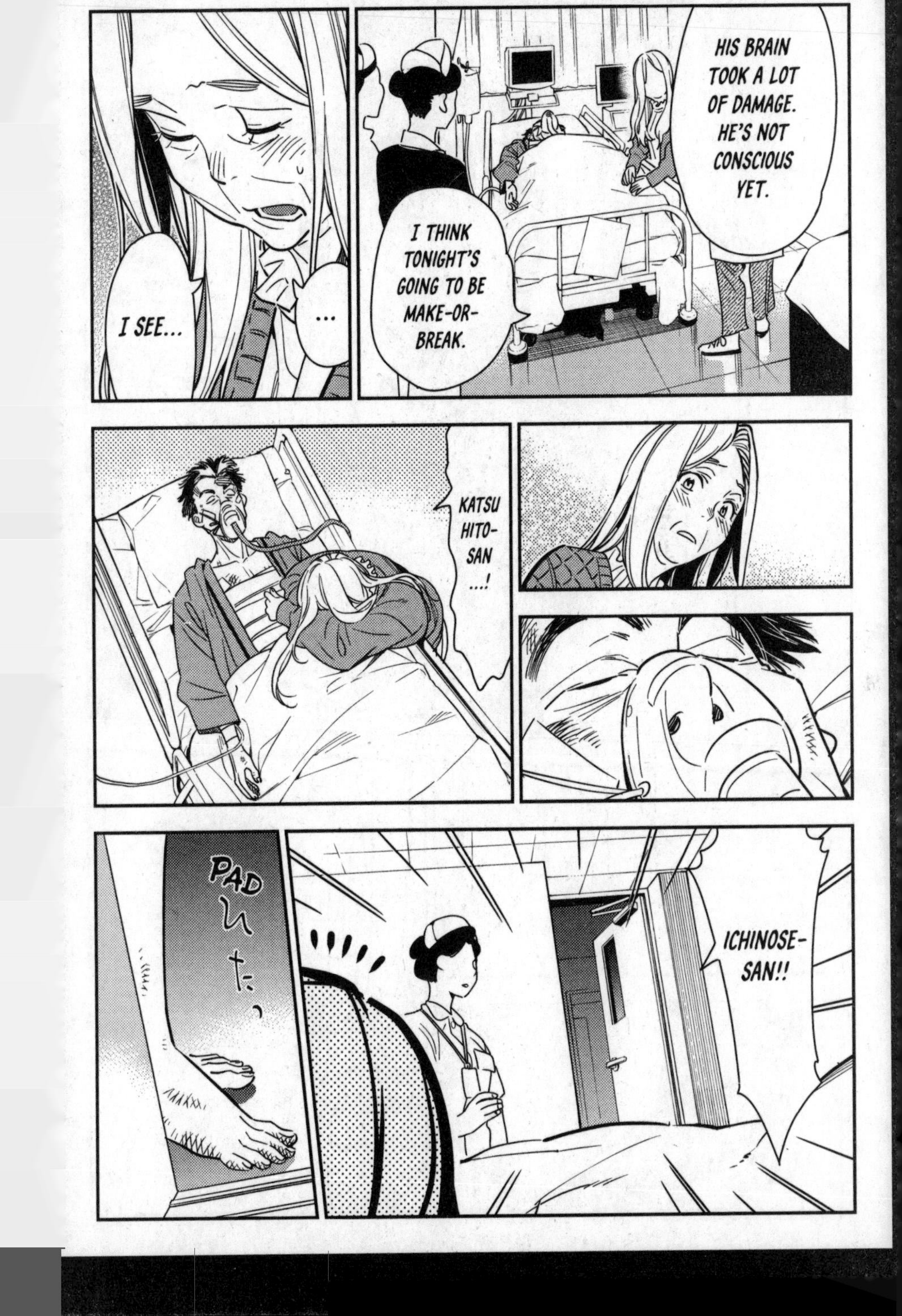
HIS BRAIN TOOK A LOT OF DAMAGE. HE'S NOT CONSCIOUS YET.
I THINK TONIGHT'S GOING TO BE MAKE-OR-BREAK.
...
I SEE...
KATSUHITO-SAN ...!
ICHINOSE-SAN!!
!!!!!
PAD
ひた、

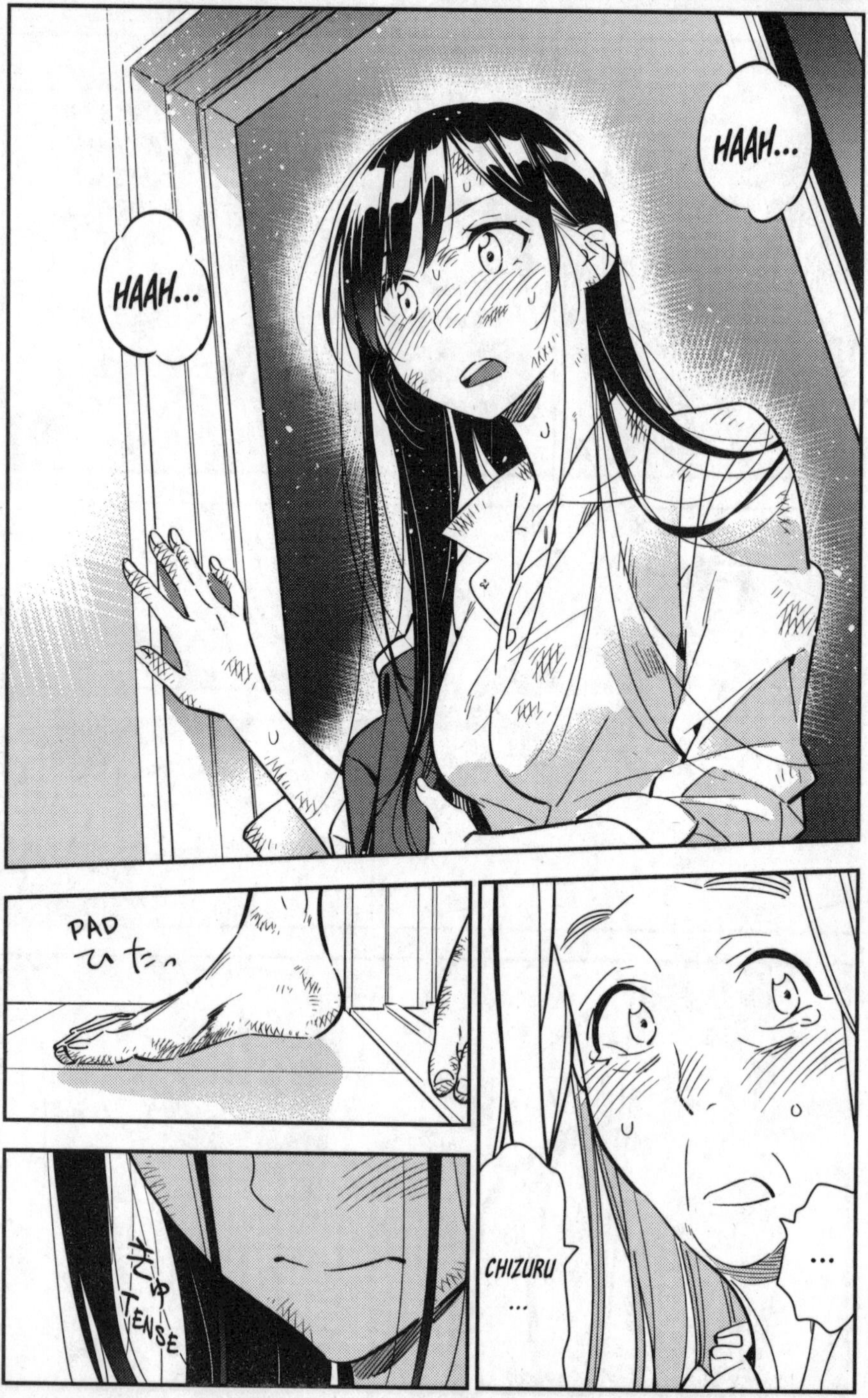
HAAH...
HAAH...
...
CHIZURU
...
PAD
ひた
TENSE

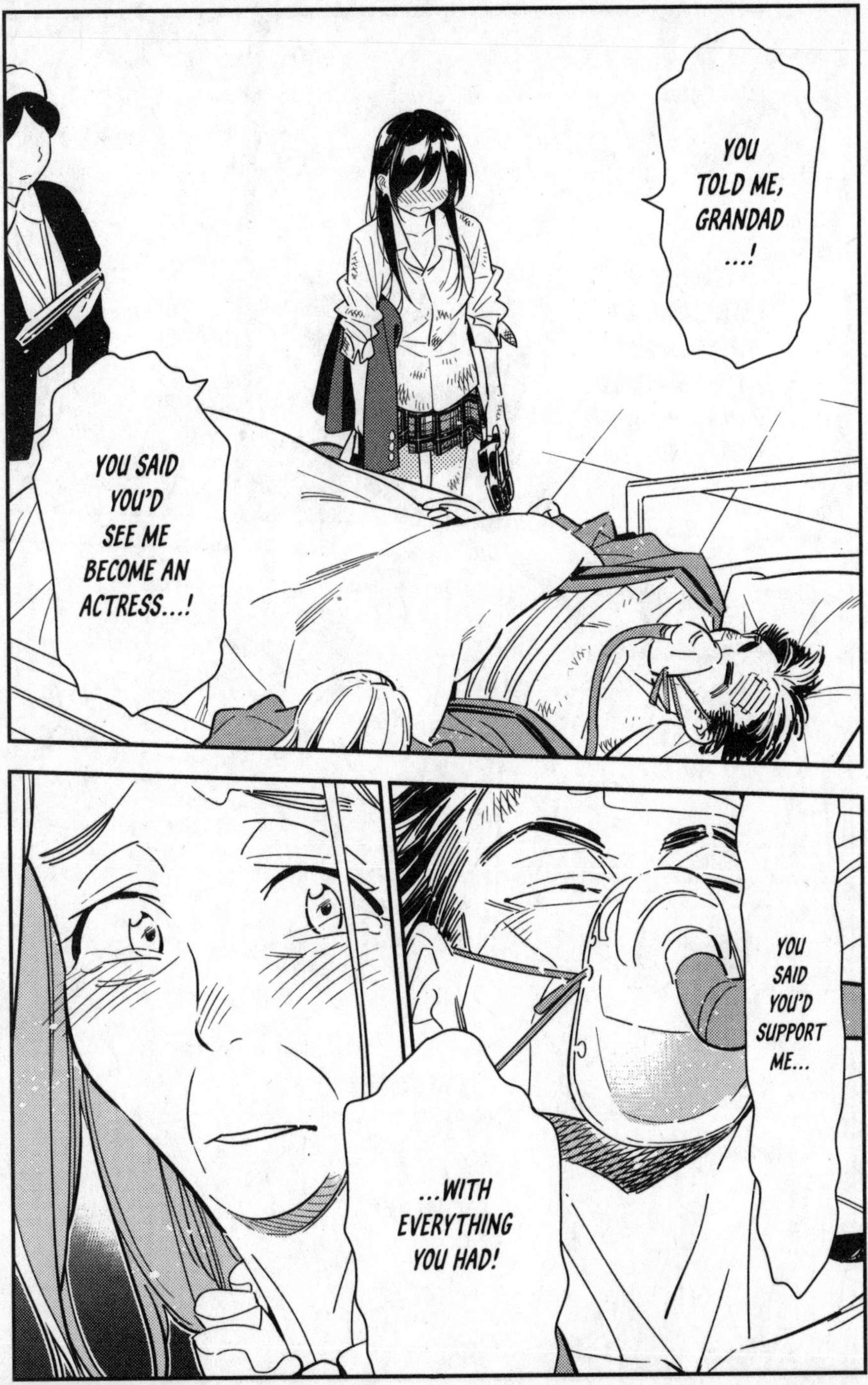
YOU TOLD ME, GRANDAD...!
YOU SAID YOU'D SEE ME BECOME AN ACTRESS...!
YOU SAID YOU'D SUPPORT ME...
...WITH EVERYTHING YOU HAD!

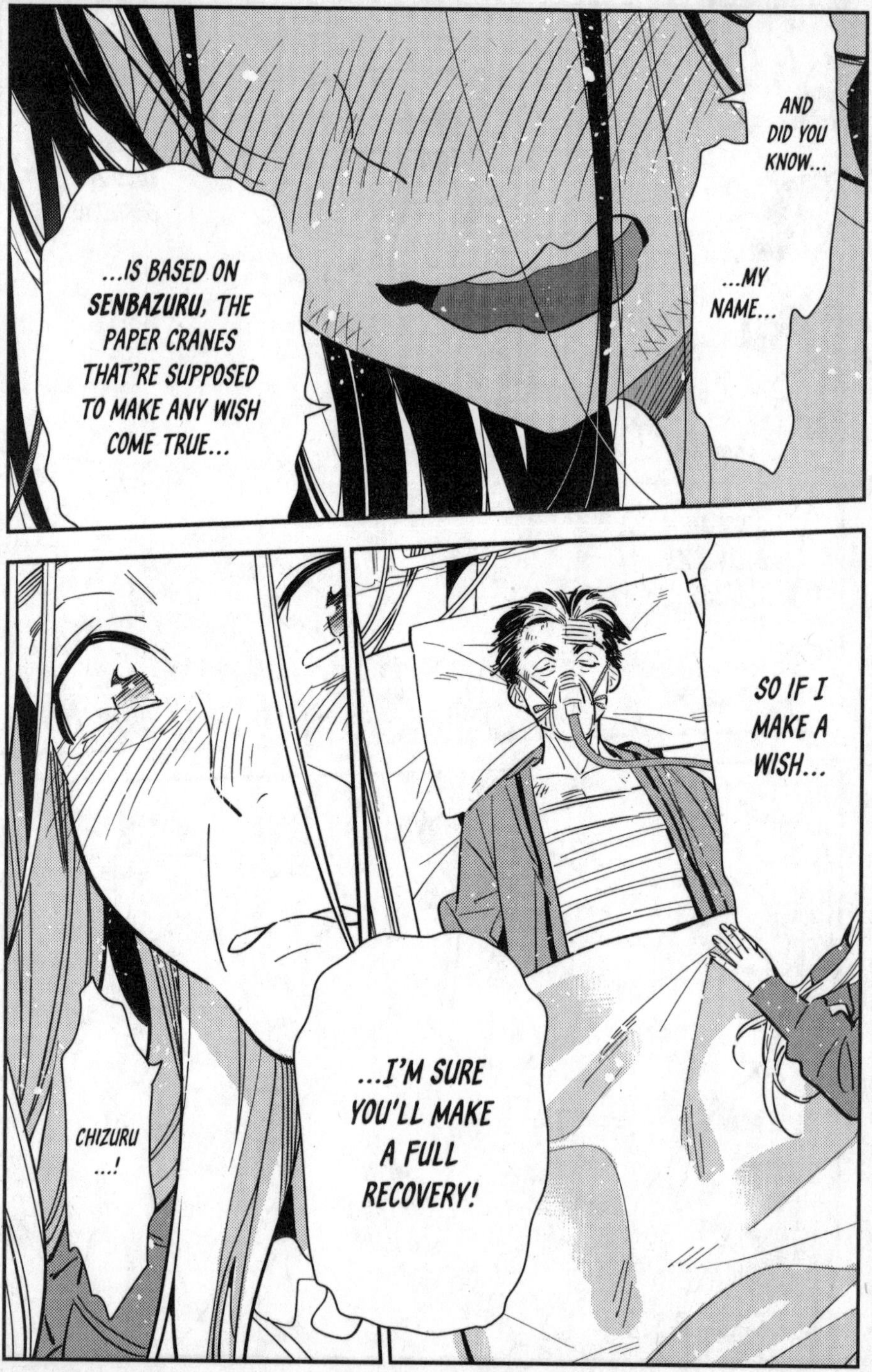
AND DID YOU KNOW...
...MY NAME...
...IS BASED ON SENBAZURU, THE PAPER CRANES THAT'RE SUPPOSED TO MAKE ANY WISH COME TRUE...
SO IF I MAKE A WISH...
...I'M SURE YOU'LL MAKE A FULL RECOVERY!
CHIZURU ...!

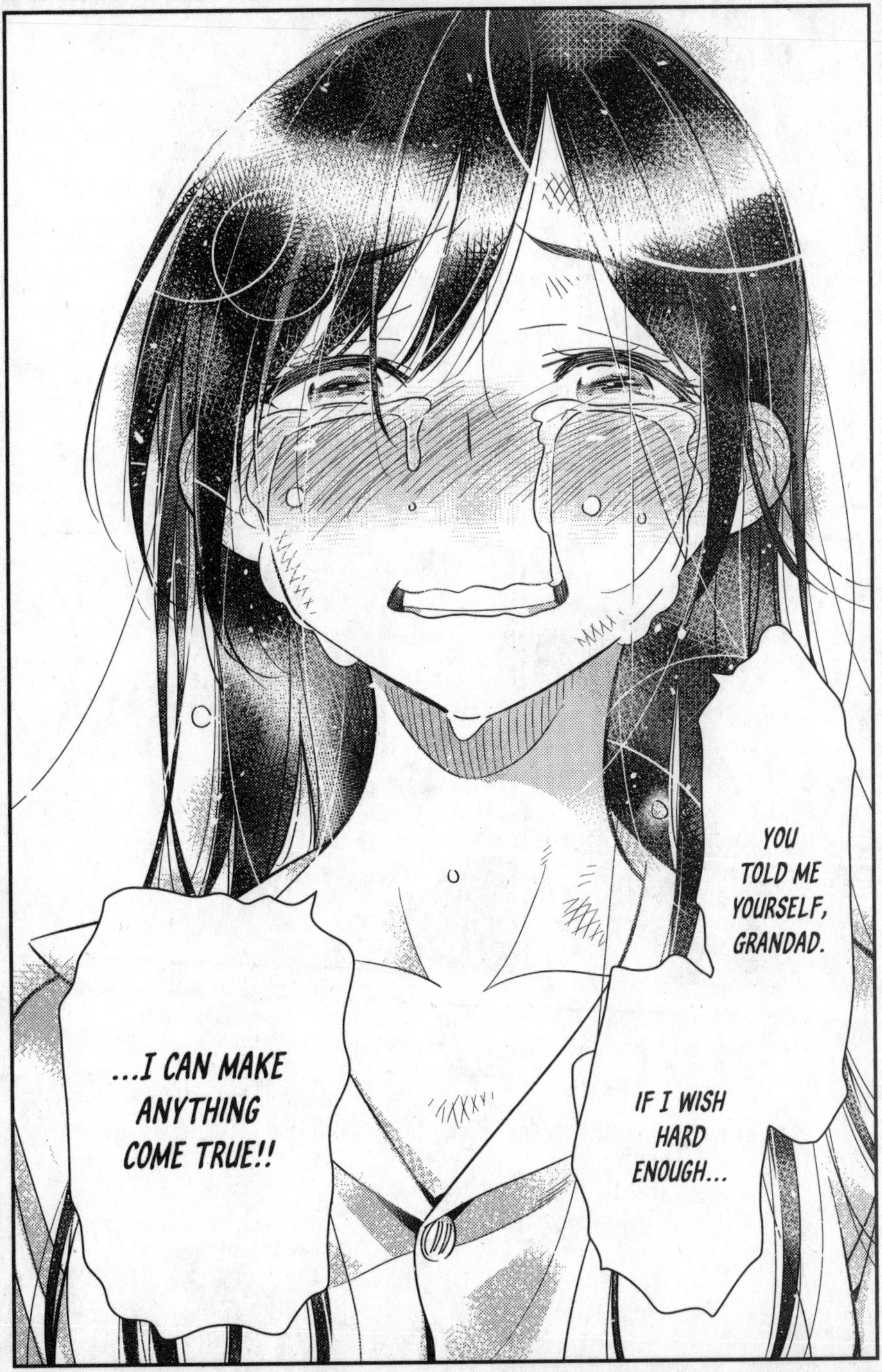
YOU TOLD ME YOURSELF, GRANDAD.
IF I WISH HARD ENOUGH...
...I CAN MAKE ANYTHING COME TRUE!!

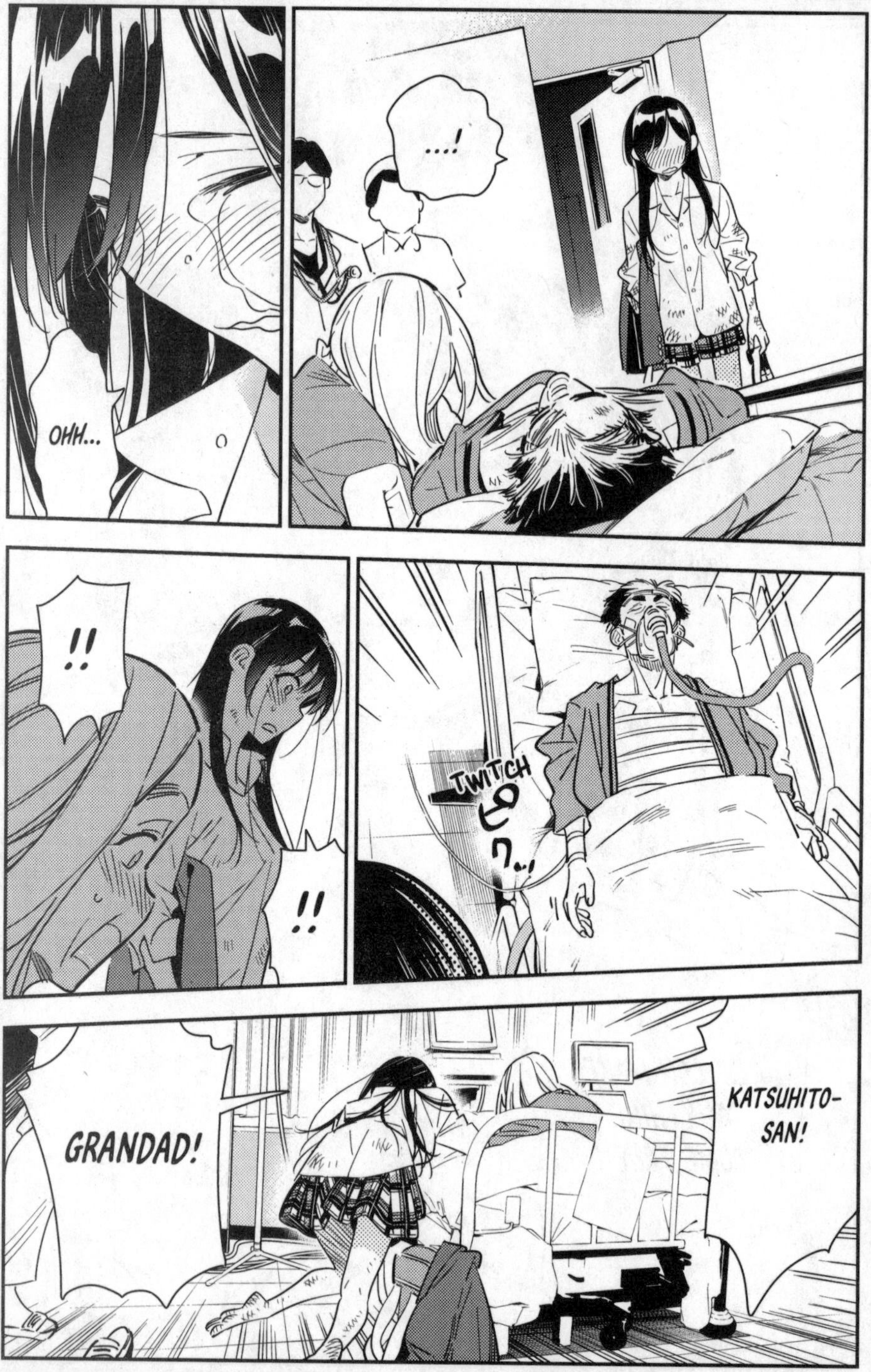
...!
OHH...
TWITCH
ピク...
!!
!!
KATSUHITO-SAN!
GRANDAD!

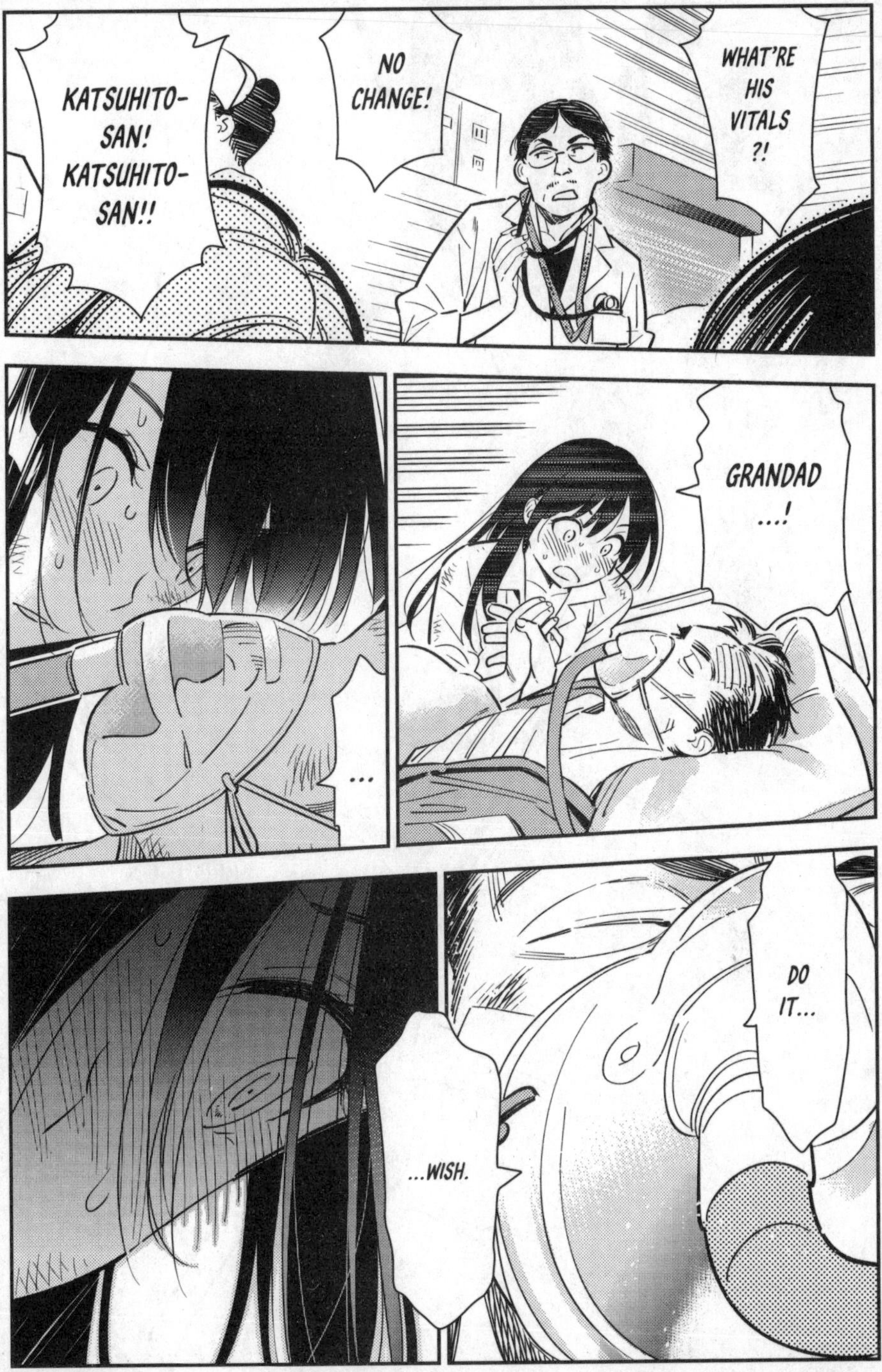
WHAT'RE HIS VITALS ?!
NO CHANGE!
KATSUHITO-SAN! KATSUHITO-SAN!!
GRANDAD ...!
...
DO IT...
...WISH.

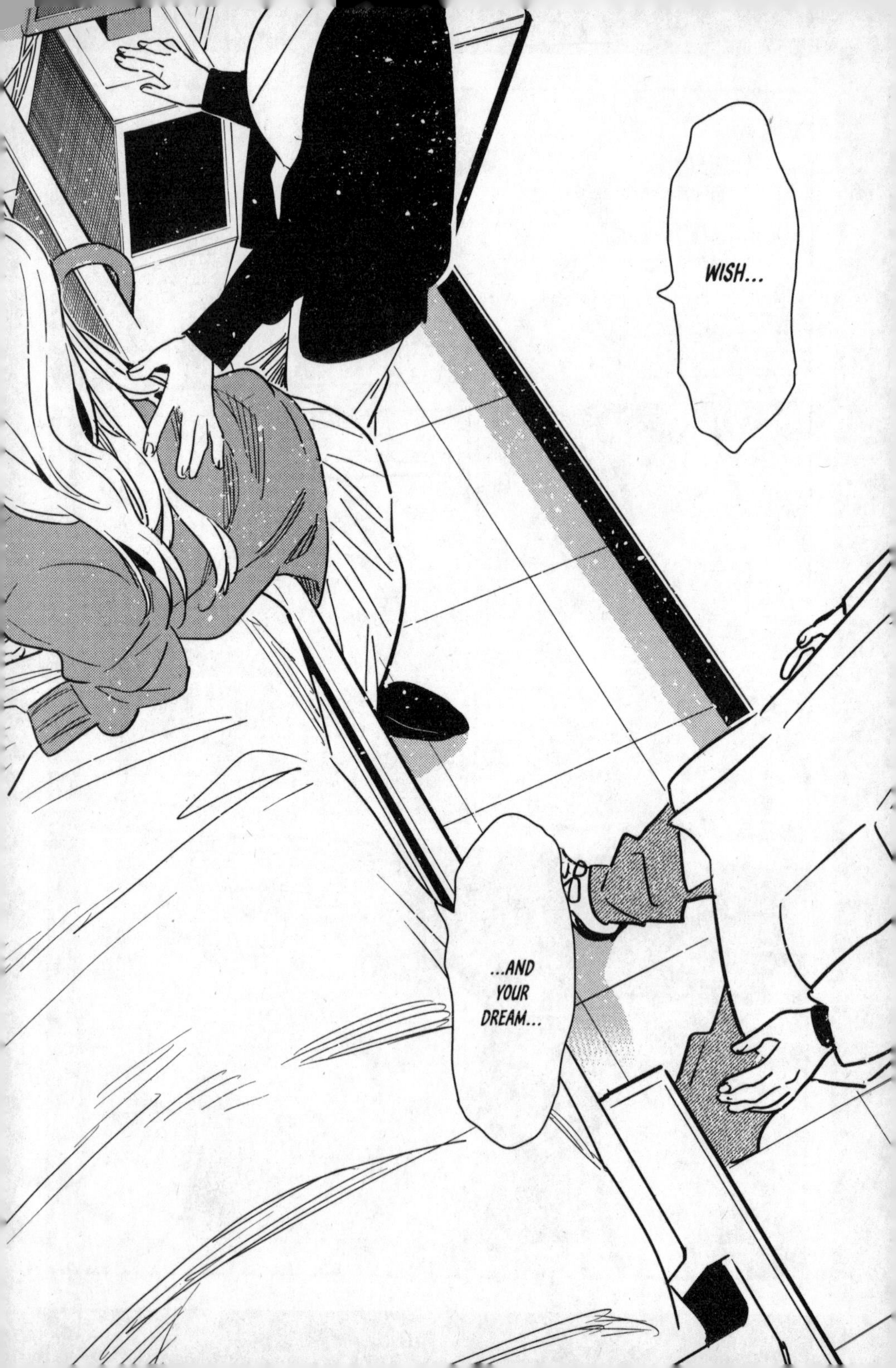
WISH...
...AND YOUR DREAM...

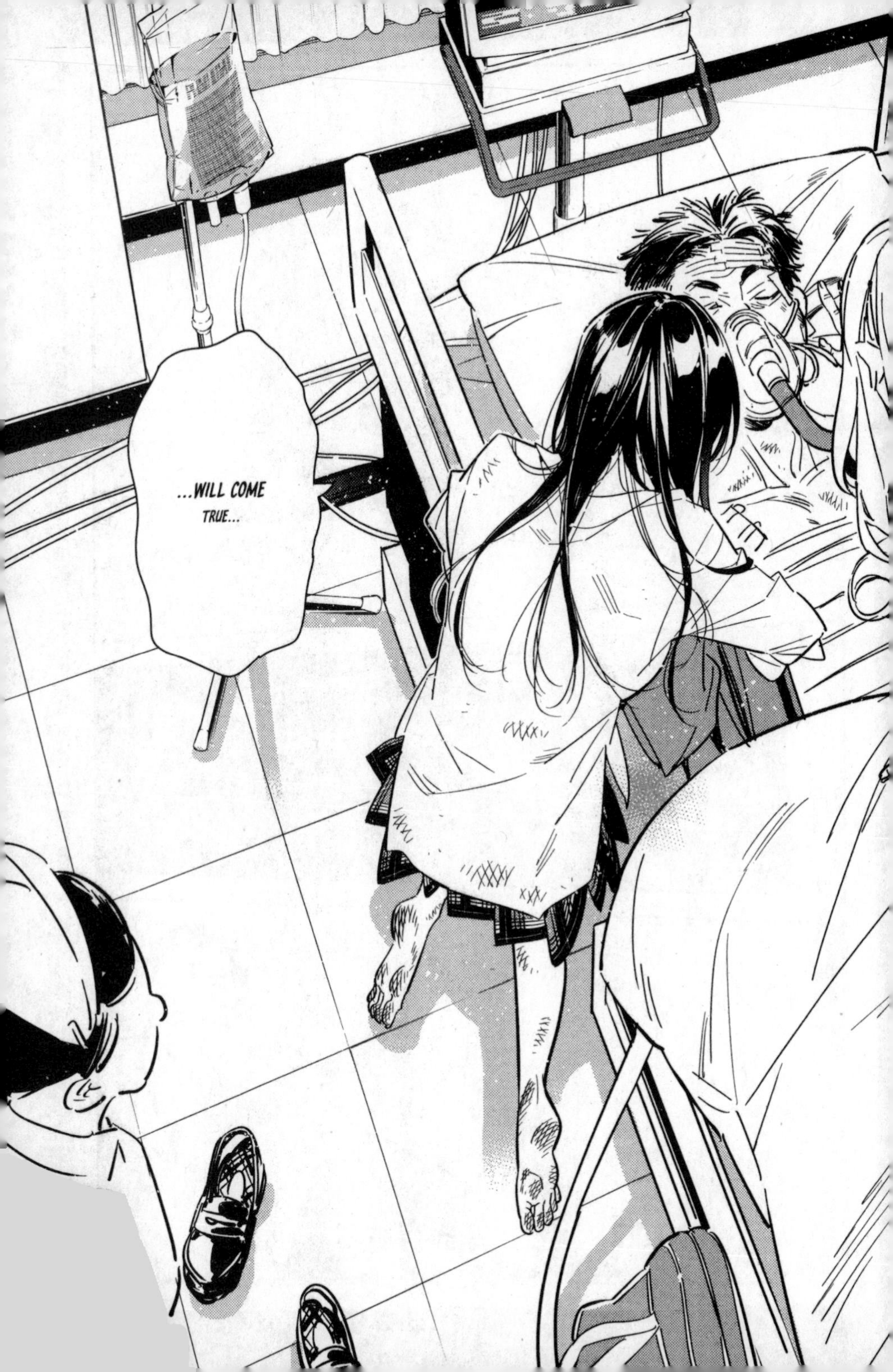
...WILL COME TRUE...

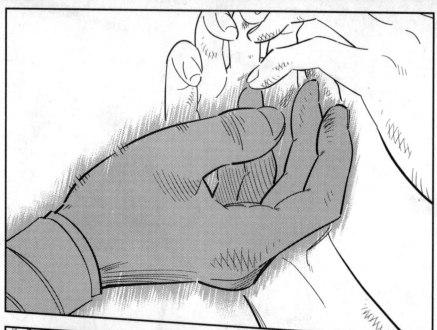

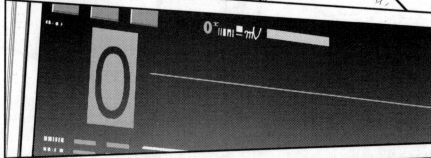

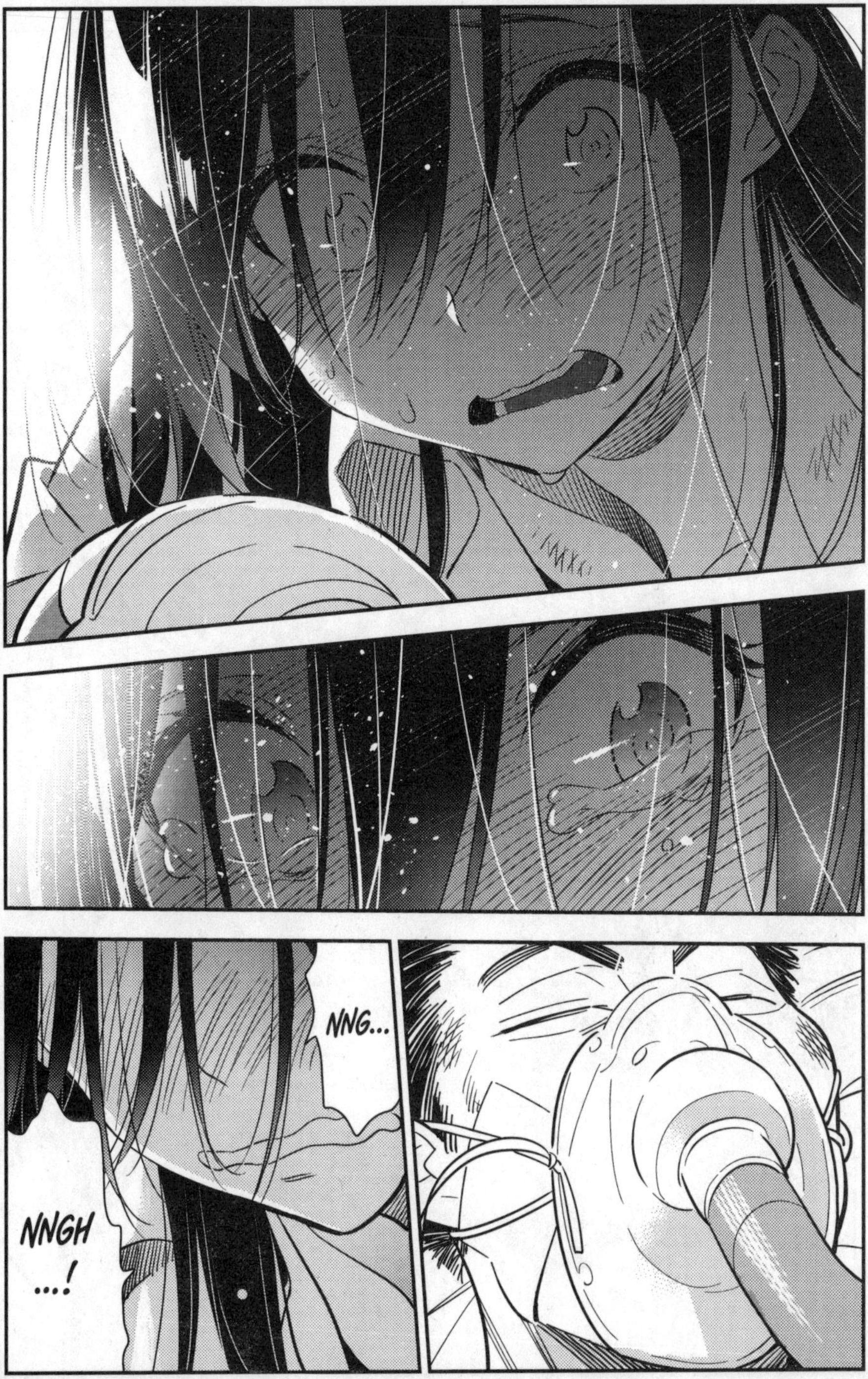
NNG...
NNGH ...!

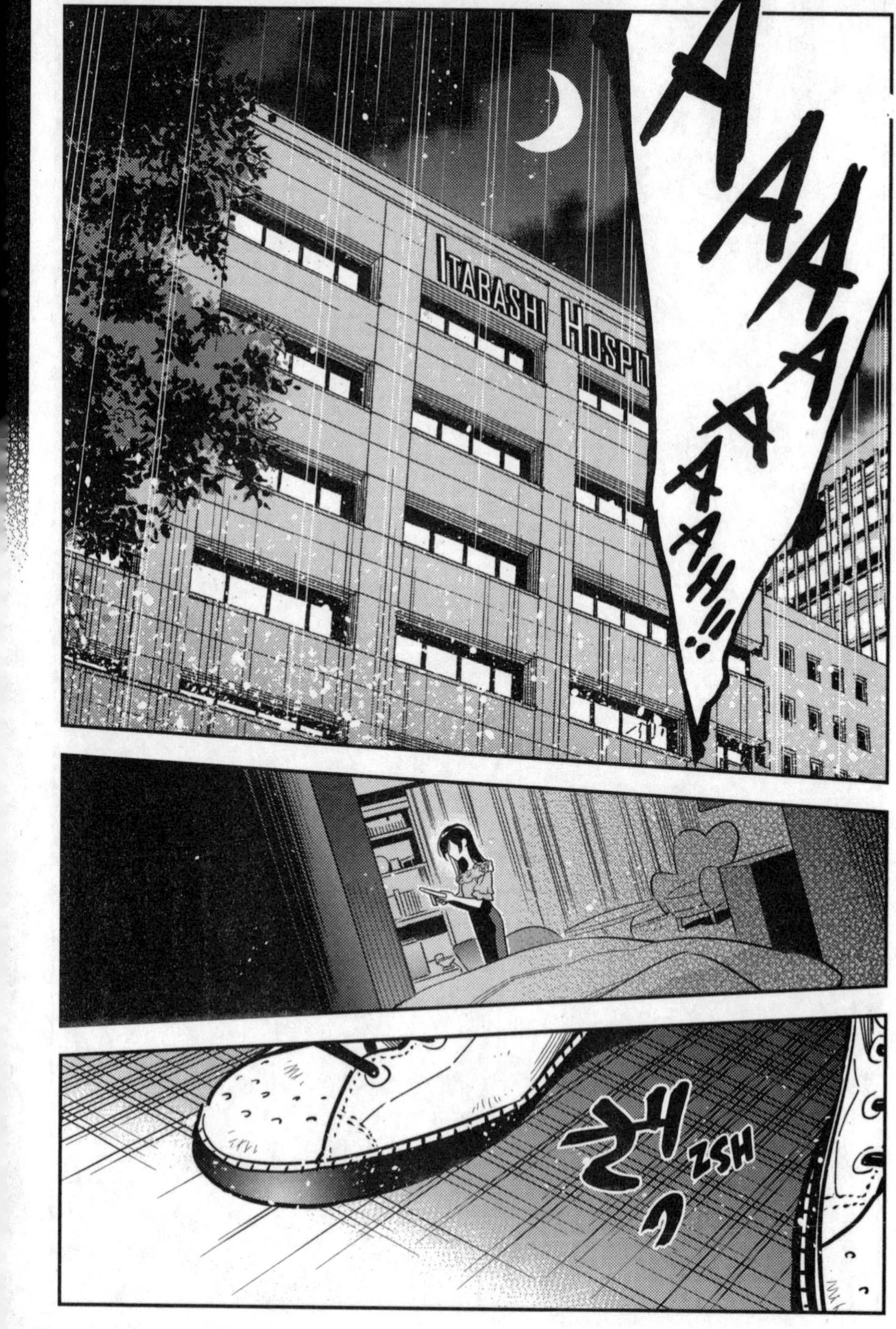
AAAAAAAAH!!!
ITABASHI HOSPIT

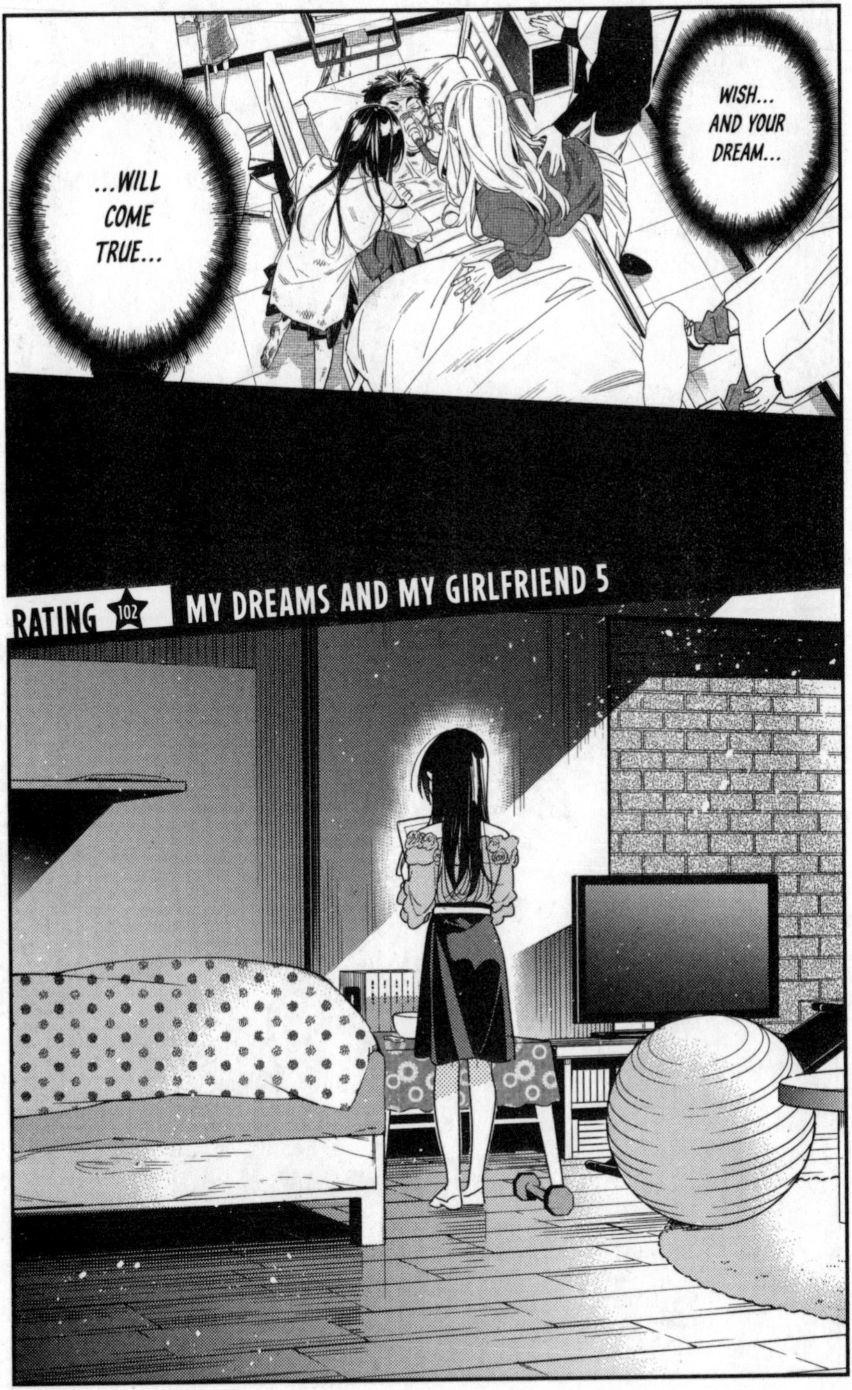
WISH... AND YOUR DREAM...
...WILL COME TRUE...
RATING 102
MY DREAMS AND MY GIRLFRIEND 5

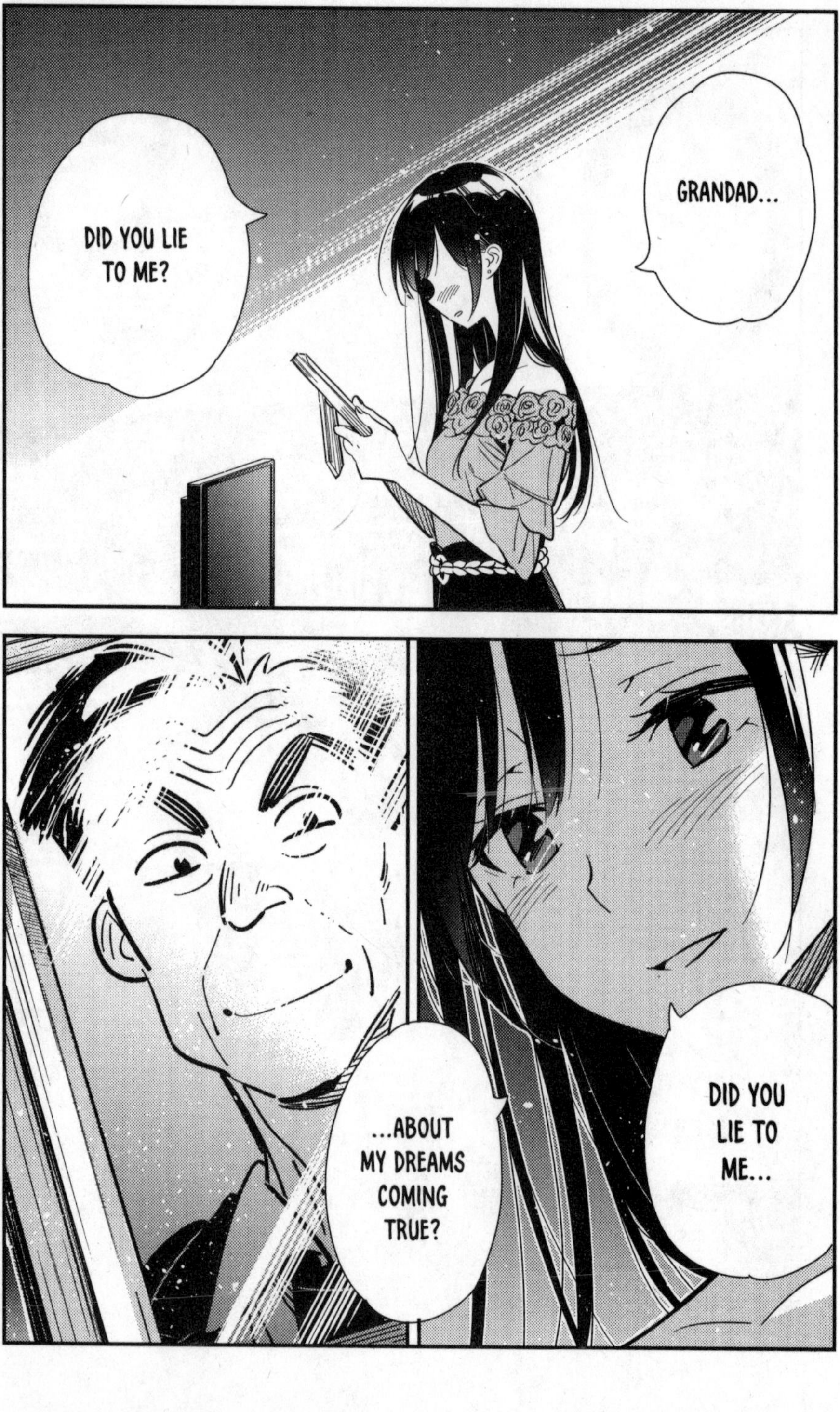
GRANDAD...
DID YOU LIE TO ME?
DID YOU LIE TO ME...
...ABOUT MY DREAMS COMING TRUE?

...

...!

SNIFFLE

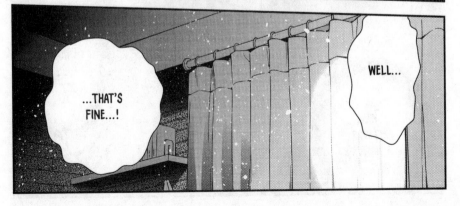

...THAT'S
FINE...!

WELL...

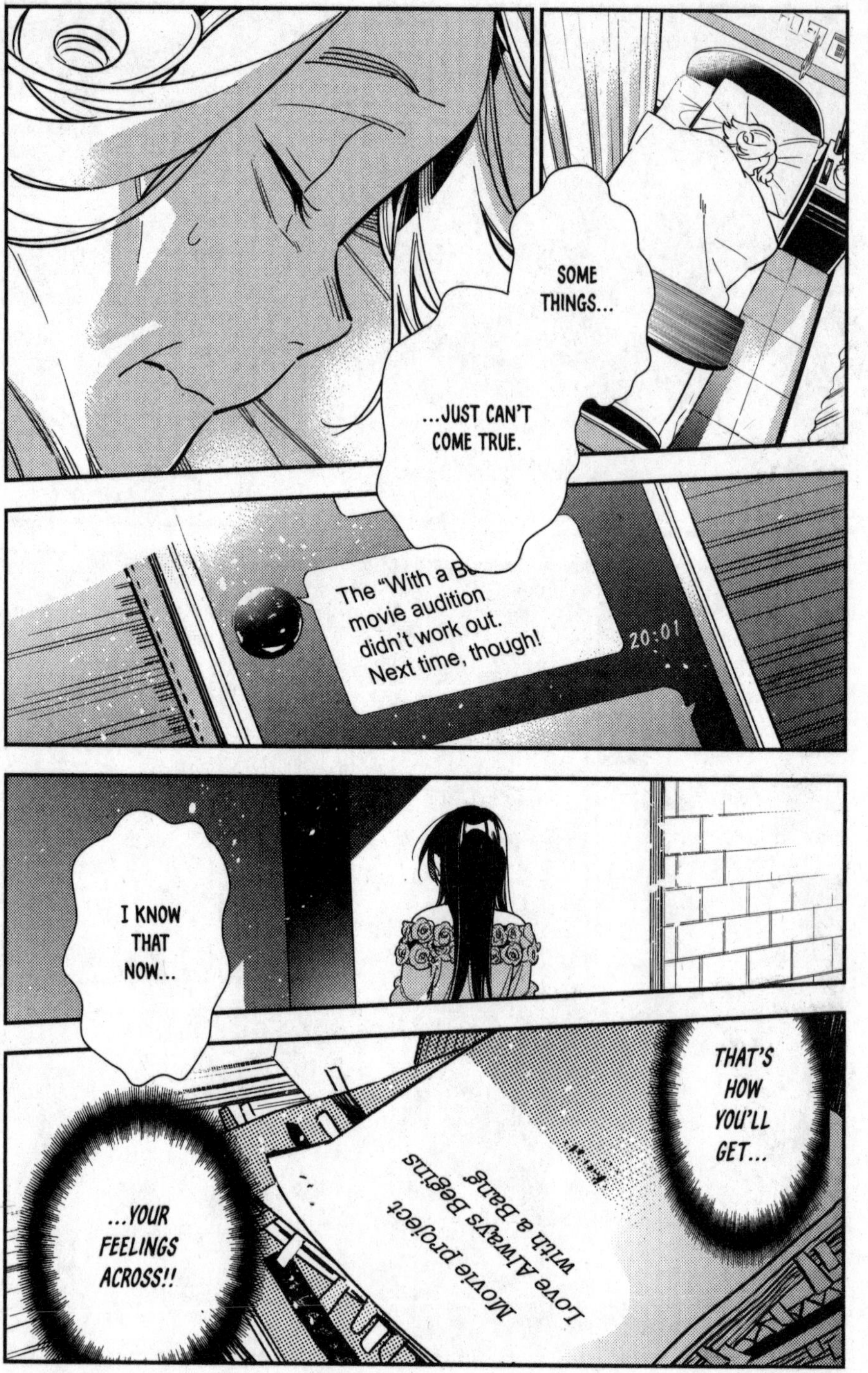
SOME THINGS...
...JUST CAN'T COME TRUE.
The “With a B
movie audition didn't work out. Next time, though!
20:01
I KNOW THAT NOW...
THAT'S HOW YOU'LL GET...
...YOUR FEELINGS ACROSS!!
Movie project
Love Always Begins with a Bang

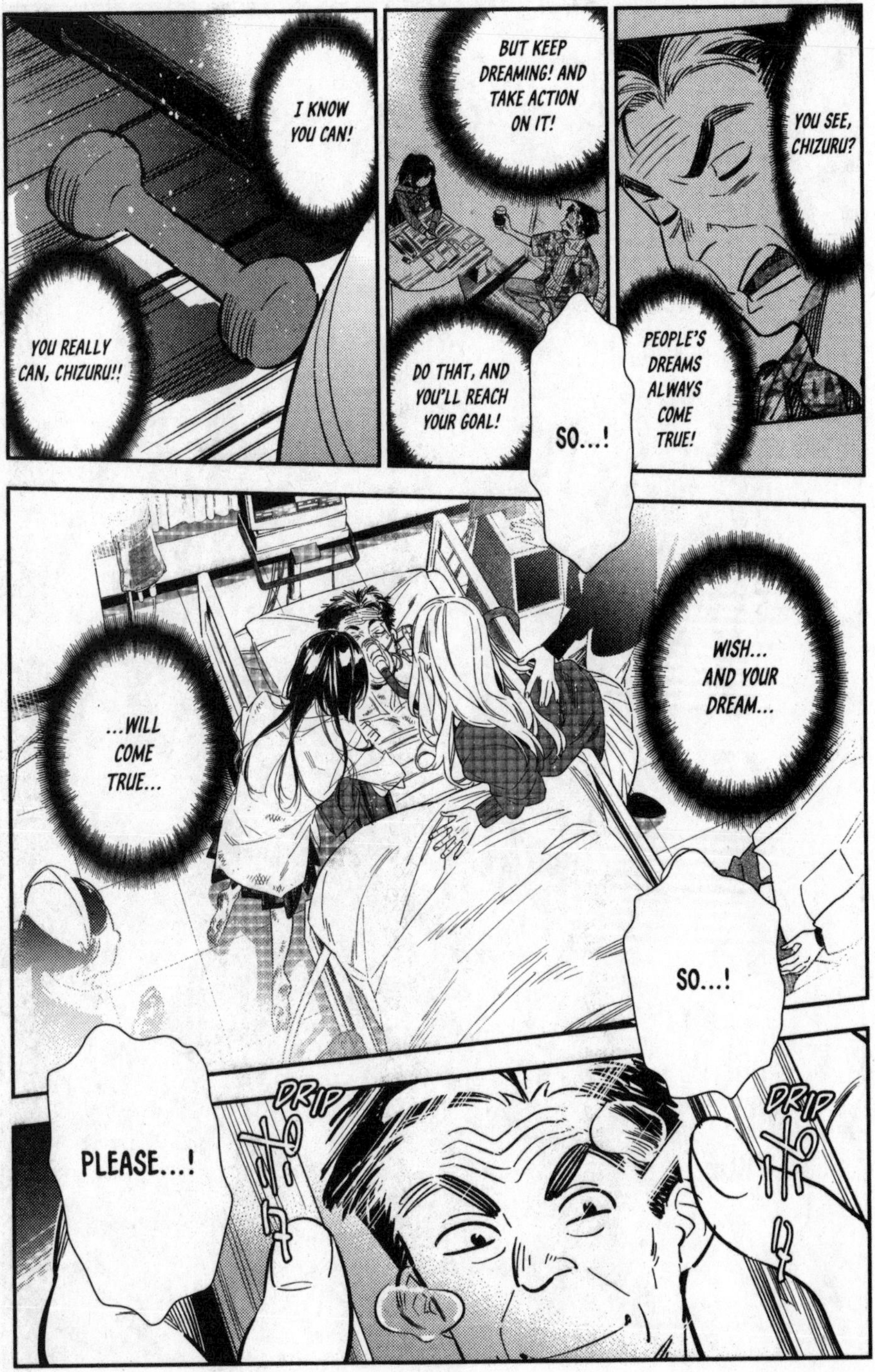
YOU SEE, CHIZURU?
PEOPLE'S DREAMS ALWAYS COME TRUE!
BUT KEEP DREAMING! AND TAKE ACTION ON IT!
SO...!
DO THAT, AND YOU'LL REACH YOUR GOAL!
I KNOW YOU CAN!
YOU REALLY CAN, CHIZURU!!
WISH... AND YOUR DREAM...
...WILL COME TRUE...
SO...!
DRIP
PLEASE...!
DRIP

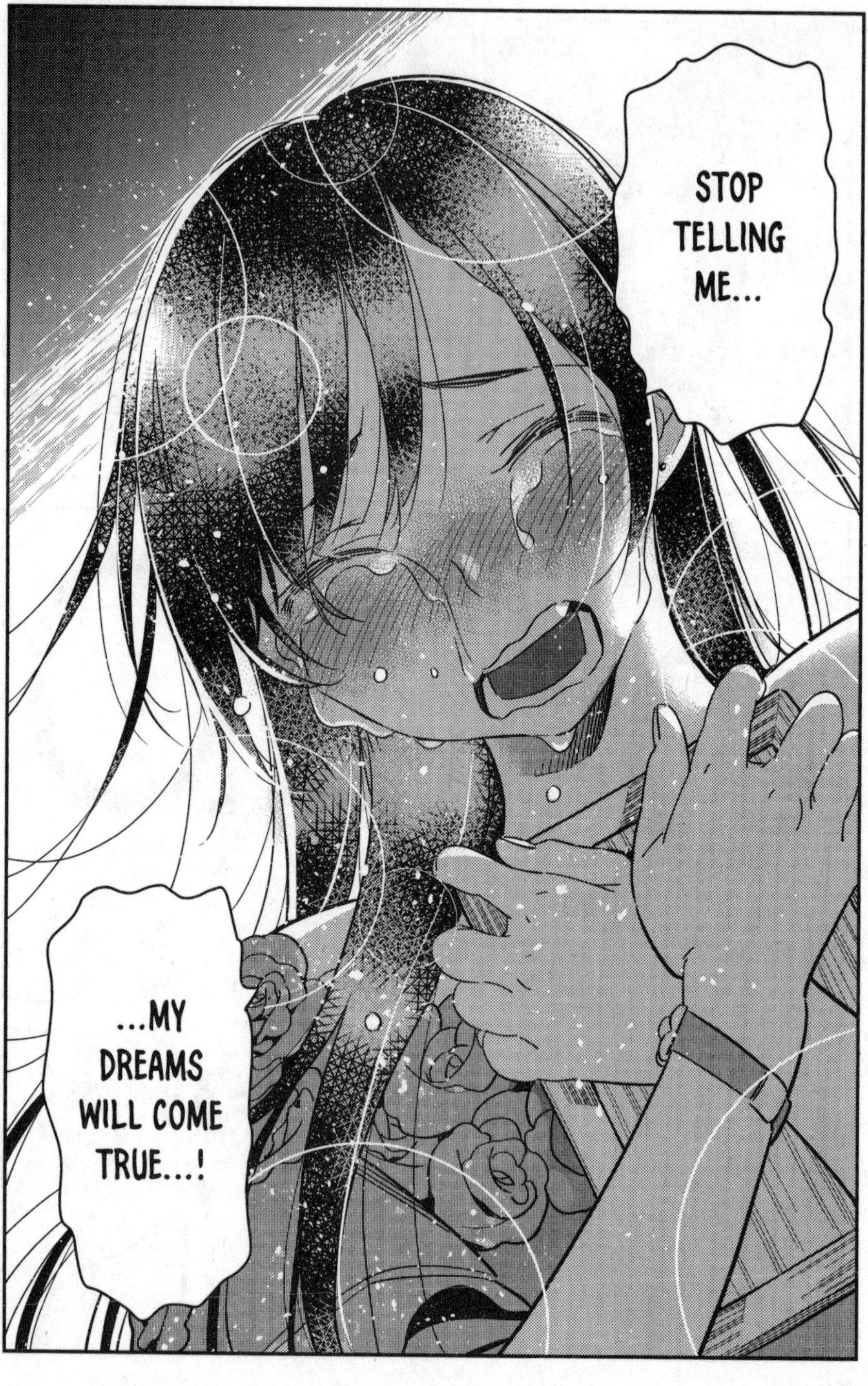
STOP TELLING ME...
...MY DREAMS WILL COME TRUE...!

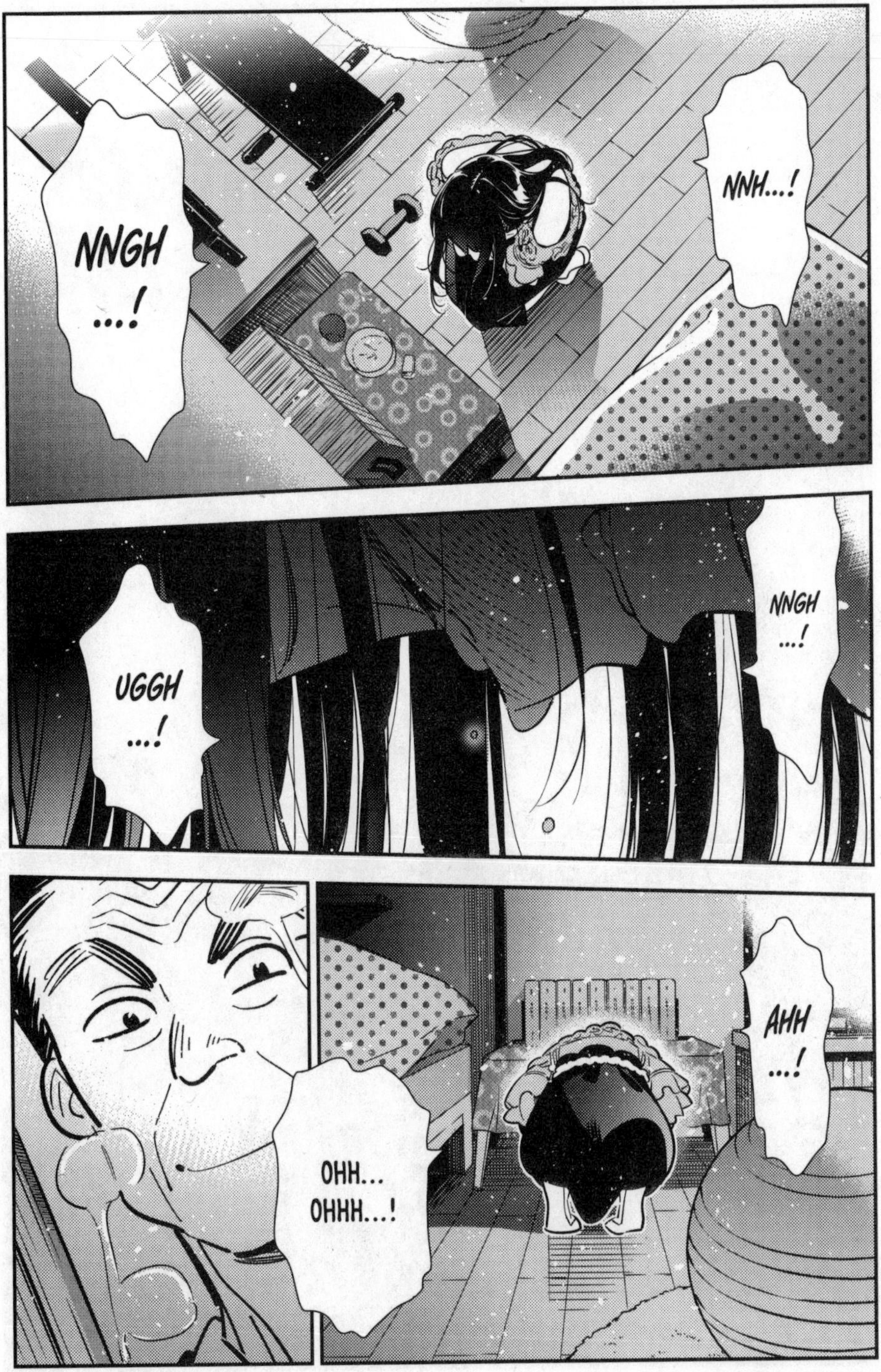
NNH...!
NNGH ...!
NNGH ...!
UGGH ...!
AHH ...!
OHH... OHHH...!

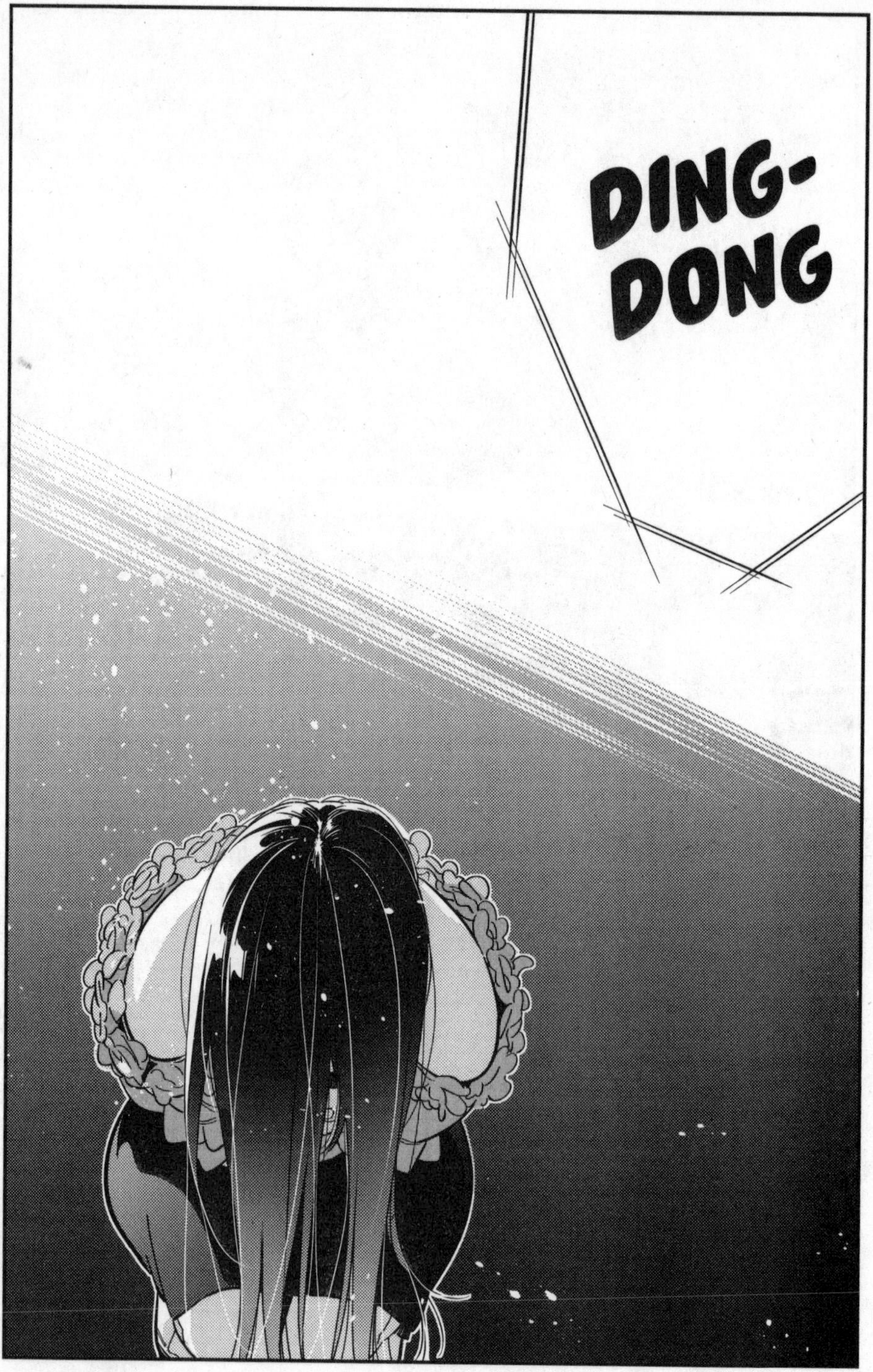
DING-
DONG

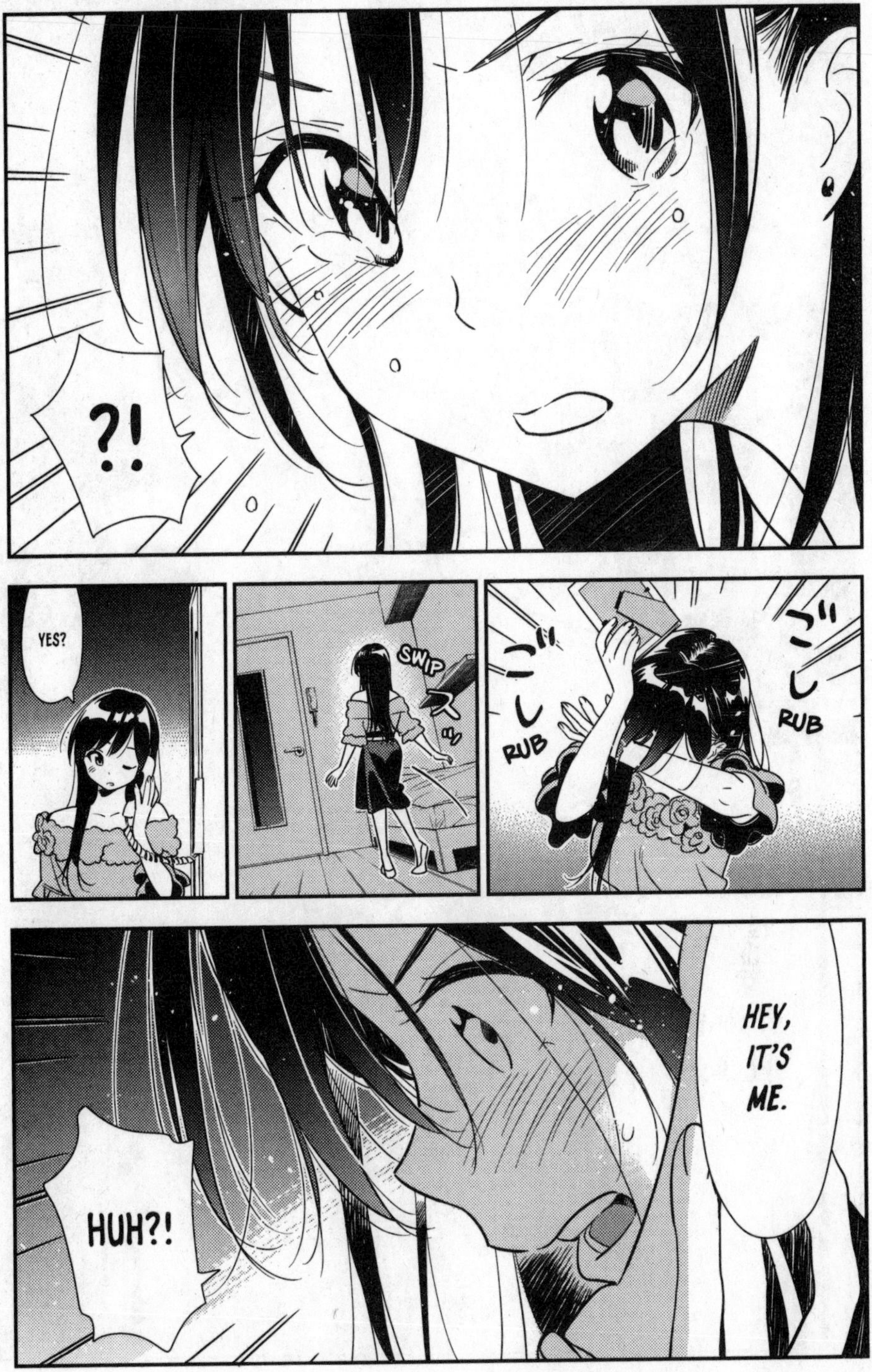
?!
ごし
RUB
ごし
RUB
SWIP
ス
YES?
HEY, IT'S ME.
HUH?!

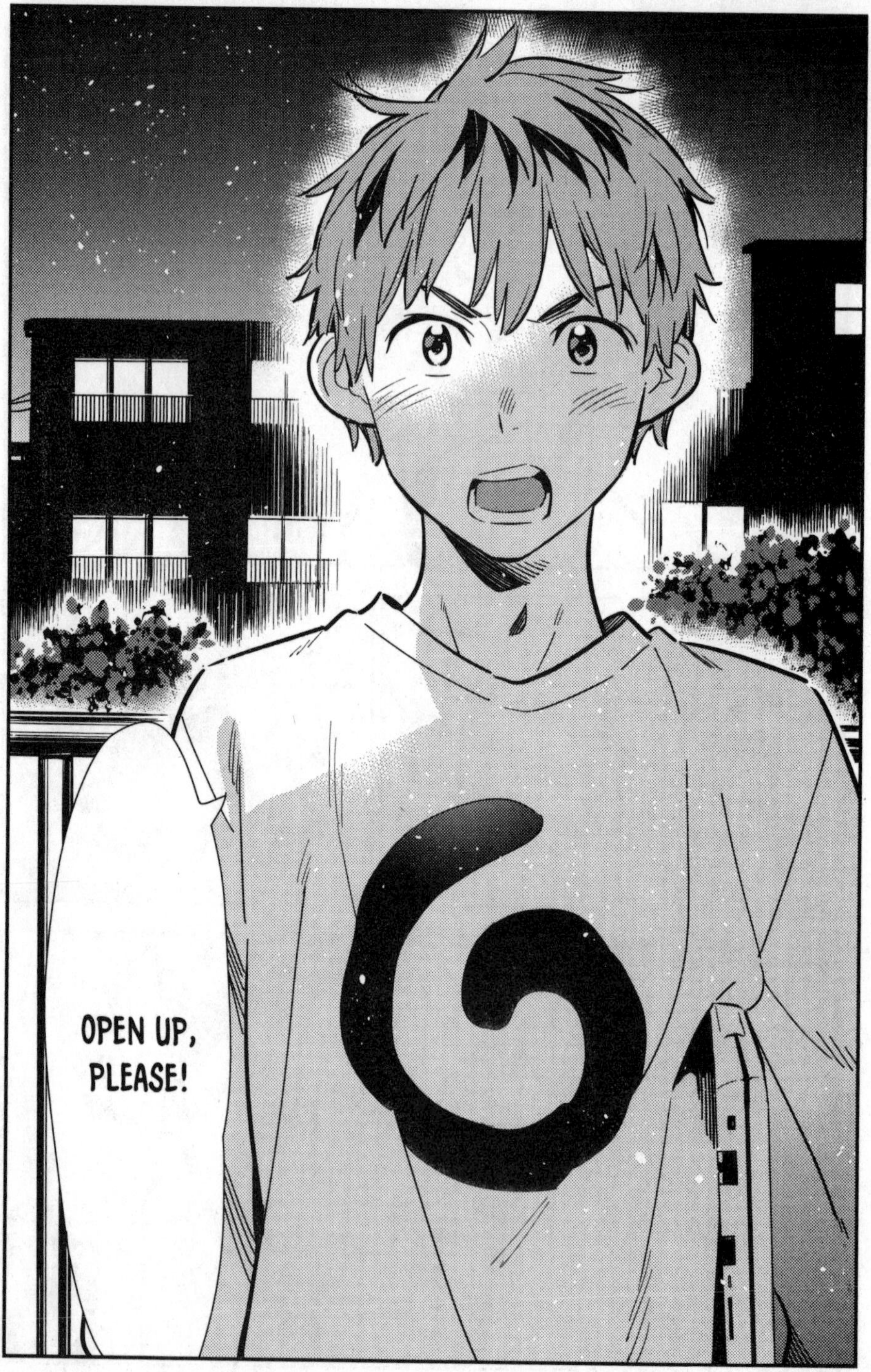
OPEN UP, PLEASE!

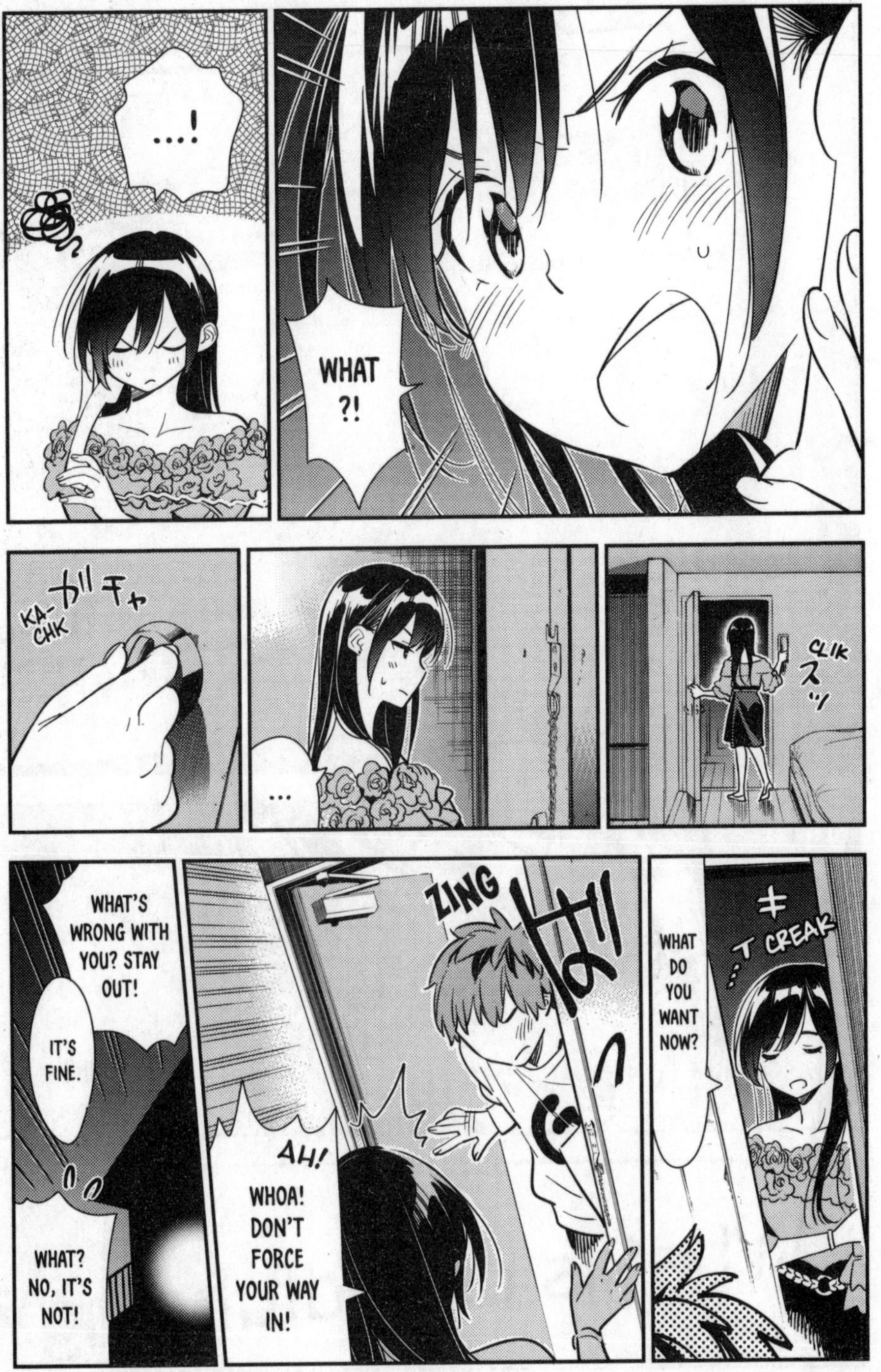
WHAT ?!
...!
CLIK
スッ
...
KA-CHK
ガチャ
キ
CREAK
WHAT DO YOU WANT NOW?
ZING
ばっ
AH!
WHOA! DON'T FORCE YOUR WAY IN!
WHAT'S WRONG WITH YOU? STAY OUT!
IT'S FINE.
WHAT? NO, IT'S NOT!

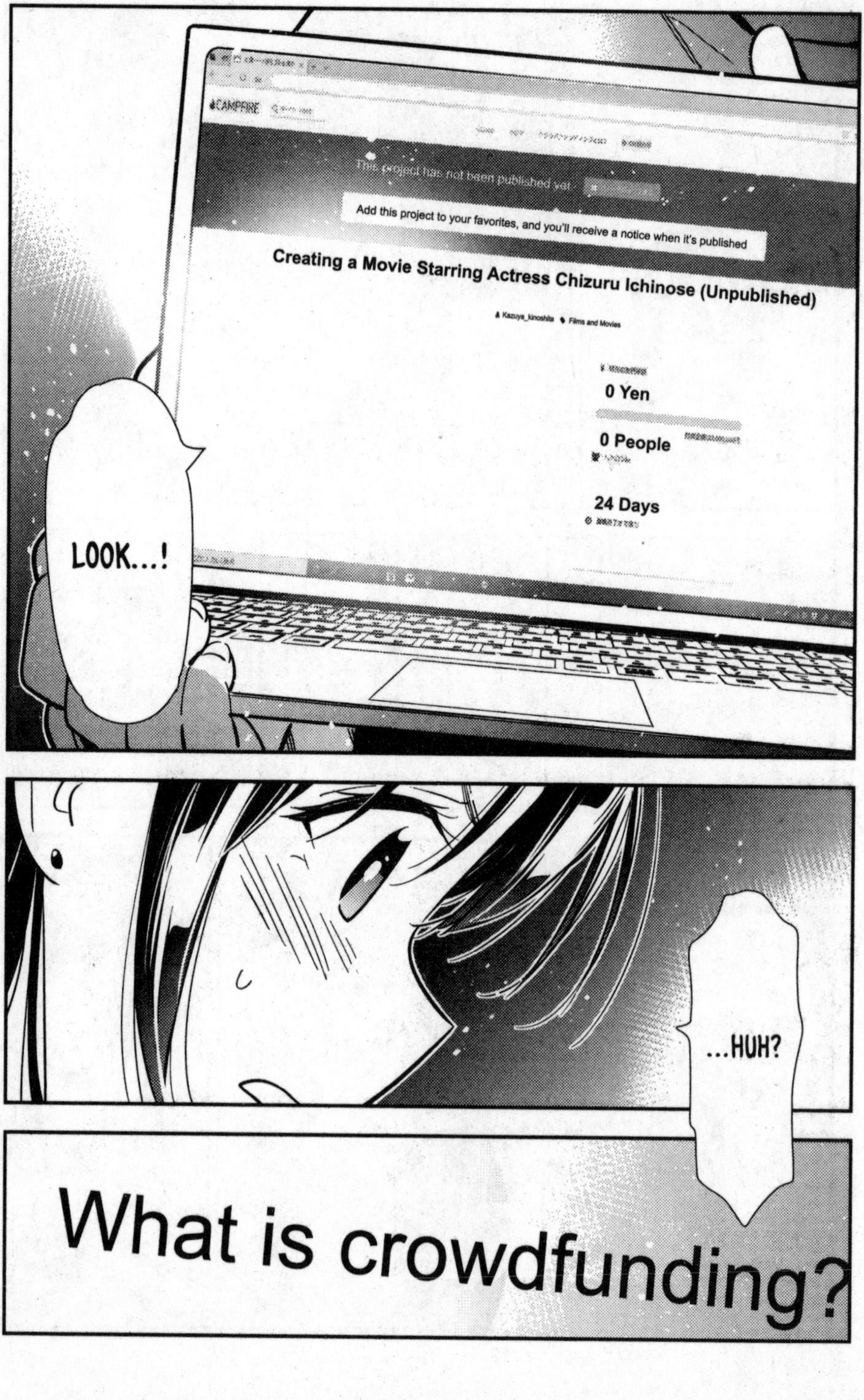
CAMPFIRE
This project has not been published yet
Add this project to your favorites, and you'll receive a notice when it's published
Creating a Movie Starring Actress Chizuru Ichinose (Unpublished)
Kazuya_kinoshita
Films and Movies
0 Yen
0 People
24 Days
LOOK...!
...HUH?
What is crowdfunding?

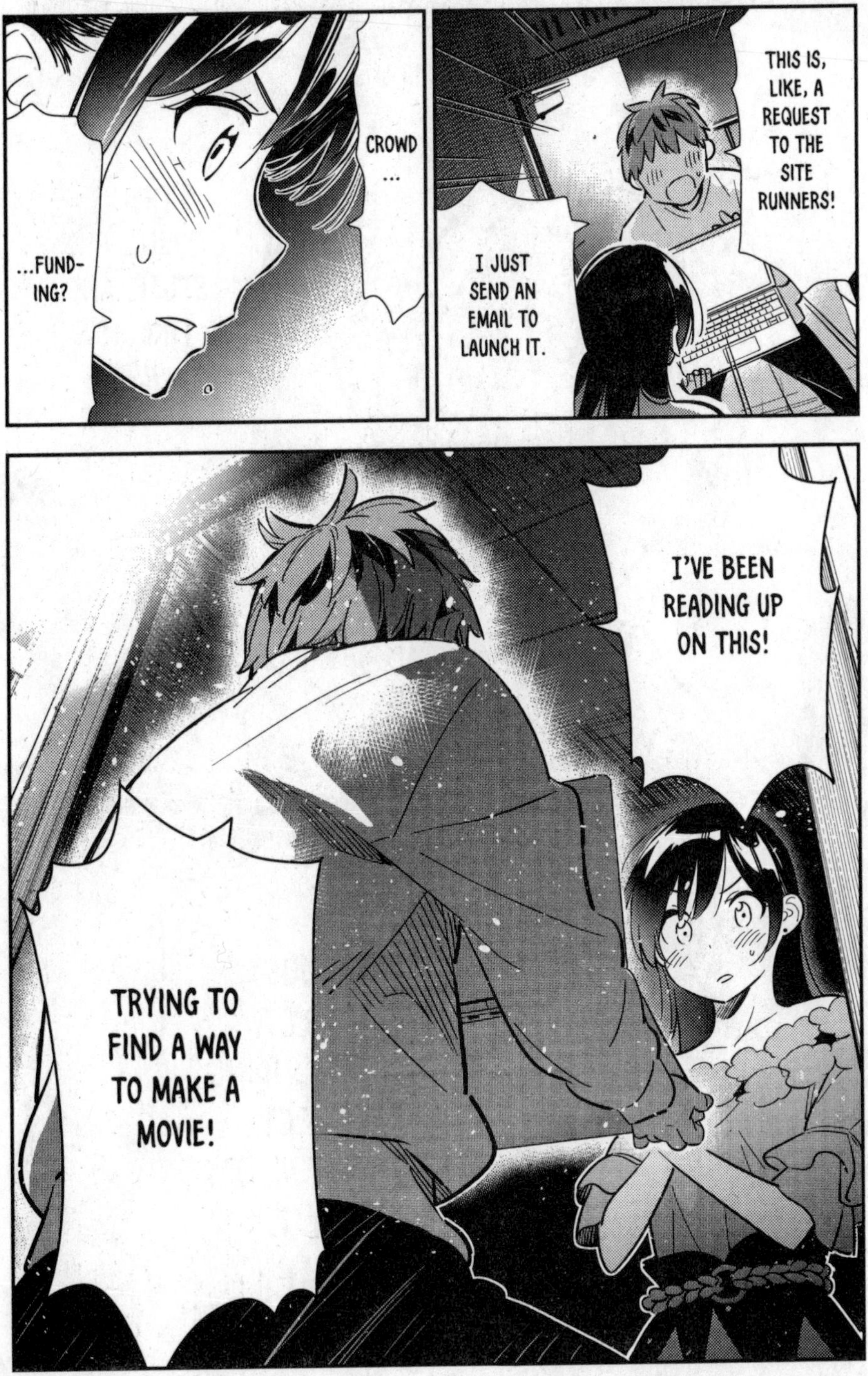
THIS IS, LIKE, A REQUEST TO THE SITE RUNNERS!
I JUST SEND AN EMAIL TO LAUNCH IT.
CROWD ...
...FUND-ING?
I'VE BEEN READING UP ON THIS!
TRYING TO FIND A WAY TO MAKE A MOVIE!

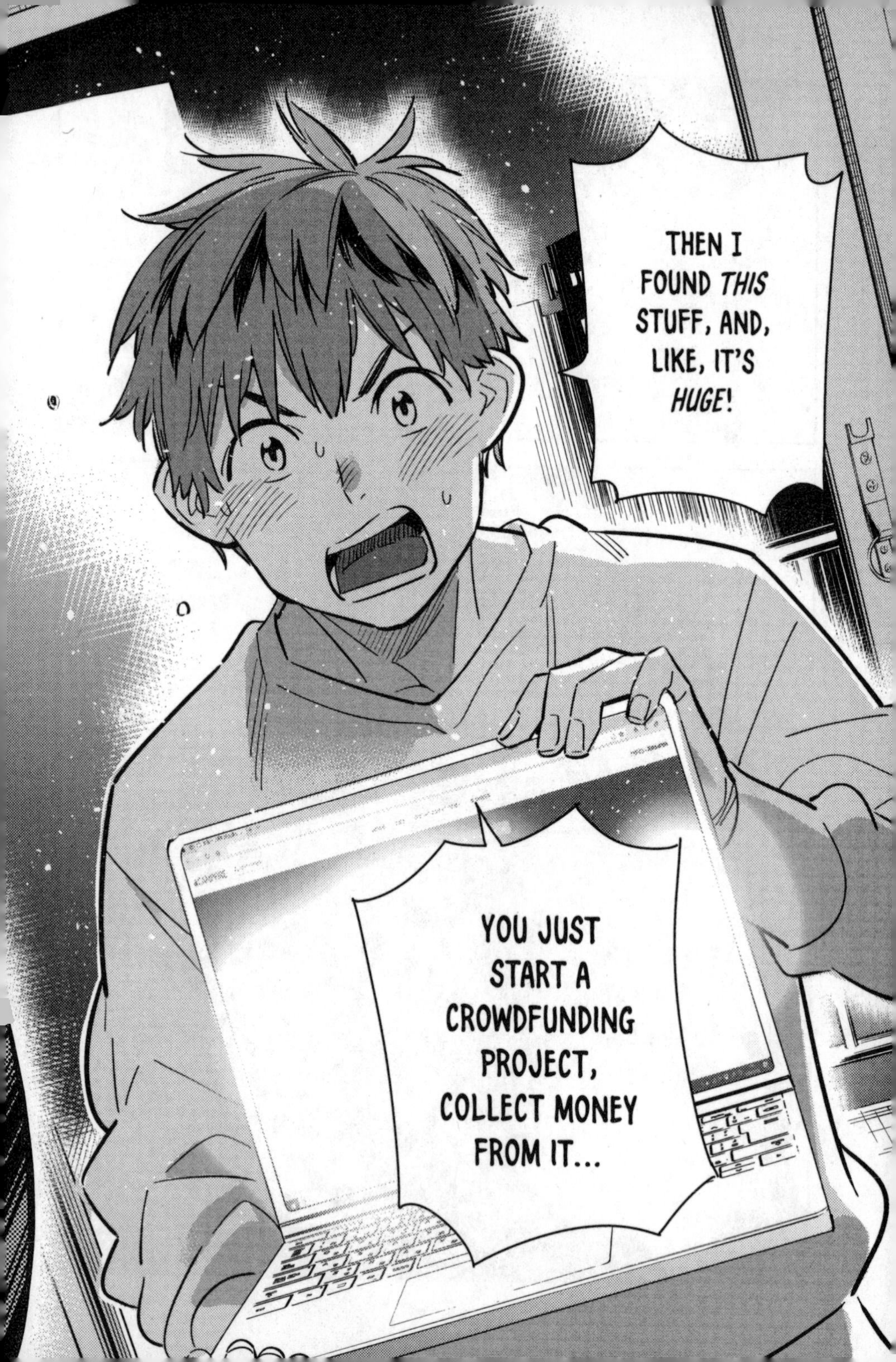
THEN I FOUND *THIS* STUFF, AND, LIKE, IT'S *HUGE*!
YOU JUST START A CROWDFUNDING PROJECT, COLLECT MONEY FROM IT...

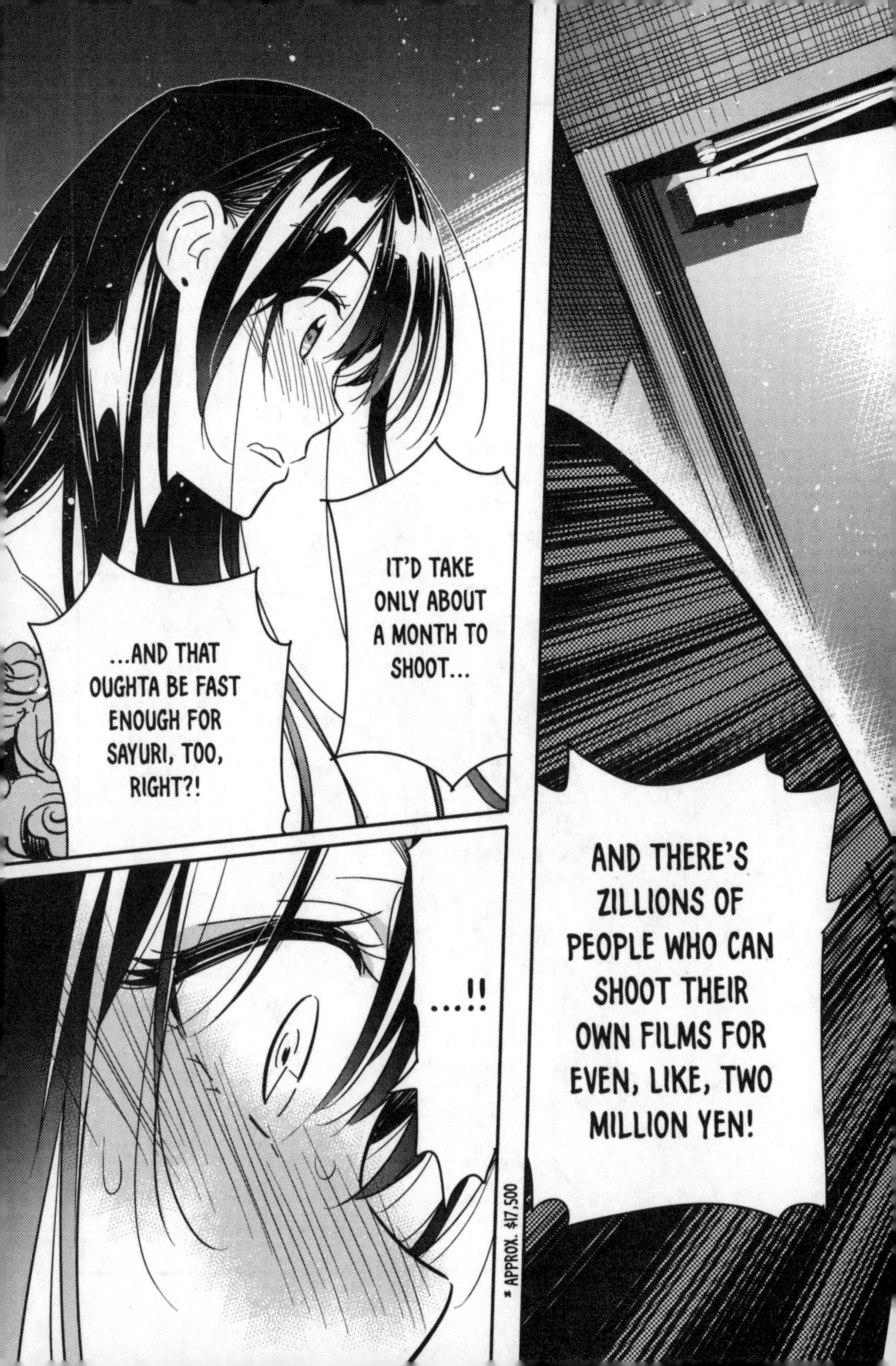
AND THERE'S ZILLIONS OF PEOPLE WHO CAN SHOOT THEIR OWN FILMS FOR EVEN, LIKE, TWO MILLION YEN!
IT'D TAKE ONLY ABOUT A MONTH TO SHOOT...
...AND THAT OUGHTA BE FAST ENOUGH FOR SAYURI, TOO, RIGHT?!
...!!

* APPROX. $17,500

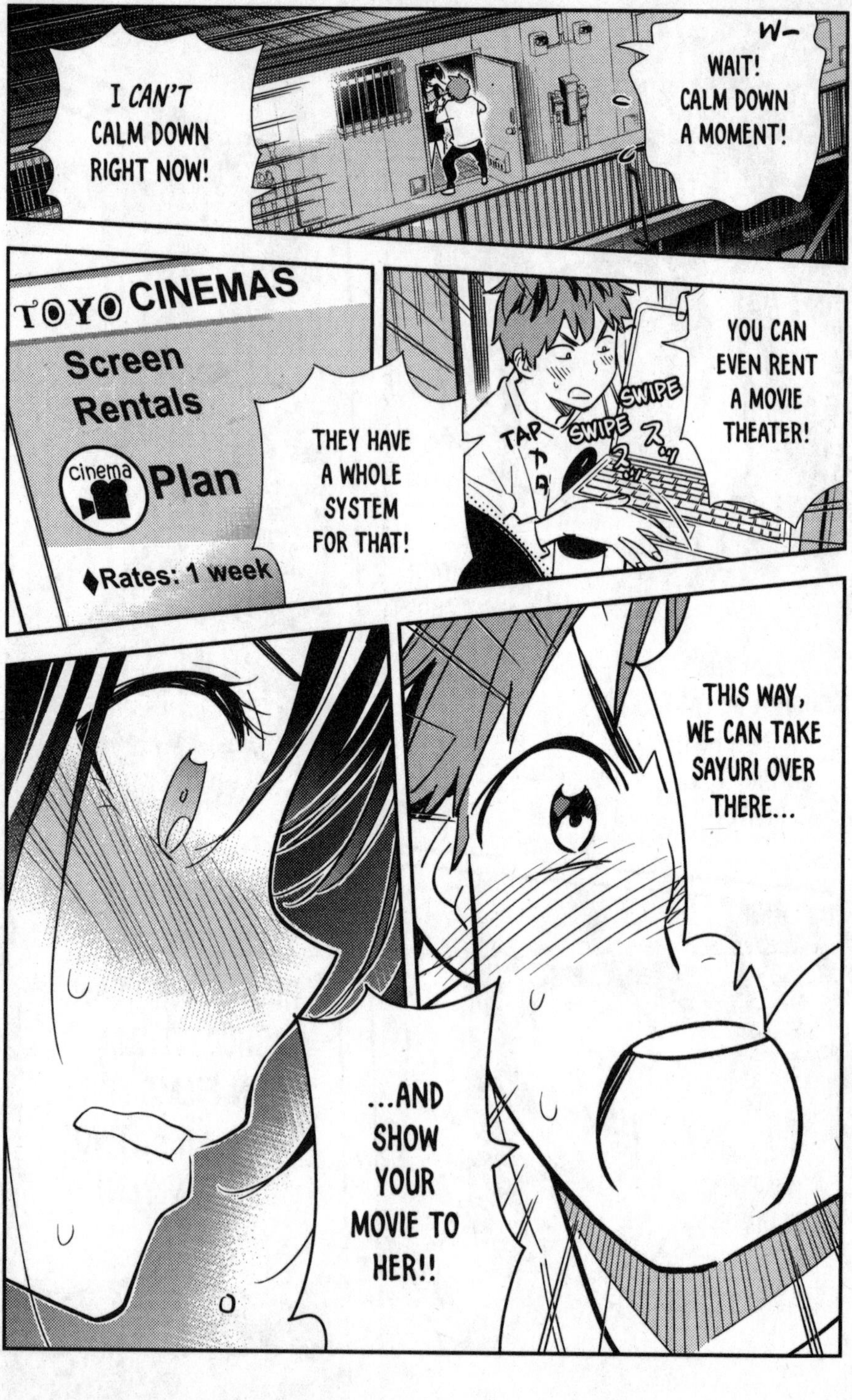
W— WAIT! CALM DOWN A MOMENT!
I CAN'T CALM DOWN RIGHT NOW!
YOU CAN EVEN RENT A MOVIE THEATER!
SWIPE
SWIPE
TAP
TOYO CINEMAS
Screen Rentals
cinema Plan
♦Rates: 1 week
THEY HAVE A WHOLE SYSTEM FOR THAT!
THIS WAY, WE CAN TAKE SAYURI OVER THERE...
...AND SHOW YOUR MOVIE TO HER!!

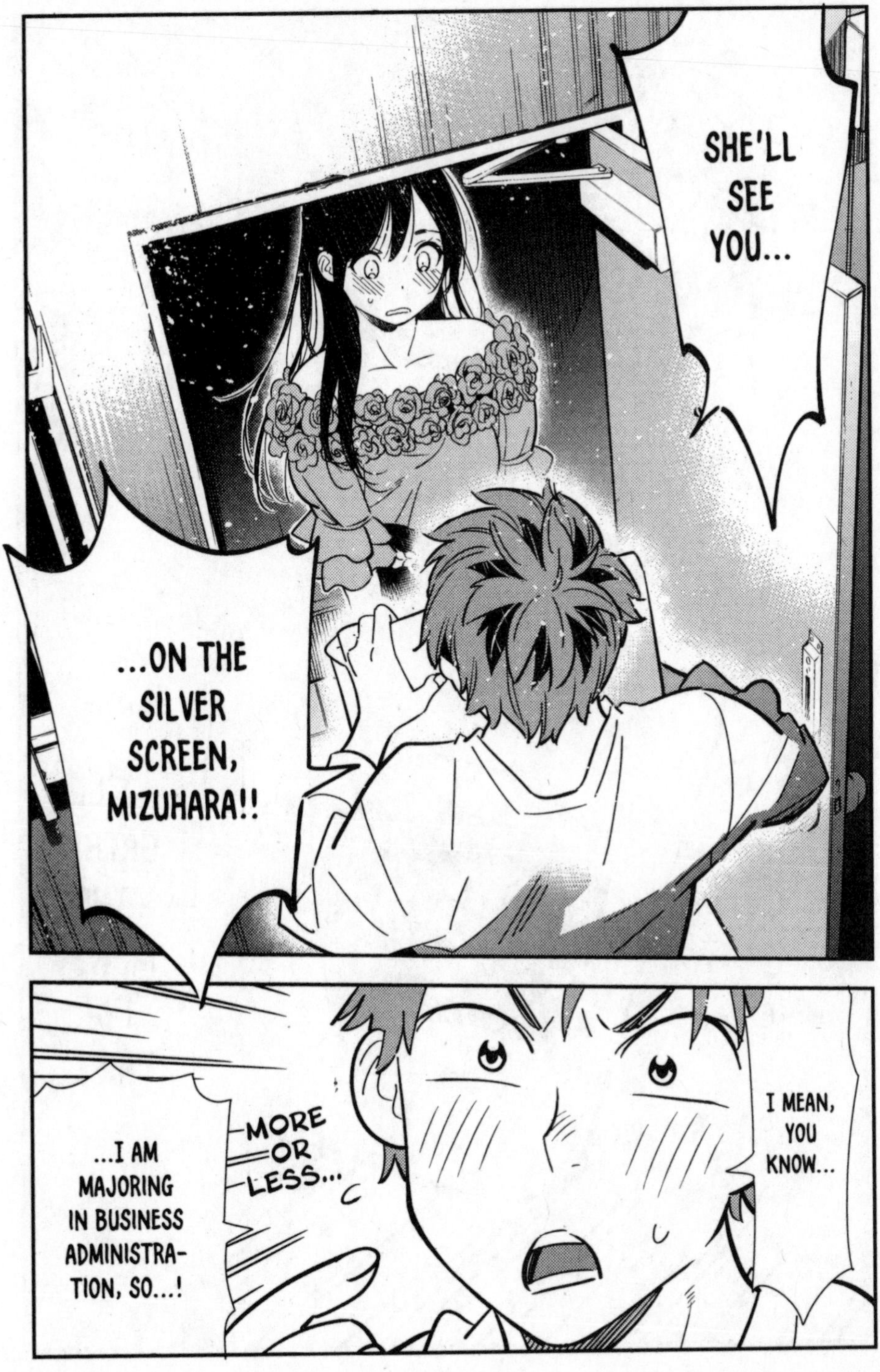
SHE'LL SEE YOU...
...ON THE SILVER SCREEN, MIZUHARA!!
I MEAN, YOU KNOW...
MORE OR LESS...
...I AM MAJORING IN BUSINESS ADMINISTRA-TION, SO...!

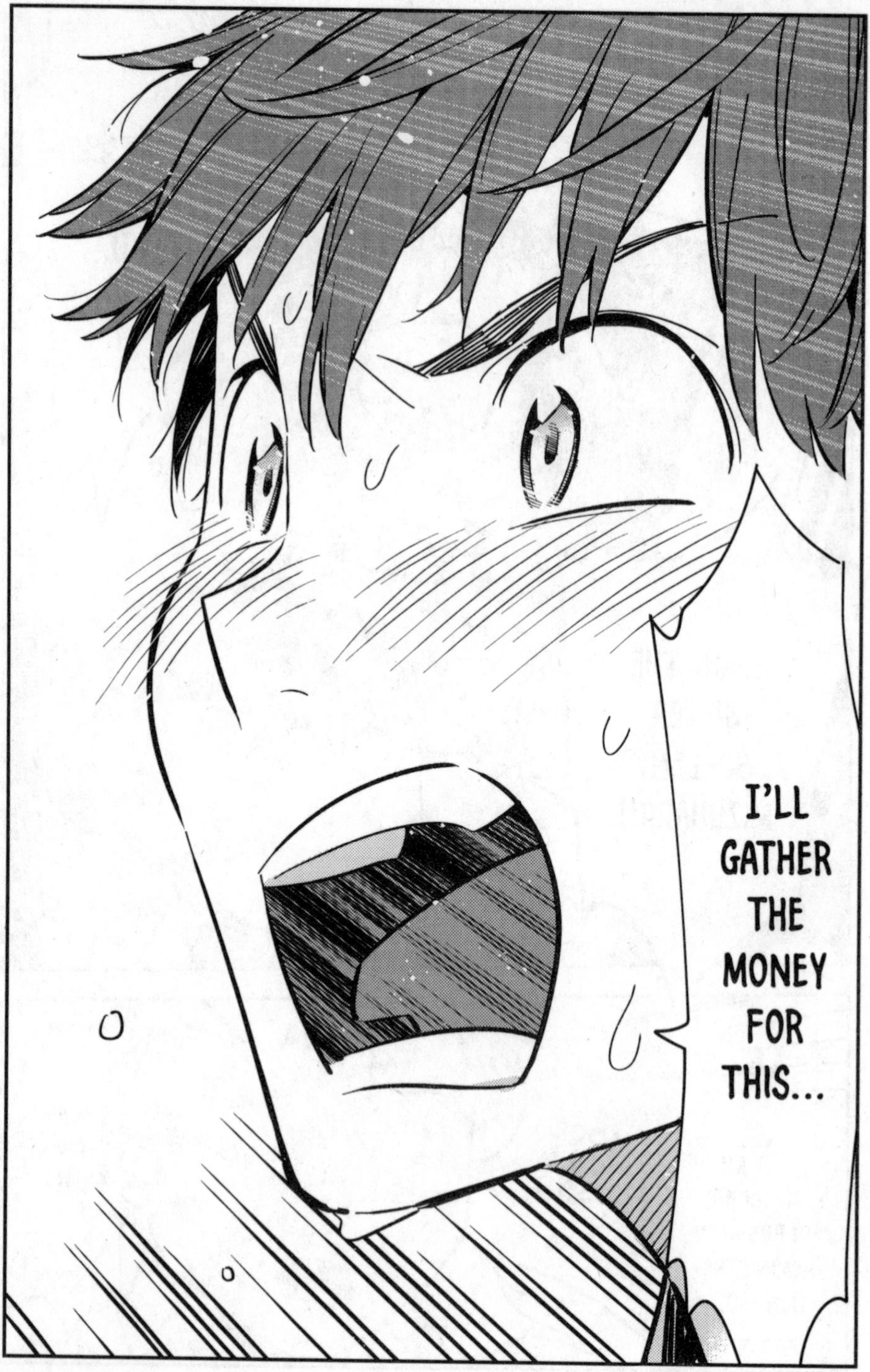
I'LL GATHER THE MONEY FOR THIS...

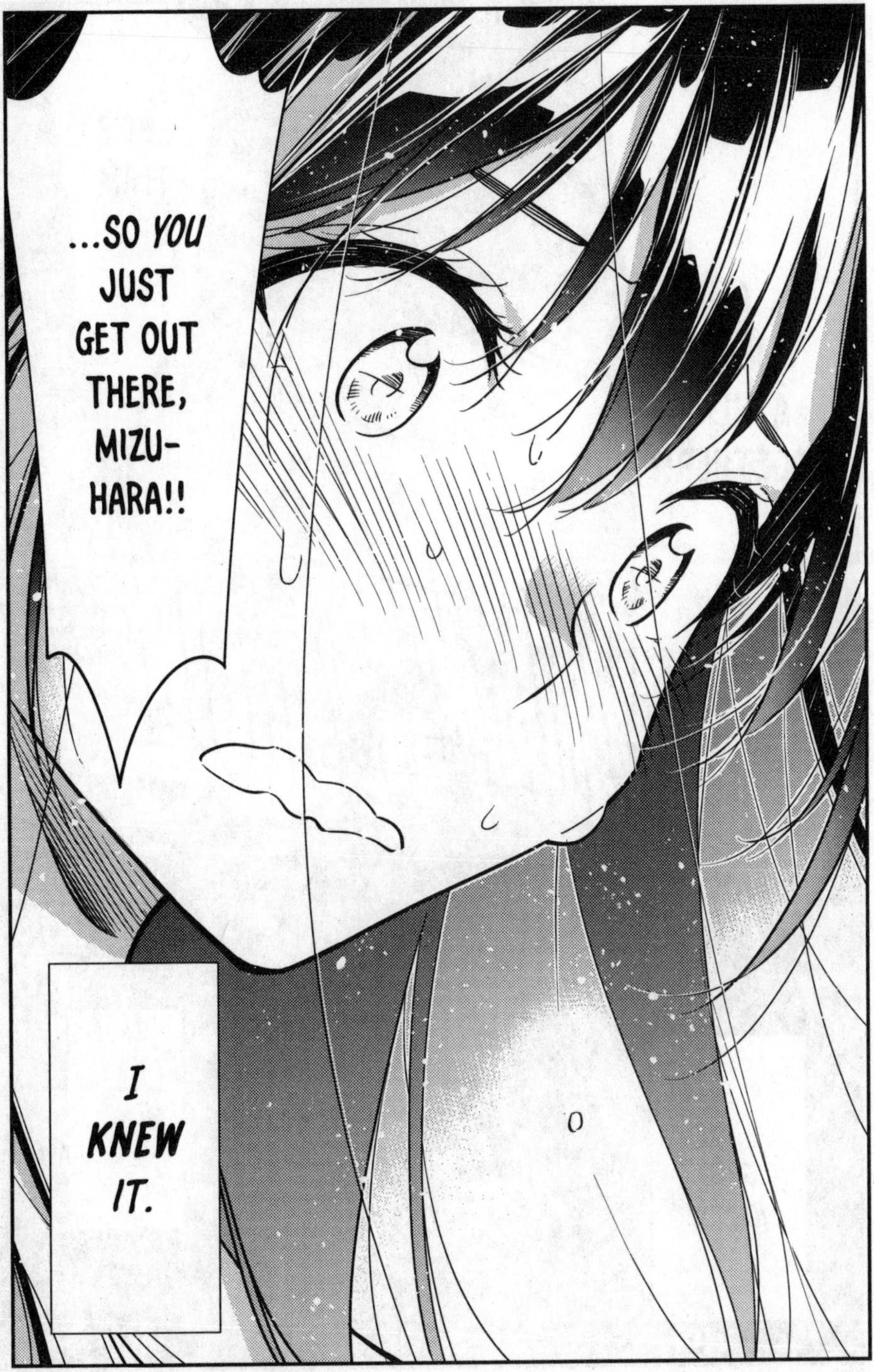
...SO YOU JUST GET OUT THERE, MIZU-HARA!!
I KNEW IT.

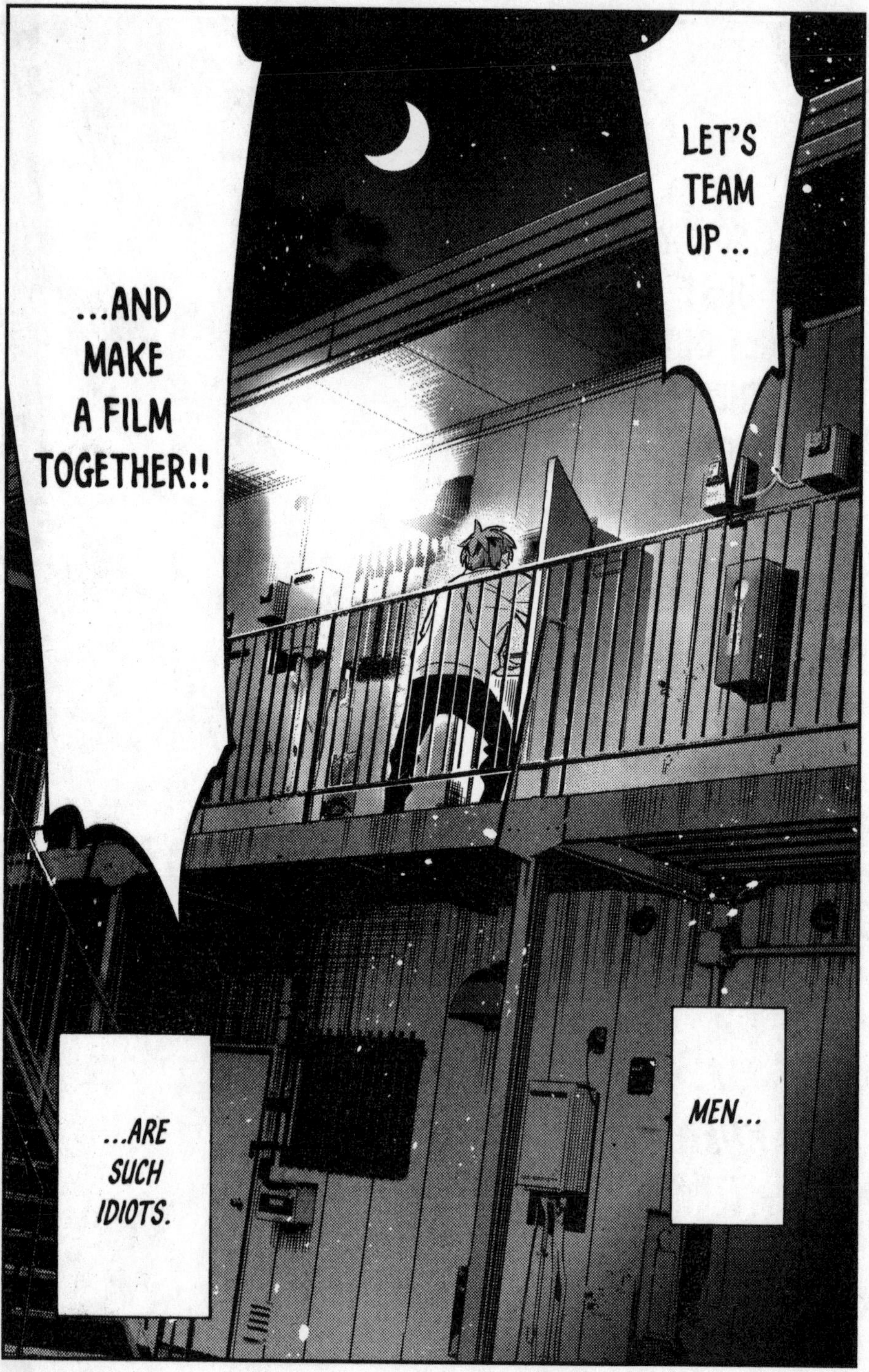

LET'S TEAM UP...
...AND MAKE A FILM TOGETHER!!
MEN...
...ARE SUCH IDIOTS.

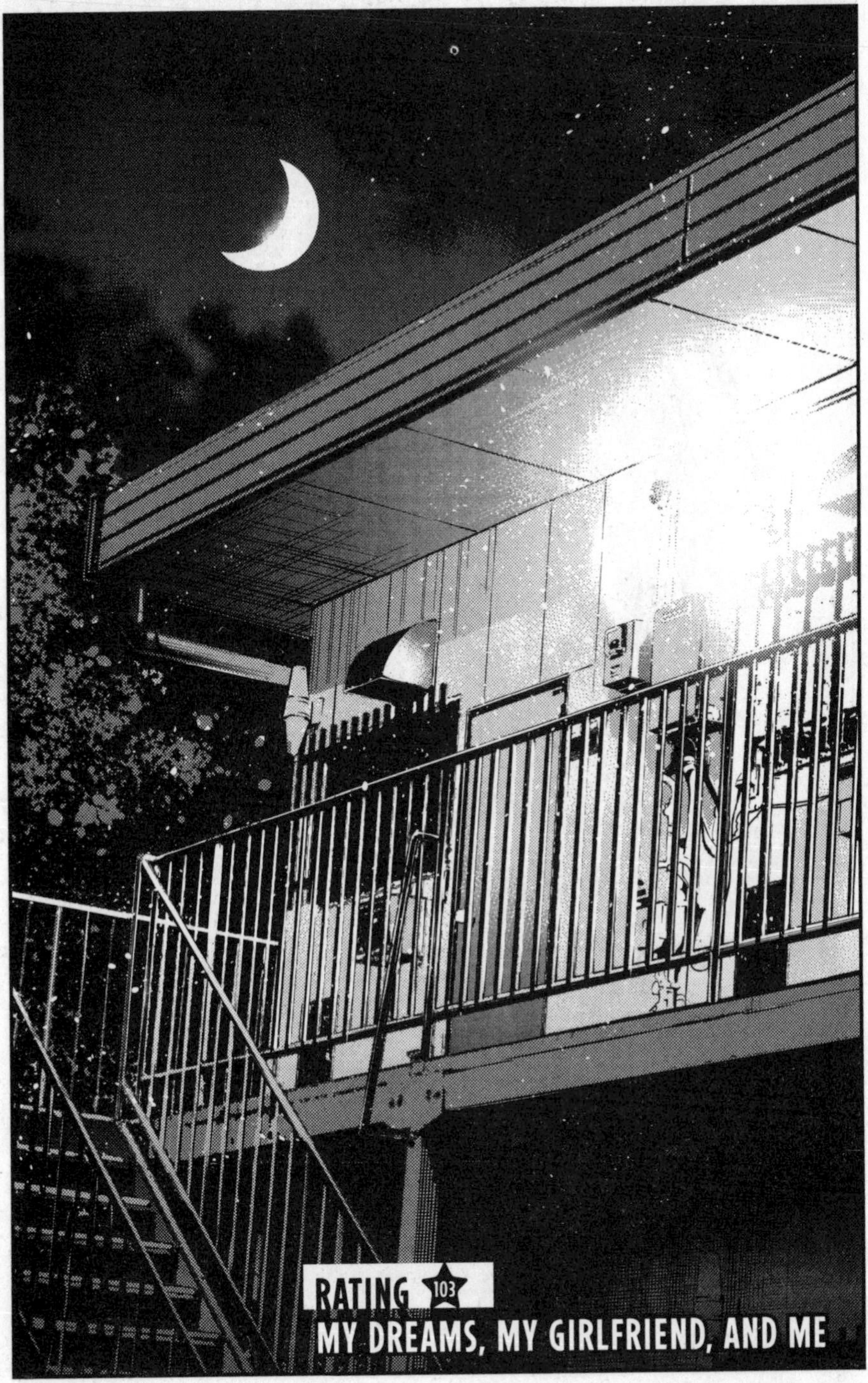
RATING 103
MY DREAMS, MY GIRLFRIEND, AND ME

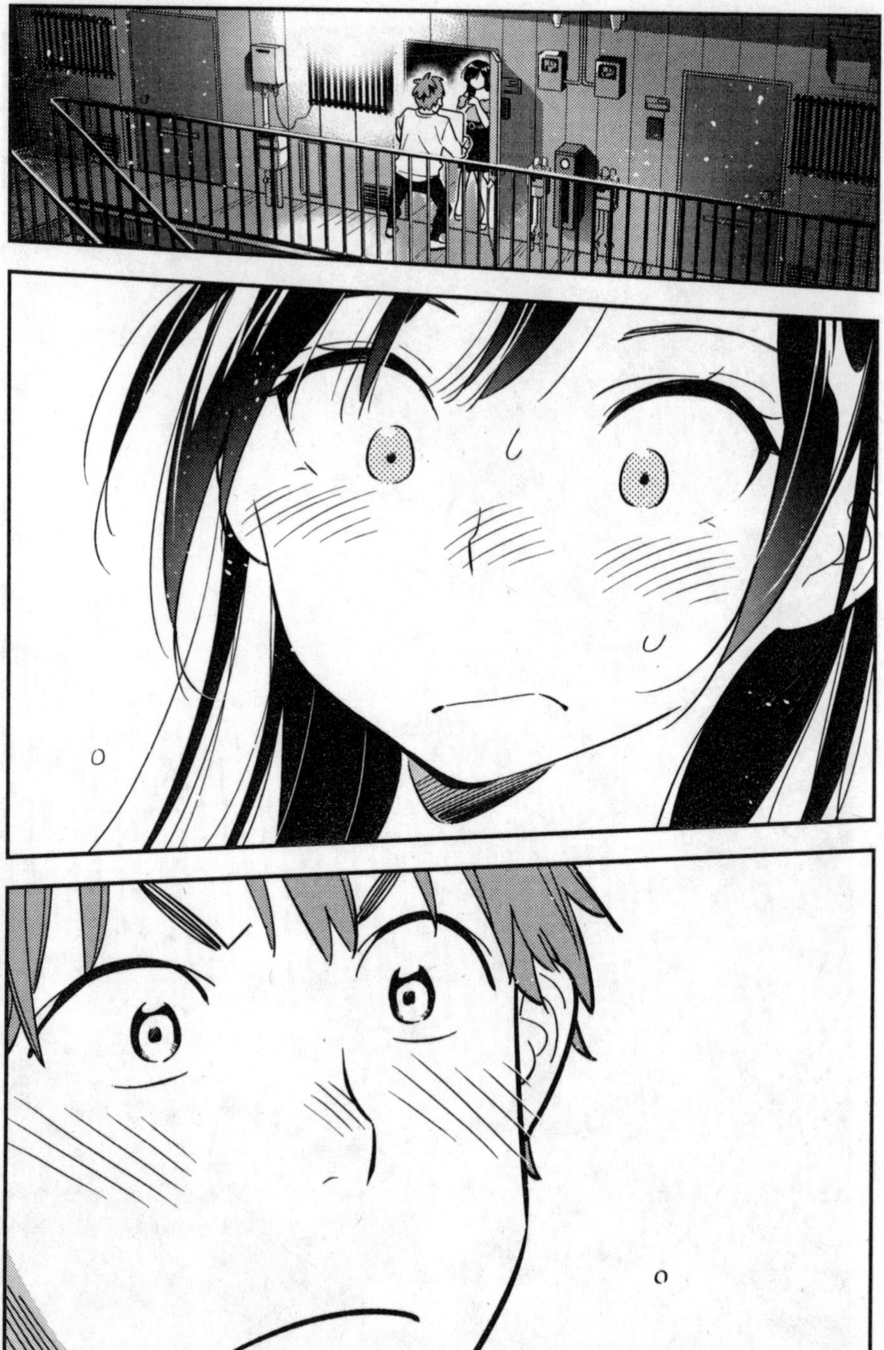

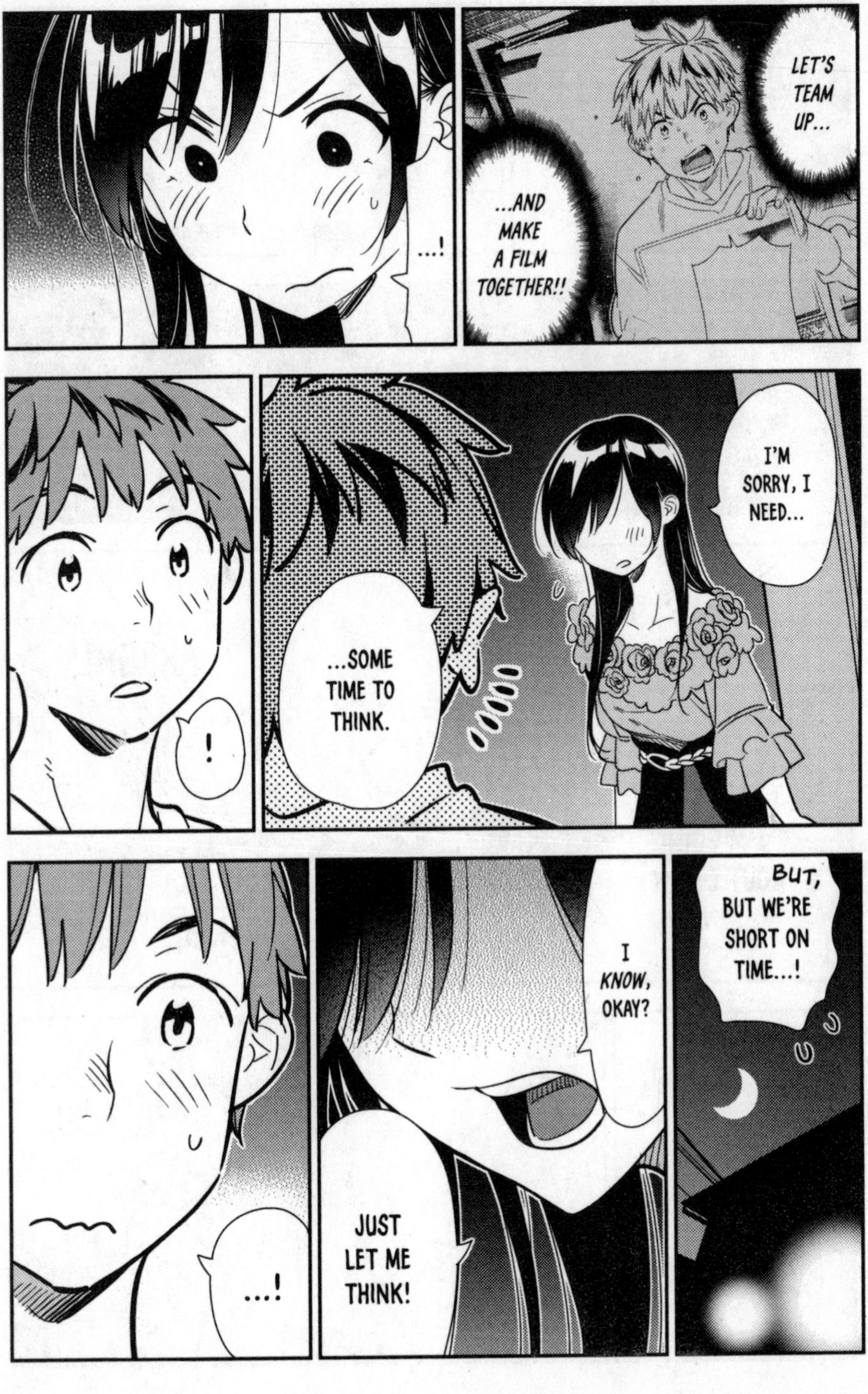
LET'S TEAM UP...
...AND MAKE A FILM TOGETHER!!
...!
I'M SORRY, I NEED...
...SOME TIME TO THINK.
!
BUT, BUT WE'RE SHORT ON TIME...!
I KNOW, OKAY?
JUST LET ME THINK!
...!

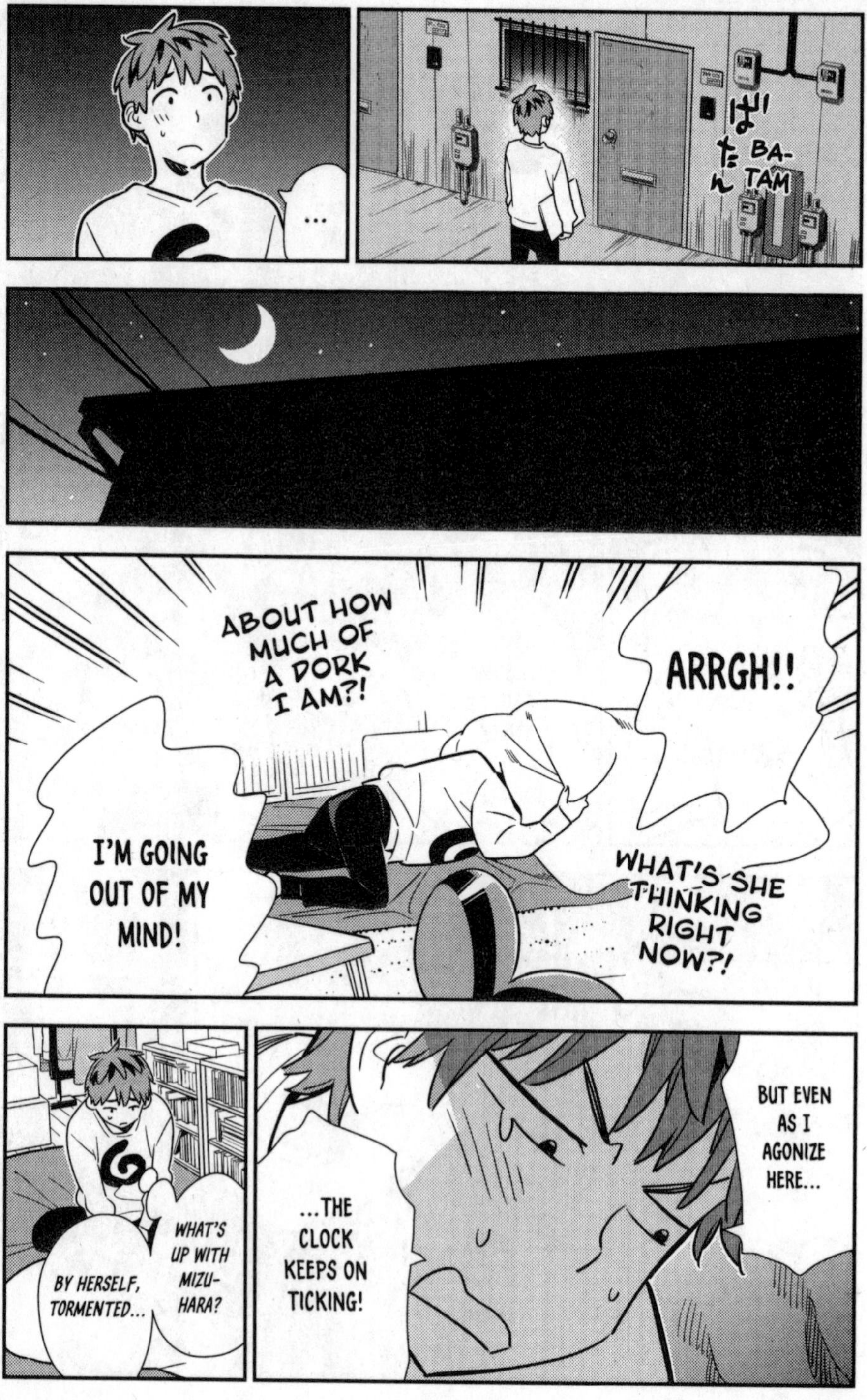
ばたん
BA-TAM
...
ARRGH!!
ABOUT HOW MUCH OF A DORK I AM?!
WHAT'S SHE THINKING RIGHT NOW?!
I'M GOING OUT OF MY MIND!
BUT EVEN AS I AGONIZE HERE...
...THE CLOCK KEEPS ON TICKING!
WHAT'S UP WITH MIZU-HARA?
BY HERSELF, TORMENTED...

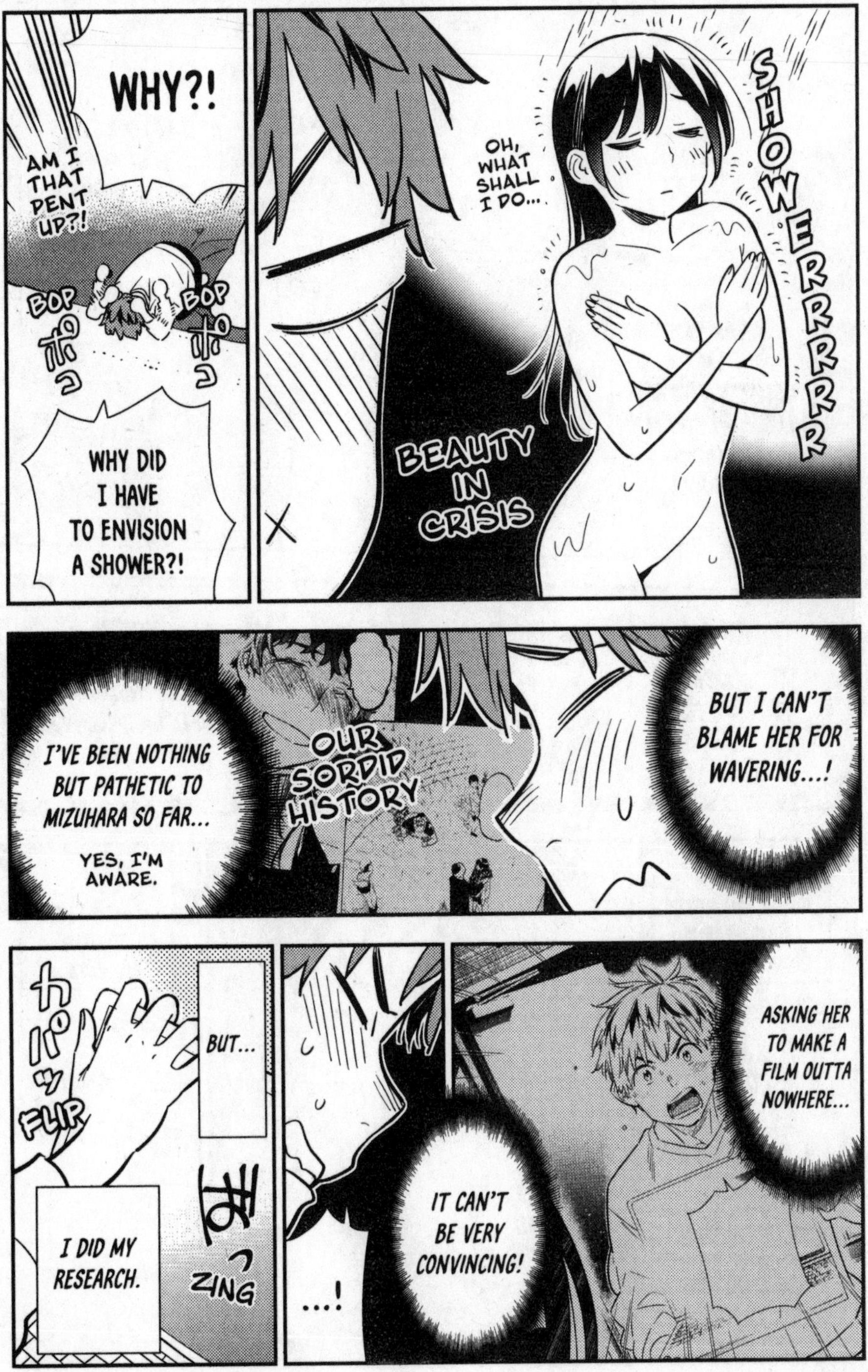
SHOWERRRRR
OH, WHAT SHALL I DO...
BEAUTY IN CRISIS
WHY?!
AM I THAT PENT UP?!
BOP ポコ
BOP ポコ
WHY DID I HAVE TO ENVISION A SHOWER?!
BUT I CAN'T BLAME HER FOR WAVERING...!
OUR SORDID HISTORY
I'VE BEEN NOTHING BUT PATHETIC TO MIZUHARA SO FAR...
YES, I'M AWARE.
ASKING HER TO MAKE A FILM OUTTA NOWHERE...
IT CAN'T BE VERY CONVINCING!
...!
BUT...
カパッ FLIP
ZING
I DID MY RESEARCH.

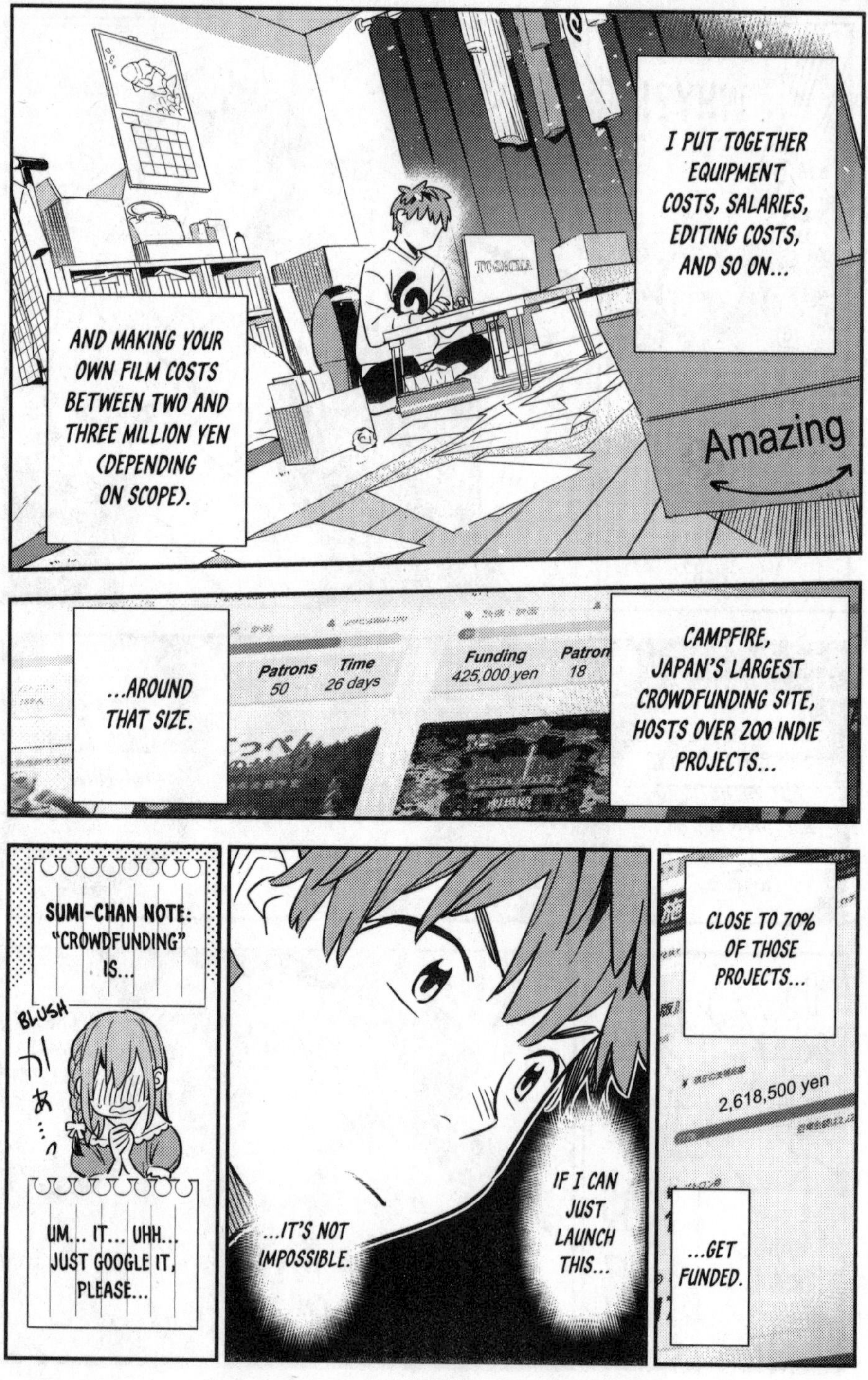
I PUT TOGETHER EQUIPMENT COSTS, SALARIES, EDITING COSTS, AND SO ON...
Amazing
AND MAKING YOUR OWN FILM COSTS BETWEEN TWO AND THREE MILLION YEN (DEPENDING ON SCOPE).
CAMPFIRE, JAPAN'S LARGEST CROWDFUNDING SITE, HOSTS OVER 200 INDIE PROJECTS...
Funding 425,000 yen
Patron 18
Patrons 50
Time 26 days
...AROUND THAT SIZE.
CLOSE TO 70% OF THOSE PROJECTS...
2,618,500 yen
...GET FUNDED.
IF I CAN JUST LAUNCH THIS...
...IT'S NOT IMPOSSIBLE.
SUMI-CHAN NOTE: "CROWDFUNDING" IS...
BLUSH
かぁ…
UM... IT... UHH... JUST GOOGLE IT, PLEASE...

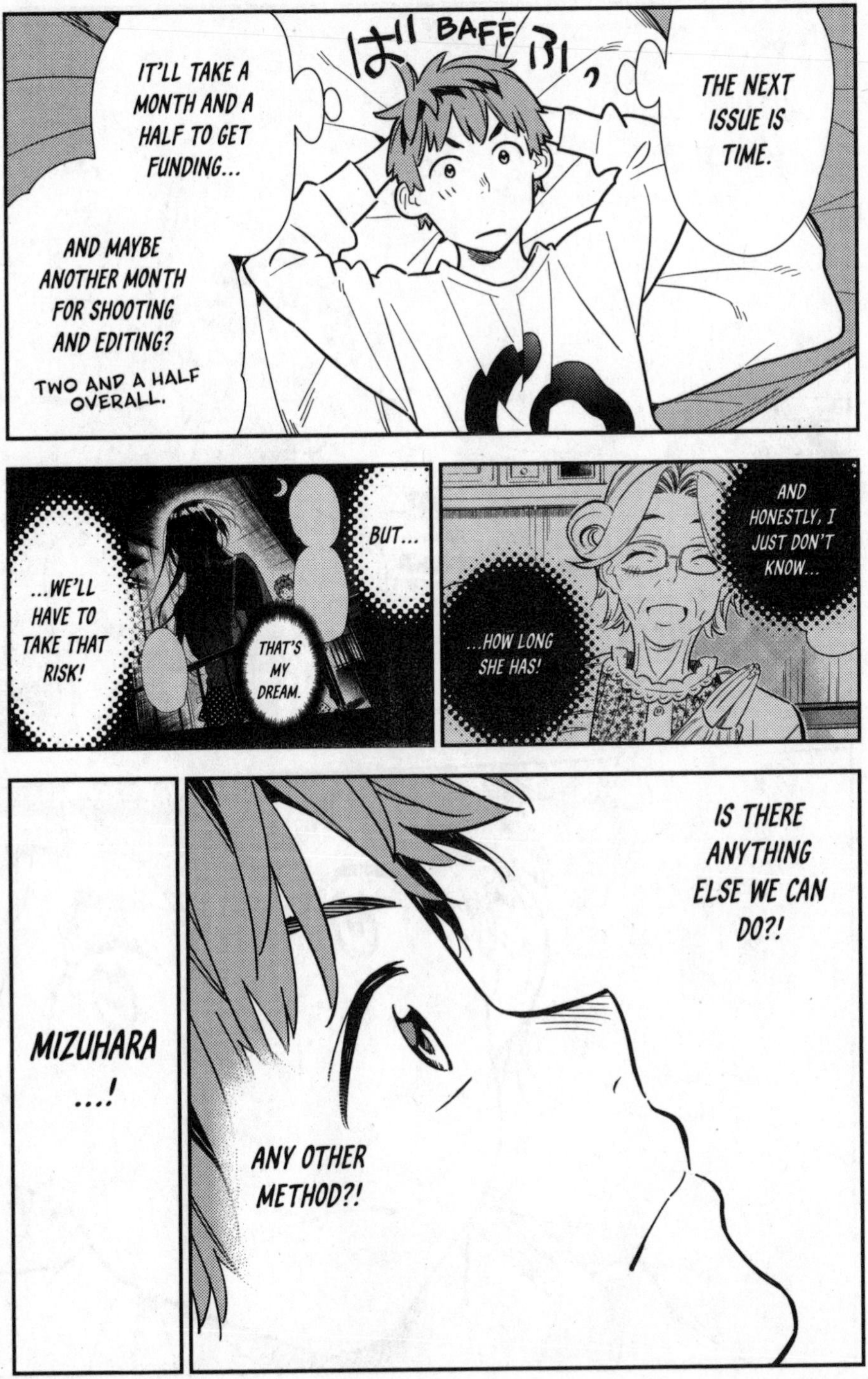

BAFF
THE NEXT ISSUE IS TIME.
IT'LL TAKE A MONTH AND A HALF TO GET FUNDING...
AND MAYBE ANOTHER MONTH FOR SHOOTING AND EDITING?
TWO AND A HALF OVERALL.
AND HONESTLY, I JUST DON'T KNOW...
...HOW LONG SHE HAS!
BUT...
THAT'S MY DREAM.
...WE'LL HAVE TO TAKE THAT RISK!
IS THERE ANYTHING ELSE WE CAN DO?!
ANY OTHER METHOD?!
MIZUHARA ...!

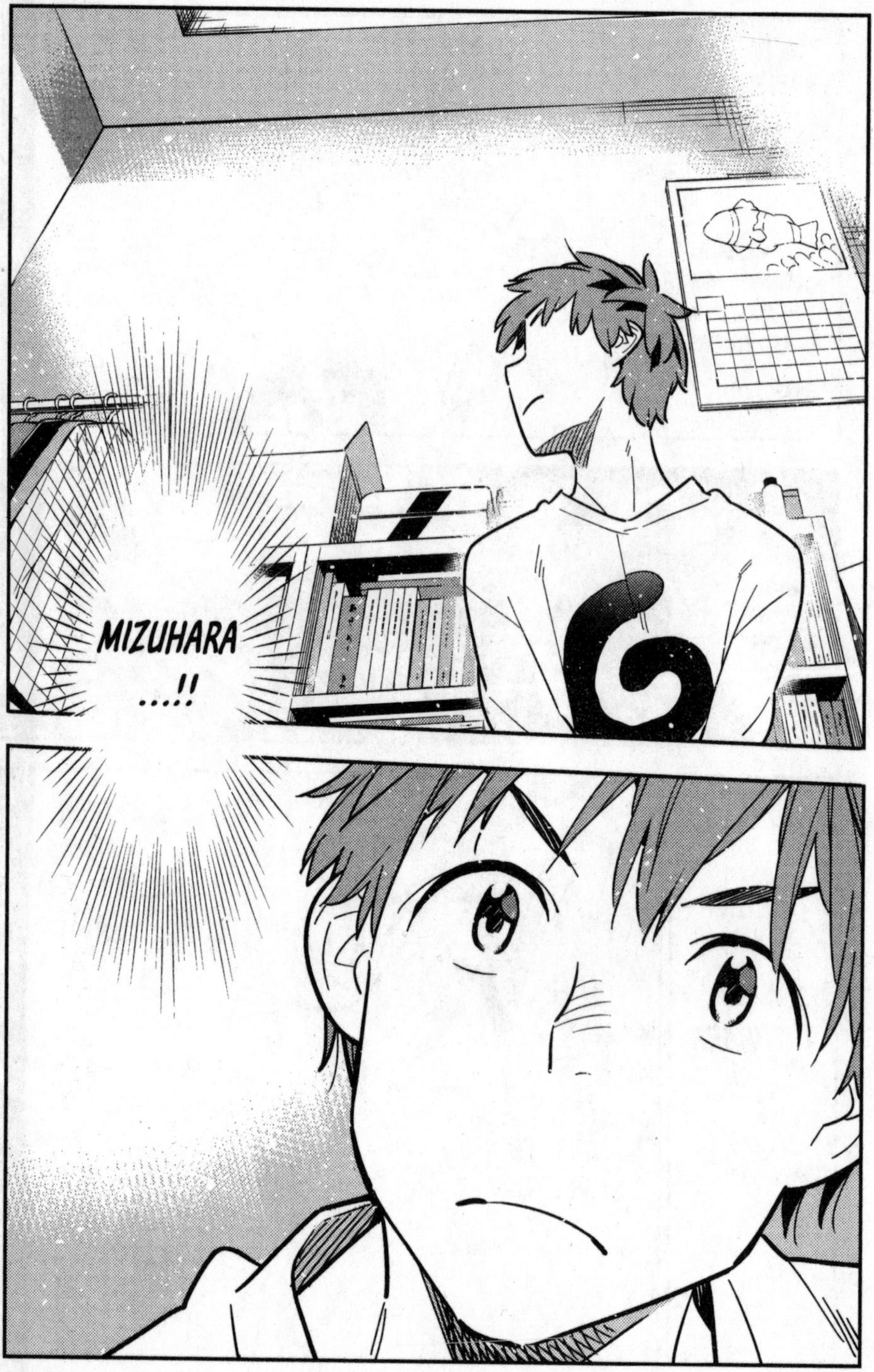
MIZUHARA
...!!

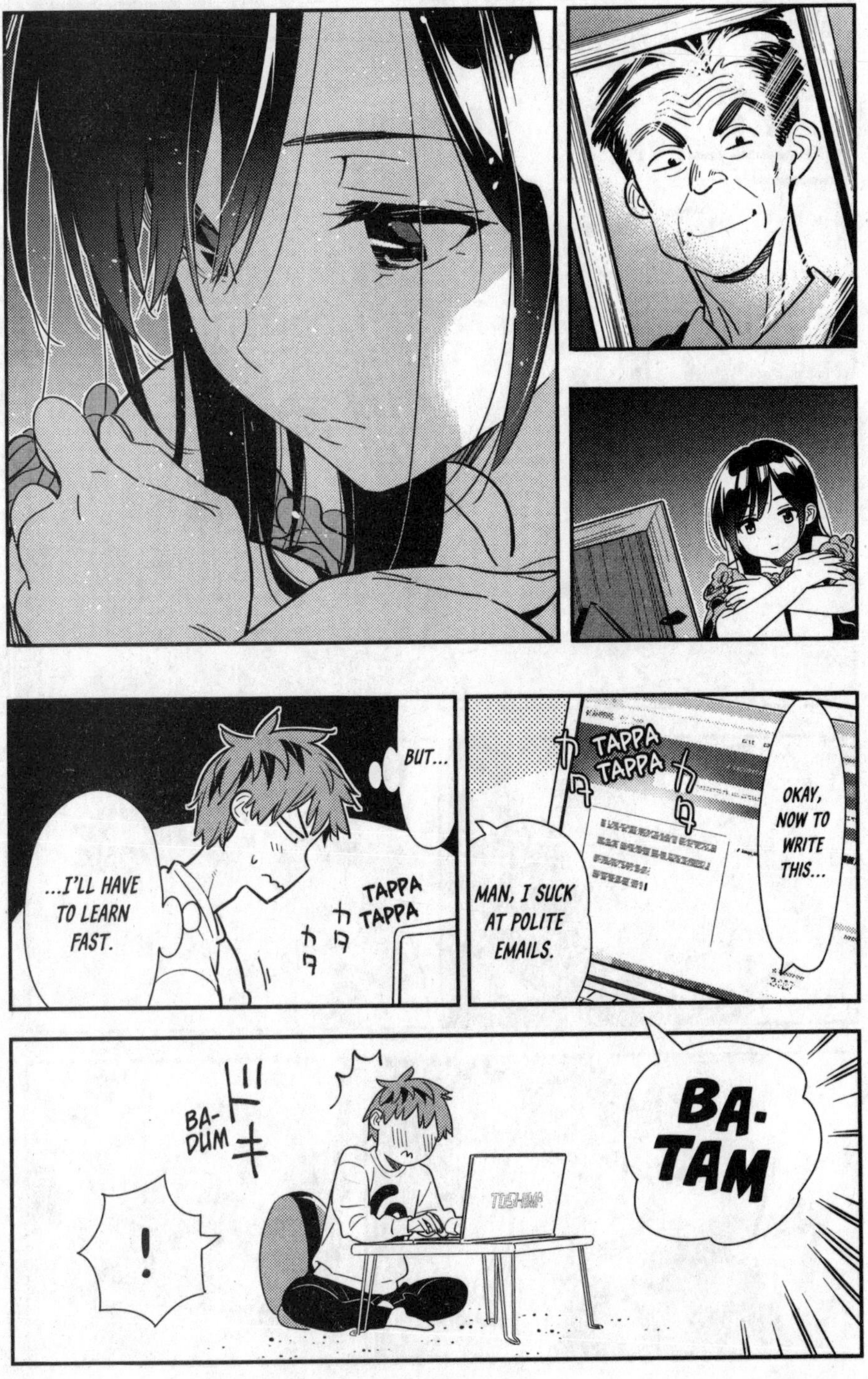

OKAY, NOW TO WRITE THIS...
TAPPA TAPPA
カタ
カタ
MAN, I SUCK AT POLITE EMAILS.
BUT...
TAPPA TAPPA
カタ
カタ
...I'LL HAVE TO LEARN FAST.
BA-TAM
BA-DUM
ドキ
!

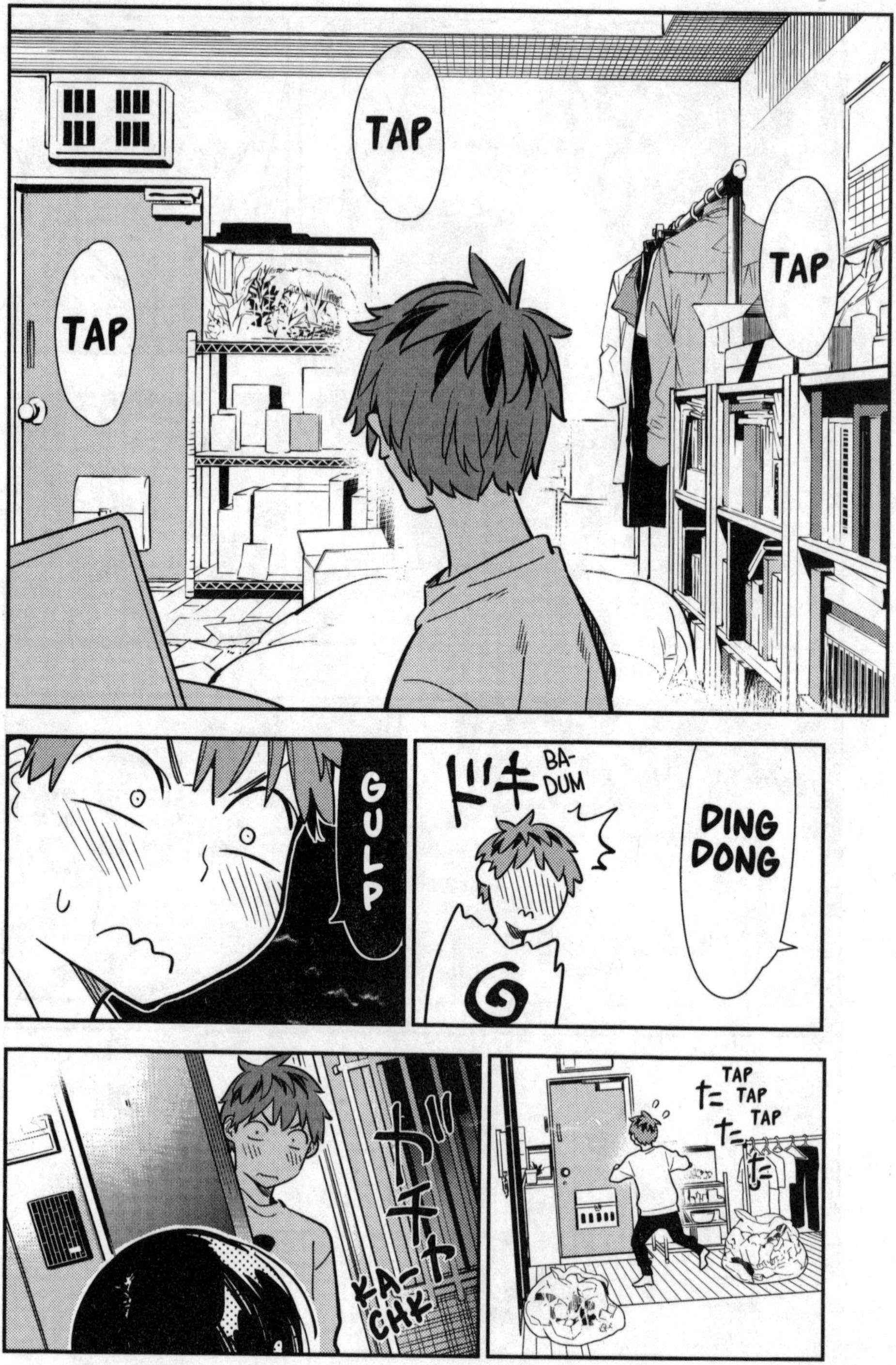
TAP
TAP
TAP
DING DONG
ドキ
BA-DUM
GULP
たたたた
TAP TAP TAP
ガチャ
KA-CHK

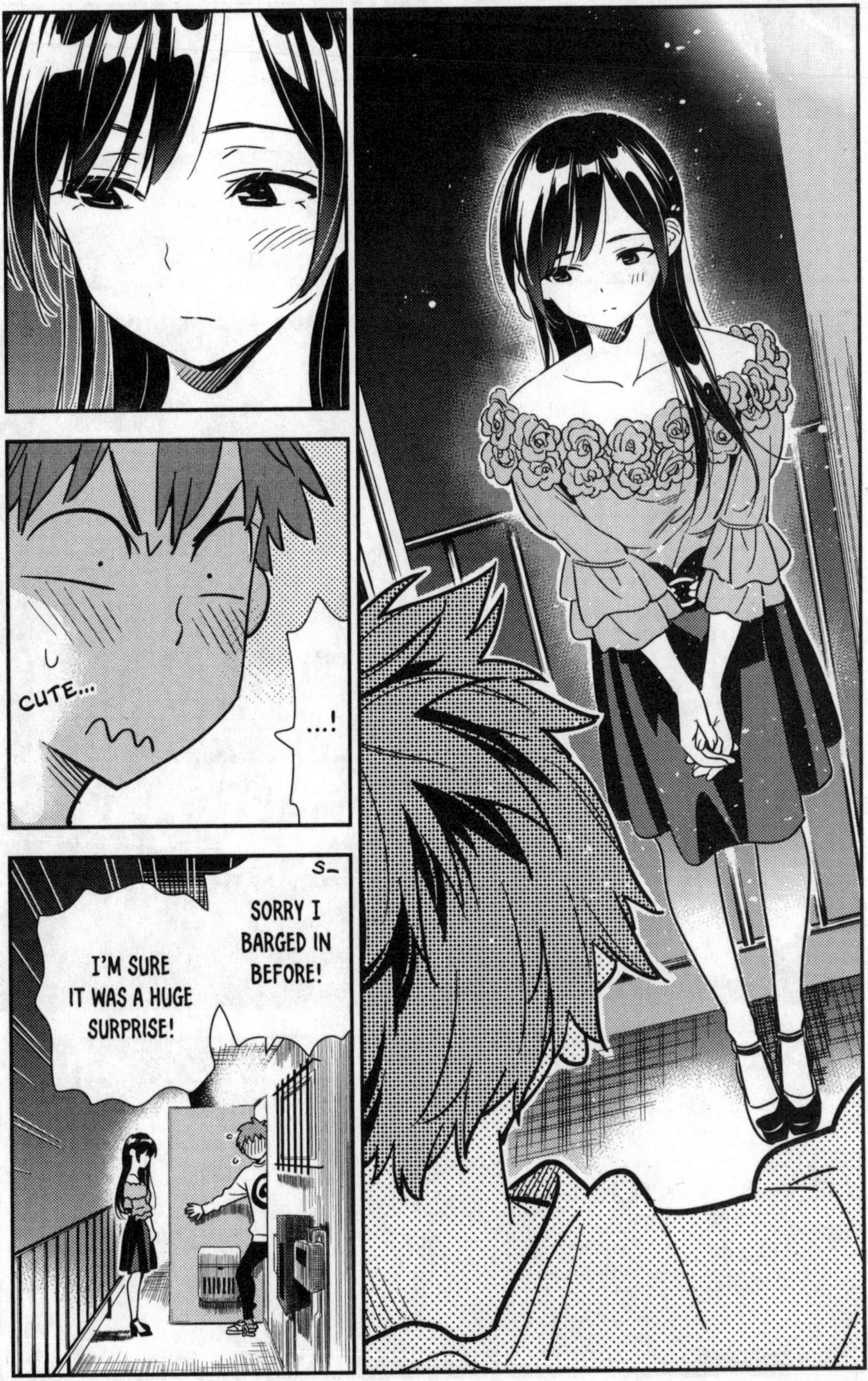
...!
CUTE...
S-
SORRY I BARGED IN BEFORE!
I'M SURE IT WAS A HUGE SURPRISE!

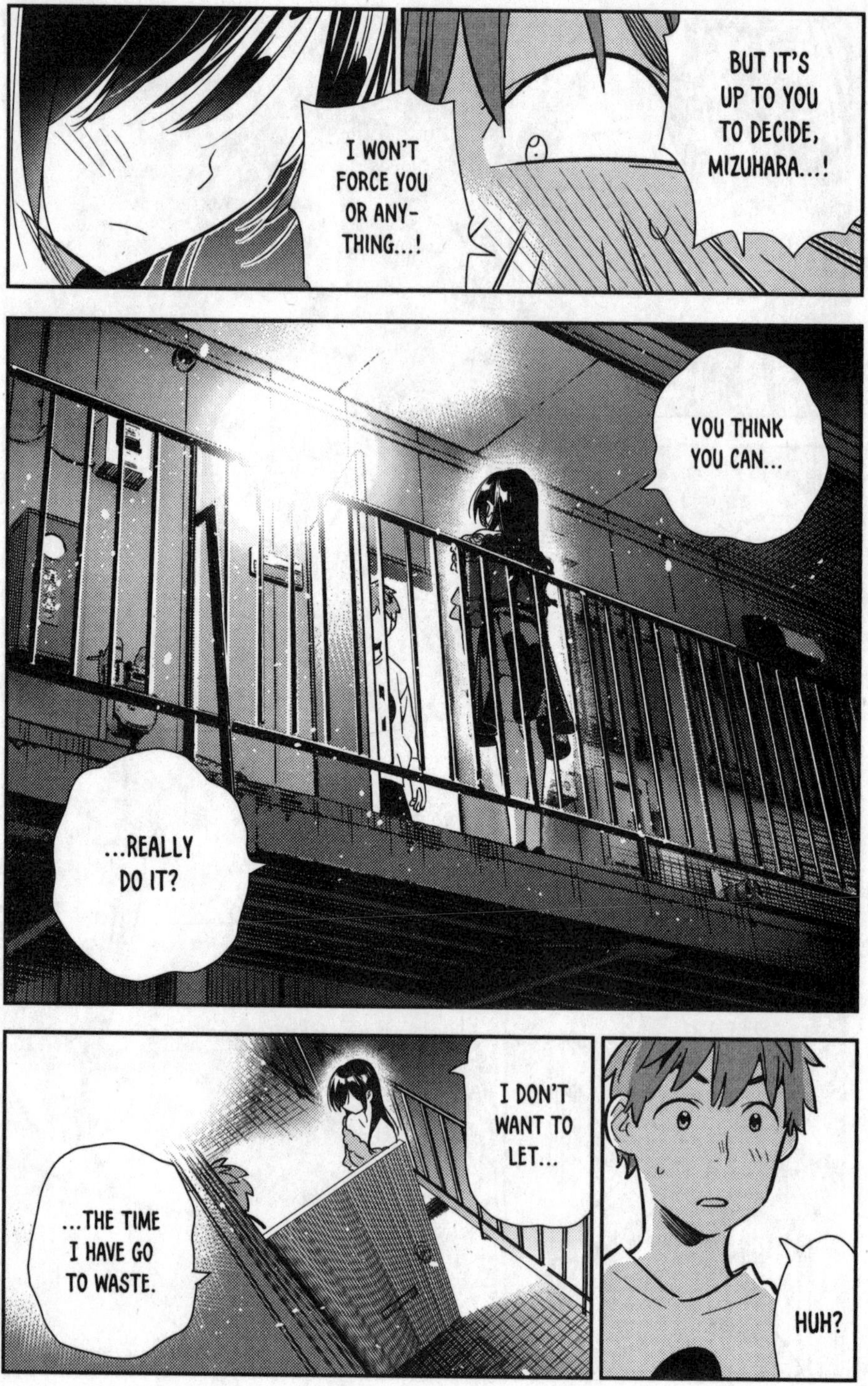
BUT IT'S UP TO YOU TO DECIDE, MIZUHARA...!
I WON'T FORCE YOU OR ANY-THING...!
YOU THINK YOU CAN...
...REALLY DO IT?
HUH?
I DON'T WANT TO LET...
...THE TIME I HAVE GO TO WASTE.

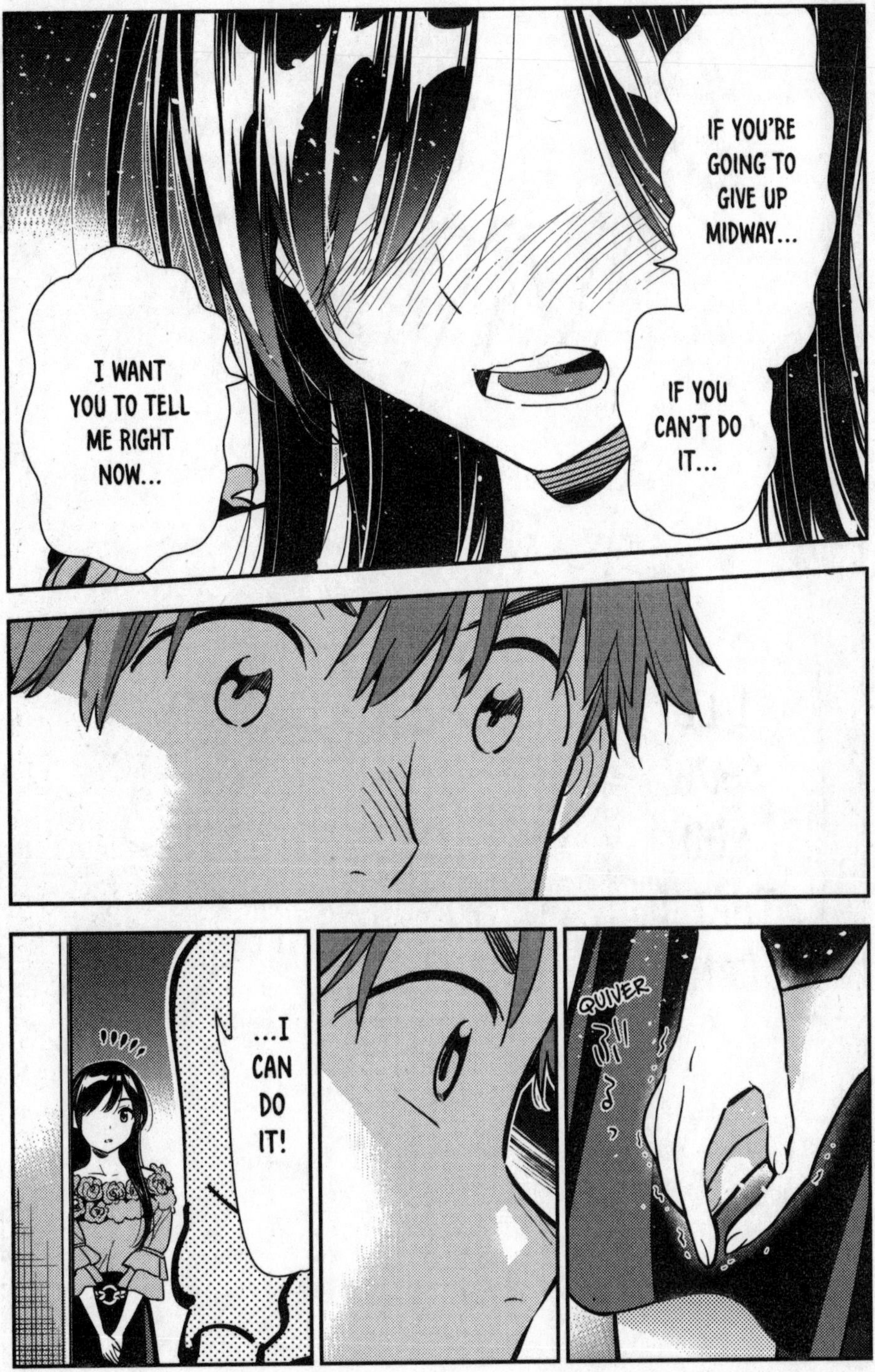
IF YOU'RE GOING TO GIVE UP MIDWAY...
IF YOU CAN'T DO IT...
I WANT YOU TO TELL ME RIGHT NOW...
QUIVER
...I CAN DO IT!

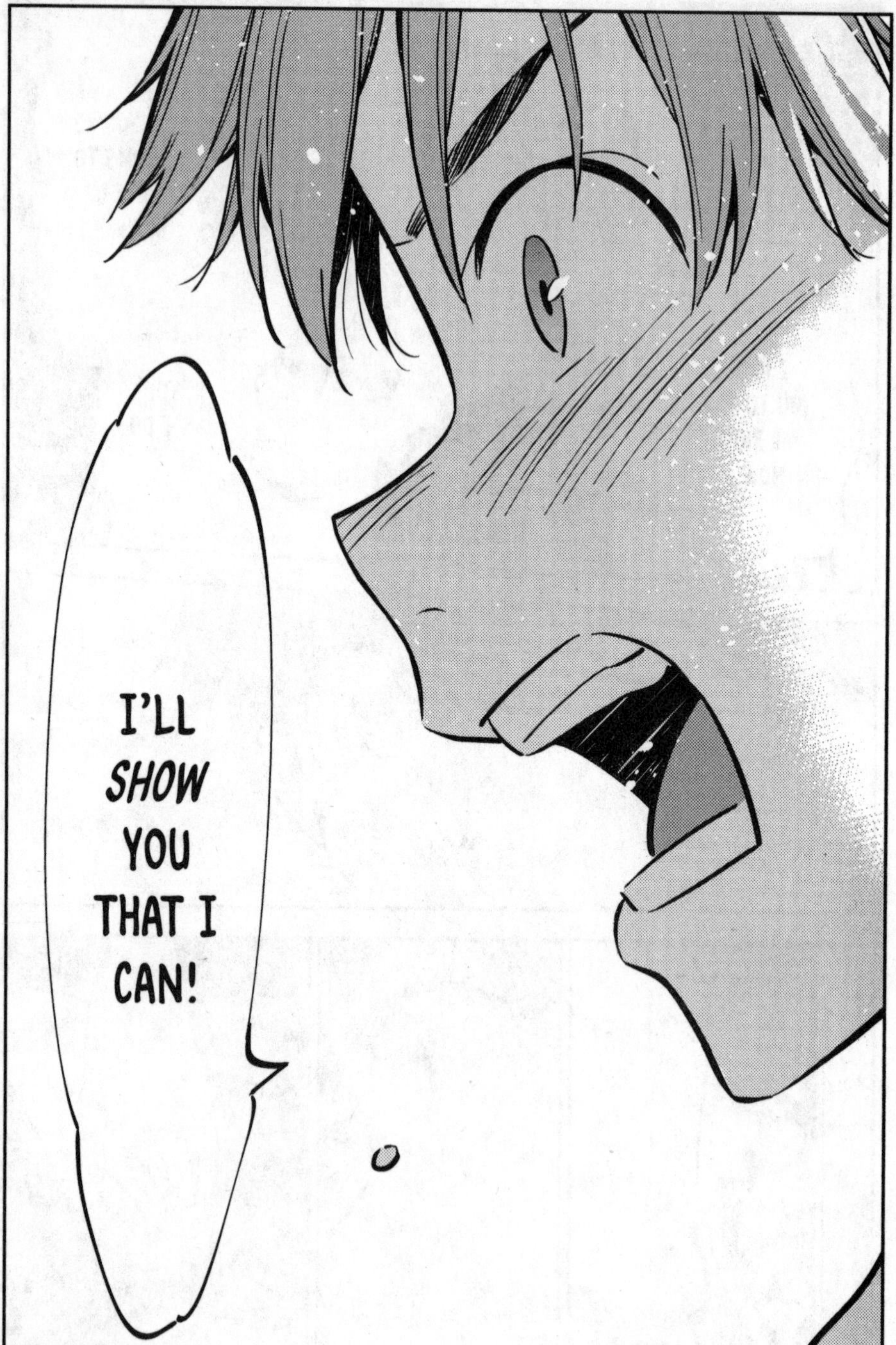
I'LL *SHOW* YOU THAT I CAN!

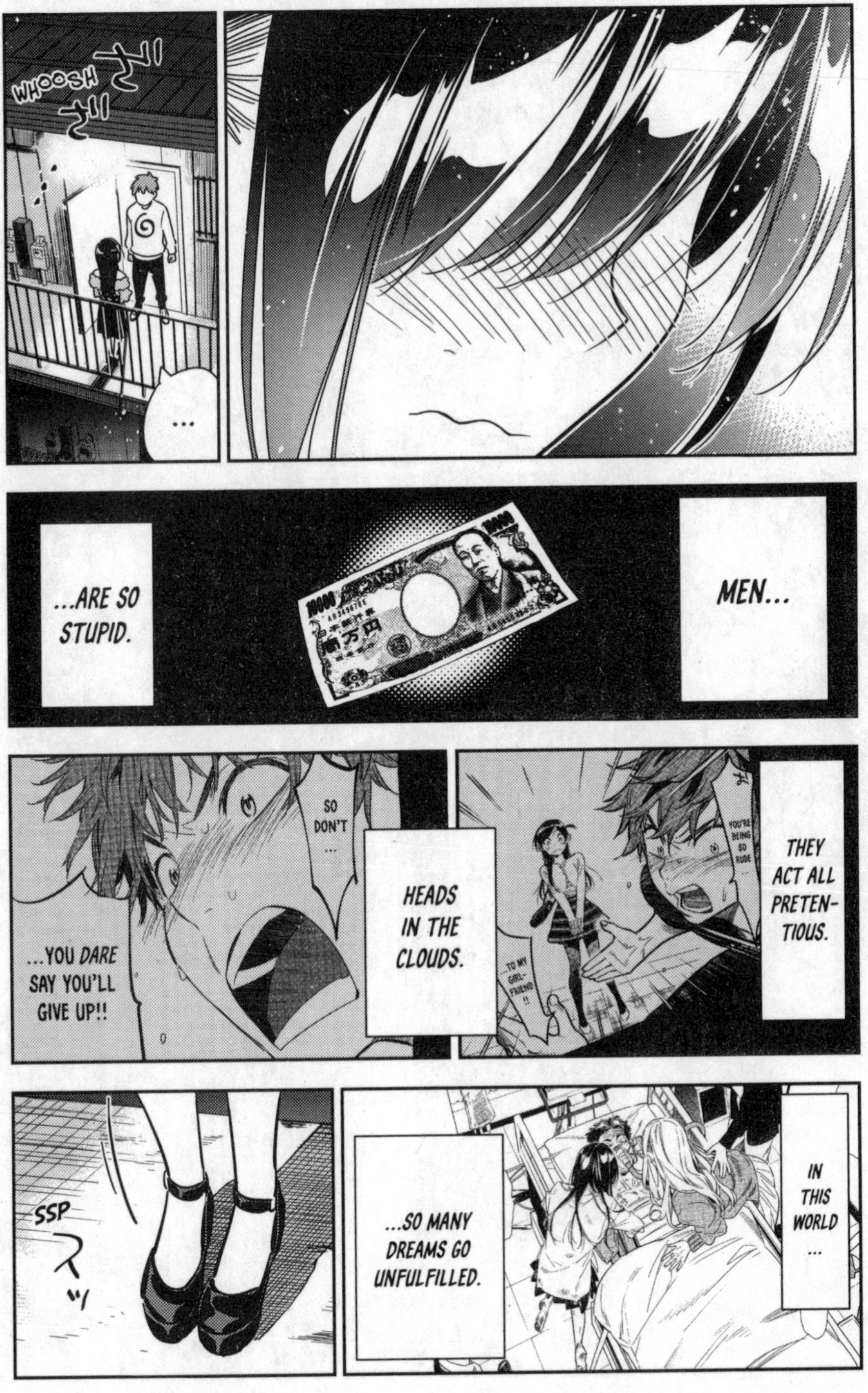
WHOOSH
...
MEN...
...ARE SO STUPID.
THEY ACT ALL PRETEN-TIOUS.
YOU'RE BEING SO RUDE
...TO MY GIRL-FRIEND!!
HEADS IN THE CLOUDS.
SO DON'T ...
...YOU DARE SAY YOU'LL GIVE UP!!
IN THIS WORLD ...
...SO MANY DREAMS GO UNFULFILLED.
SSP

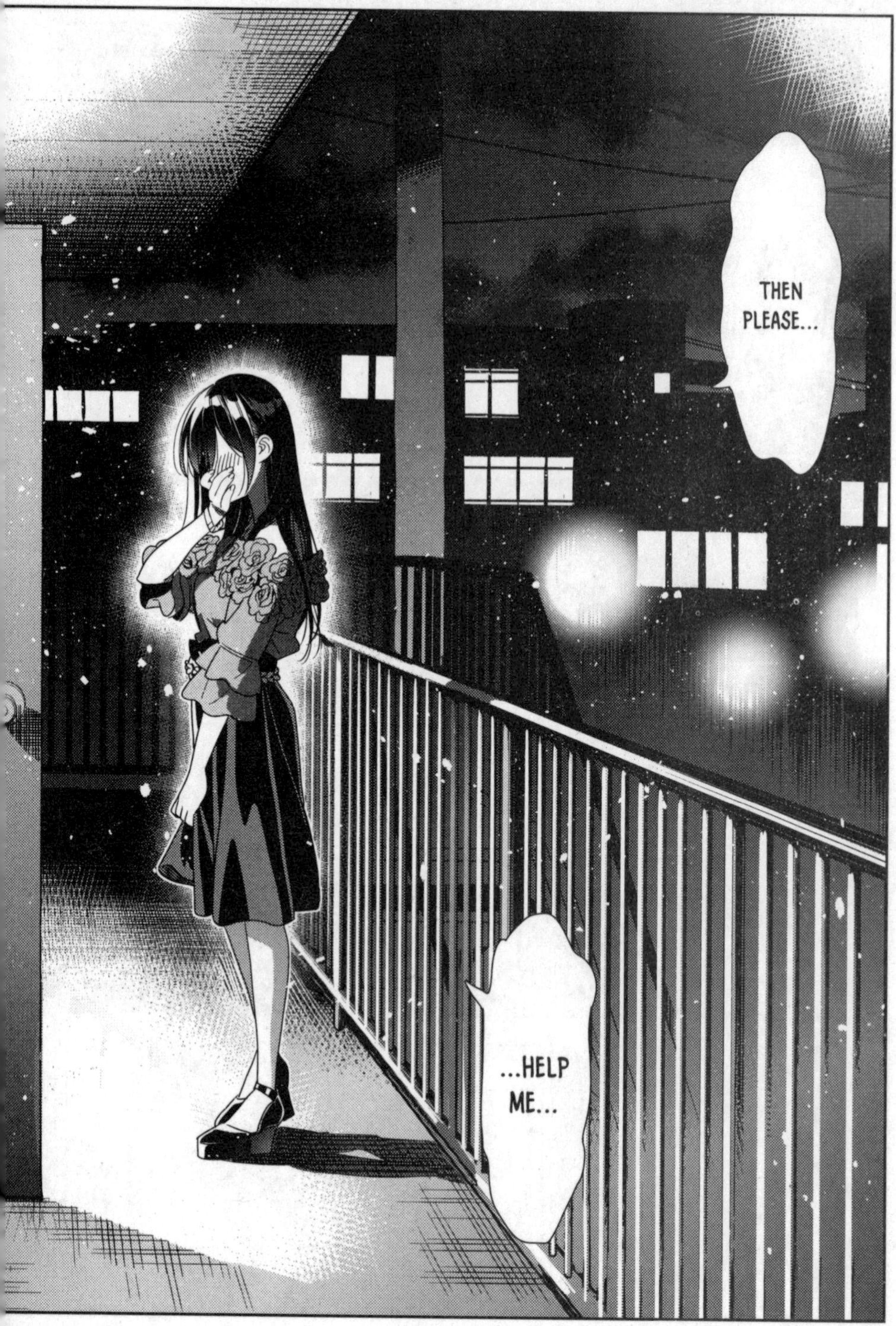
THEN PLEASE...
...HELP ME...

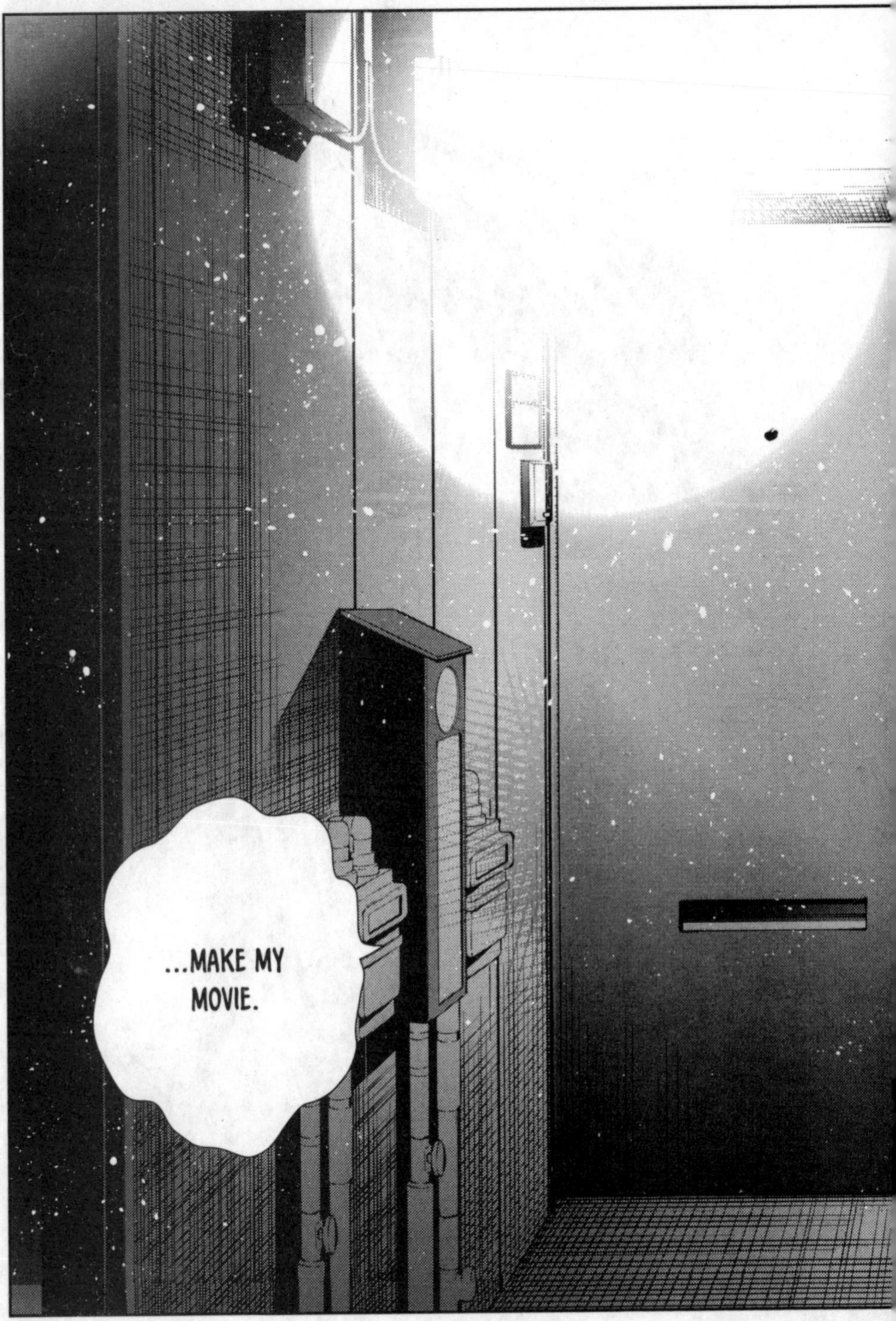
...MAKE MY MOVIE.

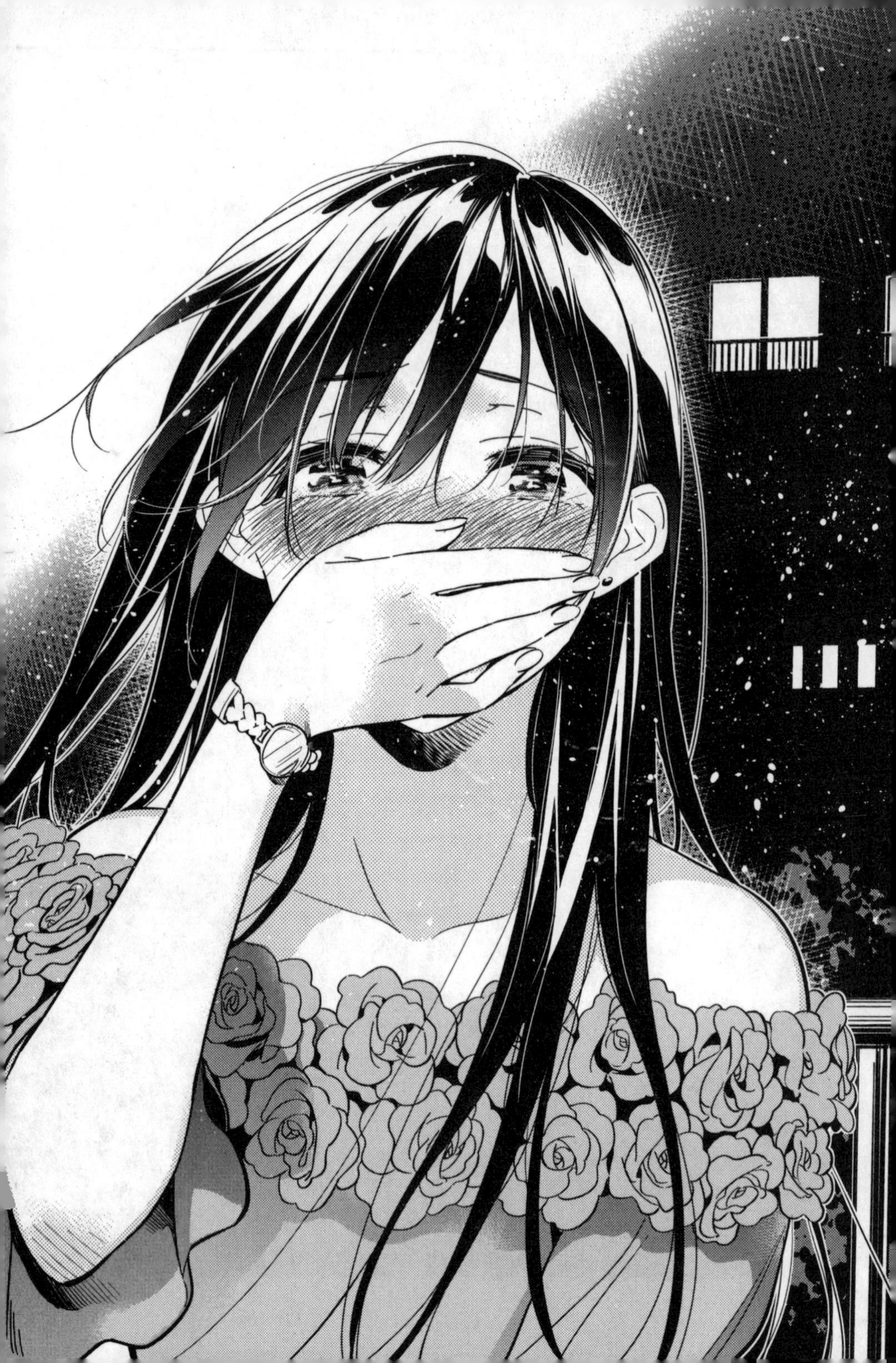

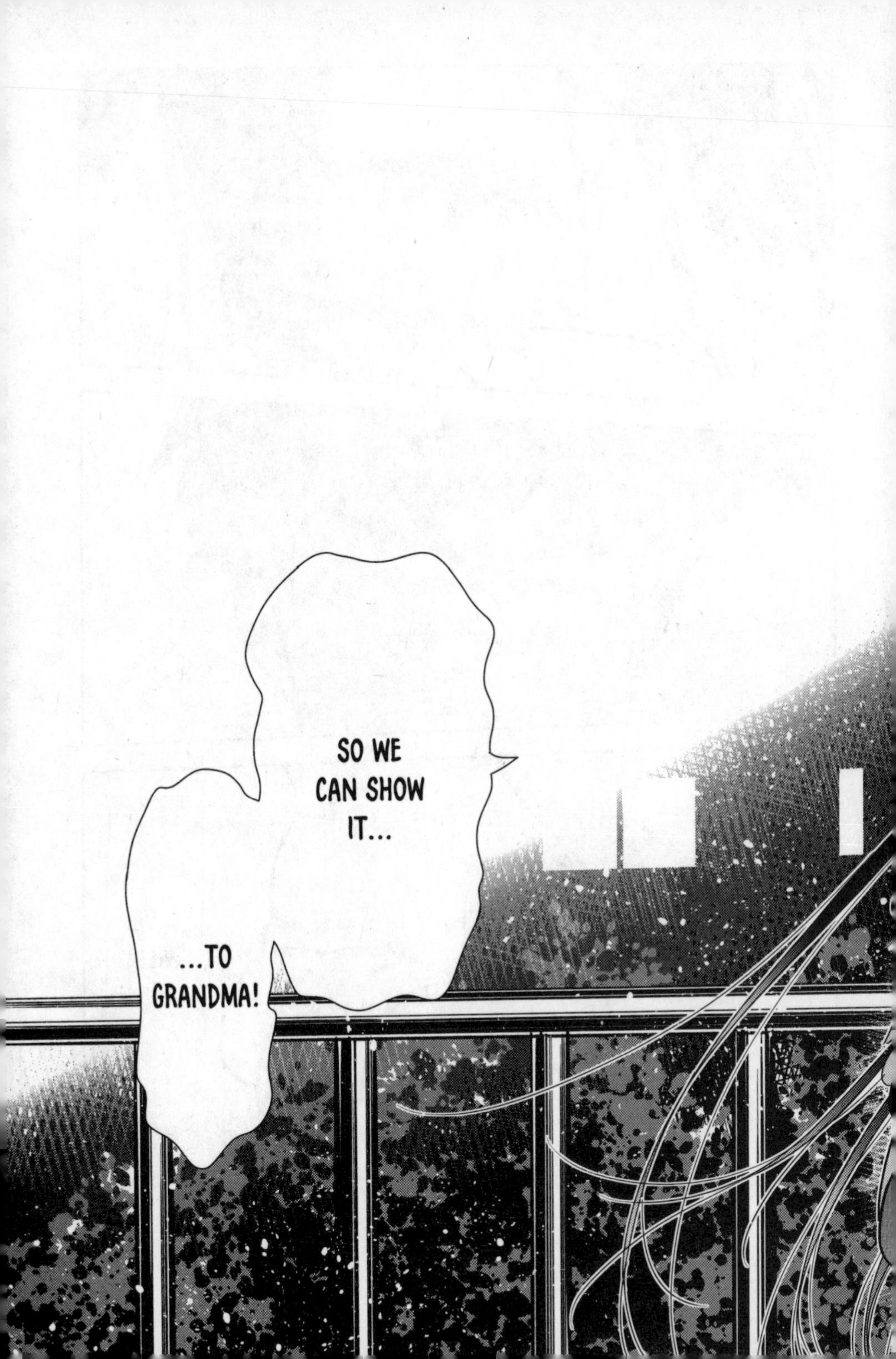
SO WE CAN SHOW IT...
...TO GRANDMA!

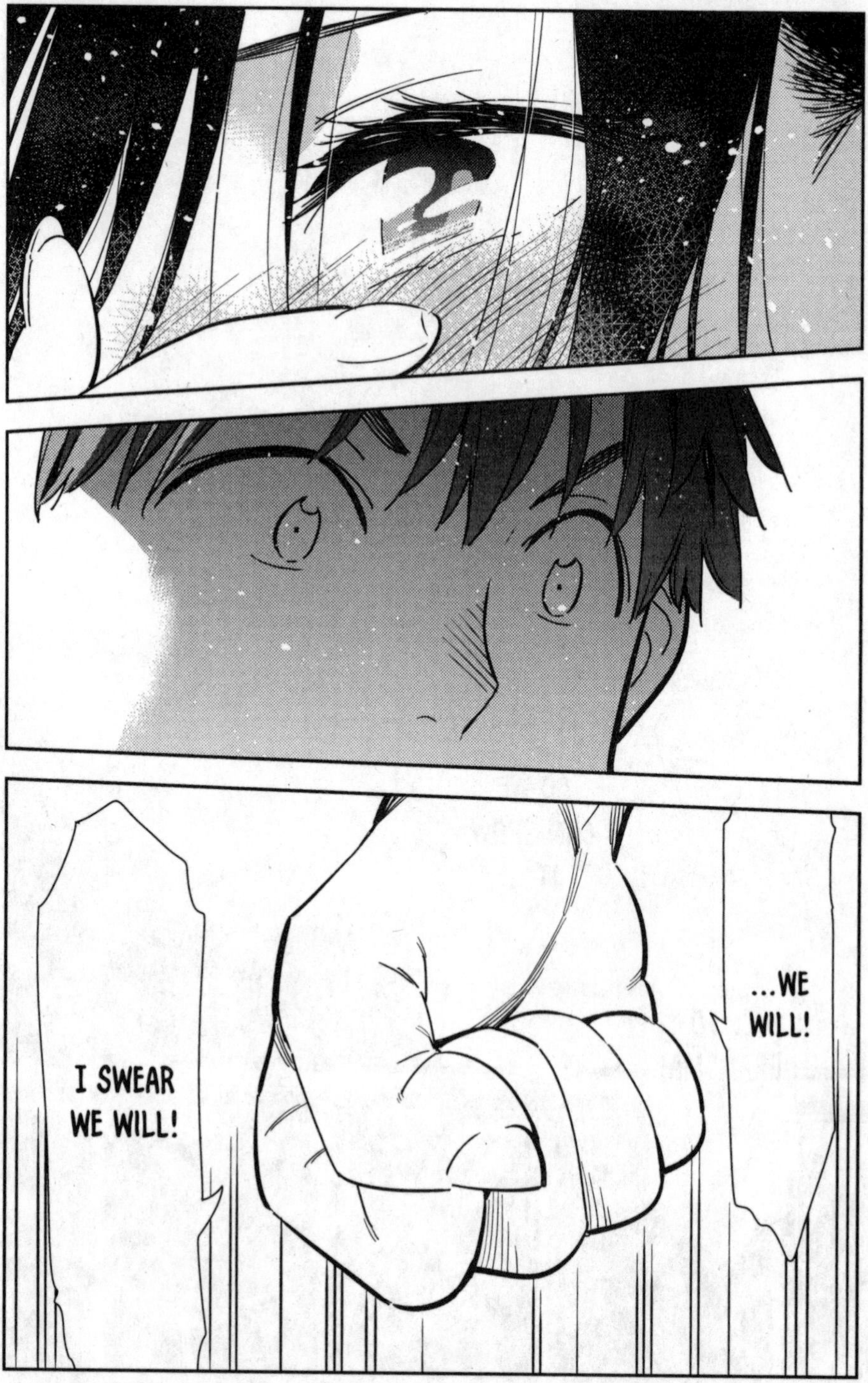
...WE WILL!
I SWEAR WE WILL!

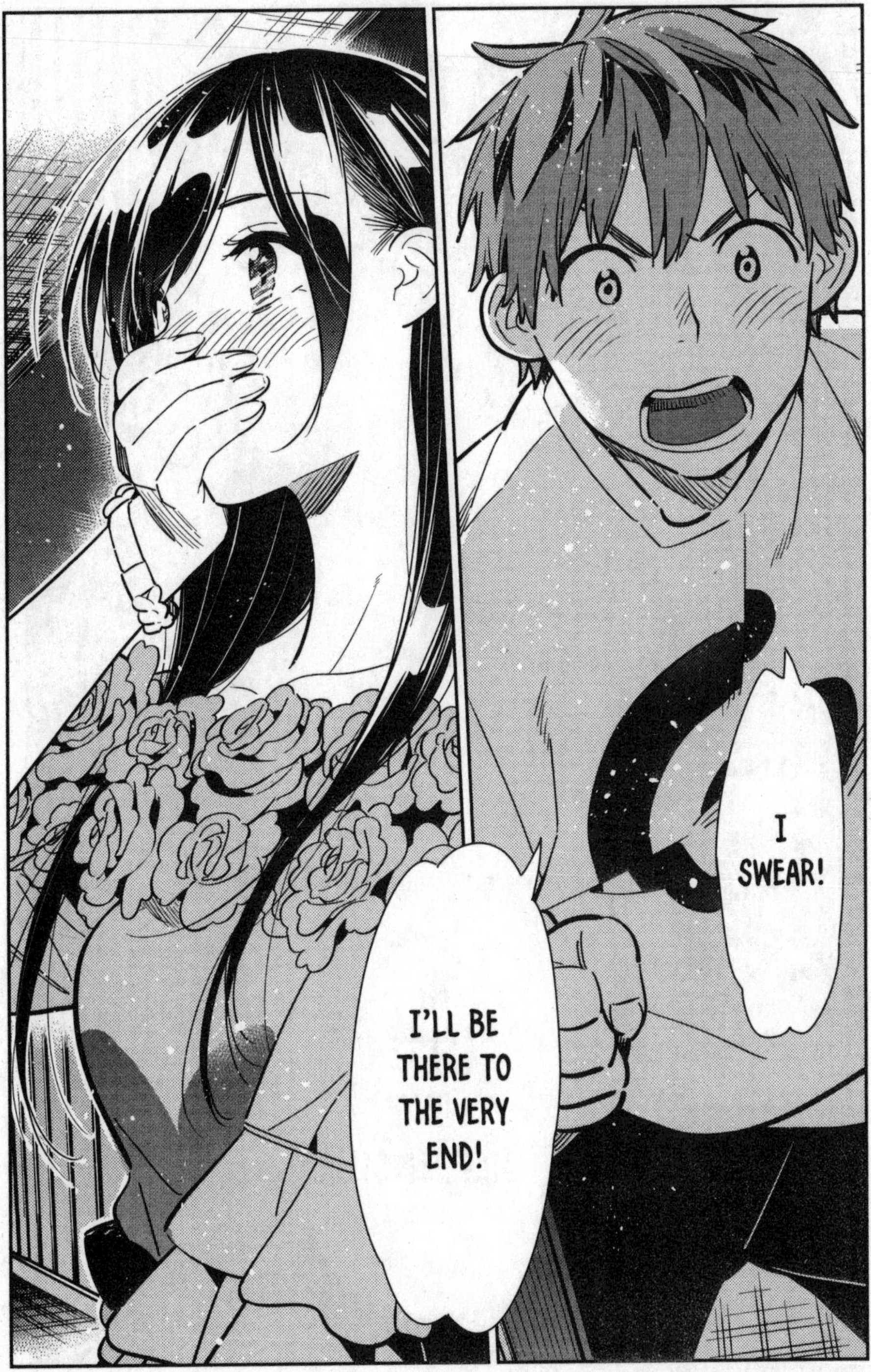
I SWEAR!
I'LL BE THERE TO THE VERY END!

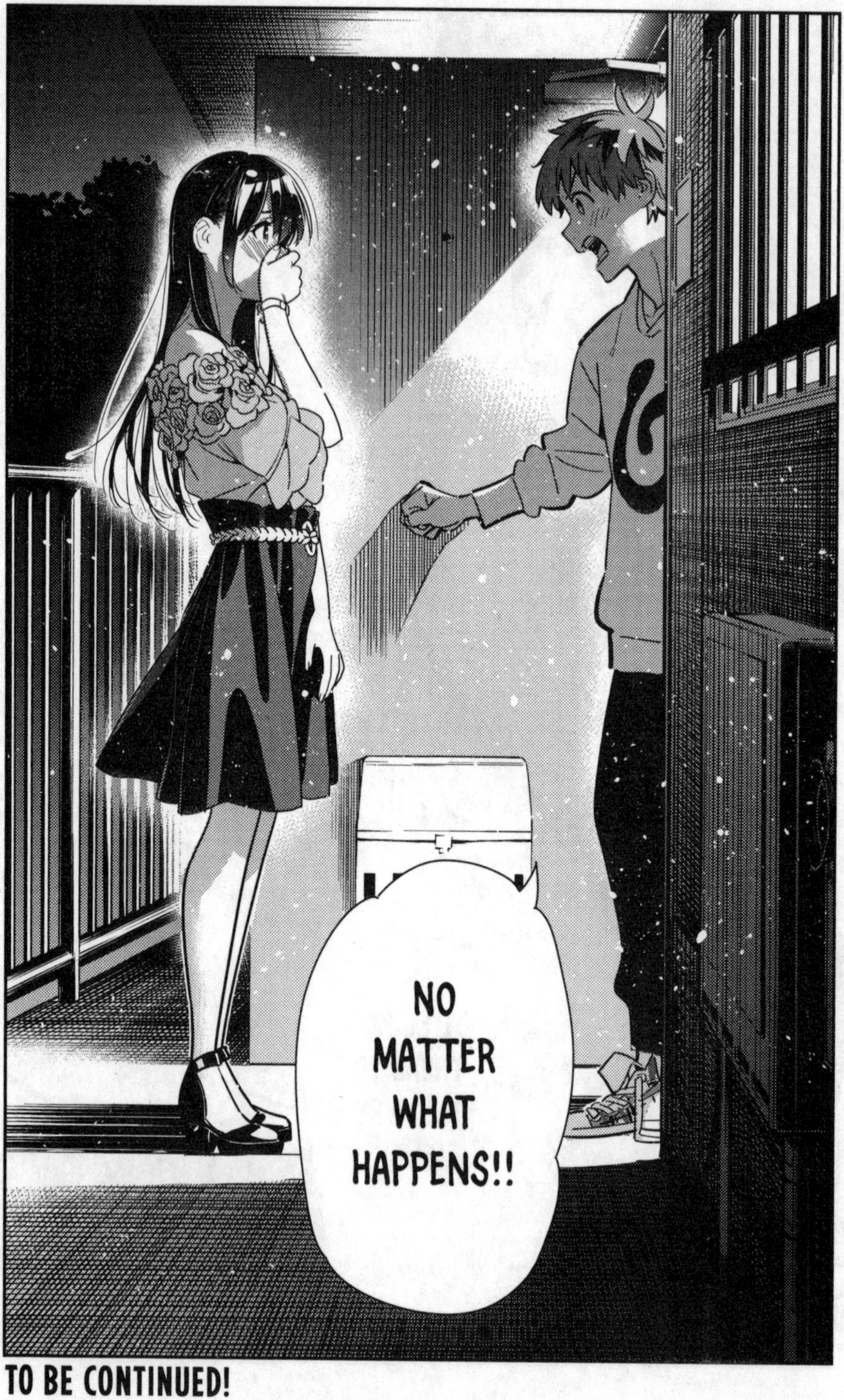
NO MATTER WHAT HAPPENS!!

TO BE CONTINUED!

THE BONUS PAGE WHERE I TRY TO FLATTER THE PAPERBACK BUYERS

THANKS FOR PURCHASING RENT-A-GIRLFRIEND VOLUME 12!

YOU CAN READ THE NEWEST CHAPTERS IN OUR ORIGINAL MAGA-POKE APP!

HAS NO IDEA WHAT THAT MEANS

MIZUHARA WAS PAID FOR HER PROMOTIONAL APPEARANCE HERE

NO, REALLY, SORRY FOR TRYING TO CURRY FAVOR WITH YOU! IF YOU BUY THE COLLECTED VOLUMES AND WE MAKE MONEY WITH THE ONLINE EDITIONS, THAT'LL MAKE ME (AND KODANSHA) SUPER, SUPER HAPPY, SO TAKE A LOOK!

MIYAJIMA

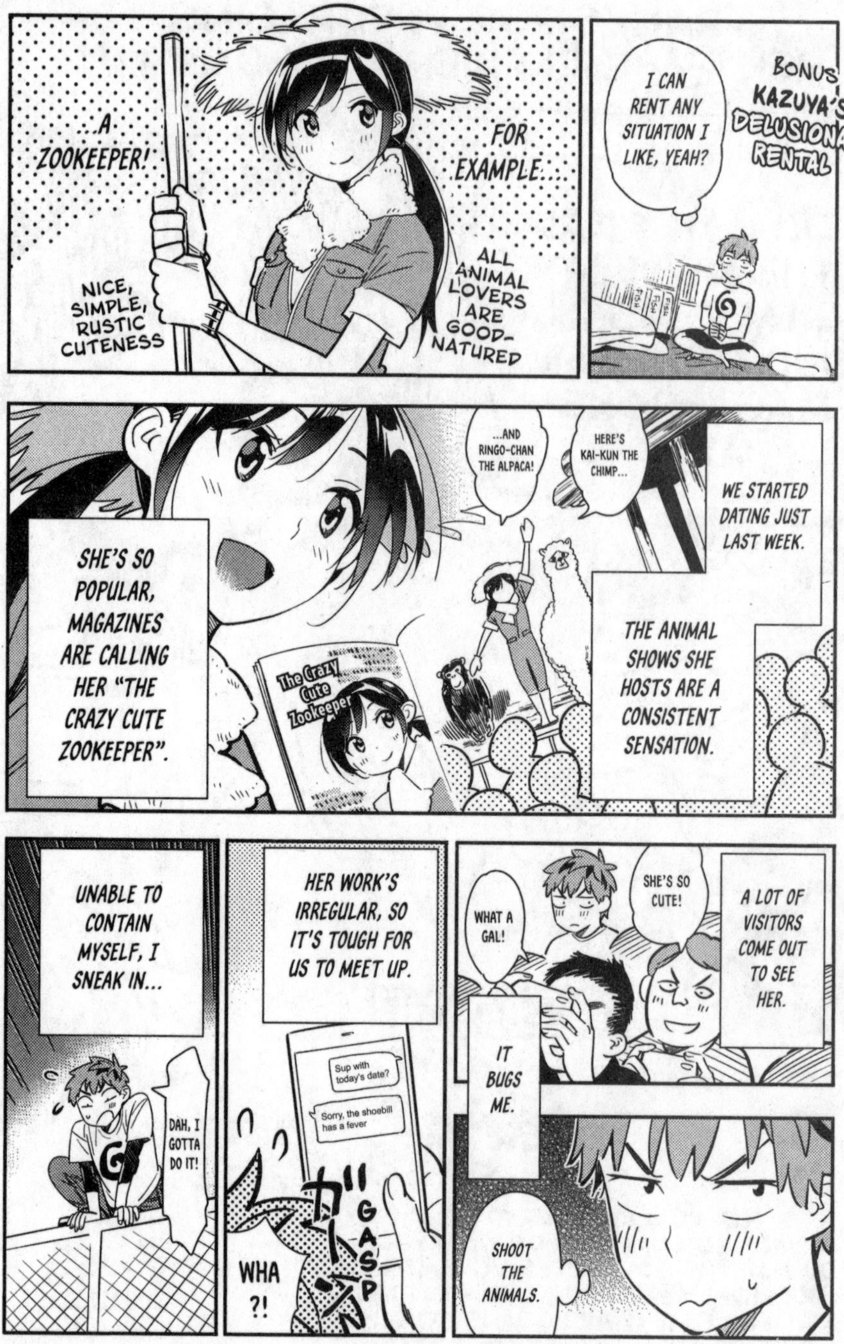
BONUS
KAZUYA'S DELUSIONAL RENTAL
I CAN RENT ANY SITUATION I LIKE, YEAH?
FOR EXAMPLE
...A ZOOKEEPER!
ALL ANIMAL LOVERS ARE GOOD-NATURED
NICE, SIMPLE, RUSTIC CUTENESS
WE STARTED DATING JUST LAST WEEK.
HERE'S KAI-KUN THE CHIMP...
...AND RINGO-CHAN THE ALPACA!
THE ANIMAL SHOWS SHE HOSTS ARE A CONSISTENT SENSATION.
SHE'S SO POPULAR, MAGAZINES ARE CALLING HER "THE CRAZY CUTE ZOOKEEPER".
The Crazy Cute Zookeeper
A LOT OF VISITORS COME OUT TO SEE HER.
SHE'S SO CUTE!
WHAT A GAL!
IT BUGS ME.
SHOOT THE ANIMALS.
HER WORK'S IRREGULAR, SO IT'S TOUGH FOR US TO MEET UP.
Sup with today's date?
Sorry, the shoebill has a fever
GASP
WHA ?!
UNABLE TO CONTAIN MYSELF, I SNEAK IN...
DAH, I GOTTA DO IT!

RENT-A-GIRLFRIEND STAFF: A, IROHKI, KUSUMI, MITSUKI, MINATO. EDITORS: HIRAOKA-SAN,
HIRATSUKA-SAN, HARA-SAN, CHOKAI-SAN. THANKS TO EVERYBODY WHO HELPED WITH RESEARCH AND PICKED UP THIS BOOK!! SEE YOU SOON! ♡

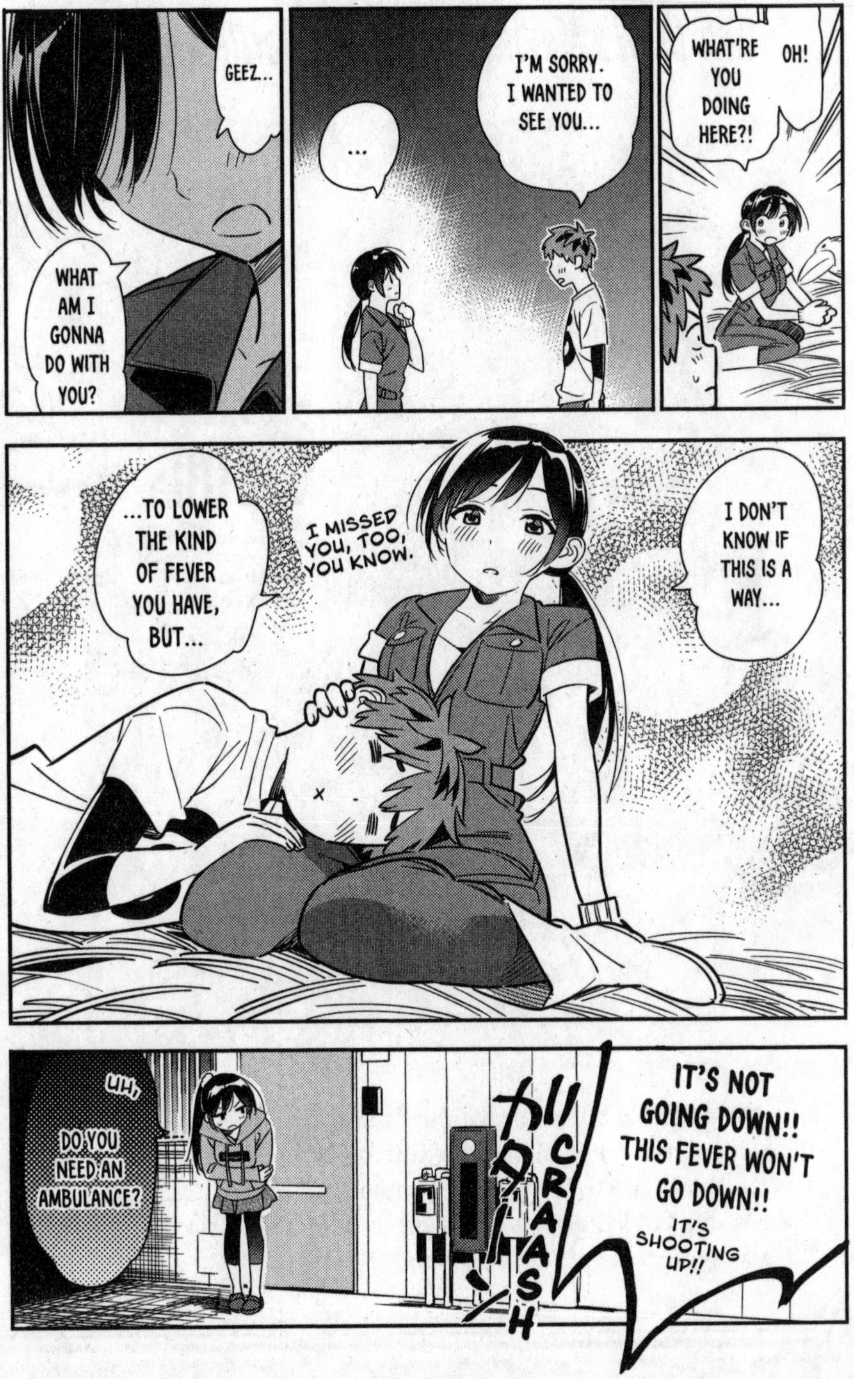
OH!
WHAT'RE YOU DOING HERE?!
I'M SORRY. I WANTED TO SEE YOU...
...
GEEZ...
WHAT AM I GONNA DO WITH YOU?
I DON'T KNOW IF THIS IS A WAY...
...TO LOWER THE KIND OF FEVER YOU HAVE, BUT...
I MISSED YOU, TOO, YOU KNOW.
IT'S NOT GOING DOWN!! THIS FEVER WON'T GO DOWN!!
IT'S SHOOTING UP!!
CRAASH
UH,
DO YOU NEED AN AMBULANCE?

# Young characters and steampunk setting, like *Howl's Moving Castle* and *Battle Angel Alita*

Beyond the Clouds © 2018 Nicke / Ki-oon

A boy with a talent for machines and a mysterious girl whose wings he's fixed will take you beyond the clouds! In the tradition of the high-flying, resonant adventure stories of Studio Ghibli comes a gorgeous tale about the longing of young hearts for adventure and friendship!

Knight of the Ice ©Yayoi Ogawa/Kodansha Ltd.

# SKATING THRILLS AND ICY CHILLS WITH THIS NEW TINGLY ROMANCE SERIES!

A rom-com on ice, perfect for fans of *Princess Jellyfish* and *Wotakoi*. Kokoro is the talk of the figure-skating world, winning trophies and hearts. But little do they know... he's actually a huge nerd! From the beloved creator of *You're My Pet* (*Tramps Like Us*).

Chitose is a serious young woman, working for the health magazine *SASSO*. Or at least, she would be, if she wasn't constantly getting distracted by her childhood friend, international figure skating star Kokoro Kijinami! In the public eye and on the ice, Kokoro is a gallant, flawless knight, but behind his glittery costumes and breathtaking spins lies a secret: He's actually a hopelessly romantic otaku, who can only land his quad jumps when Chitose is on hand to recite a spell from his favorite magical girl anime!

# A SMART, NEW ROMANTIC COMEDY FOR FANS OF *SHORTCAKE CAKE* AND *TERRACE HOUSE!*

A romance manga starring high school girl Meeko, who learns to live on her own in a boarding house whose living room is home to the odd (but handsome) Matsunaga-san. She begins to adjust to her new life away from her parents, but Meeko soon learns that no matter how far away from home she is, she's still a young girl at heart — especially when she finds herself falling for Matsunaga-san.

# PERFECT WORLD

Rie Aruga

A TOUCHING
NEW SERIES
ABOUT LOVE AND
COPING WITH
DISABILITY

An office party reunites Tsugumi with her high school crush Itsuki. He's realized his dream of becoming an architect, but along the way, he experienced a spinal injury that put him in a wheelchair. Now Tsugumi's rekindled feelings will butt up against prejudices she never considered — and Itsuki will have to decide if he's ready to let someone into his heart...

"Depicts with great delicacy and courage the difficulties some with disabilities experience getting involved in romantic relationships... Rie Aruga refuses to romanticize, pushing her heroine to face the reality of disability. She invites her readers to the same tasks of empathy, knowledge and recognition."
—Slate.fr

"An important entry [in manga romance]... The emotional core of both plot and characters indicates thoughtfulness... [Aruga's] research is readily apparent in the text and artwork, making this feel like a real story."
—Anime News Network

KC
KODANSHA
COMICS

# The art-deco cyberpunk classic from the creators of *xxxHOLiC* and *Cardcaptor Sakura*!

CLOVER © CLAMP-ShigatsuTsuitachi CO.,LTD./Kodansha Ltd.

Su was born into a bleak future, where the government keeps tight control over children with magical powers—codenamed "Clovers." With Su being the only "four-leaf" Clover in the world, she has been kept isolated nearly her whole life. Can ex-military agent Kazuhiko deliver her to the happiness she seeks? Experience the complete series in this hardcover edition, which also includes over twenty pages of ravishing color art!

KC
KODANSHA
COMICS

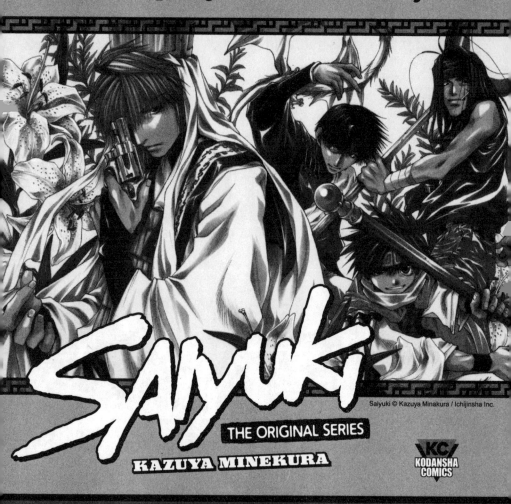

# The beloved characters from *Cardcaptor Sakura* return in a brand new, reimagined fantasy adventure!

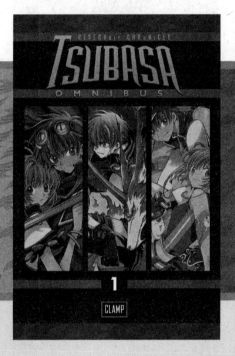

"[*Tsubasa*] takes readers on a fantastic ride that only gets more exhilarating with each successive chapter." —Anime News Network

In the Kingdom of Clow, an archaeological dig unleashes an incredible power, causing Princess Sakura to lose her memories. To save her, her childhood friend Syaoran must follow the orders of the Dimension Witch and travel alongside Kurogane, an unrivaled warrior; Fai, a powerful magician; and Mokona, a curiously strange creature, to retrieve Sakura's dispersed memories!

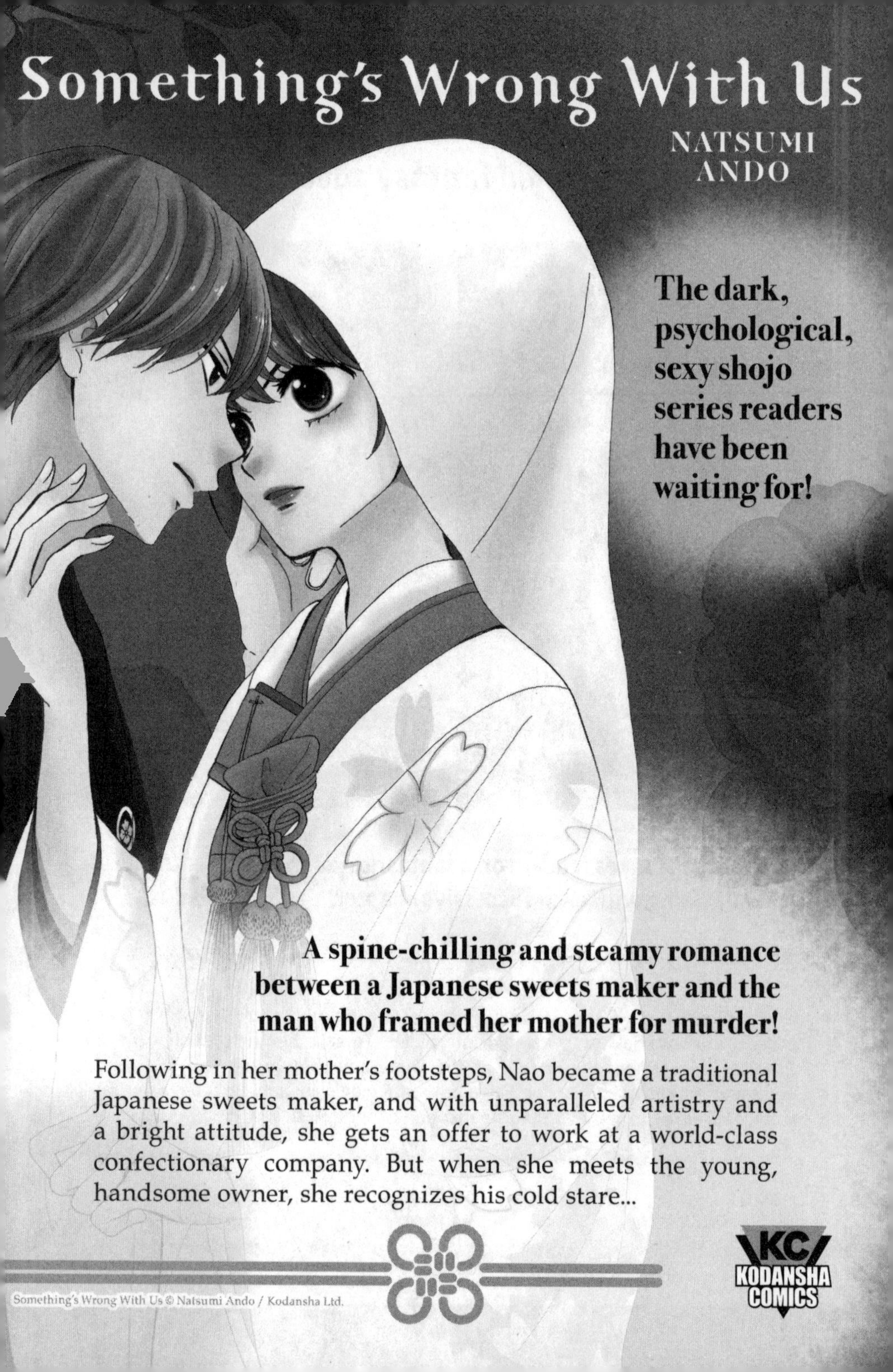
Something's Wrong With Us
NATSUMI ANDO
The dark, psychological, sexy shojo series readers have been waiting for!
A spine-chilling and steamy romance between a Japanese sweets maker and the man who framed her mother for murder!
Following in her mother's footsteps, Nao became a traditional Japanese sweets maker, and with unparalleled artistry and a bright attitude, she gets an offer to work at a world-class confectionary company. But when she meets the young, handsome owner, she recognizes his cold stare...
Something's Wrong With Us © Natsumi Ando / Kodansha Ltd.
KC KODANSHA COMICS

# THE WORLD OF CLAMP!

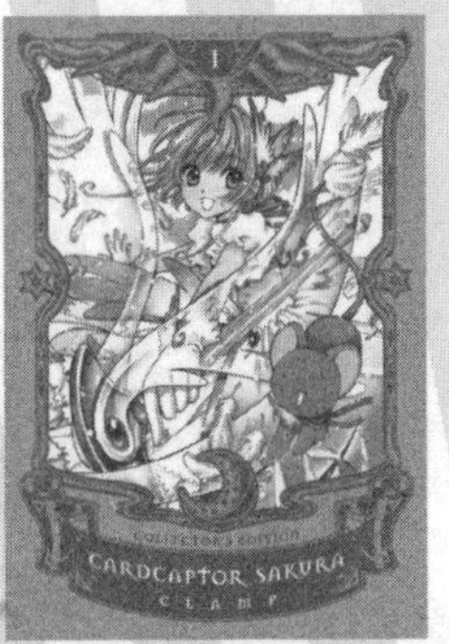
CARDCAPTOR SAKURA
CLAMP
Cardcaptor Sakura Collector's Edition

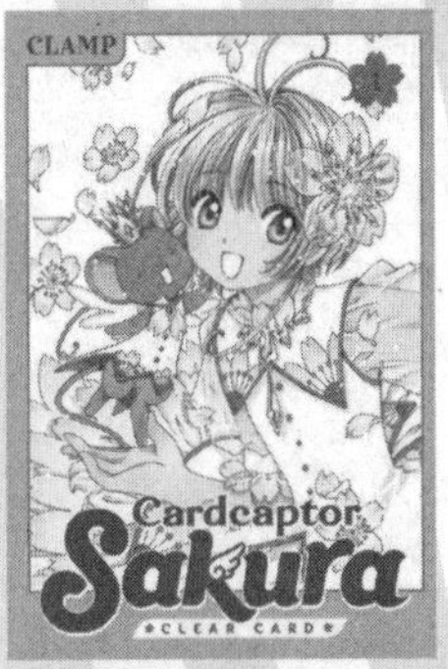
CLAMP
Cardcaptor Sakura
CLEAR CARD
Cardcaptor Sakura: Clear Card

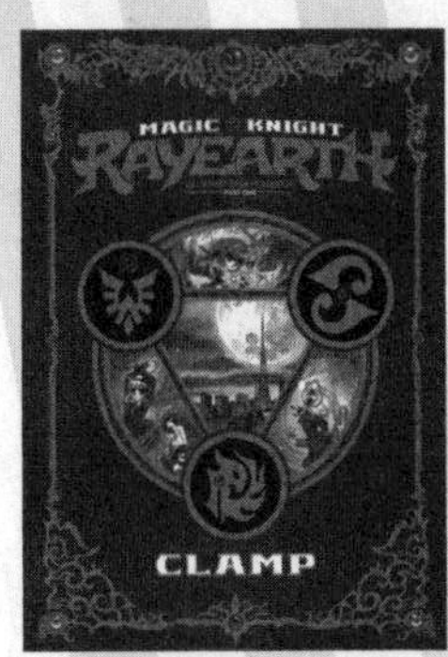
MAGIC KNIGHT RAYEARTH
CLAMP
Magic Knight Rayearth 25th Anniversary Box Set

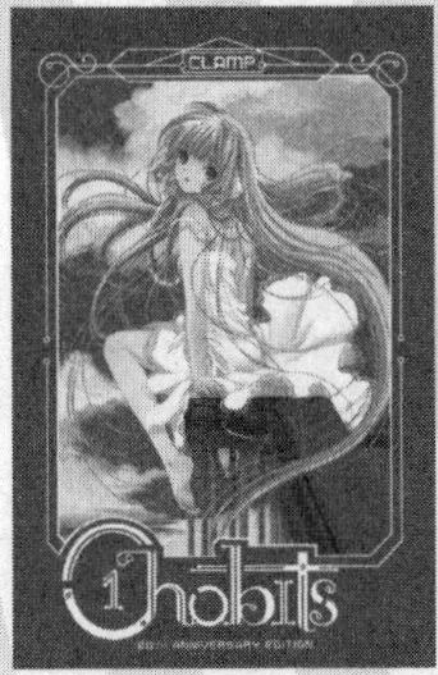
CLAMP
1 Chobits
Chobits

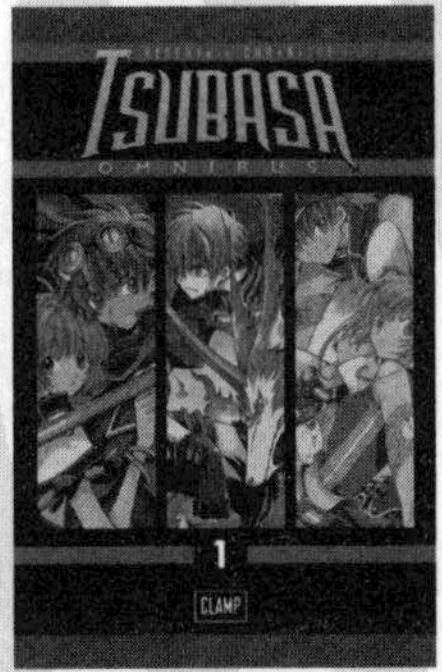
TSUBASA
OMNIBUS
1
CLAMP
TSUBASA Omnibus

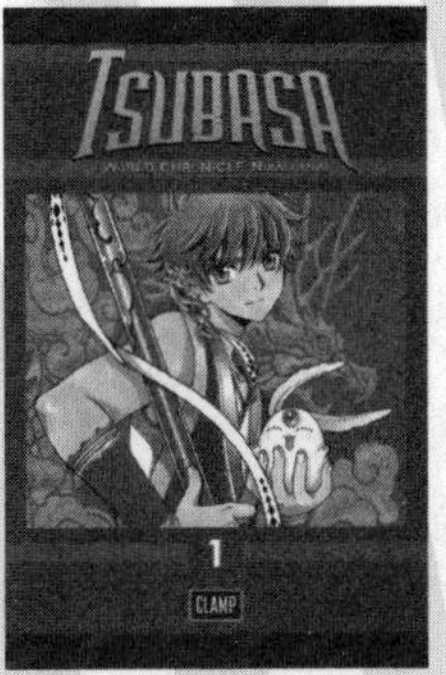
TSUBASA
1
CLAMP
TSUBASA WoRLD CHRoNiCLE

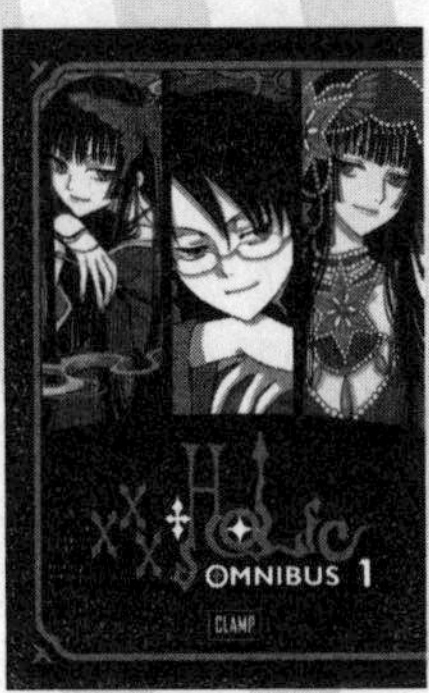
xxxHOLiC
OMNIBUS 1
CLAMP
xxxHOLiC Omnibus

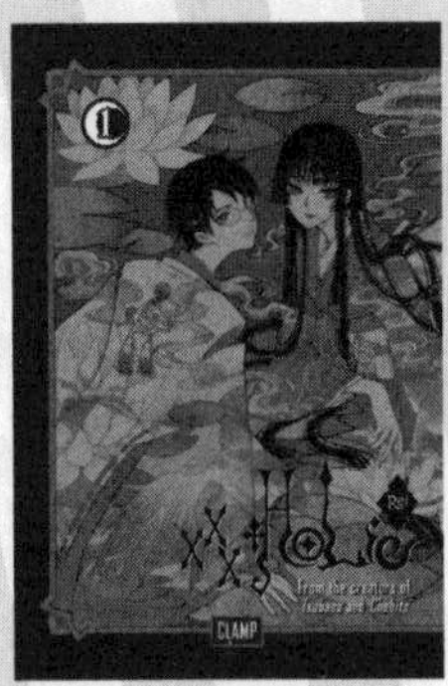
1
xxxHOLiC
CLAMP
xxxHOLiC Rei

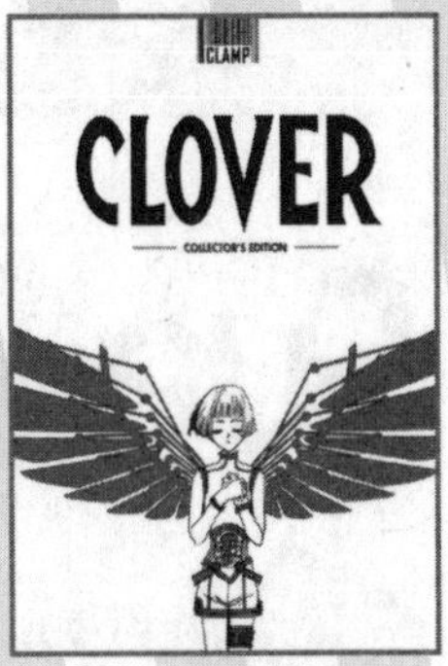
CLAMP
CLOVER
COLLECTOR'S EDITION
CLOVER Collector's Edition

KC KODANSHA COMICS

Kodansha Comics welcomes you to explore the expansive world of CLAMP, the all-female artist collective that has produced some of the most acclaimed manga of the century. Our growing catalog includes icons like *Cardcaptor Sakura* and *Magic Knight Rayearth*, each crafted with CLAMP's one-of-a-kind style and characters!

# THE SWEET SCENT OF LOVE IS IN THE AIR! FOR FANS OF OFFBEAT ROMANCES LIKE *WOTAKOI*

Sweat and Soap © Kintetsu Yamada / Kodansha Ltd.

In an office romance, there's a fine line between sexy and awkward... and that line is where Asako — a woman who sweats copiously — meets Koutarou — a perfume developer who can't get enough of Asako's, er, scent. Don't miss a romcom manga like no other!

KC KODANSHA COMICS

# CUTE ANIMALS AND LIFE LESSONS, PERFECT FOR ASPIRING PET VETS OF ALL AGES!

## YUZU THE PET VET

**1**

BY
**MINGO ITO**

In collaboration with
**NIPPON COLUMBIA CO., LTD.**

For an 11-year-old, Yuzu has a lot on her plate. When her mom gets sick and has to be hospitalized, Yuzu goes to live with her uncle who runs the local veterinary clinic. Yuzu's always been scared of animals, but she tries to help out. Through all the tough moments in her life, Yuzu realizes that she can help make things all right with a little help from her animal pals, peers, and kind grown-ups.

## Every new patient is a furry friend in the making!

# One of CLAMP's biggest hits returns in this definitive, premium, hardcover 20th anniversary collector's edition!

CLAMP

1 Chobits

20TH ANNIVERSARY EDITION

"A wonderfully entertaining story that would be a great installment in anybody's manga collection."
— Anime News Network

"CLAMP is an all-female manga-creating team whose feminine touch shows in this entertaining, sci-fi soap opera."
— Publishers Weekly

Poor college student Hideki is down on his luck. All he wants is a good job, a girlfriend, and his very own "persocom"—the latest and greatest in humanoid computer technology. Hideki's luck changes one night when he finds Chi—a persocom thrown out in a pile of trash. But Hideki soon discovers that there's much more to his cute new persocom than meets the eye.

KC
KODANSHA COMICS

A Kodansha Comics Trade Paperback Original
*Rent-A-Girlfriend* 12 copyright © 2019 Reiji Miyajima
English translation copyright © 2022 Reiji Miyajima

Published in the United States by Kodansha Comics, an imprint of Kodansha USA Publishing, LLC, New York.

Publication rights for this English edition arranged through Kodansha Ltd., Tokyo.

First published in Japan in 2019 by Kodansha Ltd., Tokyo as *Kanojo, okarishimasu*, volume 12.

ISBN 978-1-64651-393-2

Printed in the United States of America.

www.kodansha.us

1st Printing
Translation: Kevin Gifford
Lettering: Paige Pumphrey
Editing: Jordan Blanco
Kodansha Comics edition cover design by Phil Balsman

Publisher: Kiichiro Sugawara

Director of publishing services: Ben Applegate
Director of publishing operations: Dave Barrett
Associate director, publishing operations: Stephen Pakula
Publishing services managing editors: Madison Salters, Alanna Ruse
Production managers: Emi Lotto, Angela Zurlo
Logo and character art ©Kodansha USA Publishing, LLC